Pathways of
Human Development

Pathways of Human Development

Explorations of Change

Edited by Jay A. Mancini and Karen A. Roberto

Lexington Books
A division of
Rowman & Littlefield Publishers, Inc.
Lanham • Boulder • New York • Toronto • Plymouth, UK

Published by Lexington Books
A division of Rowman & Littlefield Publishers, Inc.
A wholly owned subsidiary of
The Rowman & Littlefield Publishing Group, Inc.
4501 Forbes Boulevard, Suite 200, Lanham, Maryland 20706
www.lexingtonbooks.com

Estover Road, Plymouth PL6 7PY, United Kingdom

Copyright © 2009 by Lexington Books

All rights reserved. No part of this book may be reproduced in any form or by any electronic or mechanical means, including information storage and retrieval systems, without written permission from the publisher, except by a reviewer who may quote passages in a review.

British Library Cataloguing in Publication Information Available

Library of Congress Cataloging-in-Publication Data

Pathways of human development : explorations of change / edited by Jay A. Mancini and Karen A. Roberto.
    p. cm.
 Includes bibliographical references and index.
 ISBN 978-0-7391-3686-7 (cloth : alk. paper)—ISBN 978-0-7391-3688-1 (electronic)
 1. Social change. 2. Change (Psychology) 3. Life cycle, Human. 4. Life change events. I. Mancini, Jay A. II. Roberto, Karen A.
 HM831.P375 2009
 305.2—dc22
                                                                    2009017336

∞™ The paper used in this publication meets the minimum requirements of American National Standard for Information Sciences—Permanence of Paper for Printed Library Materials, ANSI/NISO Z39.48-1992.

Printed in the United States of America

Contents

Figures and Tables ix

Preface xi

Acknowledgments xiii

Part I: Human Development, Contexts, and Change

1 A Roadmap for Understanding Human Development, Contexts, and Change 3
   Jay A. Mancini and Karen A. Roberto

Part II: Individuals, Challenges, and Trajectories

2 Positive Turning Points in the Dynamics of Change over the Life Course 15
   Robbie Gilligan

3 "We Lost Touch of Who Each Other Was": Swift Transformations in Close Relationships 35
   Susan Lollis

4 Change and Continuity in Young People's Lives: Biography in Context 53
   Janet Holland

5 African American Female Adolescent Sexuality: Creating Change Using an Ecological-Womanist Lens 75
   April L. Few and Dionne P. Stephens

6 Social Anxiety Disorder in Youth: An Ecological-
    Developmental Perspective   95
    Thomas H. Ollendick

 7 Risk and Protective Factors for Drug Use among
    American Youth   113
    Kee Jeong Kim

 8 Placing Developmental Paradigms in Context: Health and
    Adaptation in Late Life   127
    Karen A. Roberto

Part III: Families, Relationships, and Transitions

 9 Dialectics and Transactional Models: Conceptualizing
    Antecedents, Processes, and Consequences of Change in
    Parent-Child Relationships   151
    Leon Kuczynski, Robyn Pitman, and Monique B. Mitchell

10 The Dynamic Cultural Context of Emotion Socialization   171
    Julie C. Dunsmore and Amy G. Halberstadt

11 Transformation and Change: Parenting in Chinese Societies   191
    Susan S. Chuang

12 Becoming a Parent Again: An Exploration of
    Transformation Among Grandparents Raising
    Grandchildren   207
    Megan L. Dolbin-MacNab

13 Exploring Processes of Family Stress and Adaptation:
    An Expanded Model   227
    Angela J. Huebner

Part IV: Society, Systems, and Interventions

14 Community Resilience: A Social Organization Theory
    of Action and Change   245
    Jay A. Mancini and Gary L. Bowen

15 The Dynamics of Families, Social Capital, and Social
    Change: A Critical Case Study   267
    Rosalind Edwards

16	Psychosocial Impact of Illness: A Transformative Experience *Michèle Preyde*	291
17	Toward an Integrative Theory of Care: Formal and Informal Intersections *Virpi Timonen*	307
18	From Welfare to Well-Being: Turning Things Around Among Homeless Veterans *Hugh Milroy*	327

Part V: Theorizing Human Development and Change

19	Theorizing about Human Development: Identifying Antecedents, Processes, and Consequences of Change *Karen A. Roberto and Jay A. Mancini*	349

Index	367
About the Contributors	391

Figures and Tables

FIGURES

2.1	Sequence of Pre-Conditions for Enduring Turning Points in Individual Developmental Pathways	27
4.1	Dimensions and Fields of *Youth Transitions* (Henderson et al., 2007)	66
7.1	A Developmental Pathway to Adolescent Drug Use	122
7.2	A Transactional Model of Risk, Resilience, and Drug Use	123
8.1	Contextualized SOC Model (Roberto & Husser, 2007)	135
8.2	Antecedents, Processes, and Consequences of Health Changes in Late Life	136
13.1	Expanded Double ABCX Model of Adjustment for Deployment	230
13.2	Model of Relationships among Attachments	236
14.1	Social Organization and Change	250
14.2	Community Capacity Typology	258
18.1	Change Process—VA System	336

TABLES

6.1	Risk Factors for Social Anxiety Disorder	101
7.1	Odds Ratios Distinguishing Desistors, Chronic Drug Users, and Moderate Drug Users from Non-Drug Users	119
10.1	Conceptual Models Addressing Influences of Culture on Parental Emotion Socialization	173
17.1	Differences in Formal and Informal Care	310
17.2	Commonalities and Intersections of Formal and Informal Care	315
19.1	Guiding Theories and Antecedents, Processes and Consequences of Change	351

Preface

Launched on October 1, 2006, and tasked with strengthening the university's competitive position in the social sciences, humanities, and arts, the Institute for Society Culture and Environment (ISCE) (www.isce.vt.edu) at Virginia Polytechnic Institute and State University (Virginia Tech), Blacksburg, Virginia, provides organizational and financial support for targeted creative, interactive, multi- and interdisciplinary research endeavors. The programmatic focus for ISCE is the area of *Social and Individual Transformation*. Scholarship in this area focuses on the causes and consequences of the increased interdependence of economic, social, political, and institutional systems. Research based in social and individual transformation touches both societal and individual life, extending from public policy to personal identity and including explorations of the constructions of race, ethnicity, class, and gender.

In September 2008, ISCE sponsored a cross-national summit at the Virginia Tech Center for European Studies and Architecture in Riva San Vitale, Switzerland. Led by ISCE Director Karen A. Roberto and ISCE Senior Research Fellow Jay A. Mancini, the summit brought together eighteen social and behavioral scientists from Virginia Tech and other universities and the private sector in England, Ireland, and Canada to discuss antecedents, processes, and consequences of societal and individual change over the lifespan. The purpose of the summit was to explore opportunities for inter-university research collaboration in an effort to build cross-national capacity to investigate critical global issues affecting human development. During the two and a half-day summit, participants formally presented their disciplinary perspectives on human development and change. *Pathways of Human Development: Explorations of Change* is one of the initial outcomes of the summit.

Acknowledgments

The success of the Summit and this volume is a result of the efforts of many people. We were very fortunate to work with two knowledgeable and well-organized individuals who handled all the logistics. In Blacksburg, Carlene Arthur, administrative assistant for the Institute for Society Culture and Environment (ISCE), managed the entire project with great enthusiasm and humor. Daniela Doninelli, managing director of the Virginia Tech Center for European Studies and Architecture (CESA) in Riva San Vitale, graciously accommodated our needs as we prepared for, and during our time in, Switzerland. We also appreciate the additional support the Summit received from the Office of the Provost, Office of the Vice President for Research, and Office of Outreach and International Affairs. We acknowledge and appreciate the assistance received with copy editing, proofreading and reference checking from staff members at the Center for Gerontology: Erica Husser, Brandy McCann, and Marya McPherson and John L. Butler VI, from the Family and Community Research Laboratory at Virginia Tech, for preparing the artwork. The ultimate success of the Summit and of this volume is due to the professional expertise and collaboration of the Summit participants, and we are grateful to our old and new colleagues. Our own pathways are enriched by our families, Deborah, Nathan, David, and Suzanne Mancini, and Steven Sheetz, respectively.

HUMAN DEVELOPMENT, CONTEXTS, AND CHANGE

CHAPTER 1

A Roadmap for Understanding Human Development, Contexts, and Change

Jay A. Mancini and Karen A. Roberto

Understanding human development and the contexts in which development unfolds are complex activities because successful understanding requires scientists to account for the individual, for families and other important relationships, for communities that surround both individuals and their relationships, and for expansive influences of culture and society. The primary challenge to theorists and researchers involves displaying those factors that are likely to have an important bearing on human development, and to discern which are more or less powerful, and under what conditions they are so. This volume contributes to the mix of discussions about this discernment through an intentional focus on human development, contexts, and change.

Human development is awash in a sea of biology and heredity, of learning and socialization, of experience and opportunities, of failure and success, and of continuity and change. *Intersection* is a term that describes that point where human development is more fully understood. Because lives are not lived in a vacuum, development emerges from forces, situations, and processes that influence the individual, and that the individual influences. As applied to human development, the intersection is not of two lines but of multiple avenues that converge on individuals, families, and communities (depending on the ecological layer of interest). In this volume there are multiple intersections that elevate pivotal aspects of human life; some focused on the individual, others mainly about relationships, and yet others on complex systems including communities and culture. Even as lines cross, so do the myriad elements that humans are exposed to on a daily basis and over time.

CHANGE, HUMAN DEVELOPMENT, AND THE LIFESPAN

In some respects, development and change are synonymous. At its most elemental level, change is the act of either making or becoming different. As a term, develop or development, denotes an unfolding and progress, growth and advancement. Miller (2002) outlines criteria for developmental theory, including whether it focuses on change over time, whether the discussion of change is multi-dimensional, and whether it deals with transitions, processes, and sequences that contribute to change. As we developed this volume, we asked contributors to be purposive in discussing the position change has in their research and theorizing. Consequently, throughout the various chapters direct discussions about change appear, as do discussions of pivotal contexts.

Newman and Newman (2007) discuss five *special considerations* in the study of human development. The contributors in this volume address these considerations, at least implicitly, as they theorize about human development and change. First, humans have ideas and experiences that influence their outlook, so those of us who write about humans interject our own experiences, whether we recognize that or not. Second, humans are typified by representational thought. Therefore, it is important to go beyond behavior and take into account *meanings* as humans make choices over the lifespan. Next, humans have a long lifespan and therefore a substantial capacity for change over time. For this reason, identifying influences on change across the lifespan provides a fuller picture of human development. Fourth, studying humans requires looking at underlying elements for explaining change and patterns over time. Consequently, placing a premium on contexts becomes paramount. Finally, for a change to be developmental there must be some direction toward greater complexity or integration. Thus, identifying a range of consequences provides a more complete theory of human development.

ANTECEDENTS, PROCESSES, AND CONSEQUENCES

Consistent with agreed-upon qualities of human development theorizing (Miller, 2002; Newman & Newman, 2007), our approach to human development and the lifespan pivots around *antecedents*, *processes*, and *consequences* of change. By definition, development incorporates change and discussions of human development are typically located on individual trajectories. Within a trajectory is continuity, which accounts for periods in life where change is slight or not readily observable, where there may be a developmental plateau, or where staging for further development occurs. We do confess to erring on the side of change rather than continuity as we consider the pathways of life.

Antecedents

Because human development scholars typically portray antecedents, processes, and consequences sequentially, there is a tendency to view them as a linear progression. However, we do not believe that antecedents, for example, have a necessary end, as if a stage which then becomes processes. An antecedent does precede, without question. However, we maintain that an antecedent may also proceed and persist, as in the case of certain demographic, psychographic, or contextual factors that may be preludes to individual experiences. The primary importance of even considering antecedents as applied to change is their relevance for identifying leverage points that can be exploited in order to improve situations of individuals, families, and communities. From a leverage point perspective, some antecedents are amenable to intervention, so that in turn their influence on development can be modified.

Processes

Previously Mancini and colleagues (Mancini, Bowen, & Martin, 2005) have discussed the differentiation between social structure and social organization processes. This distinction is important for the analyses of antecedents, processes, and consequences. Although both structures and processes interface with prevention and intervention, the processes provide insight into how contexts are important for development. "Generally, *structure* refers to interconnecting parts, a framework, organization, configuration, and composition; *process* refers to a course of action, functions, operations, and methods of working" (Mancini et al., 2005, p. 573).

We view processes as occupying an important middle ground in any developmental portrayal or pathway, mainly because processes fill-in what occurs between A and Z. Our thinking aligns with Newman and Newman's (2007, pp. 8–9) discussion of the nature of development and of examining development. They ask six questions that are significant for the work presented in this volume:

1. What is the direction of change over the lifespan?
2. What mechanisms account for growth?
3. What is the relevance of early experience for later development?
4. How do physical, cognitive, emotional, and social functions interact?
5. How do environmental and social contexts affect individuals?
6. What factors and elements place an individual at risk?

When Newman and Newman invoke such words as direction, mechanisms, experience, functions, factors, and elements, in effect, they are using the language of uncovering and elaborating *processes* of change. The direction that change takes can be predictable, but it is also contingent; moreover, this contingency involves multiple elements that may make a difference only in combination with other mechanisms. There are mechanisms associated with change and such mechanisms often have multiple parts that function as a system. Because theorists and researchers tend to both underestimate and overestimate early experience and its place in development, they must be intentional about the linkages they make across lifespan categories. Interaction and intersection, as we have suggested, are where most of human development plays out. That is, because development is contextualized, where elements meet is where development occurs. To take an ecological approach is to have a sharp eye for environmental influences, including physical, social, and relationship contexts. The environment in some sense controls what is possible, even as the individual in some sense controls the intensity of acting on and with the environment. Theorists and researchers must address where developmental processes lead, especially because as a society, we value increasing the chances individuals have to thrive. While having certain opportunities, or lack thereof, does not necessarily place a person in a certain failure position, those experiences may increase those chances. Thus, examining consequences becomes an important part of the developmental algorithm.

Consequences

We attach the term *change* to antecedents, processes, and consequences. Even as there may be factors that precede and are directly or indirectly connected to change, as well as factors that push and pull change along a trajectory, there are also consequences of those antecedents and processes, and ultimately of change itself. We commonly refer to consequences as results or outcomes, but the key to understanding is being reasonably able to connect consequences to the change that comes from processes of human development and of whatever lurks earlier in a sequence of events, circumstances, or conditions. This connecting process is the great challenge for developmentalists and other social and behavioral scientists. We desire to attribute consequences back to primary probable causes, and concurrently account for other factors that either moderate or mediate somewhere between A and Z.

Many years ago, Zetterberg (1965) discussed the various ways elements, factors, and variables were juxtaposed. Although social science methods have now far outdistanced Zetterberg's elemental thinking, his basic message about antecedents, processes, and consequences is instructive, in particular with regard to *consequences*. Among his conclusions about determinants and results (consequences) are that a relationship between two elements may be

1. *reversible*, or it may also be *irreversible*, meaning that change in one variable may lead to a change in another variable but the reverse is not necessarily the case
2. *deterministic*, that is, change in one variable always causes change in another, or *stochastic*, in which one variable probably causes change in another
3. *sequential* or *coextensive*, meaning a side-by-side relationship
4. *sufficient*, meaning one variable influences another regardless of anything else, or *contingent*, meaning one variable influences another only in the presence of a third variable or influence
5. *necessary*, meaning if one variable is functioning, and only if it is present, then there is change in another variable, or *substitutable*, meaning that one variable can cause a particular change but so also can another variable (Zetterberg, 1965, pp. 69-74).

As we consider the process of change, including its antecedents, processes, and consequences, it is helpful to account for the assumptions we are making about linkages and connections; thus, the ways Zetterberg discusses them is instructive. For change to be more fully understood requires being mindful of how concepts and their variables are positioned. This becomes important information for charting developmental pathways, influences, and ultimately for supporting positive human development.

LEVELS AND LAYERS: CONTEXTS OF HUMAN DEVELOPMENT

A full understanding of human development is a contextual approach to human development, elaborated some years ago by Bronfenbrenner (1979). Individuals, families, and their communities cannot be understood by acontextual research or acontextual theory and theorizing. We recall a primary principle of deductive theorizing, that of *ceteris paribus*, meaning all things being equal. Because very few things are equal, nuanced approaches to human development are required, and those nuances very often are the surroundings in which we find ourselves (contexts). A primary goal of contextual thinking is to paint that portrait of human development where so many elements coalesce, merge, and cohere (in effect, intersect). Though we cannot do justice to Bronfenbrenner's thinking here, or to the other scholars who examine lives in context (e.g. Moen, Elder, & Luscher, 1995), we do elaborate a few essential matters of context. Bronfenbrenner (1979, p. 3) states, "The ecological environment is conceived as a set of nested structures, each inside the next, like a set of Russian dolls." From this simple, yet elegant, statement he went on to lay out the systems that comprise his early model: micro-, meso-, exo-, and macrosystems. Within this ecological framework, Bronfenbrenner highlighted the agency of the individual, thus making it clear that the nature of human development it not simply a matter of being acted upon but also of acting on one's own behalf. This human ecology approach is a theory of change and of contexts.

We summarize our take on contexts, and the reasons we have insured that the contributors discussed contexts throughout their chapters, as follows:

1. Words that express the nature of contexts include structure, framework, environment, situation, circumstance, surrounding, setting, background, and connection.
2. Contexts, in many respects, are *noise* or intrusions into what otherwise might be a clear, yet invalid, cause and effect scenario. This noise may moderate other elements of human development, or may mediate those elements. Rather than ignore noise, to try to suppress

it, or try to scientifically partial out its influences, we embrace it as reflective of real life. Life is experienced in that place where contexts collide, and where individuals navigate the life course.
3. Contexts are dynamic and active, rather than passive and inconsequential. To understand contexts and their intersection with the individual is to understand why some individuals thrive, and some do not.

Generally, scholars under-specify contextual effects in most analyses of contexts. For example, rarely do discussions of contexts actually describe what it is about contexts that have a place in human development. We are now beginning to conceptualize contexts in more dynamic and active ways. Contexts possess characteristics and qualities that differentiate among them. For example, some contexts may be *oppressive* whereas others may be *supportive*. Other contexts may be *malleable* or *static*, and others may be *developmental* or *chaotic*. In any case, a more complete understanding of contextual effects does not end with merely naming a context but rather explicates what it is about the context that determines or modifies human development.

THEORY AND THEORIZING

Some years ago, Weiss (1995), in making a plea for greater use of theory in the field of evaluation research contended, "there is nothing as practical as good theory" (p. 65). In some respects theory in the social and behavioral sciences lags behind advances in research methods and analysis, and has difficulty accommodating the plethora of research findings, both empirical and narrative, found in the literature. Yet theory is a primary tool for building a valid developmental science, a necessary way to capture what Reynolds (2007, p. 167) terms the "large number of subtle and interrelated processes" that are part of and surround the human condition. The practicalities of theory are several, including developing ways of thinking that coordinate research findings and provide coherence where there appears to be chaos (as in the case of those areas where there are seemingly conflicting findings). Another practicality is actually *praxis*, that is, prevention and intervention activities targeted at particular aspects of development or at dimensions of contexts.

Throughout this volume, the contributors accessed a host of extant theories to advance theie own theorizing and research (see chapter 19 for a systematic summary). We view extant theories as raw materials of a sort, and building blocks for constructing an understanding of a particular individual, family, or community phenomenon. The relationship between theory and theorizing is an interesting one, and in its own way speaks to development, in this case building the connections between the thoughts of others and one's own thoughts. When connecting frameworks with phenomena, theorizing occurs.

OVERVIEW OF PATHWAYS OF HUMAN DEVELOPMENT

This volume contains five parts, with *Part I* (*Human Development, Contexts, and Change*) being this introductory chapter that sets the stage for the following sections. Parts II, III, and IV include topical discussions on aspects of human development and change: *Individuals, Challenges, and Trajectories (Part II)*; *Families, Relationships, and Transitions (Part III)*; and *Society, Systems, and Interventions (Part IV)*. Each chapter elevates theory and theorizing, discusses contexts, and sharpens the discussion about antecedents, processes, and consequences of change. The final chapter, *Theorizing Human Development and Change* (Part V), integrates these individual contributions toward a more complete understanding of human development and change. In concert, the contributions in this volume are leading to a more nuanced conceptualization of human development with an emphasis on contexts. In particular, this volume extends an understanding of the elements of change as reflected in antecedents, processes, and consequences.

REFERENCES

Bronfenbrenner, U. (1979). *The ecology of human development: Experiments by nature and design*. Cambridge, MA: Harvard University Press.

Mancini, J. A., Bowen, G. L., & Martin, J. A. (2005). Community social organization: A conceptual linchpin in examining families in the context of communities. *Family Relations, 54*, 570–582.

Miller, P. H. (2002). *Theories of developmental psychology* (4th ed.). New York: Worth.

Moen, P., Elder, G. H., & Luscher, K. (Eds.). (1995). *Examining lives in context: Perspectives on the ecology of human development*. Washington, DC: American Psychological Association.

Newman, B. M., & Newman, P. R. (2007). *Theories of human development*. Mahweh, NJ: Erlbaum.

Reynolds, P. D. (2007). *A primer in theory construction.* Boston: Pearson.
Weiss, C. H. (1995). Nothing as practical as good theory: Exploring theory-based evaluation for comprehensive community initiatives for children and families. In J. P. Connell, A. C. Kubisch, L. B. Schorr, & C. H. Weiss (Eds.), *New approaches to evaluating community initiatives: Concepts, methods, and contexts* (pp. 65–92). Washington, DC: Aspen Institute.
Zetterberg, H. (1965). *On theory and verification in sociology* (3rd ed.). Totowa, NJ: Bedminster.

Part II

INDIVIDUALS, CHALLENGES, AND TRAJECTORIES

CHAPTER 2

Positive Turning Points in the Dynamics of Change over the Life Course

Robbie Gilligan

There is arguably a tendency towards pessimism in some of the key perspectives on developmental prospects of the individual over the life course. This pessimism reflects implicit doubts about the possibility of introducing change in established individual pathways or trajectories. In many ways, these perspectives espouse a tacit view that *the die is cast* by the relevant dominant factors. This makes it difficult, especially in the face of adversity, for individuals (or others) to alter favorably their prospects or the individual trajectory of their development. Three perspectives, (a) the decisive role of early childhood experience, (b) the decisive role of structural level social and economic forces (e.g., poverty, economic marginalization), and (c) the decisive role of the previous history of the person, all tend to play down the possibility of positive change in challenging circumstances. Yet, is it also true that in everyday life outside the academy, in the great world religions and in helping services, there is clearly discernible conviction about the possibility of change.

These pessimistic perspectives undoubtedly have broad validity, especially at the population level. In this chapter, I argue, however, that these perspectives may obscure the possibility of individual level change arising from the actions of the individual as *actor*, or from what may prove critical, if often subtle shifts in circumstances to which the person then adapts. I question excessively deterministic or linear views as to how to account for change as it may play out at the micro-level of a person's life path. This is not to say that I see the individual as having unlimited options or choices—these are clearly bounded within parameters broadly related to their unfolding immediate circumstances, to their overall trajectory of development and, as Schoon (2007) reminds us, the wider socio-historical conditions of the time. Nevertheless, I seek to encourage greater attention to the *possibility* of individual level change within these parameters and to the *agency* of the individual actor as elements that contribute to a fuller understanding of the dynamics of change in trajectories across the life course. For example, persons born in a third world slum and growing up illiterate are unlikely to have the opportunity to become a brain surgeon; however, they may eventually navigate a path carved partly by their own agency that leads them to literacy and better job opportunities in the local job market.

I explore at a micro level how change operates and is accounted for in the individual's life path, despite what sometimes might be a genuinely daunting or gloomy backdrop. How, for example, did the slum dweller ultimately learn to read and what were the key steps that opened up that opportunity, including the turning point in that process? Why did this turning point of learning to read happen in this case, but not in so many others? What were the key conditions that made this critical shift possible? I will address such questions in order to illuminate this important concept of *turning points*. Schoon (2006) describes turning points as "events or transitions that change the net probability of life-course destinations permanently, without further interventions" (p. 114). Indeed, such effects may be even more far reaching. Werner and Smith (2001) found that the impact of positive turning points in their respondents' lives often "carried forward" (p. 168) into the lives of the respondents' children, as in the case of enhanced educational opportunities or expectations

My discussion seeks to contribute to an emerging debate in which the complexity of human development across the life course is now more often understood as being driven by nature *and* nurture, and according to Lewontin (2000), *random events*, which he terms "random developmental noise" (pp. 35–36). This perspective implies a less linear view of development than might often be understood. It tends to reflect the influence of the recently emerging paradigm of complexity theory. Stevens and Cox (2008) illustrate the relevance of complexity theory with regard to understanding and predicting the weather:

> Weather systems follow principles derived from complexity theory. Hurricanes arise due to the interaction of factors such as sea temperature, moisture in the air and gravitational forces. The complex combination of multiple and contingent factors creates a complex adaptive system which

has the ability to undergo spontaneous *self-organization* (Halsey & Jensen, 2004). In other words, these factors will organize themselves to produce a hurricane. However, we cannot predict when a hurricane will form or what direction it will travel in simply by knowing these factors. Predictions can be made that there *will* be hurricanes in a particular area, but predictive ability stops at that point. So, in spite of the range of knowledge available about hurricanes, how they happen and where they occur, their actual occurrence in a time and place cannot be predicted (p. 1323).

Individual development may be a little like a weather system; we can predict that there will be development, but we cannot predict precisely the detail of its path, form, dynamics, or outcome. Yet this view departs somewhat from the more conventional linear perspective:

One of the common themes that emerges from economic theory and analysis and from other disciplines is the crucial role of early experiences in laying a foundation for ongoing development and the fact that development is a multi-period process whereby outcomes in each period build on those of the previous period (Kilburn & Karoly, 2008, p. 30).

The path of development *is* influenced by what goes before. Continuity *is* most likely across the developmental stages for the individual. However, we must still be able to accommodate and account for the possibility of shifts (or turning points) in the expected pathway. Before entering the discussion more fully, it is worth clarifying at the outset that *turning points* may arise from events that occur, possibly serendipitously, in the person's life. What turns such opportunities into positive turning points is the manner in which the person responds. As Abbott (1997) reminds us: "A major turning point has the potential to open a system the way a key has the potential to open a lock. . . . [A]ction is necessary to complete the turning" (quoted in Laub & Sampson, 2003, p. 282).

The action to open up the opportunity presented thus entails some degree of agency on the part of the relevant actor in whose life or domain the turning point presents. My inspiration for this chapter came from Abbott's quote and by an attempt to *unpack* the elements in the process of opportunity and action implied in this conception of a turning point. I use the term *turning point* here in the sense of a catalyst for an enduring *positive* shift in the trajectory of development of the individual. In approaching this task, it is also important to note that change arises not just from crisis, nor just from conscious intention or effort; change may also arise by *chance*. In this sense, the chance occurrence is *not* due to entirely random circumstances. It relates in some way to the contexts and processes in the person's life, but plays out in a way that produces outcomes that are quite unexpected or unpredictable. Here is an example from my own research: a young man of sixteen is contemplating leaving school to seek openings in the world of work. He has concluded that he lacks the academic ability to make much further progress at school. In what the boy foresees as one of his last days at school, a young teacher who has taught him English for one year asks to speak to him, possibly for the first time. The teacher tells him, "You work hard and you will do alright. You have ability." On the strength of a conversation that occurred quite out of the blue and that delivered a quite unexpected message, the boy decided to stay at school. He did well enough to earn entry to a university and is now a successful graduate working as a senior manager in a large organization. He recalls the conversation with the teacher as pivotal to a successful working life in adulthood. To return to the hurricane analogy earlier, the teacher might not have expected nor could have predicted that his conversation would have had the impact it had, but he might presumably have hoped that it might have some positive effect, that it might help to open up a space in which good things might happen in the young man's life. The conversation alone does not account for the later progress the young man made, but it seems to have been a critical pre-condition.

Change is rarely the result of some neat linear relationship between intention A and outcome C. The trouble with explaining change, of course, is there are so many multi-factorial influences interacting and recurring across A, B (the context) and C. Change does not always arise from high visibility events or processes that are evident to those not involved. In some cases, the significance of the *change moment* may not even be apparent to the person most directly involved. Further, these moments may seem innocuous in prospect, but only reveal their true significance in retrospect and in the specific context of *this* person's life. Taking the example of the teacher and the student above, it may well be that the teacher did not expect such a positive series of consequences to flow from a conversation that now he may not even readily recall. Even the boy most likely did not foresee its full significance. A key insight about change is that it may often be *unpredictable*.

Positive change in people's lives is widely sought. The public and individuals prize positive change. What accounts for positive changes in people's lives, positive changes in the trajectory of development or in the trajectory of prospects, especially in unpromising circumstances? This seems a reasonable question, but it is one not so easy to answer. From my specific perspective, change arises not just from large-scale forces. Change also can be traced at least in part to minor and seemingly *incidental moments* whose relevance may not be obvious to the onlooker. It comes by the routes of chance and small events, as well as by intention and large events.

I propose the following as an illustrative framework for considering categories of sources for change. These broad categories and their exemplars are not necessarily mutually exclusive in how they play out. Someone caught up in a military attack may also experience in the same period the death of a parent due to old age, and so on. I also suggest, somewhat counter-intuitively, that good outcomes may come from bad as well as good experiences. For example, Elder (1998) draws attention to this point in his study of the developmental outcomes of young people living through the Great Depression of the 1930s, where resulting *steeling experiences* led them to display a greater subsequent capacity for resilience in other contexts. Hard experiences, for certain contextual reasons (linked to collective survival in the face of shared adversity), made the young people stronger, a conclusion that, of course, needs to be interpreted wisely. Coming through hard times successfully teaches the young person valuable lessons about the potential gains from effort and perseverance that will influence their perception of their own efficacy (Bandura, 1989). But as Elder's study (1998) also underlines, while some individuals may thrive in difficult circumstances, this is usually with some support, whether from family or peers.

EVENTS AS SOURCES OF CHANGE

Numerous events drive change in a person's life. Firstly, there are *macro external population level* events. These events occur on a large scale, and typically have a huge impact on the largely powerless population affected. These events may arise, for example, from natural disasters impacting on whole populations such as a tsunami, serious flooding, or an earthquake. Or these events may be linked to both nature and human agency taking the form of wildfires or epidemics of disease. Or they may arise primarily due to the influence of human actors, as in the case of wars, military invasion, or terrorist attack. These violent episodes may cause not only death and injury, they may also lead to large-scale population displacement in the form of waves of refugees seeking safety. Such displacement may also involve forced removals of specific populations as in the case of indigenous children removed from their families under particular policy regimes in certain countries. Finally, economic recessions or depressions may have significant impact on people's lives through effects on the labor market and so on.

Second, *local, non-normative events* occurring within the immediate context of individuals' lives compel change. These individual or family level events may take the form of the sudden onset of illness or disability arising from an accident leading to long-term physical restrictions or psychological distress. These micro-level events may also arise from local social and economic changes impinging on the individual as in the case of a job loss due to factory closure, or the financial collapse of a family business. There may be the ensuing enforced choice of migration affecting family members left behind or those joining the migratory journey of the primary migrant. There also may be other contingencies in a person's life such as experiencing physical or sexual abuse and its longer term effects, becoming a victim of human trafficking, enlisting as a child soldier, or impending imprisonment.

Third, there are *normative events* expected within human and cultural experience that may also bring change. These include marriage, parenthood, grandparenthood, the birth of a sibling, starting school, starting work, retiring, the death of a parent, or in later life the loss of a spouse or partner. There may also be changes that arise from adaptations and choices made by the individual in response to domestic or external pressures or processes such as the choice of migration as an adult for social or economic reasons. There might be a move of house or home, a job switch out of preference rather than necessity. Other examples of change include entering a divorce, making a religious conversion, coming out as a lesbian, gay, bisexual, or trans-gender (LGBT) young person, joining the military, enlisting to serve as crew on a civilian ship, engaging seriously with addiction recovery programs such as Alcoholics Anonymous, achieving entry to higher education, undertaking re-training for a different type of job, or acquiring mastery of the host country language as a migrant.

In addition to the change driven by events at these three levels, there may be other micro-level events hidden in the fabric of the daily life of the person. These may occur *below the radar screen* of the person and his or her associates. They may occur unexpectedly. They may also occur independently or may occur embedded within events at another level. Thus, in the case of micro events, a relatively subtle or minor *moment* may, retrospectively, acquire considerable positive significance in the person's narrative, or indeed in other people's understanding of that narrative. The moment gains this status because it comes to be seen as having been pivotal in the opening up of opportunities as in the case of renewal of identity, self-esteem, or self efficacy. The moment may prove to have been the first link in what turns out to be a series of favorable chain reactions. These hidden initial turning point moments, or discrete windows of experience, often revolve around the influence of a key person. In the case of young people, this may be a relationship with an interested or supportive adult. As observed by Luthar and Zerlazo (2003), "resilient adaptation rests on good relationships" (p. 544). These formative moments may constitute the basis for a critical shift in the status quo in the person's life; they may serve as a catalyst for enduring change in some aspect of a person's life and relations. Such key moments may be constituted by, for example, representing one's branch of a family at a wider family wedding, thus connecting for the first time with one's wider family network. The simple fact of attending a wedding as an honored guest may translate into a potential strengthening of social capital in the young person's life. Social capital as used in this sense refers to the pool of helpful contacts in other spheres, trusting relations, and reciprocal helping to which a person, family, or community may have access (Putnam, 2001). Such *moments* may have a more pervasive transformative effect, as in being the first person from a family to enter, or graduate from, university.

THE POWER OF POSITIVE RELATIONSHIPS

As noted already, it should not be assumed that positive turning points emerge only from a wider positive experience in which they may be embedded. A refugee from war, for example, may eventually find safety and comfort in a host family in a neutral zone that leads onto transforming good experiences not previously available or accessible in the earlier more benign pre-war circumstances. Positive turning points may emerge unexpectedly from apparently negative experiences. However, as the following example illustrates, good things may come of the experience, despite expectations. In this instance, the boy, quoted as a man recollecting his experience of being sent to reform school where he was assigned to an electrical workshop and came to share the interest of his instructor:

> [H]e loved amateur radio. And he got me interested in radio and electrical stuff and things of that nature. . . . He saw the potentials in me. He saw I enjoyed electricity. I enjoyed radio and stuff like that. He took me under his wing. And I thought an awful lot of this guy in a short ten months I worked with him. He was a prince. . . . I prepared my whole life in ten months to do something. . . .Think about it. Those ten months were crucial in my life. Because they turned me around. [Name of prison] turned me around. Jack turned me around. Jack was a humanitarian and cared for me as an individual. Let's get down to brass tacks. What if Jack wasn't there? What if I wasn't offered the opportunity? . . . He treated me right. As a matter of fact, after I left [name of prison] year after year on a yearly basis I would take my wife and kids, we'd drive all the way to [name of prison] to see Jack (Laub & Sampson, 2003, p. 141).

The Power of Positive Expectations

The positive expectations implicit in the instructor's approach are significant here. Turning point moments with positive outcomes may often be linked to the explicit or implicit transmission of positive expectations, as in the example earlier of the young teacher making a last ditch attempt to encourage the boy to remain at school. But there are other examples involving non-professionals who also exert positive influence. Take the example of local mothers recruited by specialist public health nurses to serve as mentors in good parenting for inexperienced parents in low income communities (Johnson et al., 2000). Their purpose was to achieve positive change in the lives of the younger women and their children. But this effort often also led to positive change in the mentors' own lives as the original and largely unexpected invitation to serve had opened a vista of pathways to further engagement in community development or continuing education. This community mother model has ripple effects not just on the service recipients but also those plucked from obscurity to deliver the health messages. Take a further example of a young teenage boy in foster care visiting his friend's home. The mother of the other boy knew the boy in care quite well and struck up a conversation with both of them in which she said "when you both go to university." The phrase registered strongly with the boy in care as he had not thought of this prospect for himself before. He did indeed go to university and has had a successful career. He regards the confidence and expectation expressed by the phrase (and the woman) as very formative influences in his development, and in his motivation and progress academically.

In some cases, there may be positive changes facilitated by a demonstrated personal talent, as in this example from the military in Finland:

> [One] man emphasised that being good at sports in adolescence changed his life. After being successful in boxing he was offered an opportunity to join an army special group for athletics. This was good for his self esteem. In his own words, being good at boxing was 'kind of like the first time I felt proud of something. I felt proud of myself.' (Ronka, Oravala, & Pulkinnen, 2002, p. 55).

We have seen that change arises through events occurring at different levels and with differing visibility in people's lives. Enduring change is often supported by key others in the person's daily life. Sometimes that support is transmitted through positive expectations that encourage the person to engage and stick with change.

PERSONAL REFLECTIONS ON A POSITIVE TURNING POINT

In my personal, academic, and professional life, I have come to recognize the powerful significance of *turning points* in pathways of development, my own pathway included. I often relate a personal story to my students to illustrate this point. I tell them that I can trace my standing in front of them back to the influence of a Latin teacher. He invited and encouraged me and a group of classmates to devote some of our time to being volunteers in an inner city youth club to which the school had a long-term link. I became involved, and thoroughly enjoyed it. I went on to make choices around volunteering, study, and work that led me down a path to where I stand now. I joke to my students that, if I had been absent the day the teacher invited us, I might not be standing in front of them.

Partly, or possibly largely, because of that formative experience in the school-linked youth club, the main focus of my professional, academic, and policy work has been on vulnerable youth. The slum conditions in which many of the club members then lived made a big impression on this young man in the late 1960s and early 1970s. The north inner city of Dublin in which the club, and ironically the school, were situated, had long been probably the most deprived part of the city and country, an undoubtedly striking example of a context of structural disadvantage (e.g., Prunty, 1998).

Reflecting inter-generational change in my immediate and extended family, and wider societal change, I had the opportunity on leaving school to go to a university, the first member of my wider family to do so (although my paternal grandmother had won a scholarship to become—and worked for a time as—a primary school teacher). A number of my cousins have also since gone to university, with some also taking the academic road. I was reared as an only child in a sedate and modest middle class home with both parents who instilled in me a strong sense of social justice and the value of education. I have since been a social worker, youth worker, foster carer, volunteer, board member, policy activist, policy advisor, researcher, social work educator, and head of a university school, all of these various roles connected by a thread of interest in poor and vulnerable children, young people, and their families.

How Chance Plays a Part

This story of happening to hear the gentle invitation serves as an important reminder of how serendipity may at times play a key part in change and in the *offering* of turning points. I use the term *serendipity* to indicate some chance conjuncture of elements in context and process. School as an institution, this school with its specific culture and traditions, the teacher-student relationship, and the peer group of which I was part constituted, in part, the context for the specific interaction in which the teacher issued the invitation. In addition, the teacher and the students were engaged in their own life processes, he as a priest devoted to service and the care of others, we as students dedicated, among other things, to surviving adolescence and to finding novelty in our lives! Yet, as in my case, there are undoubtedly further sets of preceding, unfolding, and interacting reasons why I chose to stay on the path to where I find myself now (and, crucially, as to why I was in the fortunate position to be offered the opportunity in the first place). So, perhaps we should think of serendipity, where it arises, as influencing *opportunities* rather than, or as much as, outcomes. In turn, we should think of opportunities as reflecting a critical, but often *unpredictable*, juncture of process and context.

Opening Up Possibilities

That teacher's invitation could in some way be said to have changed my life, but yet the effect achieved was not part of some grand detailed plan on his part, although the teacher's actions undoubtedly fitted well with the ethos of the school. I think the story helps to underline how complex and challenging it is to attempt to deliver on the ambition of *change*, even at the level of the individual, or more realistically at the level of a *moment* in a person's life. This simple story also illustrates clearly how difficult it is to attribute credit for change or to identify the source of change. An interesting issue is whether this invitation represented a unique window, the only opportunity to move onto the path on which I now find myself.

The profound Irish saying "what is for you won't go by you" is relevant. The saying implies that ultimately we somehow will find our positive destiny—what fate has ordained for us. That is, we will find what is intended for us, even if by a circuitous route. Perhaps, if I had been missing from class the day of the invitation, I might not be on the precise path on which I now find myself, but a further relevant opportunity might have yielded a somewhat different but related pathway and outcome. This underlines the earlier point that the direction of our pathways or the nature of our opportunities is not strictly determined in some linear way but is neither chaotic nor random. Pathways open to an individual may vary somewhat, but only within certain parameters.

Why Are Some Opportunities Grasped and Others Not?

Not all the boys in the class with me that day who heard the invitation took it up. So an attempt at change may fail, or it may produce mixed results. Some boys who took up the offer were influenced in some clear ways, others appeared not to have been so influenced, and others may have been influenced, but the influence then waned, possibly because of competing demands on their time, or because of a choice they made based on deriving insufficient continuing positive meaning or satisfaction from the opportunity. Different sets of dynamics were unfolding in the case of each boy, and their response to both the opportunity and the experience.

The passage of time. The *fit* between opportunity and readiness to respond varied for each boy, at the moment of first offer, and with the passage of time. There may also have been a sleeper effect in terms of the longer term influence of the teacher's invitation. It is possible that boys who appeared uninterested or unimpressed at the time may actually have gone on to manifest a commitment to such voluntary work at a later point partly because of a seed sown by that teacher. We cannot assume a direct linear relationship in the exertion of influence, action A (teacher's invitation), leads to changed behavior C (boy's immediate and sustained engagement in voluntary work). Similarly, attempts to retain a young person in full-time education may fail at the time, but these same efforts to emphasize the value and feasibility of educational effort may bear fruit when a more mature young person re-engages with education, motivated and sustained, at least in part by positive messages they had received earlier (Sacker & Schoon, 2007).

The work of Romans and colleagues (1995) in a large study of the midlife adaptation of women who had been sexually abused in their teenage years found that positive experience in school, academically, socially, or in extracurricular activities, was associated with better functioning in mid-life. There is undoubtedly a complex set of relations and influences behind this finding, but again it flags how some positive effects of a pivotal experience may emerge or endure over long intervals of time.

Less may be more. There is also a further consideration. Insights from the field of resilience theory (Luthar, 2003; Rutter, 2006) also remind us that the notion of change in personal or collective trajectories may sometimes be quite complex. From a resilience perspective, change may need to be understood perhaps as sometimes being more about *sustaining* unexpectedly favorable trajectories of development in the face of adversity (even if only in *sub-trajectories* within certain niches or domains of a person's life). In this sense, change may need to be seen not just about altering circumstances or *doing something* proactively, but also about nurturing or sustaining the unexpected, and in some sense managing, constructively and purposefully, *not to do something*, or at least to do any something in a very subtle or unobtrusive way. The teacher who invited us was present when we used to visit the club, but he was very low key (yet supportive) in his engagement with us and was very careful to leave us *space* in which to find our own feet.

TOWARD A NEW MODEL OF TURNING POINTS AND ENDURING CHANGE

Reflecting on the conception of turning points and its applicability to my own experience in this story and other examples quoted, I suggest a four point framework for considering *turning points*: four conditions necessary for a potential turning point to lead onto enduring change based on a conjunction of opportunity, readiness, agency, and sustaining context. The model I propose is illustrated in figure 2.1 and represents how I suggest that change occurs in a trajectory of development through the mechanism of a turning point. According to the model, there is a sequence of preconditions that must be met in the specified order for enduring change to take hold and for the arch of the trajectory of development to rotate somewhat through the pivot of the turning point. The four factors listed in the necessary order are: opportunity, readiness, agency, and sustaining context and each of these is now explained in turn.

Opportunity

Opportunity represents a favorable conjuncture of process(es) and context whose potential long term value remains yet to be *harvested* and supported. In the story of the teacher and the boy about to finish school

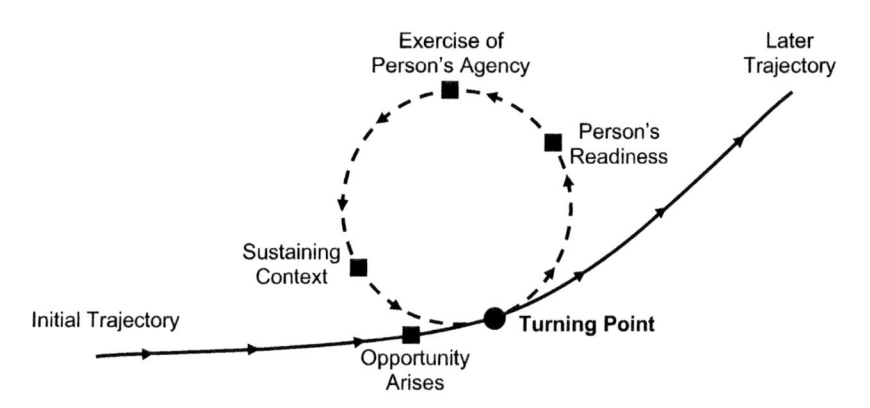

Figure 2.1. Sequence of Pre-Conditions for Enduring Turning Points in Individual Developmental Pathways

prematurely, the conversation between them represented the opportunity. However, the conversation alone did not change anything; it was the boy's responsiveness that proved important, as well as the rewards he found for any subsequent effort he invested.

Readiness

A person may show readiness to respond to an opportunity in a range of ways. Certain advice is heeded, a certain encounter registers, a certain incident resonates at a particular point for a particular person because it carries *live* personal meaning for this person at this point. This meaning may chime with key details in their personal biography and experience at that moment. It also may resonate with the example of admired role models, or the values or expectations inculcated by influential adults at earlier stages; or it may tap into socially valued talents or interests that the person already has or that are unearthed by the turning point experience. The same words of advice may mean nothing, by comparison, for another young person, even if of very similar background but not subject to a similar combination of influence. The person, who is *ready*, is, by contrast, amenable at *this* moment to influence by *this* experience.

A certain opportunity is recognized or valued at a certain moment, but perhaps not at another. In this regard, *readiness* might be considered as the *goodness of fit* between the nature of the opportunity and the person's general disposition and circumstances at the time the opportunity presents. A good fit might lead to the chance being recognized and executed; a poor fit might mean the opposite. A person being heavily committed to nursing a terminally ill relative may mean they are unable to contemplate any fresh opportunities that might seem like a distraction during that period. In such a scenario, there is a poor fit in terms of the person's readiness. Conversely, a newly arrived migrant with a limited social network may be pleased to encounter an opportunity that might open up new contacts, thus implying a good potential fit between opportunity and readiness. This notion of good or poor fit also implies that in the case of a poor fit, a person may take up the same opportunity, previously missed, at a different time when the fit is better.

In my own case, I was an only child, and a relatively shy boy from a *reserved* family with a strong sense of social justice. There was, in retrospect, a good fit for me between achieving the developmental task of moving away from the family to some degree and this opportunity that provided a feasible and legitimate way of finding space. In the short term the priest's invitation, the apparently socially useful purpose of my involvement, the apparently positive influence of older role models, the presence of the priest, and so on, all helped sustain my involvement and my parents' support or acquiescence. This is not to imply my parents were very restrictive. But overall there proved to be a good fit between what the opportunity offered me, and the developmental stage and familial and social circumstances in which I found myself.

Agency

The opportunity presents and the person recognizes it. Agency ensures that the person engages proactively with the opportunity and takes advantage of it. They need to be disposed to taking the step, to risking the change, to committing the energy required. They need to have the right mental attitude at that point. Their stance may be influenced by a complex array of micro-factors, the extent of their self-esteem and self efficacy, their values, their previous experience of risking change, and so forth. But of itself, the commitment to act for change is not of itself a guarantee that the change will stick. There is, I suggest, a fourth key ingredient in the turning point process.

Sustaining Context

In the absence of emotional return on investment and a sustaining context, the influence of the turning point may, arguably, begin to fade, erased by the absence of the necessary reinforcing conditions supportive of long term change. Returning to my own story, in the longer term, the sustaining context for my engagement with the youth work and ultimately the wider field of work included the additional and often new experiences that were opened up. These included the fun, the camaraderie, the social network, the access to valued and meaningful social roles, the positive inter-generational influences, and the insights into other worlds of poverty, of business, of management, of voluntary organizations, of adulthood, and so on. This was an intoxicating mix for a boy from a relatively sheltered background.

The sustaining context may have many elements that support the enduring change. Given our innate preference for what is familiar, change needs help to *stick*. Looking through the lens of the person's *agency*, there needs to be some reason why the change sticks based on the after-change position being better for the person than the before-change experience. At a practical or emotional level, there needs to be some tangible *gain* to motivate the person to help sustain the change and to overcome any natural resistance to change. The gain may be practical in nature. However, it may also be more subtle. The person may perceive what might be termed an *emotional return on investment*. The person perceives that, on balance, she or he gains new affirmation, recognition, and satisfaction from the new identity, role, and experience. Based on this sense, the person may develop or identify with a narrative that feeds the change and commitment, and may have access to support for their new identity and status.

There are several examples that serve to support my perspective. Take the example of an Irish gay man who was assisted in his positive adaptation to coming out in a potentially unsympathetic or ambivalent context by the supportive influence of friends and two of his sisters (Mayock, Bryan, Carr, & Kitching, 2009). In a society where conservative cultural traditions may die hard in such matters, this man describes himself nevertheless as "very content, confident . . . fully out and very happy to be gay . . . [thanks to] . . . the love and support of my friends and two of my sisters" (p. 129).

A second example is of a group of older single Irish emigrant men who had spent their adult lives working as laborers in England. They had been in treatment for severe drinking problems, often rooted in a lifetime of loneliness and isolation. A challenge for them and the treatment approach was to find a new way for them to socialize in drink-free environments and in culturally meaningful ways. They needed a sustaining context that would help their changed behavior to *stick*. One culturally adept strategy was to offer them the routine of a "dry" game of cards on a Saturday night, a night previously pivotal in their patterns of excessive and problematic drinking.

My third example is of an overweight person choosing to go on a diet. This moment of dieting only becomes a positive turning point in the person's body weight trajectory if the person finds a sustaining context for long term adherence to the diet and associated lifestyle changes. Thus, any enduring change is fed by the return on investment. This is reflected in the admiring and supportive comments that the increasingly visible physical transformation begins to elicit, or the enhanced sense of personal well-being, or the reduced anxiety at the prospect of further rebukes by fretting physicians, or the attainment of a transformed and desired physical appearance for a forthcoming event such as a wedding or beach holiday. The emotional return on investment sustains the motivation to maintain change.

Potential moments of change or turning points may arise, sometimes unexpectedly, in the unfolding story of a person's life. I have argued that whether such an opportunity is translated into an enduring change depends on fulfilling certain conditions: The opportunity has to have meaning for the person at the particular time, the person has to actively engage with the opportunity, and for the change to endure, the person must derive a sufficient return on the effort involved in engagement. The return comes in some way from sustaining elements in the person's life context, or as I have described it the *sustaining context*.

THE PROMISE OF POSITIVE TURNING POINTS

I have argued that, in accounting for change in the trajectories of development in individual lives, the concept of turning points is key to understanding positive developmental change. Sometimes highly visible, at other times apparently innocuous, such moments may prove important in opening up new possibilities, often in what may otherwise be unpromising circumstances. Resulting change of this kind requires four conditions to be fulfilled: the opportunity, the readiness of the person to grasp it, the agency of the person to take active steps to respond to the opportunity, and a sustaining context which supports the change effort and adherence to the new pathway. I assert the following as a more effective and accurate perspective for understanding change and the elements that influence change:

1. We need to avoid excessive linearity or premature closure in thinking about change and development in people's lives. While the broad parameters of a person's life course may be shaped by wider social and economic factors, there is still scope for change to emerge in response to events, large or small, and the agency of the person in engaging in that response.
2. We are in necessarily complex territory and we should be wary of overly simple formulations of what is happening and why. There are

multi-layered and reciprocal influences at work in playing out of the person's life story. My argument is that despite or indeed because of this complexity, there still remains the possibility of change, and that this change may often arise from modest sources.
3. There is a need to attend fully to context. History or adversity are not destiny, but they are still very influential, and they are likely to be key parts of the person's unfolding pathway of development. In the sense used here, context refers both to the evolving context in which the person's life unfolds over time, as well as the present moment context. It also refers to the multiple layers of social organization and systems surrounding the person, from the global economy to neighborhood norms, to family ethos and routines and so on.
4. Resilient adaptation may occur along trajectories adjusted by turning point moments or experiences. Chronic or acute adversity may jeopardize the prospects of the individual. For some, a favorable mix of supportive opportunities and positive engagement by the person may lead to resilient adaptation in at least some aspect or periods of their life in which their performance or functioning exceeds what might otherwise be expected.
5. Opportunities spurned at one point may recur. A young person may drop out of school, but may re-enter education in young adulthood. For example, positive impressions created by even some teachers and access to clear information about educational offerings and economic support may each prove important triggers or sustainers in moves to re-enter education.
6. Change may come in unexpected and unpredictable ways. For those seeking to influence positive change it is important to support the possibility and *stickability* of such change. In this chapter, I have emphasized the power of expectation. A key ingredient in the power of change is belief in the possibility of change and in the individual's own belief in their efficacy or capacity for effective responses in the face of potential change (Bandura, 1989).
7. Life course and longitudinal perspectives on the person's progress, prospective and retrospective, may yield valuable insights about developmental influences and resources for individuals in adversity. The issue of resilient development in the face of adversity remains a field rich with potential for scholarly inquiry and for application in human service policy and programs. This potential will be more

fully realized with careful attention to a long term view to trends (and shifts)—looking backward and forward.

REFERENCES

Bandura, A. (1989). Human agency in social cognitive theory. *American Psychologist*, 44, 1175-1184.

Elder, G. (1998). *Children of the Great Depression, 25th Anniversary Edition*. Boulder, CO: Westview Press.

Halsey, T. C., & Jensen, M. H. (2004). Hurricanes and butterflies. *Nature*, 428, 127–128.

Johnson, Z., Molloy, B., Scallan, E., Fitzpatrick, P., Rooney, B., Keegan, T., & Byrne, P. (2000). Community mothers programme—seven year follow-up of a randomized controlled trial of non-professional intervention in parenting. *Journal of Public Health*, 22, 337–342.

Kilburn, M. R., & Karoly, L. (2008). *The economics of early childhood policy: What the dismal science has to say about investing in children*. Occasional Paper Santa Monica: RAND Corporation.

Laub, J., & Sampson, R. (2003). *Shared beginnings, divergent lives: Delinquent boys to age 70*. Cambridge, MA: Harvard University Press.

Lewontin, R. (2000). *The triple helix: Gene, organism, and environment*. Cambridge, MA: Harvard University Press.

Luthar, S. (Ed.). (2003). *Resilience and vulnerability: Adaptation in the context of childhood adversities*. Cambridge UK: Cambridge University Press.

Luthar, S., & Zerlazo, L. B. (2003). Research into resilience: An integrative review. In S. Luthar (Ed.), *Resilience and vulnerability: Adaptation in the context of childhood adversities* (pp. 510–549). Cambridge UK: Cambridge University Press.

Mayock, P., Bryan, A., Carr, N., & Kitching, K. (2009). *Supporting LGBT lives: A study of the mental health and well-being of lesbian, gay, bisexual and transgender people*. Dublin: National Office of Suicide Prevention.

Prunty, J. (1998). *Dublin slums 1800 –1925: A study in urban geography*. Dublin: Irish Academic Press.

Putnam, R. (2001). *Bowling alone: The collapse and revival of American community*. London: Simon & Schuster.

Romans, S., Martin, J., Anderson, J., O'Shea, M., & Mullen, P. (1995). Factors that mediate between child sexual abuse and adult psychological outcome. *Psychological Medicine*, 25, 127-142.

Ronka, A., Oravala, S., & Pulkinnen, L. (2002). " I met this wife of mine and things got onto a better track:" Turning points in risk development. *Journal of Adolescence*, 25, 47–63.

Rutter, M. (2006). Implications of resilience concepts for scientific understanding. *Annals of the New York Academy of Sciences*, 1094, 1–12.

Sacker, A., & Schoon, I. (2007). Educational resilience in later life: Resources and assets in adolescence and return to education after leaving school at age 16. *Social Science Research, 36*, 873–896.

Schoon, I. (2006). *Risk and resilience—Adaptations in changing times.* Cambridge UK: Cambridge University Press.

Schoon, I. (2007). Adaptations to changing times: Agency in context. *International Journal of Psychology, 42*, 94–101.

Stevens, I., & Cox, P. (2008). Complexity theory: Developing new understandings of child protection in field settings and in residential child care. *British Journal of Social Work, 38*, 1320–1336.

Werner, E., & Smith, R. (2001). *Journeys from childhood to midlife: Risk, resilience, and recovery.* Ithaca, NY: Cornell University Press.

CHAPTER 3

"We Lost Touch of Who Each Other Was": Swift Transformations in Close Relationships

Susan Lollis

Two events happened in the world that took me out of my normal musings about close dyadic relationships of children and adolescents and into the broader context in which close relationships occur. On May 2, 2008 the cyclone, Nargis, hit the coast of Myanmar and devastated large parts of the low-lying Irrawaddy Delta; 84,500 people died and 53,000 people were missing. Homes were flattened, trees uprooted, power lines downed, and water systems devastated. Initially, the Myanmar government did not allow aid workers into the country, so the world watched as thousands of people struggled with the devastation. Then, on May 12, 2008, an earthquake with a magnitude of 6.1 devastated the southwestern province of Sichaun, China. According to official government reports, more than 69,000 people lost their lives, 18,000 people were missing, and 5 million people were homeless. Photos of people separated from family and home were in the news. I particularly remember the photos of children and adolescents in Myanmar and China who had lost most, if not all, of their family members. I found myself wondering about the effects on the countries involved, and the effects, in a wider world context, of so many children losing their close relationships so swiftly.

Two early and consistent underlying themes in my research have been the process by which children form close relationships and the effect of separation and loss of these same relationships (Lollis, 1990, 2003). As I began to consider the experiences of the children and adolescents in Myanmar and China, and by extension, other children who have found themselves swiftly separated from their close relationships, I realized that *swift transformations* in close relationships would be an important issue to explore for a book about change and human development. Swift transformations are changes to relationships that occur much more rapidly than normal. Frequently, swift transformations occur through events that are unexpected or unpredicted. In this chapter, I explore swift transformations in children's close relationships from a perspective informed by an interactional model of close relationships, theories of separation and loss, and ecological theory. My primary goal is to present an integrated theoretical framework in which the antecedents, processes, and consequences of swift transformations are understood, in light of what is already known about relationship formation and separation and loss.

INTERACTIONAL MODEL OF CLOSE RELATIONSHIPS

Robert Hinde and Joan Stevenson-Hinde (1987) described systematically how the interactions in which two people engage help to form their relationship. They conceptualized interactions as the *building blocks* for the development of a relationship over time; time which included a past, present, and future.

> When two individuals interact on successive occasions over time, each interaction may affect subsequent ones, and we speak of [the individuals] as having a relationship. Their relationship includes not only what they do together, but the perceptions, fears, expectations, and so on that each has about the other and about the future course of the relationship, based in part on the individual histories of the two interactants and the past history of their relationship with each other (Hinde & Stevenson-Hinde, 1987, p. 2).

There are five main principles contained in this quote that form the foundation of an interactional model wherein interactions, perception of the interactions, and emotions related to the interactions become the relationship:

(a) Relationships develop through interaction.
(b) Both people involved in the interaction contribute and thus both contribute to the relationship.
(c) Each relationship is a distinctive accumulation of dyadic interactions.
(d) Each relationship is based on past interactions.
(e) Close relationships have both a representation based on past experiences and a representation based on a concept of the future.

These five principles of change are at the micro-analytic level of close relationship building (Hinde & Stevenson-Hinde, 1987). Imagine that with each interaction, the relationship changes slightly. Each new interaction is added to the repertoire of past interactions, changing the concept of the past, ever so slightly. Each new interaction also contributes to the repertoire of concept of the future, changing the concept of the future, ever so slightly.

Hinde's interactional model of close relationships is an important tool to help scholars conceptualize how close dyadic relationships normally develop. The model seeks to explain *slow transformations* in which change occurs gradually between two individuals, interaction upon interaction. Originally a conceptual model, the framework needed empirical research to support Hinde's assertions. Therefore, Hildy Ross and I (Ross & Lollis, 1989) focused our early work on the first three principles of the model—interaction, mutuality, and distinctiveness. We worked to observe, transcribe, and code the interactions of young children between the ages of two and four. We were interested in showing that children, even as young as two, could develop distinctive close relationships through interaction over time. By pairing children with two other playmates, with whom they were unacquainted but met one at a time for play over eighteen play sessions, and using social relations analysis, we were able to display that children, as young as two, develop distinctive close peer relationships. Imagine our elation, and the elation of infant researchers, when we were able to display that even very young children form distinctive relationships with peers.

I initially developed the last two principles of Hinde's interactional model of close relationships (past expectations and future anticipations) with Leon Kuczynski (Lollis & Kuczynski, 1997). We were working on concepts of bidirectionality in parent-child relationships and wanted to adapt Hinde's model so that we could describe not only the contexts of bidirectionality but also the processes by which parents and children form close relationships. The model we developed displayed that as a parent and child interacted over time, the dyad developed expectations based on past interactions and anticipations of future interactions. Later, when using Hinde's interactional model of close relationships to write about bidirectionality in parent-child relationships, I began to consider more extensively the *past* and the *future* in parent-child relationships (Lollis,

2003). I speculated that in close relationships, both the past interactions and the anticipated future are the context for the present interaction with the person. Interactions that are responsive in the past, are responsive in the present, and anticipated to be responsive in the future.

The interactional model of close relationships is not only useful for conceptualizing closeness in parent-child relationships, but it also can be adapted to conceptualize other close relationships in children's lives. For example, close relationships occur between siblings (Klassen & Lollis, 2002). Recently, we engaged in a review of sibling relationships within the psychology, sociology, and anthropology literatures (Koguchi-Ames & Lollis, 2004). Five consistent themes of interaction between siblings emerged that provide the contexts for the development of close relationships: nurturance, conflict, equality, responsibility, and reciprocity. Using these themes of interaction, I adapted the model originally developed to provide insight into parent-child relationships to hypothesize how one might conceptualize and categorize the development of close sibling relationships.

To summarize, what is useful from the interactional model of close relationships for exploring swift transformations is the knowledge that children, even at a very young age, can form close relationships with parents and siblings. Each of the relationships, formed through numerous mutual interactions, is distinctive and has an experienced past and an anticipated future. Each of these relationships becomes the *antecedent* context for a swift transformation experience. This is what the child understands about relationships before a swift transformation occurs. Only recently have I realized that the interactional model's depiction of the past, present, and future resembles the conceptualization of the *working model* found in attachment theory. Working models focus on real life experiences of day-to-day interactions with parents; they are relationship specific and disrupted by separation and loss (Cassidy & Shaver, 2008).

THEORIES OF SEPARATION AND LOSS

There has been a long history of attempts in psychology, psychiatry, nursing, social work, and the aligned disciplines to understand the effect of separation and loss on children and their relationships. As early as the 1940s, Burlingham and Freud (1944), working in the Hamstead Nurseries during WWII, and Spitz (1946), working with infants born to single mothers in penal institutions, documented the effect of separation and loss on children. In 1952, James Robertson issued a film titled, *A Two-year-old Goes to the Hospital*, followed by a set of articles and another film documentary on responses of young children to loss. Later, the Tavistock Child Development Research Unit in London sponsored the Tavistock Seminars and invited prominent researchers interested in close relationships and separation. Participants included Harry Harlow, who studied love and affection in primates (Harlow, 1961), John Bowlby, who studied children who were hospitalized and separated from their parents (1961), and Mary Ainsworth, whose work focused on parent-child attachment (Ainsworth & Wittig, 1969). Eventually, Ainsworth and her colleagues (researchers, graduate students, and students of her students) over multiple generations would observe, document, record, code, and categorize the effects of separation from the primary caregiver (Ainsworth, Blehar, Waters, & Wall, 1978; Cassidy & Shaver, 2008).

The amount of attention and concurrent research generated in the area of separation and loss was immense. All of the studies pointed to the emotional effects on children (and primates), when separated from their primary caregivers. Brief separations resulted in searching for the caregiver, calling, or crying. The majority of young children in these studies temporarily suffered a lost sense of security (Ainsworth et al., 1978). Longer separations, well documented first by Bowlby and his colleagues and then by others, resulted in sadness, anxiety, anger, despair, and, in the absence of reunion, changes to the child's working model of close relationships (Bowlby, 1973; Cassidy & Shaver, 2008). What is useful from theories of separation and loss for this chapter on swift transformation, is the overwhelming convergent findings that separation from a close relationship causes predictable responses in children. If the close relationship is the antecedent context for understanding swift transformations, then separation and loss is the causal event that leads to predictable change and consequences.

ECOLOGICAL SYSTEMS THEORY

Urie Bronfenbrenner's Ecological Systems Theory (1979) is useful in considering the different levels or contexts in which children might experience swift transformations. His model contains five nested levels of systems or contexts important for child development. The model begins with a central sphere representing the child. This sphere is surrounded by four concentric spheres representing the microsystem context of close dyadic relationships including (a) parents, siblings, peers; (b) the mesosystem context (two microsystems in interaction); (c) the exosystem context of external environmental institutions that directly influence development including school, church, and other group contexts; and (d) the macrosystem context, which represents the larger socio-cultural context of ideology, laws, customs, culture. Later, Bronfenbrenner added the chronosystem context of time into his model. Certainly, in the microsystem context of close dyadic relationships, family and friends are of importance when considering swift transformations. However, the ever-widening rings of contextual influence including institutions such as schools in the exosystem, as well as a country's laws in the macrosystem are also of extreme importance. Ecological theory depicts the different levels or contexts in which swift transformations of close relationships can occur. However, regardless of the context, it is the dyadic close relationship that transforms. What follows is a brief discussion of swift transformations and three examples viewed from the microsystem, the exosystem, and macrosystem, respectively.

SWIFT TRANSFORMATION IN CLOSE RELATIONSHIPS

Recently, I have begun to ask the following questions, "What could cause a swift transformation in a close relationship?" "How would the individual describe this transformation?" "What might aid or help the individual through in this swift transformation?" "Could things learned in slow transformations help us to understand what individuals need to recover from swift transformations?"

The interactional model of close relationships is a *slow (and steady) transformation* model of relationships. That is, over time, often a long period, as two individuals interact their interactions and perceptions of the interactions create the relationship. Over the course of a long, close relationship, the *building blocks* of interaction mount up and create dependable expectations from past interactions and possibly dependable anticipations of the future. Over a long period the working model is developed. I have come to believe that the longer the relationship, the less of an impact that each individual interaction might have on either person's understanding of the past, present, and future of the relationship if the interaction is within what has been experienced and what is anticipated. This is a slow transformation model.

Yet, events can occur within children's lives that cause a quick and clear change in the child's interaction within the relationship as constructed. We have many examples of large numbers of children within North America experiencing swift transformations in their close relationships.

Swift Transformation caused by Sibling Cancer: Microsystem

Approximately 80 percent of individuals in Europe and North America grow up with a sibling (Dunn, 2004). The sibling relationship is often the longest relationship that most people experience. Additionally, sibling relationships are intimate. Most children spend even more time in interaction with their siblings than with their parents (McHale & Crouter, 1996). Siblings know each other well and frequently provide emotional support to one another. Children, in particular, may rely on this source of support when faced with stressful experiences.

Chronic or life-threatening conditions in one member of a family can be a cause for a swift transformation, particularly if separation and/or loss is likely to occur. Research regarding the effects of pediatric cancer on family members has focused primarily on the child or adolescents diagnosed with pediatric cancer and their parents (Barlow & Ellard, 2006). Recently, however, researchers and practitioners have turned their attention to the experiences of non-cancer siblings, particularly the psychosocial needs of these non-cancer siblings during the time of diagnosis and treatment of the sibling with cancer (Wilkins & Woodgate, 2005).

I have worked to understand the transformation of sibling relationships when one of the siblings develops cancer. We wanted to explore with non-cancer siblings how the experience of having a sister or brother diagnosed with cancer influenced them not only during the occurrence of cancer, but also in their present lives and possibly into the future. Thus, our research focused on the individual's understanding of the influence of the cancer experience in the past relationship, the present relationship, and into the future relationship with the sibling with cancer. We interviewed individuals who were old enough at the time of their siblings' diagnosis of cancer to retain memories of the experience and who were several years beyond the cancer experience at the time of the interview. We wanted to know about the context of the cancer experience on their present lives as distinguished from the time of the cancer. The interviews focused on three main open-ended questions, "How do you think your sibling's diagnosis (a) influenced your relationship with your sibling in the past (at the time of diagnosis), (b) continues to influence your relationship with your sibling in the present, and (c) will possibly influence your relationship with your sibling in the future?" All interviews were transcribed and open coded. We recorded categories relating to the family, the sibling relationship, and the self for past, present, and future time (Lollis & Hamelin, 2008).

Among our findings is the discovery that non-cancer siblings described the experience of the sibling relationship after the diagnosis of cancer as having a past, but not a particularly useable past. Expectations from the past seemed no longer useful for the present. Possibly the *internal working model* of the relationship was suddenly no longer useful. Here is one of the most revealing quotes from a participant describing the swift transformation of her sibling relationship following her sister's diagnosis.

> It became almost like a non-existent, superficial relationship that we had after that [diagnosis of cancer], because I would know, I wouldn't want to go down to the hospital, but I'd go down, and I'd be sitting in her hospital room, watching TV, talking about how the day was, you know, "What did you do today? What did you do today?" Uh huh. Not wanting to say too much because we didn't know each other's boundaries, we didn't know how far to go. So, I think not knowing the boundaries, or not knowing what to say to each other, um and how to accept the fact that this was happening at the beginning hurt our relationship when she was diagnosed, and when she was sick in treatment, simply because it's not that we didn't understand what was going on, but that we lost touch of who each other was before and we became who each other were then." (Sarah, age 16 at sibling's cancer diagnosis).

The phrases, "we didn't know each other's boundaries" and "we lost touch of who each other was before" were striking. The history of interaction of the relationship, the antecedent context of the relationship, seemed no longer useful to the present needs of the individual. In attachment terms, it seemed as if the working model of the sibling relationship no longer fit the present needs of the relationship. The past expectations were no longer pertinent to the present and the diagnosis of a serious life-threatening illness called future anticipations into question.

Swift Transformation caused by School Transition: Exosystem

Focusing on close relationships in the exosystem, there are contexts in which large numbers of children and adolescents interact within close relationships, including neighborhoods, health and welfare systems, and schools. Within Canada, all children from the ages of six to sixteen are required to enroll in school. Parents who choose to home-school their children must register their intent with the government. There are at least two large school-related transitions identified in the literature that influence not only the child entering school, but also the family. These are the transition that occurs at school entry and the transition that occurs from a junior level of education to a more senior level of education.

It is well-documented that the move from a junior level of education to a more senior level of education changes the patterns of relationships for children and adolescents. This occurs not only with their friends (Hardy, Bukowski, & Sippola, 2002), but also with their parents (Falbo, Lein, & Amador, 2001). Friendships are susceptible to change upon entry into high school, but the increase in school population and organization of classes offers opportunities to meet new people (Hardy et al., 2002). Both adolescents and parents (Falbo et al., 2001) anticipate changes in peer relations as adolescents enter high school. Research findings suggest parents attempt to steer their adolescents toward activities in order to link their children with positive academic and peer networks (Falbo et al., 2001). The transformation in relationships that occurs for children as they enter school is within the normative model of transformations for North America.

There are other examples of school transition in which children experienced swift transformations in their close relationships and experienced discontinuity with the past through separation and loss. Although I could choose many different school transition examples, I have chosen the one that occurred for many First Nations people within Canada from the 1880s through the early 1980s (Gagne, 1998). The schooling of First Nation children came under colonial control in 1867 with the *British North America Act* and further in 1876 through the *Indian Act*. Both of these acts set up an education policy that would last one hundred years with four generations of First Nation children passing through residential schools. Indian agents and clergy took children from their families and placed them in residential schools, often without their siblings, cousins, or friends. The schools did not allow the children to use their native language or go home on holidays. In 1880 there were eleven residential schools for indigenous children in Canada, increasing to seventy-seven by the early 1900s, and finally sixty until the late 1970s when the National Indian Brotherhood of Canada called for the end of federal control of First Nations' Schooling (First Nations Health Commission, 1994). According to records of the Canadian federal government, during that one hundred-year period, tens of thousands of First Nations children attended residential schools.

After interviewing individuals who experienced residential schools, the First Nations Health Commission (1994) summarized the impact of the residential school experience on First Nations children. When asked about memories of the experience of being placed in residential school one individual said:

> My mother and grandmother were gone. . . . This place and everyone in it was so strange. I didn't know anything or anyone there. The thing I remember was standing at a window and looking out into the dusk and it seemed like I could look forever and ever and ever into the sky. . . . I remember feeling my tininess, my littleness. I felt so lost and so alone (p. 23).

Another individual explained the experience in the following manner:

> I didn't trust anyone. I didn't feel anything, and I didn't talk to anyone. I didn't even trust myself (p. 33).

Both of these quotes are remarkable. In the first quote, the individual uses the word "lost," as it was used in the sibling quote earlier in the chapter, but this time "lost and so alone." In the second quote, the individual speaks about losing trust in others and in oneself. These descriptions of young children's feelings acutely describe the swift transformation experience. The closest relationships are no longer available. What was presumed from past relationships seems no longer useful.

Another quote illustrates that this particular context of the exosystem not only affected the children, but their family relationships as well.

Dad started to drink, and then mom joined him, and then he stopped working and then there was all this fighting and drinking. My older brothers got into that stuff too. Every time I came back, things were worse. . . . My family just kept breaking a little more, until finally, it was all broken (p. 32).

Bull (1991) argues that residential schools contributed significantly to the social breakdown of families. One might ask how children navigated this transition to residential school, a transition that swiftly transformed most close relationships. The interactional model of close relationships (Hinde & Stevenson-Hinde, 1987; Lollis, 2003) and previous research on separation and loss are useful for answering this question. In *Breaking the Silence* (First Nations Health Commission, 1994), the people interviewed about their experience in residential schools tell how they realized that they needed to band together. They needed to create close relationships with each other. Children turned to other children for protection, emotional support, and reassurance. "By developing close connections with each other (some relationships which lasted into adulthood), other children became part of one's family" (p. 43). Collectively, the interactional model of close relationships and research on separation and loss suggest that children formed new relationships through interactions, possibly building from the working models of relationships that they already possessed.

Swift Transformation caused by Translocation: Macrosystem

The next ring of Bronfenbrenner's model represents the macrosystem, which involves the laws and customs of a country. Over the past decade, there has been increasing interest in the issues of cross-cultural relocation and acculturation. In part, this is due to the increase in the number of individuals and families are moving from one area of a country to another.

During World War II, after the attack on Pearl Harbor on December 7, 1941, 120,000 individuals of Japanese descent in the United States (two-thirds of whom had become American citizens) and 22,000 individuals of Japanese descent in Canada (most of whom were native-born Canadians or naturalized citizens) were relocated to internment camps, mainly up and down the Pacific Coast. From 1941–1945, families of Japanese descent, in both countries, were moved from their homes on the Pacific Coast to "holding" locations, often cattle yards or fairgrounds, and then eventually into the interior of the two countries. Canada had eight internment camps in British Columbia, Kaslo, New Denver, Tashme, Roseberry, Slocan City, Lemon Creek, Sandon, and Greenwood. The United States had ten internment camps scattered in various states, two in Arkansas including Gila River and Poston, two in Arizona including Jerome and Rohwer, two in California including Manzanar and Tule Lake, and one each in Amache, Colorado, Minidoka, Idaho, Topaz, Utah, and Heart Mountain, Wyoming. Both countries also had work camps and prisoner of war camps. Families were asked to move from their homes and lease, sell, and place in storage their household and business possessions. Sometimes, husbands and fathers were separated from their wives and children (Nagata, 1998).

In Canada, readers can obtain the history of these camps from the Canadian Broadcast Corporation (2009). In the United States, an oral history of personal accounts of adults looking back on their experience as children is available through *Densho: The Japanese American Legacy Project* (2009), a website committed to "preserving the past and imaging the future." The word *Densho* means "pass on to the next generation." The Densho Project contains 230 interviews with individuals who experienced the internment camps and over 6,000 photos of that time in history in North America. On the site are accounts of adults who were children at the time of the internment. I choose one quote from the Densho project for this chapter. Frank Fujii remembers a bittersweet reunion with his father after three years separation. This is a vivid memory of the moment in which Mr. Fujii's relationship with his father transformed immediately. His father was in a camp in Santa Fe, New Mexico while he and his family were in a camp in Tule Lake, California.

> When the Justice Department OK'd his release from Santa Fe, New Mexico to Tule Lake, I said, "Dad's (snaps his fingers) coming back. Man!" [. . .] "He's coming back." And so we knew what day, they didn't tell us what time. So waiting for a truck to drop him off and we waited and waited. I remember it was in the afternoon and it was a hot day and the truck dropped him off and he had to get off the back and I grabbed his luggage and I brought it inside. Now, I didn't see him from '41, Dec 7th, 'till, uh, '44 something, uh, '44 . . . so that's a few years and I think when I'd grown up so much, my . . . my body'd changed, my looks changed, and I'm more of a man. I mean I've grown about 5 . . . 6 inches. So as he looked around the family, [. . .] my dad's grandson, and he looks at mom and then some

guests that knew him, some people in Tule and Seattle who knew him [. . .] But the whole scenario was (pauses and then continues) . . . there was a lot of his peer group who dad sorta 'membered and didn't because I think he was, he was too tired that day . . . but the bad scenario was as he went around the room nodding his head and kinda greeting everybody by looking at them and kinda saying, "I think I know you, but 'hi' how are you," but then he points to me, of all people, and he says, "Who is this boy?" And you know that (chokes up) . . . that really shook me (chokes up again and puts his hand to his chin) . . . but uh . . . I, I never forgot that because, uh . . . I felt lost at that time. And I think that, uh, mental part of it all, that's what I think the effect of camp does to you. And uh, it isn't the monetary kind of things that get to you, it's the, because you can always sorta adjust, but the loss of, uh, family tie . . . (waves hand back and forth in front of him) . . . it was tough. And, uh, but I was glad, I was glad he was there. In fact, I tried to be this nice guy to dad. I said, "Dad, I heard you play shogee a lot" . . . you know it's that Japanese chess game . . . and I said, "If you teach me, I'll play with you," 'cause you know I wanted him to have something to do. [. . .] But, uh, you know it was hard, I think I lost that, that tie and ever since then it's been, it was down hill, down hill . . . (Fujii, 1997)

The impact of separation on the relationship between Mr. Fujji and his father is evident. Mr. Fujii refers to "the bad scenario" as the moment in which his father, who Mr. Fujii has been separated from for three years, is unable to recognize him and asks, "Who is this boy?" Mr. Fujii further describes how his father's inability to recognize him affected him, "that really shook me" and "I felt lost at that time." He also describes how he never forgot that event and proceeds to express what he felt was the effect of separation, "I think that, uh, mental part of it all, that's what I think the effect of camp does to you. And uh, it isn't the monetary kind of things that get to you, it's the, because you can always sorta adjust, but the loss of, uh, family tie . . . , I think I lost that, that tie and ever since then it's been, it was down hill, down hill."

SWIFT TRANSFORMATIONS: IMPLICATIONS FOR INTERVENTION

Swift transformations due to separation and loss in children's close relationships can happen in many different ecological contexts. It is not surprising, then, that researchers who are working to understand resilience in children and adolescents suggest three interrelated contexts that need attention for interventions (Walsh, 1996): the individual, the family, and the social support network. The individual needs support in order to develop positive self-esteem and good intellectual ability to address the vulnerability caused by the loss of close relationships. The family, not just the child, experiences the swift transformation. It may be difficult for the family to organize itself and reconstruct itself. The family needs support to re-develop into a context that nurtures, guides, and supports the child and adolescent. Walsh (1996) particularly notes that the family needs a context of "warmth, affection, emotional support, and clear-cut, reasonable structure and limits" to help bolster a child or adolescent's resilience. Finally, the social support networks of friends, neighbors, teachers, and mentors need support to continue to re-engage the child and adolescent in relationships that happen outside the family. The above three contexts for the development of resilience are comparable to Bronfenbrenner's (1979) context of the child, the microsystem, and the exosystem.

There are at least two other contexts that need supportive intervention. First, researchers who study resilience rarely address the context of the macrosystem. It is at the macrosystem level that laws and customs of the country have an impact on the child or adolescent. The people who develop policies that affect children's close relationships need information about relationship formation and the impact of separation and loss on close relationships. Policy makers need to work with science-practitioners who can translate research and help develop laws that are supportive, rather than destructive to children's close relationships. Policy makers have a particular responsibility to protect close relationships, since the institution of a law can affect thousands of children and adolescents at any moment in time.

The other context for intervention is the dyad. A law may affect large groups of children and adolescents, but the law is felt child-by-child and dyad-by-dyad. When a close relationship swiftly changes, through unforeseeable circumstances—a family member or friend becomes ill with a life threatening illness, a child is removed from his or her home and placed within another home or institution, possibly along with large numbers of other children, or an entire family is translocated from one location to another—any time a close relationship is transformed swiftly, the child or adolescent may need help in re-creating the close relationships that were lost or creating new close relationships.

Children and adolescents need support to begin again in interactions with the people who were "lost" or begin interactions with others in order to form close relationships. The First Nations Health Commission (1994) suggests a *healing model* that includes reconnecting with family members and learning the necessary skills involved in how to "be close" with others. Reconnecting with family members includes having an opportunity to interact repeatedly, talk at length, and grieve the sudden loss of the relationship.

In returning to my *microanalytic roots*, I suggest that the interactional model of close relationships may not only be useful in understanding how close relationships are formed, but also useful in providing answers to how close relationships can be reformed. In fact, many of the individuals who are quoted in this chapter mentioned what they needed when they felt "lost," or "alone," or "lost touch with who each other was before [the swift transition]." The quotes in this chapter provide hints of what the children, themselves, needed to regain a close relationship that was "lost." For example, for the individual who had a sibling diagnosed with cancer, merely watching TV together appeared helpful:

> I wouldn't want to go down to the hospital, but I'd go down, and I'd be sitting in her hospital room, watching TV, talking about how the day was, you know, "What did you do today? What did you do today?" (Sarah, age 16 at sibling's cancer diagnosis).

Or from Frank Fujii, playing a game with his father:

> But I was glad, I was glad he was there. In fact, I tried to be this nice guy to dad. I said, "Dad, I heard you play shogee a lot . . ." you know it's that Japanese chess game . . . and I said, "If you teach me, I'll play with you," 'cause you know I wanted him to have something to do.

Or from the literature on First Nations children's experiences of separation and loss, turning to others for protection, emotional support, and reassurance. "By developing close connections with each other (some relationships which lasted into adulthood), other children became part of one's family" (First Nations Health Commission, p. 43).

The children and adolescents needed time and repeated interaction to re-form the relationship that had been close. It may be possible to re-learn the necessary skills involved in being close or intimate by considering again the interactional model of close relationships. It is through interactions that people build and develop relationships. It may be in the mundane interactions of everyday life, as the children have suggested, such as watching television together, asking how the day was, playing a game together, helping each other, that one learns to regain what was lost. Possibly the way back into close relationships, after a swift transformation, is through the numerous, sometimes mundane, interactions that inform each who the other is presently. Each of these interactions, added together over time, create again the relationship, a relationship that once again has a past and a present and gives hope for a future together.

REFERENCES

Ainsworth, M. D. S., Blehar, M. C., Waters, E., & Wall. S. (1978). *Patterns of attachment: A psychological study of the strange situation.* Hillsdale, NJ: Erlbaum.

Ainsworth, M. D. S., & Wittig, B. A. (1969). Attachment and exploratory behavior of one-year-olds in a strange situation. In B.M. Foss (Ed.), *Determinants of infant behavior* (Vol. 4, pp. 129–173). New York: Barnes & Noble.

Barlow, J. H., & Ellard, D. R. (2006). The psychological well-being of children with chronic disease, their parents and siblings: An overview of the research evidence base. *Child: Care, Health & Development, 32*(1), 19–31.

Bowlby, J. (1961). Separation anxiety: A critical review of the literature. *Journal of Child Psychology and Psychiatry, 1,* 251–269.

Bowlby, J. (1973). *Attachment and loss: Vol. 2. Separation.* New York: Basic Books.

Bronfenbrenner, U. (1979). *The ecology of human development.* Cambridge, MA: Harvard University Press.

Bull, L.R. (1991). Indian residential schooling: The native perspective. *Canadian Journal of Native Education, 18,* 3–63.

Burlingham, D., & Freud, A. (1944). *Infants without families.* London: Allen & Unwin.

Canadian Broadcast Corporation. (2009). *Japanese internment: British Columbia wages war against Japanese Canadians.* Retrieved March 15, 2009, from http://history.cbc.ca/history/?MIval=EpisContent&series_id=1&episode_id=14&chapter_id=3&page_id=3&lang=E

Cassidy, J., & Shaver, P. R. (2008). *Handbook of attachment: Theory, research, and clinical applications* (2nd ed). New York: Guilford.

Densho: The Japanese American Legacy Project (2009). Retrieved March 15, 2009, from http://www.densho.org/archive

Dunn, J. (2004). Sibling relationships. In P. K. Smith & C. H. Hart (Eds.), *Childhood social development* (pp. 223–237). Oxford, UK: Blackwell.

Falbo, T., Lein, L., & Amador, N. (2001). Parental involvement during the transition to high school. *Journal of Adolescent Research, 16*, 511–529.

First Nations Health Commission. (1994). *Breaking the silence.* Ottawa, ON: Assembly of First Nations.

Fujii, F. (September 3, 1997). A bittersweet reunion with father at Tule Lake (Densho ID: denshovh-ffrank-01-0025). Larry Hashima & Beth Kawahara (Interviewers), *Densho Visual History Collection.* Seattle, WA: Densho. Retrieved March 15, 2009, from http://www.densho.org/archive

Gagne, M.-A. (1998). The role of dependency and colonialism in generating trauma. In Y. Danieli (Ed.), *International handbook of multinational legacies of trauma* (pp. 355–372). New York: Plenum.

Hardy, C. L., Bukowski, W. M., & Sippola, L. K. (2002). Stability and change in peer relationships during the transition to middle-level school. *Journal of Early Adolescence, 22*, 117–142.

Harlow, H. F. (1961). The development of affectional patterns in infant monkeys. In B. M. Foss (Ed.), *Determinants of infant behavior* (Vol. 1, pp. 75–100). New York: Wiley.

Hinde, R. A., & Stevenson-Hinde, J. (1987). Interpersonal relationships and child development. *Developmental Review, 7*, 1–21.

Klassen, T. M., & Lollis, S. (2002). Moments of intimacy: Co-creation of themes and coordination of action within sibling pretense. *Canadian Journal of Infancy and Early Childhood, 9*, 29–41.

Koguchi-Ames, Y., & Lollis, S. (2004, August). *Japanese and Euro-Canadian parental socialization of siblinghood.* Poster session presented at the 17th International Congress of the International Association for Cross-Cultural Psychology, Xi'an, China.

Lollis, S. P. (1990). Effects of maternal behaviour on toddler behaviour during play and separation. *Child Development, 61*, 99–103.

Lollis, S. (2003). Conceptualizing the influence of past and future in present parent-child relationships. In L. Kuczynski (Ed.), *Handbook of dynamics in parent-child relations* (pp. 67–87). Thousand Oaks, CA: Sage.

Lollis, S., & Hamelin, J. (2008, April). *Changed lives: The experience of siblings of children with cancer.* Poster session presented at the biennial conference of the Society for Research on Adolescents, Chicago, IL.

Lollis, S., & Kuczynski, L. (1997). Beyond one hand clapping: Seeing bidirectionality in parent-child relations. *Journal of Social and Personal Relationships, 14*, 441–461.

McHale, S. M., & Crouter, A. C. (1996). The family context of children's sibling relationships. In G. Brody (Ed.), *Sibling relationships: Their causes and consequences* (pp. 173–195). Norwood, NJ: Ablex.

Nagata, D. K. (1998). Intergenerational effects of the Japanese American internment. In Y. Danieli (Ed.), *International handbook of multinational legacies of trauma* (pp. 125–139). New York: Plenum.

Robertson, J. (1952). *A two-year-old goes to hospital* (16 mm film; 45 min). London: Tavistock Child Development Research Unit.

Ross, H. S., & Lollis, S. P. (1989). A social relations analysis of toddler peer relationships. *Child Development, 60*, 1082–1091.

Spitz, R. (1946). Anaclitic depression. *Psychoanalytic Study of the Child, 2*, 313–342.

Walsh, F. (1996). The concept of family resilience: Crisis and challenge. *Family Process, 35*, 261–281.

Wilkins, K., & Woodgate, R. (2005). A review of qualitative research on the childhood cancer experience from the perspective of siblings: A need to give them a voice. *Journal of Pediatric Oncology Nursing, 22*, 305–319.

CHAPTER 4

Change and Continuity in Young People's Lives: Biography in Context

Janet Holland

Theorists of late modernity are largely concerned with change, transformation, and breaks with the past that current times seem to represent. Change at every level—social, political, economic, and individual—becomes important in theories that describe change over time. At the broadest level of grand- or macro-theories, our lives are said to be played out against changes in epoch, the move from modern to post-modern, high, or late modernity. At the meso- or mid-level theories, we see descriptions of and efforts at explanation for changes in institutions, changes in demographics, and for the new economies generated through global economic changes. At the micro-level, we see changes in individuals' lives, relationships, experiences, and trajectories. In this maelstrom of change, some voices call our attention to the existence of continuity. In this instance new theories reformulate old theoretical and conceptual categories, or theorists argue that old categories, for example social class, instead of being irrelevant and empty, are being reworked and reconfigured in new ways, leading to persistent inequalities. Feminists, for example, argue that gendered power relations may well be undergoing a process of reconfiguration, but that the old gender hierarchy seems to be substantially resilient in the new formulations. These different levels of theory influenced the conceptualization, design, and interpretation of *Inventing Adulthoods*, the study I draw on in this chapter. As our research team pursued our own understandings of the data, we generated in an iterative process of analysis and theorization. I use data from this study to illustrate more general points about change and continuity, transformation, and the processes, contexts, and consequences of change.

In *Inventing Adulthoods*, time becomes a central part of the story, integral to theory development, data generation, and data analysis. Time operates on at least three levels: biographical time, social time, and historical time. The ten-year study tells a story of individual lives viewed over time in the flow of social and historical time. Social time consists of social institutions, policies, and practices, both local and global. Historical time covers the broad sweep of historical events and epochs. Biographical time refers to the life of the individual in all its relational complexity.

At this historic juncture, where theorists of late modernity suggest that social and traditional supports for the individual are being swept away, and we are cast into an uncertain world of risk and insecurity where it is for us to construct and create ourselves, our identities, our trajectories, and our futures, young people are exemplars of these changes. They are the vanguard generation facing the postmodern risk society in all its ramifications. Insights from their lives can provide support for or challenge the theories that try to capture such changes, as well as provide grounds for developing appropriate policies to support young people.

INVENTING ADULTHOODS

Design, Method, and Interpretation

The *Inventing Adulthoods* study has followed a group of 100 young people (aged 11–17) over more than ten years from 1996 with up to six interviews with each participant.[1] The context of the young people's lives and experiences was important. Drawing from five socio-economically contrasting sites in the United Kingdom, our sample is comprised of residents of a leafy suburb, an inner city, a disadvantaged estate in the north of England, an isolated rural area, and a city in Northern Ireland, where the areas involved also varied by sectarian identification. We used a range of methods and data generation techniques in the study, including a questionnaire on youth values at the start, followed by focus groups, lifelines, and memory books (a form of diary), but the main method was repeated biographical interviews at intervals varying with the status of our funding. This method allowed us to follow the development of young lives and identities through time using their own narration of those lives.[2] We also generated data and developed rapport via phone calls, e-mail, cards, and so forth. Additional data, generated later in the project, includes a DVD on a small group made in connection with an Open University course and a follow-up of the Northern Irish subgroup.

In qualitative longitudinal research the analysis is theoretically driven, with a focus on meaning, process variables, and change over time. The analysis works in two temporal dimensions: diachronically through time and synchronically cutting across at one point in time, and articulates these analyses through a third integrative dimension. Researchers have varied ways of approaching the challenges of integration (Saldana, 2003; Thomson & Holland, 2003). Also taken into account are researchers' different positionalities that highlight different interpretations of the data over time. In this type of research, interpretation is an integral part of the analysis, and the researcher engages in and becomes a part of a reflexive process of reconsidering and reinterpreting the meaning of the data and analysis.

The cross-sectional, synchronic analysis captured a moment in the life of participants at each interview. Computer aided analysis enabled comparison of similarities and differences across the sample of young people based on age, gender, social class, geographical location/community, and other factors. The sequence of analyses constituted a repeat cross-sectional study of the group, compared for change over time and contextualized in social and historical time (McGrellis, 2005). The longitudinal diachronic dimension of the analysis consisted of examining the narratives of each individual through time, following the complexity and contingencies of individual trajectories. We identified critical moments and change, making the process of interpretation explicit as the research process progressed. Integration of the two modes of analysis largely took place in writing and publications, as in this chapter (see also Henderson, Holland, McGrellis, Sharpe, & Thomson, 2007; Thomson et al., 2002, 2004).

Across the three component studies, the major focus for investigation shifted from agency, to values, to social capital.[3] But the core of our investigation has remained the same. First is agency and the *reflexive project of self* (Giddens, 1991). Second is a focus on values and the construction of adult identity, particularly in relation to processes and consequences of change. Third is how the resources to which young people have access and the social and material environment in which they grow to adulthood act to shape the values and identities that they adopt. The contexts in which young lives are lived and the resources to which they have access are crucial to their life chances, and the adult identities they take up. Through longitudinal case studies, we have tracked the trajectories of young people in different geographical and social contexts to highlight and illustrate the importance of these factors, and the processes of change and continuity of which they are part.

THEORETICAL SOURCES: LATE MODERNITY AND THE RISK SOCIETY

The concepts of late modernity and the risk society derive from the work of a number of theorists engaged in exploring social change at this historical juncture. They argue that industrial capitalism has been superseded by an individualized, globalized economy, precipitating a new age of late (high or post) modernity. These theorists include Giddens and Beck, who take a relatively positive stance towards social change, and Bauman. Bauman is more negative, and sees a conflation of citizenship with consumption (rather than as formerly with production) in these New Times, with a consequent loss of meaning and values (Bauman, 2000). Giddens argues that a process of detraditionalization is taking place, where traditional institutional supports for belonging and identity are being eroded, and individuals are becoming increasingly free to engage in a "reflexive project of self whereby self-identity is constituted by the reflexive ordering of self narratives" (Giddens, 1991, p. 244). Through this reflexive ordering people can be, indeed are, responsible for constructing their own identity, and so Giddens attributes individual agency to this process of choice. Beck proposes a theory of individualization, "a concept which describes a structural, sociological transformation of social institutions and the relationship of the individual to society" (Beck & Beck-Gernsheim, 2002, p. 202). He postulates a process in which we are moving from "normal biographies," in which pre-existing roles and life plans are followed, to "choice biographies" where we are responsible for who and what we become. Differing from Giddens, Beck sees this process less as agentic, but more as choices that we are obliged to make given the context(s) of contemporary society.

Each theorist regards late modern society to be a risk society, where levels of insecurity and uncertainty are high, but which provides new choices, opportunities, and access to new and multiple information sources. They each see the changing balance of power between men and women, and a redefinition of the relationship between them, as important in the processes of change in late modernity. Each sees the couple relationship as becoming more significant in these shifting sands. For Giddens (1992), it is the pure relationship, made between equals, and lasts for as long as it works for them. For Beck (1992), it is the loss of other meaningful relationships that can lead to considerable weight being placed on the couple, which may not be able to meet the relational needs of the individual. Here there is a tension between the overcommitment to the couple relation, for which the young people in our study have a definite desire, and the "throwaway" society, where if the relationship does not work you move onto the next, creating yet more uncertainty and insecurity.

Despite considerable criticism of these approaches from those who base their critique on contrary empirical evidence (Jamieson, 1998), these theories remain important in youth studies because they emphasize intergenerational change. The context in which young people now live no longer provides the predictable patterns of the past where lives were shaped by strongly structured factors, such as gender and social class; these are eroding and losing their power. Beck, for example, talks of class and family as zombie categories, dead yet still alive, losing their meaning in postmodern society since they are eaten away from inside by individualization, globalization, changing labor markets, and welfare states. In this situation, young people must forge their own way and create their own future in a rapidly changing society without the traditional supports of family and the collective identities of class.

Youth researchers have drawn attention to the increasingly fragmented pathways through transitions to adulthood and used Beck's distinction between normal and choice biographies to understand them. Du Bois-Reymond (1998), for example, describes a *gender specific normal biography*. Here young people "aim for a clearly defined profession and employment at an early stage and enter fixed relationships in order to start a family—or at least they intend to" (p. 66). She contrasts this with a *non-gender specific choice biography*. Du Bois-Reymond argues that while gender is losing its determining influence, in practice the pull of tradition is still felt, and felt most acutely by young women, whom she sees as more willing to accommodate their careers with family demands than young men.

Nilsen and Brannen (2002) are wary of adopting these conceptual tools and argue that the distinction between normal and choice biography is too simplistic. They bring structural features, particularly class, back into the frame, drawing attention to the continuing significance of structural inequalities that provide the parameters within which people make individual choices. These sets of parameters often go unrecognized, and individuals tend to blame themselves rather than social and economic factors when things go wrong. They say:

> When structural forces and personal resources, such as gender and social class, support one another, there is a tendency for the structural resources to take on an "invisible" quality (p. 42).

Furlong and Cartmel (1997) suggest that this leads to self-blame for factors beyond the individual's control, and call it *the epistemological fallacy*. Aapola and her colleagues (2005) comment:

> Economic insecurity and risk are now imagined to be best addressed through individual resiliency and a capacity to change and adapt to a volatile educational and labour market. Individuals need to be prepared to return to education to re-skill themselves, to negotiate wages and conditions through private arrangements, to change career paths when necessary, to manage livelihoods without a "job for life," and to take personal responsibility for their economic security (p. 59).

This situation reflects current forms of government that shift responsibility from the state to the individual, who must make choices about work, health, employment, and intimate life in order to access opportunity and resources. However, as empirical data on all areas of social life suggests, familiar inequalities continue to profoundly shape life chances. Critics of the self government approach suggest that it privileges particular forms of cultural and social capital that tend to be more characteristic of the middle classes, so enhancing their ability to secure material, social, and affective resources for themselves (Skeggs, 2004). This has clear implications for social justice.

We have found some of the concepts developed by theorists of late modernity useful and productive in our work. For example, we have used Giddens' notion of the reflexive project of self to examine the process of construction of identity and adulthood that the young people follow (see below). We do not think the process of individualization is as thorough-going as Beck envisages, nor do we believe that the family is a zombie category, but regardless of the specific form that a family might take, it is often a source of support for young people in the uncertain times that both theorists portray. We see social class differences and distinctions in our data in terms of material and other resources available to the young participants, life chances and trajectories, as well as cultural distinctions between different class groups, although the situation is complex with many intersecting facets. The zombie categories live on, and like other critics, we see old inequalities and distinctions resilient in reconfiguration.

THEORY AND DATA: AN ITERATIVE PROCESS

Critical Moments

Giddens (1991) introduces the notion of the "fateful moment," in which reflexivity, agency, and choice are key "transition points, which have major implications not just for the circumstances of an individual's future conduct but for self-identity. For consequential decisions once taken, will reshape the reflexive project of identity through the lifestyle consequences which ensue" (p. 143). For Giddens, the fateful moment is an antecedent of a change process, even of a transformation in the life of those experiencing it. The focus is on individuals as rational choice-making agents who take control of their life and seek information on which to make decisions about the direction to take from this key moment. We distinguished between fateful and critical moments (Thomson et al., 2002). Giddens' concept of fateful moments is a theoretical explanation of possible responses to change and risk. We saw the concept of critical moments as descriptive, grounded in and deriving from our analysis of the interview narratives of the young people, a practical analytical device. For us a critical moment was an event described in an interview that the interviewee (and/or the researcher) understood as having important consequences for the young person's life and identity, a potential tool in understanding change. And just as hindsight and a longer perspective have helped us as researchers to see different events as important in the process of the young person's life moving through time, so it enabled the young people themselves to reassess and reconsider what were and were not critical moments, as they reflected on their experiences in later interviews.

A Biographical Model

In the first interview we asked the young people to reflect on the meanings of the terms *adulthood* and *maturity*, and on times, places, and situations when they felt adult or not. Two major strands in their understanding of adulthood emerged. The first is a *relational* understanding, stressing relationship, interdependence, and care; the second is an *individualized* understanding, stressing independence, autonomy, and pleasure. Examining individual cases, we found that young people might employ both, or move between them in their accounts. We understood these as discursive positions that young people can move in and out of over time, and which may be congruent with aspects of their social locations in distinct ways. In an attempt to capture, conceptualize, and compare empirical examples of adult identity expressed by individuals at any one time we developed a simple analytic model. The young people felt adult in different ways and different contexts; thinking and feeling themselves as adult related to feelings of competence, and recognition received for demonstrating that competence, which would lead to further investment in those activities or areas. Areas of adult lives where identities were accessed and constructed and competences recognized included education, employment, leisure, and consumption, and the domestic environment (including family relationships and care). Recognition for success in education, for example, might lead to a greater investment in education for the young person. However, this clearly did not take place in a vacuum, and the choices that they perceived as available to them were highly structured in terms of gender, locality, ethnicity, and social class, as are the resources to which they have access.

Grounded in a cross-sectional analysis of all of the young people's responses in the first interview, we used our model to understand the experiences of individuals through time. Findings are articulated through contextualized case studies that demonstrate the different trajectories experienced in different social, gender, and class locations and indicate the resilience and continuity of these structural factors. They also illustrate how identities can change over time in response to changing conditions, and that the configuration of resources available to the young people are themselves structured by time and timing. We can see the effects of contingency and timing, continuity and change in the individual trajectories.

In our latest iteration, we contextualized our model in the theoretical understanding of nested social conditions suggested in the introduction. We see three dynamic levels through which identity is constructed. Nested at the core, the micro or individual level is the reflexive production of self that links lived experience with narrative production. At the meso or relational level are the constellation of relationships of which the individual self is a part and includes social contexts such as educational settings, domestic environments, work places, and leisure activities. At the macro level are the social structures and formations of which the individual is a part. Individuals may experience critical moments at each level of this nested system, which sits in social, generational, historical, and global time. Our longitudinal study enabled us to make linkages and explore explanatory possibilities across these levels. It also highlighted the tensions between the individual narratives provided for us by the young people in our study and the contradictory picture that emerges from the juxtaposition of multiple narratives over time.

CHANGING CONTEXTS, CHANGING TRANSITIONS

In the UK, traditional youth transitions referred to movement from school (or education) to work (or a career), with other markers of the transition to adulthood—leaving home, marriage, and family—following soon after; the trajectory varied by class, gender, and ethnicity. In recent decades the effects of globalization, technological change, recession, de-industrialization, part-time labor, and increasing gender equity, have brought havoc to the 'normal' biography of youth transitions (MacDonald & Marsh, 2001). There is a consensus that youth transitions have become fragmented and stretched. Jones (2005) describes these changes as making young people's transitions to adulthood more: (a) *extended*, with economic independence deferred; (b) *complex* as there is no longer a conventional timetable (Dependence and independence may combine, for example when a young person is economically dependent and living at home, but sexually active and independent in that regard. Critical moments can also play a part in disrupting a conventional timetable, for example becoming pregnant, or a bereavement.); (c) *risky*, involving backtracking, risk taking, and parent-child conflict; and (d) *polarized*, with inequalities more sharply defined in relation to more elite slow track transitions and more risky fast track transitions.

In the light of this flux in the lives of young people, some researchers in youth studies have moved to a more holistic approach to conceptualizing and theorizing about young people's varied pathways into adulthood, trying to take into account all aspects of their experience. There is also a shift from thinking of work as employment toward more embedded, located, yet fluid notions of work that slip across categories of public and private. Both of these characterize our study of youth transitions (Henderson et al., 2007).

ILLUSTRATIVE FINDINGS FROM THE INVENTING ADULTHOODS STUDY

Critical Moments

The kind of situations, events, and experiences that the young people identified as critical moments during the initial interview and over time varied extremely. They included family issues (being kicked out of home, parents splitting up, parental unemployment); illness and bereavement (a parent's death, suicide, death of a baby, diagnosis of chronic illness); moving (house, school, town, country); and education issues (formal—exams, changing schools, and informal—bullying, relationship with teachers). Situations defined as *trouble* also appeared (teen pregnancy, drug taking, illegal or criminal activity), as did leisure and consumption (learning to drive, clubbing), and rites of passage (coming out, discovering religion). Relationships were a continuing source of critical moments, with changes in family relationships, friendship circles, dating relationships, and sexual experience providing important biographical markers throughout the study.

Some examples of critical moments that the young people discussed include Alf who lost both grandparents, and was bullied at school, Maisie who had a miscarriage, and Stan, who had a potentially fatal accident.

> *Alf*: My granddad died and I was pretty upset after that, and then my gran as well, I was upset then, I just didn't want to go to school or anything, just felt the whole world was against me and didn't wanna do anything and when I come back to school and the bullying started then, I just used to go home and lock myself in my room and didn't come out.

Maisie: Because in the holidays I did lose a baby. . . . It made me think, I don't know, because I do like babies, love babies . . . but then you think if you had the baby now, seventeen is too young I think to have a baby, to have one on purpose anyway . . . you should wait anyway until you've at least finished college.

Stan: Last summer I did a bit of scuba diving and I had a kind of a bit of a close scrape under water, and that changed my outlook quite considerably . . . I kind of a bit live for the moment now, and there's a few things I wanna do in the near future that I'll do, like travelling and snowboarding.

Belinda and Sandy had close relationship encounters, and Devon decided that perhaps coming out was not a critical moment because it was so inevitable.

Belinda: The only thing I really think of, that has really, really changed me, would have to be my one night stand. Because it just changes a whole lot of things. Yeah, it's like, I was so stupid.

Sandy: I've done a lot of growing up I think cause a lot of things happened to me in that year . . . embarrassing things. I don't tell people cause people just say to me 'you don't know what that is, you're not well.' I think I fell in love. It's very sad sometimes when I think you can't always have what you want.

Devon identifies two critical moments, one joining a college to take a training course and the other moving in with friends. His training course led to one job after another and finally to one he has now. Of his job he says, "I love [it] so, that was one of the most crucial things for me." The other critical moment was when he realized that he could not live alone. He joined a flatshare with friends who have "influenced [him] to become who [he is] and really to become more grounded." But he was sure that coming out was not a critical moment.

I don't consider coming out to be a turning point, I had a choice whether my life could have gone one way, it could have gone another, because as far as I'm concerned that had already been decided for me, I can't do anything about that. The timing, I suppose could have affected me, but I don't think it would have affected me that much.

While critical moments related to family, education, and relationships occurred across the group, others identified with particular locations. For example, in the socially disadvantaged estate critical moments related to chronic illness and death were more prevalent, whereas in the leafy suburb critical moments were more likely to relate to leisure, consumption, and mobility. These differences reflected the material conditions of life and resources available to the young people in these highly contrasted sites.

The lives of some young people were particularly vulnerable to events beyond their control (e.g., illness, violence, family disruption) while others reported critical moments that expressed a growing sense of autonomy. Some critical moments are more consequential than others, with some leading to a transformation in the expected path of life. In practice the configuration and timing of these events, when they occur and in conjunction with what other events, becomes significant in the young person's trajectory, as seen from examples given in this chapter. Also important is the extent to which young people are able to respond with resources, which depends on material and structural aspects of their situation, and resourcefulness, which can depend on material resources, but also requires psychological and affective resources. Bereavement, for example, can provide a turning point from which a young person takes control of his or her life or enters into a downward spiral of depression and despair, reinforcing a sense of powerlessness and limiting possibilities (Henderson et al., 2007).

A brief case study indicates the provisionality of the kind of Giddens' fateful moment in conceptualizing identity work. It also illustrates the provisionality of interpretation in cross-sectional longitudinal research by both researcher and participant, highlighting the importance of a longitudinal perspective, and ongoing biographical features that appear only over time.

A Case Study: Robin

Robin (at fifteen) described a critical moment and its consequences. He had been caught smoking marijuana, "busted for smoking the old puff" with two friends at school. The drama included a visit from the headmaster and the police. As a result, Robin reported, "I didn't sleep a wink that night." He described the whole event as "the worst time of my life." In his account of events and of his and his parents' reaction to them, Robin's case seemed to fulfill Giddens' criteria for fatefulness. He provided a reflexive account of his experience: "I look back now and think how pathetic I was. I knew I was going down a bad track, but I didn't care." His [separated] parents made a desperate and successful attempt to intervene and prevent his expulsion. He began to re-evaluate his identity as a "bad boy" and his likely future, vowing that "I'd never put myself in that position again." We interpreted his account as indicating that the fateful moment was important to a change process.

However, using the theoretical approach of the fateful moment to understand the significance of life events, an approach that privileges individual choice, can obscure relationships, investments, and the wider power structures that might constrain choice. Crucial for Robin was his access to the social and cultural capital of his parents, which they instantly, fiercely, and successfully deployed in his defense. This parental intervention, and the fact that Robin's fellow smokers [who were expelled] clearly did not have access to these kinds of resources (Holland, 2006), supports the suggestion that a particular form of cultural capital is crucial for the kind of reflexivity to which Giddens appears to give universal status (Skeggs, 2004). In broader perspective, the longitudinal approach reveals underlying processes influencing responses and narratives at any particular point in time.

Although Robin's agentic response to being discovered smoking cannabis did save him from expulsion from school in the short term, it did not represent an enduring identity in broader longitudinal perspective. Over time, it appeared not as a turning point, but as part of what was to become a pattern of confession, self-inspection, and experimentation. By the second interview, Robin had reverted to his *bad boy* identity, and drug and alcohol use continued to be an enduring part of his pattern of behavior throughout the period we met with him. Although not narrated as such, the breakdown of Robin's family and establishing of two families of father and stepmother, and mother and stepfather could be seen as a more consequential life event for both Robin and his elder brother, helping to explain their investment in rebellion and bad boy images.

Models of Adulthood

Education. In relation to our model, various patterns of experience emerged from investments in the different areas of life including education, employment, leisure, and consumption, and the domestic sphere. Educational achievement brings with it rewards of recognition, and this encourages young people to invest more in this area as they progress toward an imagined adulthood. Such an investment can be associated with deferred youth. In the young people's narratives, this trajectory involved a mature period of studiousness, being a sensible student and *grown up*, while taking relevant examinations to enable them to go to university, followed by a youthful lifestyle while at university. This route can lead to a form of adulthood associated with professional work, and was often, but not exclusively, found in those with a middle-class background.

Various patterns emerged for young people who failed to secure a sense of competence or recognition in education: possible trajectories

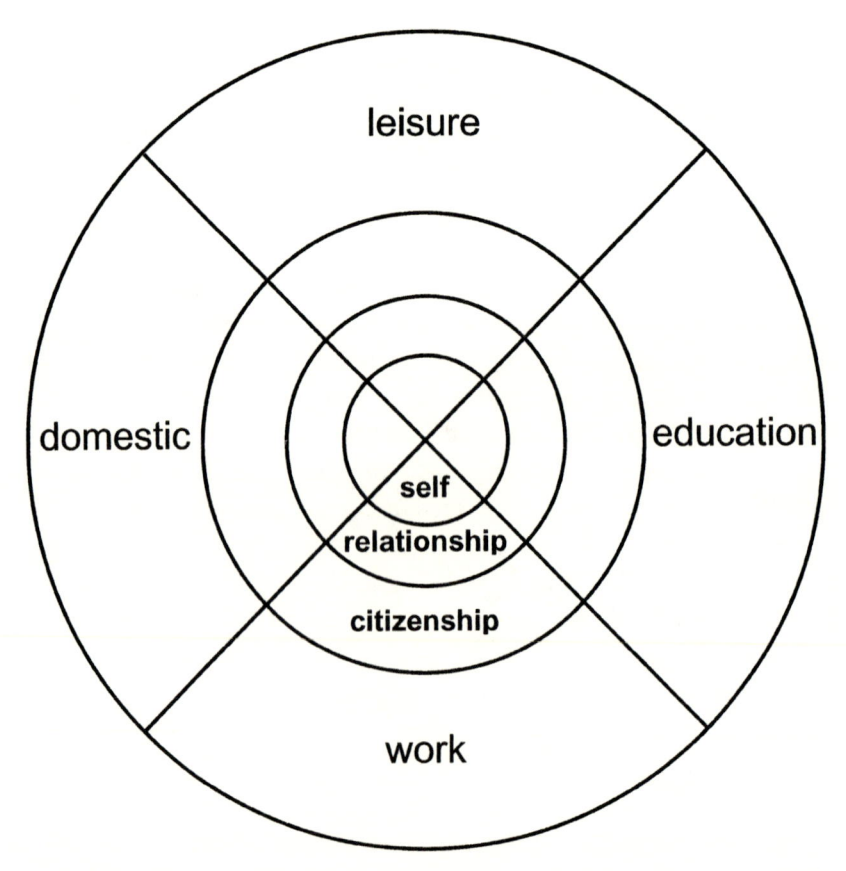

Figure 4.1. Dimensions and Fields of Youth Transitions (Henderson et al., 2007)

included pursuing an accelerated adulthood, a more traditional pattern of leaving school and entering work as soon as possible, starting a steady relationship, and *settling down*. Alternatively, they pursued an extended youth lifestyle. Some young people attempted to maintain a connection with education and took vocational courses often leading nowhere, while at the same time working in *McJobs*. A pattern we found that has emerged throughout the United Kingdom for young people is that of moving between short periods of employment, training schemes or vocational courses, and unemployment. The different sites in our study offered different opportunities for employment, depending on the local labor market (Henderson et al., 2007).

Employment. Like many young people in the United Kingdom, most participants in the study undertook high levels of part-time work while engaged in education. Those unable to find a sense of recognition in education were more likely to prioritize the demands of work in the competition for their time and energy. The young people who invested in education tended to view part-time work while in school as useful for financing a certain lifestyle or as valuable experience for their further educational or professional career. Those who invested less in education were more likely to see part-time work as providing personal affirmation in their role as worker. The money they earned also allowed some independence from their family or contributed to family finances. The appeal of full-time wages and a working life evaporated for many who took this route on leaving school, leading to regret about not pursuing education.

Leisure and Consumption. Leisure and consumption were important for the young workers. In a number of cases, young people who were alienated from education creatively deployed their leisure identities, such as engaging in club culture in a way that enabled them to develop alternative careers, to rework traditional boundaries, and to access cultural and social capital. Young people also were involved in less commercial forms of leisure including participation in community projects, self-help groups, organized youth movements, and paramilitary activities. Again, these forms of activity gave young people a sense of responsibility, competence, and recognition that in biographical terms may have been highly significant in shaping their future trajectories.

The Domestic Arena. Often hidden for young people is the domestic arena. We found that many young people took on an extremely high level of responsibility within the home for child care, housework, and care of sick or unhappy parents. This was particularly pronounced in young women's narratives, although several young men were also involved in forms of caring. A sense of competence in relation to the home and family was particularly important in the accounts of working class young people, many of whom were highly conscious of the details of household budgets, and avoided placing additional financial or emotional burdens on their parents. Many gained a sense of self-worth from the care they expressed and enacted for their families and this investment shaped or constrained their plans for the future. They might curtail educational investment if they thought their family could not afford to support them or plan to live close to parents for whom they would expect to provide care as their parents grew older. Moreover, establishing a family of their own was central to their imagined futures, with adulthood firmly defined through the couple relationship and parenthood. This contrasted with more individualized orientations toward family life, in which particularly middle-class young people considered parental support and higher education as a right, and where they deferred establishing a family life of their own to the distant future.

A Case Study: Cheryl

Cheryl's case illustrates changing investments in different arenas of her life related to age, available resources, and contingency. It also is a medley of change and continuity. At her first interview at sixteen, she lived at home with her parents and sister, studying for examinations at school. Enmeshed in a range of community organizations and social and family networks, Cheryl lived in a working class, protestant community in Northern Ireland. At this time, she invested in education, hoping to go on to take further examinations and possibly higher education. The relationship with her twenty-year-old boyfriend also was important, but she explained that she was in "no hurry" to become an adult with all of the associated responsibilities. In particular, she wanted to delay motherhood. She was enjoying a life with many of the "trappings" of adulthood made accessible through her boyfriend, which counterbalanced her investment in education.

By her second interview (at seventeen) the balance had shifted. While still committed to education, Cheryl also talked about the temptation of entering the world of work and the financial and emotional independence that it offered. She resented that at school teachers treated her as if she was still a child. While her heterosexual relationship offered her an area where she could experience adult-like competence, as the couple's practices became more domestic, she was finding her life increasingly boring and routine.

We discovered a very different young woman for whom "everything" had changed at her third interview (at eighteen). The interviewer described Cheryl as "buzzing with energy" and "hungry for new experiences and new people." The pressures evident in her second interview had led Cheryl to leave school and take a job. She explained this decision in terms of frustration at her lack of freedom and spending power in comparison with her friends, although she did not rule out more education at a later point.

> That job that I'm in now they're very into investing in people and so hopefully they'll put me through [a course] next year and I might go on and do my degree in a couple of years time. But, I want to save up some money and enjoy my life for a couple of years now.

She expressed some regret about abandoning education, but suggested, "You can't have the best of both worlds."

The decision to move into employment was a critical moment in Cheryl's life. In the same week, Cheryl began her new job and moved out of her parental home into rented accommodations with a friend. Soon afterwards, her relationship with her boyfriend ended, partly because of Cheryl's frustration with his parents' refusal to treat their relationship as sufficiently adult. As a result, Cheryl was no longer staying at home and living for the future, but going out, partying, and living for the moment. Work not only provided her with the material resources to become independent of her boyfriend and parents, but also with access to social and cultural networks that made different forms of adulthood available. She had begun to go clubbing and to develop a more cosmopolitan outlook, which culminated in having a Catholic boyfriend. She still talked about university as a possible option for the future, although recognizing that recent choices made this a difficult route. Cheryl believed that she had matured and become more adult, making her own decisions and accepting responsibility for the consequences of those decisions, but paradoxically was at the same time living a more carefree and hedonistic life, contemplating travel and excitement. She said, "There's a whole world out there that you never see . . . I definitely feel no bind to here." Cheryl was drawing on more individualized notions of adulthood.

> I can see me growing up and maybe never seeing my friends that I run about with now because I only am eighteen, I could have completely different friends in a couple of years time than what I have now and grow completely apart from them.

Her world had become broader and more flexible, itself the historically specific consequences of the rapid development of cultural and leisure industries in the wake of the Northern Irish peace process. Her pathway is highly contingent and open to resequencing.

At her fourth interview (at nineteen) Cheryl's circumstances had once again changed significantly in a way that demonstrates the contingency of contemporary youth transitions and the pull of class and gender based securities and continuities. Her experiments with a more individualized adulthood constructed through leisure and work practices was replaced by an adulthood wholly realized in the domestic sphere. Cheryl had returned to the family home after a few months of independent living, missing the relationality and support of the close-knit family. She also had begun a new relationship with a man a few years older than herself. Within months, she was engaged to be married, bought a house with her partner in the same neighborhood as her parents, and became pregnant. The pregnancy was unexpected, and she has now given birth.

It appears that her choices have became limited and many of the alternative options and pathways she courted at the third interview (e.g., travel, university, exploration) relinquished. However, we can also understand her as securing much of what she had been looking for within the various domains in her life over the course of the interviews. Consumption had always been important to her sense of herself as competent and free. As a homeowner, she and her partner have invested significant amounts of time, money, and energy into creating their home. Through the security of both a couple and a parenting relationship, she achieved independence from her family and created her own. The experience of experimenting with a more cosmopolitan lifestyle did enable her to imagine more easily a future where she might return to education or progress within the work field. Although Cheryl disrupted a traditionally gendered relational route to adulthood, the alternative of an individualized route, though initially exciting, liberating, and fulfilling, was ultimately unsustainable. When the opportunity to attain adulthood through a more traditional route presented itself, Cheryl grasped it.

Change had characterized Cheryl's life as recounted in her interviews, and between the second and third interviews, the relational model of adulthood gave way to the individualized model. But there is also continuity; the domestic and consumption areas provided a basic core to her construction of adulthood, to which, after an exploration of a different route, she resorted when circumstances and resources (i.e., a new heterosexual relationship), gave her the opportunity. Her exploration at the time of the third interview reflected more the transitions of high modernity, the fragmented and elusive adulthood experienced by the current vanguard generation. However, by the fourth interview she seemed to have returned to a traditional, gendered route, although she postponed her marriage because the consumption demands of reproduction and providing a home for the new family precluded the expense of a wedding.

FUTURE SPACES

Our sociological perspective emphasizes social contexts, rather than individual psychological processes, in the transition from youth to adulthood. However, individual trajectories through the social, historical, and biographical landscape provide the data for our considerations. Our discussion and theorization of young people in turbulent times is grounded in a longitudinal study that has given unique insight into young lives in a variety of social, material, and geographical contexts within the United Kingdom. While the times are changing, it was perhaps ever thus. Those inside any period or epoch may perceive themselves to be in the vortex of grand historical changes. While these are indeed turbulent times, we found continuity in young lives: on the positive side in the support and relationality offered by community and family life, regardless of the form of family; on the negative side in some basic characteristics of social institutions and structures, including continuing inequalities associated with social class, gender, and ethnic differences.

Transformations can come about through fateful and/or critical moments in young lives, but the key difference in a fateful moment is the rational decision-making process that individuals pursue in understanding, learning from, and reacting to the fateful moment by changing their trajectory and life style. The critical moment might be less fateful in terms of changing futures, but can help to explain some of the mechanisms that lie behind particular trajectories. Close inspection of critical moments, the resources that are accessed and deployed by young people, and those that they can call on to resolve or deal with these moments can indicate the types of policy approaches that might be appropriate for a variety of issues confronting young people. Policy approaches tend to fragment young lives into policy relevant segments, such as education, employment, and delinquency, but taking a holistic approach to the complex web in which social lives are enmeshed as advocated here, while making policy decisions more difficult, might make them more apt.

NOTES

1. Funded throughout by the UK Economic and Social Research Council on a series of programs of research (L129251020, L134251008, M570255001), Inventing Adulthoods (www.lsbu.ac.uk/inventingadulthoods) is now in archiving and longitudinal analysis mode as a part of *Timescapes: Changing relationships and identities through the life course*, (www.timescapes.leeds.ac.uk; RES-347-25-0003). London South Bank University also provided support.

2. Sheila Henderson, Janet Holland, Sheena McGrellis, Sue Sharpe, and Rachel Thomson. This chapter draws on the collective work of this team.

3. In this regard we have followed Bourdieu, using his interrelated set of capitals (economic, social, cultural, and symbolic) as indicating resources that can be bestowed upon or accessed by an individual by virtue of family or group membership. Social capital itself consists of social networks and connections—"contacts and group memberships which, through the accumulation of exchanges, obligations and shared identities, provide actual or potential support and access to valued resources" (Bourdieu 1993, p. 143). Also see Holland, 2006.

REFERENCES

Aapola, S., Gonick, M., & Harris, A. (2005). *Young femininity: Girlhood, power and social change*. Houndmills, UK: Palgrave.

Bauman, Z. (2000). *The individualised society*. Cambridge, UK: Polity.

Beck, U. (1992). *Risk society: Towards a new modernity*. London: Sage.

Beck, U., & Beck-Gernsheim, E. (2002). *Individualization*. London: Sage.

Bourdieu, P. (1993). *Sociology in question*. London: Sage.

Du Bois-Reymond, M. (1998). "I don't want to commit myself yet": Young people's life concepts. *Journal of Youth Studies*, *1*, 63–79.

Furlong, A., & Cartmel, F. (1997). *Young people and social change: Individualization and risk in late modernity*. Buckingham: Open University Press.

Giddens, A. (1991). *Modernity and self identity: Self and society in the late modern age*. Cambridge UK: Polity.

Giddens, A. (1992). *The transformation of intimacy: Sexuality, love and eroticism in modern societies*. Cambridge UK: Polity.

Henderson, S., Holland, J., McGrellis, S., Sharpe, S., & Thomson, R. (2007). *Inventing Adulthoods: A biographical approach to youth transitions*. London: Sage.

Holland, J. (2006). Fragmented youth: Social capital in biographical context in young people's lives. In R. Edwards, J. Franklin, & J. Holland (Eds.), *Assessing social capital: Concept, policy and practice* (pp. 163–177). Newcastle: Cambridge Scholars Press.

Jamieson, L. (1998). *Intimacy*. Cambridge UK: Polity.

Jones, G. (2005). *Thinking and behaviour of young adults 16–25: A review*. Annex A, Report on Young Adults with Complex Needs. London: Social Exclusion Unit, ODPM.

MacDonald, R., & Marsh, J. (2001). Disconnected youth? *Journal of Youth Studies*, *4*, 373–391.

McGrellis, S. (2005). Pure and bitter spaces: Gender, identity and territory in Northern Irish youth transitions. *Gender and Education*, *17*, 515–529.

Nilsen, A., & Brannen, J. (2002). Theorising the individual-structure dynamic. In J. Brannen, S. Lewis, A. Nilsen, & J. Smithson (Eds). *Young Europeans, work and family: Futures in transition* (pp. 30–47). London: Routledge.

Saldana, J. (2003). *Longitudinal qualitative research: Analyzing change through time*. Walnut Creek, CA: AltaMira Press.

Skeggs, B. (2004). *Class, self, culture*. London: Routledge.

Thomson, R. (2009). *Unfolding lives: Case histories in personal and social change*. Bristol: The Policy Press.

Thomson, R., Bell, R., Holland, J., Henderson, S., McGrellis, S., & Sharpe, S. (2002). Critical Moments: Choice, chance and opportunity in young people's narratives of transition. *Sociology*, *36*, 335–354.

Thomson, R., and Holland, J. (2003). Hindsight, foresight and insight: The challenges of longitudinal qualitative research. *International Journal of Social Research Methods – Special Issue on Longitudinal Qualitative Methods*, *6*, 233–244.

Thomson, R., Holland, J., McGrellis, S., Bell, R., Henderson, S., & Sharpe, S. (2004). Inventing adulthoods: A biographical approach to understanding youth citizenship. *Sociological Review*, *52*, 218–239.

CHAPTER 5

African American Female Adolescent Sexuality: Creating Change Using an Ecological-Womanist Lens

April L. Few and Dionne P. Stephens

Sexually transmitted diseases (STDs) affect racial-ethnic minorities disproportionately. For example, AIDS affects significantly more African Americans than members of other racial-ethnic groups. In 2006, rates of AIDS cases were 47.6 per 100,000 for African Americans, 15.6 for Hispanics, and 5.4 for Whites. Among adults and adolescents, rates of AIDS cases were highest for African American males (82.9 per 100,000), followed by African American females (40.4) and Hispanic males (31.3). Several factors contribute to these disparities. As noted by the Center for Disease Control (CDC, 2005), racial-ethnic minorities often live in impoverished communities with higher prevalence of diseases, have limited access to quality health care and health promotion education, and experience multigenerational poverty. They also may have to negotiate certain cultural barriers (e.g., racial and gender socialization practices; sexual meanings constructed from media venues that foster hypersexuality; conservative religiosity that fosters shame of body and guilt). Because low-income and working class African Americans are overrepresented in sexual health disparities, there is a profound need for practitioners and researchers to develop sexual practices interventions that target this population early in adolescence and to further understand the role that family, peers, and culture play in shaping African American adolescent sexuality.

Given the precarious state of African American adolescent sexual health, we focus on this developmental period to theorize about possible trajectories of sexual health behavioral change through an examination of factors at play within a specific cultural context, Hip Hop. Adolescence is a dynamic period marked by rapid and dramatic changes across many domains, including the development of intimate friendships, social and sexual experimentation and debut, peer relations, and social comparisons. How post-pubescents respond to the biological, social, and psychological changes co-occurring depends on the social context in which they occur (Kipke, 1999). The social context not only includes a part of African American culture but also adolescent interactions with parents and peers, including sexually intimate partners. Adolescents develop sexual meanings through these social interactions and make choices about how they express and enact their sexuality.

In this chapter, we contemplate influences on the sexual decision-making of African American adolescents and their bearing on designing sexual health intervention targeting African American adolescents. We posit that effective intervention begins with understanding how culture influences change in individual behavior because sexual knowledge of consequences alone does not translate into sexual behavioral change (Kirby, 2000). It is the meanings that emerge from sexual messages that are important for understanding how knowledge affects behavior. We also propose that family researchers examine African American adolescent sexuality using a theoretical lens that is representative of African American experiences—an integrated ecological and womanist theoretical lens that is inclusive of parent-child interactions, peer group influences, and media effects, all encapsulated within the cultural milieu of Hip Hop. Because Hip Hop is embedded simultaneously within African American culture and mainstream commercialism within the United States, researchers are afforded a unique site to examine the influences of Hip Hop as a transformational force in the unfolding of young African American adolescents' sense of self, sexual identity, and timing of sexual practices.

Through this theoretical framework, we can situate and hypothesize how Hip Hop-generated sexual messaging is internalized by African American adolescents, and the extent to which parental and peer communication about sexual behaviors and consequences act as a filter of Hip Hop sexual messages. Our focus here is the internalization of Hip Hop sexual messaging as a primary antecedent that endorses a social acceptability of high sexual risk behaviors among youth throughout the ecological system of African American female adolescents. We also, however, recognize other antecedents of adolescent sexual risk-taking that interact within this social context and may be exacerbated by the behavioral expectations set by Hip Hop culture. Antecedents may constitute either risk or protective factors.

These risk factors include sexual onset, initiation, and non-coital sexual behaviors (Grello, Welsh, & Harper, 2006), previous sex-risking activities (Grello et al.), compliance to traditional gender relations, alcohol and substance abuse (Grello et al.), self-esteem and mental health status (Grello et al.), family histories of transition (Moore & Chase-Lansdale, 2001), and neighborhood context (Browning, Levanthal, & Brooks-Gunn, 2005). Protective factors that modify or mediate those risk factors endorsed by Hip Hop culture include the effectiveness of parent-child communication about media consumption, parent-child communication about sexual attitudes and behaviors (Stephens & Few, 2007), peer influences (Wallace, Miller, & Forehand, 2008), and neighborhood context (Browning et al.).

HIP HOP CULTURE: A TRANSFORMATIONAL FORCE FOR AFRICAN AMERICAN YOUTH

There is a growing body of social science research examining the influence of Hip Hop culture on African American female adolescents' sexual attitudes and behavioral outcomes. Hip Hop, which emerged as a cultural movement out of the creativity of urban African Americans during the early 1970s, is a socially constructed system in which cultural narratives of masculinity and femininity are constantly (re)produced, resisted, and consumed (Kitwana, 2002). Hip Hop culture began as a venue to express racial solidarity between black men and women, the bonds of brotherhood and sisterhood, black pride, and the challenges of urban life. Some Hip Hop female artists emphasized safe sex and aspects of womanism (e.g., women's empowerment, women's equality, spirituality, community) in their work. The voices of Hip Hop female artists were included (to a limited extent) until a shift occurred in the 1990s that emphasized defining sexuality, particularly exploiting African American women's sexuality, and reflected the co-occurring rise of individualism and materialism among all youth in mainstream culture. And thus, attitudes toward sexuality and sexual scripts among African American youth (as well as other racial or ethnic consumers) evolved in a way that elevated men's power and sexual needs over those of women and perceived weaker men. Hip Hop became a testosterone-fueled cultural catalyst for the transformation of gender relations, and consequently, sexual practices among certain African American communities and generations of Hip Hop consumers.

Within our discussion of the layers of an ecological-womanist theoretical framework, we submit examples for understanding how antecedents—protective factors and risk factors—influence sexual health developmental outcomes for African American adolescents who live in this Hip Hop era. Using our integrative theoretical framework, we elucidate how African American adolescents' negotiate their consumption of Hip Hop sexual imagery and their interactions with parents and peers through a discussion of Afrocentric gender and racial socialization practices. Finally, we contemplate how this interdisciplinary theoretical framework could inform the development and application of an effective sexual practices intervention for African American adolescents of the Hip Hop generation.

INTEGRATIVE THEORETICAL APPROACH FOR STUDYING ADOLESCENT SEXUALITY

Historically, culturally insensitive theories and deviance and negative developmental outcomes have been the dominant foci of studies on black family life (Few, Stephens, & Rouse-Arnett, 2003). Additionally, African American experience continues to be distilled and qualitatively distorted through comparative quantitative data collected from predominantly White populations. We recognize that the study of African American adolescent sexuality requires a theoretical framework that facilitates multi-layered intersectional analysis. We propose an integration of Bronfenbrenner's (1979) ecological theory and womanist theory (Walker, 1983) to guide our examination of how Hip Hop culture, as a transformative force, shapes sexual scripts enacted by African American female adolescents. Bronfenbrenner's ecological theory is particularly useful for it allows family scholars to cast a wide lens in examining variables of African American female adolescent sexuality socialization and development by being inclusive of both psychological characteristics and various Hip Hop cultural environmental factors. According to Bronfenbrenner's ecological theory, individuals' perceptions and beliefs of their reality do not develop in a vacuum, but are products of the larger ecology. Bronfenbrenner's ecological model is particularly relevant for examining African American female adolescent sexuality as it is inclusive of both individual and interpersonal factors. Behavior is a result of interplay between the psychological characteristics of the person and of a specific environment. Thus, we cannot simply look at African American female adolescents' sexual health issues or decision-making processes as isolated individual acts and/or consequences; they must be assessed in relation to the world around them.

Womanist theory is a racial-ethnic-based theory that places African American women at the center of analysis and allows researchers to explore African American women's unique socio-cultural-spiritual standpoint (Walker, 1983). Phillips (2006) identifies five overarching core characteristics of womanism: (a) anti-oppressionist (i.e., simultaneously rejecting of all forms of oppression); (b) vernacular (i.e., street-level sensibilities); (c) non-ideological (i.e., dialogical); (d) communitarian (i.e., concerned with the wellness of the whole group); and (e) spiritualized (i.e., affirming the importance of spirituality). Womanist theory is a viable framework to use in any study focusing on the variables of race and gender because it affirms the inextricable intersectionality of identities and oppressions in the lived experiences of women of the African Diaspora. Although racial-ethnic theorists position race and ethnicity as the primary social locations in which all social locations intersect, racial-ethnic theorists (in this case, womanist theorists) do not overlook that sexism is a domain that remains to be contested in private and public relationships and at times, at great risk to women's personal safety (Few, 2009). As previously mentioned, Hip Hop has become a cultural space where sexism is mainstream and women are visual and tangible objects of male sexual desire.

The integration is found in that one must use an Afrocentric, gender-sensitive lens to interpret events, timing, behaviors, and interactions in each level of an individual's ecosystem. Womanist theory provides a culturally-based, culturally-sensitive, and gender-specific filter to integrate into an ecological framework; thus, enhancing the explanatory power of Bronfenbrenner's ecological theory and creatively advancing how we, as family scholars, theorize about observed phenomena and practices of racial-ethnic groups. Womanist theory brings a critical lens to interpret the symbolic context for the internalization, emulation, mimicry, or rejection of Hip Hop sexual imagery across the multiple systems of a female adolescent's social world. In the case of African American adolescents, womanist theory provides a rich foundation for the theorizing phenomenon within a unique racialized historical context that has shaped the diverse Afrocentric belief and value systems of African American families and communities.

With the integration of these two theories, our queries must progress beyond capturing frequencies and typologies of sexual behaviors or the degree of affect indicated by attitudes scales. Using a critical lens, we tap into how individuals make sense of the symbolism, meanings, and consequences of sexual behaviors and attitudes, all of which is embedded within a specific cultural context. We ask questions that interrogate cultural values, deconstructing the social context in which individuals interdependently interact and make choices. We ask participants to label artifacts (e.g., cultural representations such as art or imagery) and rituals specific to their culture and identify behaviors and attitudes that are appropriate or justifiable within a larger ecosystem. In conducting sexual health intervention, it is important to recognize where and how cultural beliefs may conflict with medical realities or intervention goals. For example, religious beliefs may preclude the use of condoms or any form of contraceptive that protects against STD transmission. Culture (e.g., beliefs, values, practices) becomes more than a dormant variable that we so often divorce from analysis; culture becomes a meaningful factor in defining, in this case, sexual practices as well as possible effective points for intervention, change, adaptation, and transformation.

We believe that this theoretical integration is a useful contribution to the growing body of social science research, which indicates that multiple Hip Hop cultural contexts do influence various sexual risk-taking beliefs and behaviors among and about African American adolescents and emerging adults (Wingood et al., 2001). The knowledge that can be gained from using more than one theory to examine this issue is particularly pertinent given that this population is at the highest risk across their age and gender cohort for the majority of negative sexual health outcomes, including unplanned pregnancy, sexually transmitted disease and/or infection acquisition (e.g., HIV/AIDS), non-voluntary intercourse, and early sexual onset.

DOING INTERSECTIONAL ANALYSIS USING AN ECOLOGICAL-WOMANIST THEORETICAL LENS

African American female adolescent sexual socialization in the context of mainstream Hip Hop culture takes place at multiple locations. Further, according to ecological theory, the degree of influence of these locations may differ as a function of various sources of influence. Our integration of ecological and womanist theories allows us to examine Hip Hop culture's influence on the interaction of structures within a layer as well as interactions of structures between layers (Darling, 2007). In doing so, we have situated ourselves to better understand or hypothesize strategies to increase the likelihood of change, specifically reducing sexual risk-taking. The goal of our intersectional analysis is to gain knowledge about the complexity of African American female adolescent sexual socialization processes and resulting sexual practices. In this section, we interpret each layer of Bronfenbrenner's ecological theory through a womanist lens. We incorporate the work of Africana studies scholars, family sociologists, and psychologists to broaden our examination of the influences of parents, peers, intimate partners, and Hip Hop culture on the formation of sexual identity, behaviors, and practices of African American female adolescents.

Chronosystemic Analysis: Evolution of an Afrocentric Cultural Phenomenon

When considering the role of mainstream Hip Hop within a chronosystem framework, we explore the internal and external factors that create, continuously develop, and maintain the parameters of gender relations and a unique world view over time. In the mid-1980s, a distinctly womanist/feminist trend developed as Hip Hop woman artists articulated women's empowerment messages against sexism and intimate and community violence as increasingly misogynistic (i.e., hatred of women) themes were being expressed by mainstream male artists. During the late 1990s, however, the culture of Hip Hop transformed in that misogynistic themes were being popularized in gangsta rap (which emphasizes *justified* violence and posturing) and Dirty South rap (which is closely associated with Southern strip club culture and pornography) while women's empowerment messages received less of an audience (Kitwana, 2002).

While an African American female adolescent's sexual sense of self may have been formed by self-respect and safer sex discourses during the 1980s and early 1990s, today's female adolescent is inundated with verbal messages and visual imagery that promote the strip club culture and the pornography industry. Within this context, an African American woman's value is male-defined such that her greatest commodities to possess are her body and hypersexualized sense of sexual self. The sexual and material desires of African American men (and white men, as they are not only consumers but producers of Hip Hop music and related media) define a *heteronormative* (Oswald, Blume, & Marks, 2005) context for what is appropriate female sexual behavior and practices. Womanist and feminist scholars define heteronormativity as a system of privilege formed by intersections of the socially constructed institutions of gender, sexuality, and family. It encompasses heterosexual principles such as traditional gender role adherence, traditional family structure of husband-wife pairing, and heterosexual sexual orientation.

The Hip Hop generation is now large enough to encompass both mothers and daughters and in some cases, granddaughters. This is an important consideration when thinking of how parent-child communication mediates Hip Hop consumption. For instance, an African American woman who grew up during Hip Hop's early period, a time in which Hip Hop artists espoused gender equality, might emphasize the importance of self-esteem and safe sex practices to her daughter and grandchild. This Hip Hop-identified grandmother/mother might encourage abstinence until the attainment of a committed relationship, talk about the joys and risks of sexuality, and warn against the advances of uncommitted men or the possibility of gaining a "used bad girl" reputation. This same grandmother/mother may even highlight the centrality of spirituality as a component of women's self-worth. Such conversations may influence the timing of sexual intercourse or contraceptive use by her daughter. This political analysis, or full engagement of both the secular and spiritual nature of female sexuality, is a parental protective factor. This type of active engagement is also a source for nurturing a positive sense of self for female adolescents as they negotiate emerging adulthood. Phillips (2006), a renowned womanist scholar, found that there are Hip Hop identified mothers who engage in a layman's political analysis of race and gender with their daughters. Phillips, however, also notes that these same mothers may be averse to social change strategies that pit African American women against African American men. For example, some Hip Hop identified mothers communicate that women should be protective of African American men because of the historical mistreatment of African American men in the legal system or workplace. While others may encourage their daughters to attain a man of financial means irrespective of his fidelity or commitment; in this scenario, gender differences are ignored in favor of individual or family sustainability. We believe that the *space* of parent-child communication is a fruitful opportunity for intervention practice to include the influential family context in deconstructing high-risk Hip Hop sexual scripts.

Macrosystemic Analysis: Hypersexualization of African American Women's Bodies

The macrosystem is comprised of cultural values, customs, and laws. Within the macrosystem, family researchers interpret how cultural values and laws justify or explain the behaviors of the population under study and the population's interactions with the overarching institutional structures that reflect a society's cultural values (Bronfenbrenner, 1979). Mainstream Hip Hop culture projects a sexual materialism that has led to the hypersexualization of women for economic gain. Toward this end, lyrics, video portrayals, and general cultural values have presented African American women as sexually lascivious and available. Because of the power of African American and white men within Hip Hop as artists, industry operatives, and consumers, their ability to influence sexual scripts for women in ways that reflect patriarchal, exploitative, or simply hedonistic desires is considerable. Most Hip Hop women artists have been relegated to the position of performers, not mass producers or CEOs. Thus, there are few images of women of equal status to men in videos. Rather, if women are not the lead singers, then they perform the role of video vixens, amorous for male performers.

We recognize that negative presentations of African American womanhood as highly sexualized are not new and reflect a colonialist Eurocentric history and racist values (Collins, 2005). Remnants of the Jezebel, Mammy, Welfare Mother, and Matriarch imagery have transmorphed into modern day stereotypical images that personify and outline even more sexually explicit sexual scripts—the Diva, the Gold Digger, the Freak, the Dyke, the Gangster Bitch, the Sister Savior, the Earth Mother, and the Baby Mama (Stephens & Phillips, 2003). These eight scripts are widely accepted frameworks used to illustrate beliefs about African American female adolescent sexuality within the African American-based heterosexual male-dominated youth culture of mainstream Hip Hop (Stokes, 2007). In other words, adolescents have expectations about how a woman *should or will* behave based on their preconceived characterizations of Hip Hop sexual imagery and the corresponding sexual scripts. Thus, this hypersexualized imagery and corresponding belief system may serve as an antecedent for timing of sexual onset and unsafe sexual practices that place women's health at risk. These representations of African American womanhood contribute to sexual identification processes and the ritual progression of sexual behaviors and practices of African American female adolescents in the context of Hip Hop culture (Stokes, 2007). They should be considered as sexual scripts, as sexuality is *socially scripted* in that it is a *part* that is learned and acted out within a social context, and different social contexts have different social scripts. How an individual perceives herself, relates to others, and how others relate to an individual are based on shared symbolic meanings about sexuality. It is important for researchers to examine the influence of these scripts on sexual behavioral outcomes at this macrosystemic level as activating a stereotype usually leads people to engage in behaviors that reinforce the stereotype.

Exosystemic Analysis: Site of Mass Media Effects on Adolescent Sexuality

The exosystem represents external institutions in which African American female adolescents are not direct participants (Bronfenbrenner, 1979). These external institutions and policies of these external forces affect African American female adolescents' decisions. Such institutions include the mass media, legal settings, social services, educational institutions, health systems, governmental agencies, and other political venues. African American female adolescents do not hold positions of power in these settings. An integrated womanist perspective allows researchers to examine critically the ways in which African American female adolescents simultaneously accept, resist, change, and reproduce similar or different images of themselves and sexual attitudes within and apart from commercialized Hip Hop culture (Stephens & Phillips, 2005).

Mass media messages are important tools for exploring exosystemic constructs, as they serve to both emulate and reproduce a range of racialized and gendered sexual stereotypes. Mainstream Hip Hop cultural consumption takes place primarily through television and online viewing of music videos (Stokes, 2007). Women in mainstream Hip Hop videos are depicted as simultaneously having great sexual desires and quenching these sexual needs by allowing themselves to be degraded for male pleasure. In these videos, women are not people with feelings and emotions but rather, they are characterized as female caricatures and as quick-flashed disembodied body parts for males' consumption.

Several studies have found a common risk factor for adolescent engagement in sexually risky behaviors: African American adolescents who watch large amounts of sexualized images in mainstream Hip Hop music videos are more likely to endorse and engage in sexually risky behaviors (Brown et al., 2006). Research on young adult consumption of pornography and the associated sexual script enactments suggests that these portrayals do directly affect sexual behavior attitudes and outcomes. Cline's (2000) study of six hundred American males and females of junior high and high school age found that 82 percent of the females and 91 percent of the males had been exposed to X-rated, hard-core pornography. Of these, over 66 percent of the males and 40 percent of the females reported wanting to try out some of the sexual behaviors they had witnessed.

In our study of sexualized imagery in Hop Hop culture (Stephens & Few, 2007), we found that African American adolescents not only recognized stereotypical sexual scripts in mainstream Hip Hop videos, but saw them as accurate portrayals of real life behavioral guidelines of their peers. Wingood et al. (2001) found that African American female adolescents who viewed films with high levels of African American sexual content were approximately twice as likely to have multiple sex partners, have sex more frequently, not use contraception during last intercourse, and have a strong desire to conceive. These studies indicate that Hip Hop culture may have a profound effect on the sexual decision-making processes, sexual health outcomes, and sexual practices of African American adolescents. Therefore, we propose that Hip Hop media is a potential intervention site for behavioral transformation for at-risk adolescents. We theorize that interventions should provoke adolescents to reframe and analyze the sexual imagery that they consume in such a way that encourages sexual wellness instead of risky sexual behaviors.

Given that women in this age group want to achieve the life task of entering intimate relationships and that they are at the highest risk for sexual violence, it is important to examine the influence of Hip Hop culture on adolescent intimate relationships (Grello et. al, 2006). In particular, we assert the need for an examination of how African American adolescents may condone acts of intimate violence and sexual risk-taking based on perceived adoption and performance of certain Hip Hop sexual scripts.

Gillum's (2002) study investigating the link between stereotypic images of African American women and intimate partner violence found that a large percentage of African American men endorsed stereotypic images of African American women. Similarly, those with higher rates of endorsement and acceptance of these images were more likely to justify violence against women. We found that male and female adolescents felt that women who enacted highly sexualized scripts from Hip Hop culture were at fault if they were the victims of rape (Stephens & Few, 2007). They viewed these women harshly and saw them as sexually unacceptable. In contrast, the adolescents viewed the less sexualized scripts as ideal friends and people to have in your personal circle. Responses of preadolescent males to scripts that were considered highly physically attractive and less sexually experienced indicated that they were less likely to use safer sex practices with women they perceived as enacting these scripts. Specifically, when they viewed females to be religious, virginal, or beautiful, a condom was not necessary. A condom was not necessary because the boys perceived these women as sexually safe (e.g., STD/HIV-negative, sexually inexperienced). Thus, through the anti-oppressionist lens of womanist theory, we acknowledge and can hypothesize that adolescent peers determine and communicate the *value* of certain women as being *sacred* or *disposable* as they weigh the messages of Hip Hop media imagery. In other words, Hip Hop in its current form is not healthy for African American girls or women because it views women as objects for sexual consumption, either in a marital bed or as a one-night stand. Regardless of perceived virtue, a woman finds her place and roles only within the context of male desire in this culture.

Mesosystemic Analysis: Gathering Place to Practice Gender Relations

The mesosystem is "a set of interrelations between two or more settings in which the developing person actively participates" (Bronfenbrenner, 1979, p. 25). For African American female adolescents this could include the family context, community center context, and church settings. These places also serve as connectors between microsystem and macrosystem forces, creating a unique cultural space for the socialization of African American female adolescents. Here we use the example of Hip Hop night clubs as defined spaces for adolescent (and emerging adult) consumers and one of the few places where Hip Hop fans cross all sectors of society (e.g., different neighborhoods, work environments, and educational and income levels), come to intermingle, express themselves verbally and non-verbally, and meet potential friends and intimate partners. Hutchinson (1999) conducted an ethnographic study to explore male-female relationships in a night club setting. He found gendered hierarchies reflecting Hip Hop cultural scripts for both men and women. Specifically, males were evaluated on the basis of monetary acquisitions (e.g., drug dealers) and women were evaluated on their sexuality [e.g., *good girls* (sexually conservative) versus *sluts* (hypersexual)]. Hip Hop nightclubs are also the physical site where safe and unsafe sexual practices are negotiated. Muñoz-Laboy et al. (2008) reported that the more frequently men went to a Hip Hop night club, the lower the probability they used condoms during intercourse. They suggested that having sexual intercourse within a context that supports risky sexual behaviors is likely to be the major reason for limited condom use. From a womanist perspective, we can examine nightclubs as a cultural venue where adolescents and emerging adults consciously and subconsciously engage actively antecedent protective and risk factors in their negotiation of sexual and emotional risk. At this *variable-rich* site, we can analyze the extent to which parental messages about sexuality intersect and interact with peer (pressure) factors, such as the promotion or avoidance of alcohol and substance abuse and the engagement in sexual risk-taking and/or anti-social behaviors.

Microsystemic Analysis: Gender and Racial Socialization by Parents, Partners, and Peers

The microsystem is the immediate social settings in which African American female adolescents are involved. This layer emphasizes the role and bi-directional influences of family and primary relationships when explaining human behavior (Darling, 2007). Racial and gender identity socialization processes inform African American females' understandings of appropriate sexual behaviors (Stephens & Few, 2007). At this level of analysis within our theoretical framework, we understand that parents and peers are primary sources of sexuality information and values for African American female adolescents and that these relationships are the most influential relationships this population will have during adolescence.

Family relationships. Families play an important role in microsytems, particularly in the context of sexual health messaging. Parental communications about sexuality has been widely noted to be instrumental in shaping African American adolescent behavioral outcomes (Barr & Neville, 2008). Familial socialization processes inform both racial and gender identity processes. We believe that parental messages that frame African American femaleness or womanhood as a positive identity and social position within the community increases African American female adolescents' levels of self-esteem and decreases their risk for negative sexual behavioral outcomes (Barr & Neville, 2008). Further, we recognize from the literature that African American female adolescents who report higher self-esteem, more knowledge about their racial group, and more favorable in-group attitudes had parents who emphasized their ethnic or racial group's culture, history, and heritage.

Unfortunately, few social science studies have specifically examined the influence or role of familial processes as it pertains to the engagement of Hip Hop culture. In this dearth, we see the contributions of our budding work on the interplay of Hip Hop sexual imagery and African American adolescent sexual behaviors. We found that African American pre-adolescent girls viewed their mothers as the parent most responsible for monitoring mainstream Hip Hop sexual image consumption (Stephens & Few, 2007). Specifically, the girls in this study believed that their mothers influenced their attitudes toward sexual scripting in Hip Hop not only through direct communications, but also through maternal enactment and/or modeling of the sexual images. Similarly, fathers' attitudes about inappropriate and appropriate sexual scripts in mainstream Hip Hop culture influenced the girls' attitudes as well. These results highlight the importance of developing future research and interventions that specifically explore the ways in which families can serve as protective factors or buffers against negative sexual scripting messages in Hip Hop culture.

Peer and intimate relationships. Peers also inform racial and gender identity socialization processes for African American adolescent females. By participating in peer culture groups, adolescents satisfy their needs for acceptance and differentiate from the adults in their life (Wallace et al., 2008). As African American adolescents tend to have peers from the same racial group, they communicate their understandings about racial identity and stereotyping through verbal and non-verbal communications. Racial messaging research shows that African American adolescents share memories for racially stereotyped portrayals and race-based peer preferences. Race schematicity was positively and significantly associated with same-race peer preference bias (Levy, 2000). Further, we found that African American adolescents believed that Hip Hop sexual scripts were behavioral guidelines used by their peers (Stephens & Few, 2007). These adolescents predicted behaviors of their peers and potential partners through these script frameworks. This greater focus on Hip Hop culture and peer relationships in our research and that of others may be a result of the obvious link between the two forces.

THEORETICAL APPLICATION TO CULTURALLY RELEVANT SEXUAL HEALTH INTERVENTION

In developing effective interventions, researchers must take care to capture both sexual health behavioral outcomes as well as the symbolic meanings that adolescents assign to the concepts evaluated as indicators of change. In this section, we discuss the development toward effective culturally relevant sexual health intervention by first deconstructing symbolism assigned to sexual meanings and practices and identifying a crucial pitfall for researchers and practitioners. We then present a practical model to capture the nuances and fluidity of change in African American adolescent sexual health outcomes and practices.

Deconstructing Symbolism: Moving Focus from Sexual Behaviors to Sexual Practices

While sexual behavior can be similar across time and place, sexual practice is a diverse phenomenon. All sexual behavior is sexual practice; it is produced and performed in particular interpersonal, social, historical, and cultural contexts. From an ecological-womanist theoretical framework, we assume that the meanings for sexual risk differ in terms of how risk is understood and practiced with respect to dominant discourses of sexuality. This would include *sex drive, love and romance*, and *permissiveness*, as well as reference to discursive understandings of sexually transmitted diseases, pregnancy, and public health messaging within African American families and communities. Womanist theory provides researchers with a historical context to examine how dominant racialized and gendered discourses define moral and medicalized parameters around appropriate sex and the characteristics of positive sexual relationships and behaviors. From womanist theory, we must study how these discourses are internalized and challenged at a vernacular or street level. For example, in what ways do fathers and mothers talk about sex and the risk of sexually transmitted diseases to their children? Is oral and anal sex considered as *real* or *condemnable* sex across different African American communities? Researchers cannot study sexual practice apart from social conditions and sexual discourses that have been socially constructed collectively and intersubjectively. Effective intervention targets the point where meaning is negotiated and changed, not simply individual behaviors or knowledge. To measure only individual indicators of sexual behavior using surveys and measures is to risk being misled, receiving only a partial account of human cognition and experience, or a *thin* rather than *thick* description.

The complexity of meaning assigned to sexual practices and behavior requires a theory that captures the interpretative exchanges of symbolic meanings and a multi-method approach to studying sexuality. We propose our ecological-womanist framework to encapsulate symbolic meanings colored by cultural influences and the resulting behaviors and practices. Womanist theory compels us to examine the context in which diverse African American women live: specifically, the low number of desirable African American men as marital partners for educated and undereducated African American women; the high number of African American men incarcerated because of drug offenses, felonies, and racial profiling; motherhood as a status marker; historical distrust of mental health services; and internalized racism and sexism. By understanding how these circumstances influence daily living, we can identify points and resources for relevant intervention as well as positive transformation for this at-risk population.

Investigating Change Through a Culturally-Relevant Intervention Model

Evaluating change to decrease sexual risk-taking is a basic goal of most sexual health and practices intervention. Using the *Sexual Health Model* (Robinson, Bockting, Rosser, Miner, & Coleman, 2002), researchers can identify barriers to intervention, motivators for change, and the conditions in which change is acceptable and accessible to targeted populations. The Sexual Health Model is an intervention model which allows discussion of how cultural values and beliefs influence ten domains of sexuality. The Sexual Health Model outlines ten critical areas of inquiry and intervention:

1. sex education knowledge
2. exploring cultural and sexual identities
3. sexual anatomy knowledge
4. sexual health and safe sex practices
5. barriers to change in sexual behavioral outcomes and practices
6. body image perceptions
7. cultural acceptability of masturbation and fantasy
8. positive sexual health factors identification
9. quality of intimacy and relationship interactions
10. spiritual influences on sexual behaviors and practices.

The ecological-womanist theory is well suited for the Sexual Health Model in that a racialized and gendered context can be examined through multiple methods (e.g., interviews, focus groups, surveys) in all ten domains. Findings from the analyses of various forms of data will inform the best culturally-specific strategies that may promote African American female adolescents' transformation—the self-motivated agency to conceptualize or lend meaning to one's own sexuality, with accountability for one's sexual health and that of others.

AN INTEGRATIVE FRAMEWORK FOR PROMOTING HEALTHY SEXUAL PRACTICES

Our interdisciplinary framework, an ecological-womanist theoretical framework, allows researchers the ability to identify multiple variables for changes in sexual behavior outcomes and sexual practices. Connections between the sexual scripts and sexual behaviors influence the extent to which an African American female adolescent can identify with or imagine herself within the sexual scripts she consumes and enacts, as well as the messages about her sexuality received from those with whom she directly interacts. We recognize that adolescence is a critical period for researchers interested in sexual practices interventions because it is during this tumultuous developmental time that adolescents rehearse, internalize, and endorse sexual scripting and practices. For African American adolescents, this transition from childhood to emerging adulthood includes additional negotiated constructions of a distinct racial and gender identification.

Effective intervention programs are those that focus on a narrow range of behavioral goals, promote a particular set of social norms, provide information through active learning methods, address social pressures on behaviors, provide skill rehearsal opportunities, and are culturally relevant (Kirby, 2000). We propose that the Sexual Health Model (Robinson et al., 2002) has potential as an intervention that can focus attention on sexual (e.g., developmental outcomes), relational (specifically, familial and peer relationship influences), and emotional variables (e.g., sexual fulfillment and satisfaction, intimacy needs, and affirmation of both racial and gender identities) within a culturally-embedded context. The cultural context of Hip Hop may be a promising spark to build innovative research on African American adolescent sexual health. We believe that guiding adolescents to deconstruct and challenge Hip Hop sexual imagery is the key to instigating effective change in individual behaviors, practices, and values.

REFERENCES

Barr, S. C., & Neville, H. A. (2008). Examination of the link between parental racial socialization messages and racial ideology among Black college students. *Journal of Black Psychology, 34*, 131–155.

Bronfenbrenner, U. (1979). *The ecology of human development.* Cambridge, MA: Harvard University Press.

Brown, J. D., L'Engle, K. L., Pardun, C. J., Guo, G., Kenneavy, K., & Jackson C. (2006). Sexy media matter: Exposure to sexual content in music, movies, television, and magazines predicts black and white adolescents' sexual behavior. *Pediatrics, 117*, 1018–1027.

Browning, C. R., Leventhal, T., & Brooks-Gunn, J. (2005). Sexual initiation in early adolescence: The nexus of parental and community control. *American Sociological Review, 70*, 758–778.

Centers for Disease Control. (2005). HIV transmission among Black women—North Carolina, 2004. *Morbidity and Mortality Weekly Report, 54*, 89–93.

Cline, V. B. (2000). *Pornography's effects on adults and children.* New York: Morality in Media.

Collins, P. H. (2005). *Black sexual politics: African Americans, gender, and the new racism.* New York: Routledge.

Darling, N. (2007). Ecological systems theory: The person in the center of the circles. *Research in Human Development, 4*, 203–217.

Few, A. L. (2009). Theorizing with racial-ethnic feminisms. In S. A. Lloyd, A. L. Few, & K. R. Allen (Eds.), *Handbook of feminist family studies* (pp. 28–42). Thousand Oaks, CA: Sage.

Few, A. L., Stephens, D. P., & Rouse-Arnett, M. (2003). Sister-to-sister talk: Transcending boundaries in qualitative research with Black women. *Family Relations, 52*, 205–215.

Gillum, T. L. (2002). Exploring the link between stereotypic images and intimate partner violence in the African American community. *Violence Against Women, 8*, 64–87.

Grello, C. M., Welsh, D. P., & Harper, M. S. (2006). No strings attached: The nature of casual sex in college students. *Journal of Sex Research, 43*, 255–267.

Hutchinson, J. F. (1999). The Hip Hop generation: African American male-female relationships in nightclub settings. *Journal of Black Studies, 73*, 62–84.

Kipke, M. D. (1999). *Risks and opportunities: Synthesis of studies on adolescence.* Washington, D.C.: National Academy Press.

Kirby, D. (2000). School-based interventions to prevent unprotected sex and HIV among adolescents. In J. L. Peterson & R. J. DiClemente (Eds.), *Handbook of HIV prevention* (pp. 83–101). New York: Plenum.

Kitwana, B. (2002). *The Hip Hop generation: Young Blacks and the crisis in African American culture.* New York: Basic Books.

Levy, G. (2000). Individual differences in race schematicity as predictors of African American and White children's race-relevant memories and peer preferences. *The Journal of Genetic Psychology, 161*, 400–419.

Moore, M. R., & Chase-Lansdale, P. L. (2001). Sexual intercourse and pregnancy among African-American girls in high-poverty neighborhoods: The role of family and perceived community environment. *Journal of Marriage and the Family, 63*, 1146–1157.

Muñoz-Laboy, M. A., Castellanos, D. H., Haliburton, C. S., del Aguila, E. V., Weinstein, H. J., & Parker, R. G. (2008). Condom use and Hip Hop culture: The case of urban young men in New York City. *American Journal of Public Health, 98*, 1081–1085.

Oswald, R., Blume, L. B., & Marks, S. (2005). Decentering heteronormativity: A model for family studies. In V. L. Bengtson, A. C. Acock, K. R. Allen, P. Dilworth-Anderson, & D. M. Klein (Eds.), *Sourcebook of family theory and research* (pp. 143–165). Thousand Oaks, CA: Sage.

Phillips, L. (2006). *The womanist reader.* New York: Routledge.

Robinson, B. E., Bockting, W. O., Rosser, B. R. S., Miner, M., & Coleman, E. (2002). The sexual health model: Application of a sexological approach to HIV prevention. *Health Education Research: Theory & Practice, 17*(1), 43–57.

Stephens, D. P., & Few, A. L. (2007). Hip Hop honeys or video hos: African American preadolescents' understandings of popular culture-based female sexual scripts. *Sexuality & Culture, 11*, 48–69.

Stephens, D. P., & Phillips, L. D. (2003). Freaks, gold diggers, divas and dykes: the socio-historical development of African American adolescent females' sexual scripts. *Sexuality and Culture, 7*, 3–47.

Stephens, D. P., & Phillips, L. D. (2005). Integrating Black feminist thought into conceptual frameworks of African American adolescent women's sexual scripting processes. *Sexualities, Evolution and Gender, 7*, 37–55.

Stokes, C. E. (2007). Representin' in cyberspace: Sexual scripts, self-definition, and hip hop culture in Black American adolescent girls' home pages. *Culture, Health & Sexuality, 9*, 169–184.

Walker, A. (1983). *In search of our mother's gardens: Womanist prose.* San Diego, CA: Harcourt Brace Jovanovich.

Wallace, S. A., Miller, K. S., & Forehand, R. (2008). Perceived peer norms and sexual intentions among African American preadolescents. *AIDS Education and Prevention, 20*, 360–369.

Wingood, G. M., DiClemente, R. J., Harrington, K., Davies, S., Hook, E. W., & Oh, K. (2001). Exposure to X-rated movies and adolescents' sexual and contraceptive-related attitudes and behaviors. *Pediatrics, 107*, 1116–1120.

CHAPTER 6

Social Anxiety Disorder in Youth: An Ecological-Developmental Perspective

Thomas H. Ollendick

Age-related increases in social evaluative anxiety are part of normal development. As youth emerge from infancy into childhood and adolescence, they place increasing importance on how peers, friends, and adults perceive them and how they *come across* in their social worlds. Transient episodes of social anxiety are common and part of normal development. However, for a small but significant number of youth, normal developmental processes go awry and social anxiety disorder (SAD) develops.

In this chapter, I explore SAD from a contextual perspective that is informed by social ecology and development. My primary objective is to present a coherent theoretical framework in which knowledge of the antecedents, processes, and consequences of change that occur with development can be incorporated in the understanding of SAD and its sequellae. The chapter concludes with a discussion of further use of this model for theory, research, and practice.

SOCIAL ANXIETY DISORDER

Social Anxiety Disorder (SAD; American Psychiatric Association, 1994) consists of a marked and persistent fear of social or performance situations in which embarrassment or humiliation might occur. Frequently, when exposed to possible scrutiny by others, youth with SAD fear they might do something wrong or act in a way that will be embarrassing or humiliating to them. Exposure to social or performance situations frequently provokes an immediate anxiety response that is excessive or unreasonable. In children, this anxiety response may take the form of crying, screaming, or clinging to familiar persons or objects. Adolescents may also experience panic-like symptoms when confronted by anxiety-provoking social situations. Other behavioral manifestations of SAD include gaze aversion, slumped shoulders, nail biting, and a trembling voice. Although behavioral avoidance of social or performance situations is common among socially anxious adolescents and adults, socially anxious children rarely have the opportunity to avoid these social situations. As a result, they may evince disinterest in age-appropriate social, academic, and athletic activities. Adults frequently perceive youth who attempt to avoid anxiety-provoking situations as oppositional, negativistic, or noncompliant because they refuse to do as they are asked (Beidel & Turner, 1998; Hofmann & DiBartolo, 2001; Ollendick & Hirshfeld-Becker, 2002).

Middle-aged children and adolescents with SAD often report anxious thoughts concerning embarrassment, inadequacy, and self-criticism. Alternatively, some youth report that when confronted by anxiety-provoking social situations they are overcome by maladaptive thoughts and are unable to think clearly and become inept or awkward in their social interchanges. Although adolescents and adults typically recognize their fears as irrational, children may not. They report feeling justified in their *distorted* and *dysfunctional* beliefs. Thus, one of the most important contextual factors associated with the expression of SAD is age.

The average age of onset for social phobia is mid-adolescence (APA, 1994) and coincides with the normal vulnerability to social embarrassment seen in adolescents. However, a number of researchers report diagnoses of the disorder in prepubertal children as young as seven (Ollendick & Hirshfeld-Becker, 2002). SAD is the most common anxiety disorder seen in late adolescence and adulthood and ranks third among all psychiatric disorders, following major depression and alcohol dependence. Results of the National Comorbidity Survey indicate that the adult lifetime prevalence of social anxiety disorder is 13.3 percent (Kessler et al., 1994). Research also indicates SAD lifetime prevalence rates of between 10 and 15 percent in adolescents in the United States (Heimberg, Stine, Hiripi, & Kessler, 2000) and Germany (Wittchen, Stein, & Kessler, 1999). Although prevalence rates for children are not well established, most adults with SAD are frequently unable to recall a period in their lives when they were *not* socially anxious. Of course, professionals must view these retrospective reports with appropriate caution. Still, it is common for adolescents with SAD to report their social anxieties began at an early age and are longstanding. Findings also suggest that SAD, at least in adolescence, follows a chronic, unremitting course in the absence of effective treatment (Ollendick & Hirshfeld-Becker, 2002; Ollendick & March, 2004). Thus, SAD represents a disorder of considerable magnitude and significance in childhood and adolescence. What are the antecedents to this disorder and what processes characterize this development gone awry? Although the answer to this question is complex, developmental psychology and developmental psychopathology provide us important clues.

BASIC PREMISES OF DEVELOPMENTAL PSYCHOLOGY AND DEVELOPMENTAL PSYCHOPATHOLOGY

Developmental Theory

Within the field of developmental psychology, theorists have long debated which developmental model best helps researchers and clinicians understand the many changes that occur in individuals throughout their development and across their life spans, and the processes responsible for them. Early debates focused attention on issues of autonomy and organization and were tied to two major worldviews in what came to be known as the *mechanistic* and *organismic* models of development. Supporters of the mechanistic model (Baer, 1982; Skinner, 1938), viewed organisms as similar to machines; they were acted upon largely by forces from the outside world. Specifically, with regard to development, these theorists viewed organisms primarily as passive recipients of information and relatively passive respondents to increasingly complex and varied stimulus input (i.e., a tabula rasa). Furthermore, they believed that changes in behavior over time reflected gradual modifications in antecedent and consequent stimuli with explanations for development derived largely from principles of learning theory (e.g., conditioning, reinforcement). Skinner (1938), for example, asserted "the basic premise of behavioral psychology (was) that all organisms, human and subhuman, *young and old* (italics added), were subject to the same law of effect (principle of reinforcement) and could be studied in the same basic manner" (p. 27). From this perspective, many clinicians and researchers viewed development and developmental processes as possessing relatively little clinical or societal significance (for an extended discussion of this point see Ollendick & Cerny, 1981).

In contrast to the passive qualities of the organism portrayed in the mechanistic point of view, proponents of the organismic model of development asserted that organisms were not passive; rather, they viewed them as agents who were actively involved in the construction of their own environments. Furthermore, organismic theorists often described development as if it passed through discrete and oftentimes invariant stages (e.g., Piaget's stages of cognitive development, Freud's psychosexual stages, and Erickson's stages of identity development). These various theories maintained that basic structures and functions changed across age and that they reflected emerging, qualitatively different ways of interacting with the environment. In its simplest form, this model proposed that change resulted largely from maturational processes occasioned by intrinsic organismic factors rather than extrinsic environmental ones.

Extensive debate among proponents of these opposing models as well as increasing recognition of their limitations led to the advent of a third model of development, namely, the *transactional* model. Also known as *developmental contextualism*, the transactional model moved beyond the mechanistic and organismic models (Lerner, Hess, & Nitz, 1991; Ollendick & Vasey, 1999) and was highly consistent with the tenets of social learning/social cognitive theory (cf. Bandura, 1977, 1986; Ollendick & Cerny, 1981). Advocates of this model proposed that developmental changes occurred because of continuous reciprocal interactions (i.e., reciprocal determinism, transactions) between an active organism and its active environmental context. Organisms affected their own development by being both products and producers of their environments. Although differences in theory and philosophy remain, most developmental theorists agree that development involves systematic, successive, and adaptive changes within and across life periods in the structure, function, and content of the individual's cognitive, emotional, behavioral, social, and interpersonal characteristics (Silverman & Ollendick, 1999). Because developmental changes occur in an orderly and sequential fashion (i.e., they are systematic and successive), changes observed at one point in time will likely influence subsequent events (although not necessarily in a direct linear fashion, see below). Changes that occur at one point in time (whether due to learning, an unfolding of basic predetermined structures, or some complex, interactive/transactional process) have an impact on subsequent development. Thus, the diversity or variety of changes over the life span is constrained by, but not solely determined by, changes that occurred at an earlier point in time.

Developmental Psychopathology

Developmental psychopathology and developmental psychology are closely inter-connected (Rutter & Garmezy, 1983). Sroufe and Rutter (1984) defined developmental psychopathology as "the study of the origins and course of individual patterns of behavioral maladaptation, whatever the age of onset, whatever the causes, whatever the transformations in behavioral manifestations, and however complex the course of developmental pattern may be" (p. 18). Implicit in this definition is concern with development and developmental deviations or distortions (i.e., clinical psychopathologies) that occur throughout and across the life span and the processes associated with those perturbations. The study of psychopathology, from this perspective, organizes itself around milestones, transitions, and sequences in physical, cognitive, and social-emotional development. This theory views development as a series of qualitative reorganizations within and among systems. The character of these reorganizations is determined by factors at various levels of contextual analysis (e.g., genetic, constitutional, developmental, physiological, behavioral, environmental, and sociological) that are in dynamic transaction with one another (Cicchetti, 1989). Pathological development constitutes a lack of integration among the very systems that contribute synergistically to adaptation at particular developmental levels (i.e., toddlerhood, childhood, adolescence). Development goes awry at such times and under such conditions (Ollendick & Vasey, 1999).

Although development at one level affects later development, direct or isomorphic continuity of behavior is not expected. Rather, developmental outcomes may occur through multiple pathways. Normal *and* pathological development results from individually distinct and unique transactions between a changing organism and its ever-changing environmental context. This notion is captured in the developmental principle of equifinality—the principle that any one outcome (i.e., SAD) may result from multiple and diverse pathways. From a developmental perspective, the expectation that a singular pathway to a given disorder exists would be the exception, not the rule. In contrast to equifinality, the principle of multifinality asserts that varied outcomes can eventuate from the very same common starting points. Thus, any one risk factor for the development of SAD (e.g., behavioral inhibition to the unfamiliar) is likely to result in a variety of diverse outcomes, not just SAD (Kagan, 1994). It is therefore important to identify and understand intra- and extra-individual characteristics (i.e., antecedents) that promote or inhibit early deviations or maintain or disrupt early adaptation and development (i.e., outcomes). Thus, the field of developmental psychopathology examines the origins and course of a given disorder, its precursors and sequellae, its variations in manifestation with development, and more broadly, its relations to non-disordered behavior patterns (Ollendick & Vasey, 1999; Rutter, 1985; Toth & Cicchetti, 1999).

As may be evident, the developmental psychopathology perspective does not subscribe to nor prescribe a particular theoretical orientation or explanation for the origins of diverse child psychopathologies (i.e., medical model, psychodynamic theory, social learning theory, family systems theory), nor does it supplant particular theories; rather, it sharpens our awareness about connections among phenomena that may otherwise seem unrelated or disconnected. In this sense, it is a macroparadigm, which serves to bridge a variety of conceptual models (i.e., microparadigms in themselves).

ANTECEDENT PATHWAYS TO SOCIAL ANXIETY DISORDER AS AN OUTCOME

Several antecedent factors can lead to the development of SAD as a developmental outcome, including genetic factors, temperamental factors, parental influences, conditioning events, information processing styles, peer interpersonal factors, and more broad ecological and developmental forces (see table 6.1). Our etiologic model of SAD posits an interaction of biological, psychological, and social antecedent factors that intersect with negative thoughts, feelings, and avoidance behaviors in the individual child (Ollendick & Hirshfeld-Becker, 2002). An examination of all of these factors is beyond the scope of the present chapter. Rather, one of these factors—the temperamental characteristic of *behavioral inhibition to the unfamiliar* (Kagan, 1994), will be highlighted to illustrate the sometimes unexpected findings associated with development and the delicate interplay of ecological-developmental forces that lead to development gone awry.

Table 6.1. Risk Factors for Social Anxiety Disorder

	Antecedent Factor	Description	Source Data	Comments
Genetic Factors	Specific vulnerability to SAD Broader vulnerabilities for anxiety proneness or anxiety and affective disorders	Family history of SAD Family history of panic disorder or major depression	Twin, family-genetic, and high-risk offspring only studies	Twin studies have been carried out for females Family studies suggest higher familiality for generalized than non-generalized SAD
Temperament	Behavioral inhibition to the unfamiliar (BI) Behavioral disinhibition (BD)	Temperamental tendency to be silent, behaviorally restrained, or fearful in novel situations The tendency to exhibit increased exploration, spontaneity of speech, and approach in unfamiliar situations	Prospective longitudinal and cross-sectional observational studies; retrospective self-report studies Prospective longitudinal cross-sectional observational studies	Unknown if BI is a specific risk factor for social anxiety or for more general anxiety-proneness or anxiety and depression. The difference may be related to assessment differences (measurement of inhibition to social vs. non-social novelty) Most BI children do not develop SAD; moreover some with BD develop SAD
Parental Influences	Behavioral modeling Parental attitudes and actions Relationship quality	Modeling of social avoidance and fear of social evaluation Attitudes of low affection/warmth, over-protection, restrictiveness, rejection criticism, shame	High-risk studies, retrospective reports Retrospective and concurrent self-reports by adults and children with SAD	Heavy reliance on correlational studies or retrospective self-report instruments Child symptoms may elicit parental behaviors or interact reciprocally

(*continued*)

Table 6.1. (continued)

	Antecedent Factor	Description	Source Data	Comments
		inducement, over-concern with opinions of others Facilitation or encouragement of social avoidance Non-optimal fostering of social interaction Insecure attachment	Observation studies (including children with anxiety disorders other than SAD) Extrapolated from studies of parents of peer-rejected children Prospective study	Influences may operate differently on children in the same family as a function of child temperament or vulnerability Included children with anxiety disorders other than SAD
Conditioning Events	Traumatic or vicarious conditioning or information transfer Socialization experiences	Experiencing, observing or hearing about humiliating social experiences Peer neglect Peer rejection	Retrospective self-reports by adults with SAD Retrospective reports and cross-sectional and longitudinal observations of peer relations of anxious or inhibited children	Self-reports of etiology may be inaccurate Peer neglect or rejection may be a response to temperament or anxious behaviors, or may interact reciprocally
Cognitive	Distorted perceptions and cognitions which exacerbate or maintain social anxiety Thoughts which interfere with coping	Overestimation of threat Underestimation of social competence Selective attention to own arousal, signs of negative evaluation Negative self-talk	Observational studies of SAD adults, self-reports by SAD children	Maintaining factor (no evidence for etiological influence)

Note. SAD = Social Anxiety Disorder; BI = Behavioral inhibition to the unfamiliar. BD = Behavioral disinhibition to the unfamiliar.

Research has pointed to the temperamental characteristic of *behavioral inhibition to the unfamiliar* (BI) as one of the precursors to social anxiety disorder. Originally described by Kagan, Reznick, and Snidman (1987), BI represents an enduring tendency, observable in 10-15 percent of infants and toddlers, to demonstrate fear, avoidance, or quiet restraint and reticence when exposed to unfamiliar situations, objects, or people. BI overlaps with shyness to be sure; however, it is broader in scope in that it encompasses inhibition to non-social as well as social stimuli. In practice, however, assessment of BI often emphasizes inhibition to unfamiliar adults and peers. The characteristic manifests itself differently at different developmental ages: inhibited toddlers react to novelty with fear, clinging, and avoidance; preschoolers react with hesitancy, restraint, and reticence, inhibited spontaneous conversation, and limited smiling in unfamiliar situations; school-age children manifest inhibition through reticence and constriction with unfamiliar adults, and through quiet isolation with unfamiliar peers; and, adolescents demonstrate inhibition through a potpourri of problems including talking in public, dating, and other social intercourse. Thus, age, a developmental marker serves as a context for the form of the disorder across development. In their research, Kagan and colleagues followed two independent cohorts of children identified as inhibited as toddlers and found that BI was moderately stable through middle childhood and early adolescence (Kagan, 1994). Other longitudinal studies, which vary widely in the ways in which they defined behavioral inhibition, have found similar stability of BI from toddlerhood through middle childhood and from early childhood to middle and late childhood, as well as early adulthood (Caspi & Silva, 1995).

BI is a complex phenomenon characterized by its own set of antecedent factors and developmental processes. At a biological level, BI reflects a lower threshold to arousal in response to novelty (Kagan et al., 1987). Support for this hypothesis comes from studies finding correlations between behavioral markers of inhibition and increased sympathetic nervous system activation (see Hirshfeld, Rosenbaum, Fredman, & Kagan, 1999 for a review). Somewhat different physiologic reactions characterize BI at different ages: increased baseline morning salivary cortisol levels at ages five-and-a-half and seven-and-a-half, high and stable heart rates at ages four, five-and-a-half and seven-and-a-half, and a tendency at all ages for heart rate to accelerate in novel situations (Kagan, Reznick, & Snidman, 1988). Moreover, findings from two small studies (Calkins, Fox, &

Marshall, 1996; Davidson, 1994) suggest that highly reactive or inhibited infants (ages 9–10 months) show asymmetries in cerebral activation indicative of increased right hemisphere activation (of hypothesized *withdrawal centers* including areas of the right frontal region, the amygdala, and the temporal polar region) or decreased left hemisphere activation (Davidson, 1994).

Twin studies demonstrate a genetic component to BI, with heritabilities estimated in the .4 to .7 range at fourteen to twenty-four months (DiLalla, Kagan, & Reznick, 1994; Robinson, Kagan, Reznick, & Corley, 1992). Studies also suggest that changes in inhibited or shy behaviors from toddlerhood to early preschool age are more similar in monozygotic than dizygotic twin pairs (Plomin et al., 1993).

Other studies link BI with family risk for SAD. Inhibited children from the Kagan cohort had parents with higher rates of social phobia than parents of non-inhibited control children (Rosenbaum et al., 1988; Rosenbaum, Biederman, Hirshfeld, Bolduc, & Chaloff, 1991). Similarly, mothers of four-year-olds identified as extremely *shy* have elevated rates of lifetime history of SAD (Cooper & Eke, 1999).

Moreover, BI appears prospectively associated with social anxiety in the children of both normal and anxiety-disordered parents. Children from the Kagan cohort demonstrated significantly more phobic disorders at age 7–8 years than controls. The most common feared situations included speaking in front of others, meeting strangers, being in crowds, and being called on in class (Biederman et al., 1990). Furthermore, stability of BI throughout early childhood increased the risk for phobias and for parental history of SAD (Hirshfeld et al., 1992). BI children whose parents themselves had anxiety disorders were most at risk (Rosenbaum et al., 1992). By age thirteen, social anxiety was significantly higher in youngsters from both Kagan cohorts who had been inhibited as toddlers compared with those who had been uninhibited (34% vs. 9%), with the effect more robust for girls (44% vs. 6%).

Similar results have emerged in other cohorts of children evincing BI. One study, for example, compared rates of anxiety disorders among 216 inhibited and non-inhibited children from a sample of offspring of parents with panic disorder, major depressive disorder, and non-anxious, non-depressed controls (Biederman et al., 2001). This study found that inhibited youngsters (mean age 6) had significantly higher rates of social anxiety disorder than noninhibited children (17% vs. 5%). At follow-up when these children were approximately ten (Biederman et al, 2006; Hirshfeld-Becker, Biederman, et al., 2007), BI was shown to be selective in its prediction of SAD: inhibited children were significantly more likely than noninhibited children to manifest SAD (28% vs. 14%). In addition, BI children were significantly more likely to show new onset of SAD (22% vs. 8%) during this follow-up period. These differential patterns are in accord with other longitudinal studies that have found specific links between BI and SAD (Hayward, Killen, Kraemer, & Taylor, 1998; Schwartz, Snidman, & Kagan, 1999).

These results suggest that BI is associated specifically with the development of maladaptive social anxiety in childhood and adolescence. However, it is clear from these studies that not all children with BI develop SAD (in fact, only about one-third do so), suggesting that there must be other pathways to SAD. Recent studies show that *Behavioral Disinhibition* (BD) may also be related to the development and course of SAD in youth. BD is the polar opposite of BI. It is the tendency to exhibit increased exploration, spontaneity of speech, and approach in unfamiliar situations (see Hirshfeld-Becker, Biederman, Calltharp, Rosenbaum, & Rosenbaum, 2003). How should we understand that a temperamental characteristic that is the polar opposite of BI also serves to occasion the development of SAD? Although perplexing, such a prospect is consistent with developmental theory and the developmental psychopathology perspective. There are multiple and diverse pathways to any one outcome.

Specifically, in an early study, BD was associated with elevated risks for disruptive behavior disorders at age six (32% vs. 6%) and age ten (44% vs. 17%; Hirshfeld-Becker, Henin, et al., 2007), just as BI was related specifically to SAD at these different ages. However, in a more recent analysis of the children of parents with panic disorder who were at risk for disorder, Hirshfeld-Becker and her colleagues (2009) showed that children with BI and BD differed at age six in presence of SAD (26% vs. 9%), as expected, but not at age ten (42% vs. 37%). Thus, within these offspring at risk for development of an anxiety disorder (children of parents with panic disorder), BI predicted SAD at age six but BD did not. At mean age of ten, however, both offspring with BI and offspring with BD had significantly elevated rates of SAD compared with children who were not at extremes of these temperamental dimensions. These findings are surprising and counterintuitive. Although BI and SAD show similar biological and physiological underpinnings (e.g., lower threshold to sympathetic arousal, hypothalamic-pituitary axis activation, and amygdalar reactivity to novelty) and *map onto* one another, BD and SAD do not. Although speculative, we propose that general dysregulation in the approach-avoidance system may predispose both groups of youngsters to later social anxiety disorder. If so, perturbations in the motivational system of approach or withdrawal from novelty at either extreme may be associated with development of social anxiety disorder. In either case, normal development has gone awry.

CONCLUSIONS AND IMPLICATIONS

The development of SAD is not straightforward nor is its course easily predicted. SAD may result from multiple antecedent pathways (i.e., the developmental principle of equifinality); moreover, any one pathway associated with the development of SAD can lead to outcomes other than SAD (i.e., the developmental principle of multifinality). Although genetic and temperamental factors, parental influences, conditioning events, cognitive factors, peer relationships, and diverse environmental factors are all associated with SAD, they do so in a complex, transactive manner that is dependent upon contextual factors such as age of the child and the broader familial and community context in which the child is embedded. Any one of these antecedent factors alone is likely not sufficient, nor necessary, to occasion the onset of this (or any other) disorder. Specificity of the developmental outcome results from the combination, timing, and circumstances surrounding these influences (Ollendick & Hirshfeld-Becker, 2002; Ollendick & Horsch, 2007; Ollendick & Vasey, 1999; Vasey & Ollendick, 2000). Put simply, antecedent risk factors serve to predispose youth to the development of an outcome such as SAD; however, they do not directly occasion it. A complex interplay of factors serves to precipitate its expression and maintenance.

Implications for Theory, Research, and Practice

Five different types of studies would be helpful in testing the viability of the developmental psychopathology model and in advancing theory, research, and practice. First, we need to conduct longitudinal prospective studies of at-risk children (offspring of parents with SAD), which begin in infancy or toddlerhood and assess children temperamentally, behaviorally, and diagnostically, as well as monitor the course of parental symptoms, parenting behaviors, and peer and sibling influences. With such studies, we could advance our theory and empirical findings related to the role of family and peer contextual variables and the onset of SAD. Such studies are critical if we are to progress beyond mere correlational studies and examine the causal pathways leading to this disorder. Given that developmental outcomes are not linear and the pathways are not direct, very large numbers of participants will be required.

Second, we need to undertake twin studies, which assess both behavioral inhibition *and* behavioral disinhibition along with childhood anxiety disorders. It will be important for such studies to model the associations between temperaments and disorders over time. Such studies will help us disentangle important genetic and constitutional factors and help us better understand why disparate temperaments such as behavioral inhibition (BI) and behavioral disinhibition (BD) result in different disorders at some times in development and the same disorders at other times in development. These studies will likely require large multi-site samples to examine the delicate interplay of these important antecedent markers of SAD and the changes associated with them.

Third, we need to conduct adoption studies of at-risk children (i.e., those whose biological or adoptive parents have SAD), in which biological and adoptive parents, as well as their children, are assessed temperamentally, behaviorally, and diagnostically over time. It will be important in these studies to examine the presence of social anxiety and related disorders in the children *and* their parents. For too long, we have assumed that causal patterns are uni-directional and that parents cause disorder in their offspring. We need to be open to bi-directional pathways and the possibility that disorders in children lead to disorders in parents. That is, children who evidence social anxiety disorders may contribute to the development of similar disorders in their parents, rather than the other way around (Ollendick & Horsch, 2007).

Fourth, we need complex, large scale studies such as that reported by Wickrama and Bryant (2003) that assess structural community characteristics (e.g., poverty, ethnicity), community social resources (e.g., social integration, extended families), family social resources (e.g., involved parenting, parent-child relations), and specific developmental outcomes. Such studies would allow for an examination of the ecological-developmental model within a set of multi-level social contexts as recommended by Bronfenbrenner (1986). It would be important for such studies to be longitudinal in nature and to utilize structural equation modeling techniques to test out the complex interactions involved in such relations.

Finally, we desperately need to undertake intervention studies with at-risk offspring with behavioral inhibition *and* behavioral disinhibition in which antecedent factors that contribute to the onset of SAD are the focus of intervention. In such studies, it will be important to monitor family and developmental processes that result in diverse developmental outcomes. Although interventions cannot tell us about etiologic factors, they can inform us about maintaining factors, and importantly, about how to prevent or mitigate the course of SAD. Ultimately, comparisons of such interventions for children with and without different antecedent risk factors will help determine which factors are important to target and under which conditions. The factors intervened with might include factors in the child (e.g., cognitive factors, tendency to cope through avoidance, lower threshold to sympathetic arousal), family (e.g., parental modeling, parental facilitation or avoidance of socialization, criticism/shaming), peer group (e.g., neglect or rejection), and community (e.g., schools, churches). Intervention methods might include psychosocial and psychopharmacological interventions that address all of these interacting and transacting components (Hirshfeld-Becker et al, 2008; Ollendick & Hirshfeld-Becker, 2002; Ollendick & March, 2004). Such studies will not only help us understand the development and course of these disorders but also help us reverse the negative sequellae associated with this impairing disorder.

In short, researchers have their work cut out for them. Although we have learned much about SAD in recent years and its antecedents, causes, and consequences, we have only begun to scratch the surface of what we need to do. In many respects, the study of SAD is in its own infancy. Still, we are making progress, even if only by baby steps.

REFERENCES

American Psychiatric Association. (1994). *Diagnostic and statistical manual for mental disorders* (4th ed.). Washington, DC: Author.

Baer, D. M. (1982). Behavior analysis and development. *Human Development, 25,* 357–361.

Bandura, A. (1977). *Social learning theory.* Englewood Cliffs, NJ: Prentice-Hall.

Bandura, A. (1986). *Social foundations of thought and action: A social cognitive theory.* Englewood Cliffs, NJ: Prentice-Hall.

Beidel, D. C., & Turner, S. M. (1998). *Shy children, phobic adults: Nature and treatment of social phobia.* Washington, DC: American Psychological Association.

Biederman, J., Faraone, S. V., Hirshfeld-Becker, D. R., Friedman, D., Robin, J., & Rosenbaum, J. F. (2001). Patterns of psychopathology and dysfunction in a large sample of high-risk children of parents with panic disorder and major depression: A controlled study. *American Journal of Psychiatry, 158,* 49–57.

Biederman, J., Petty, C., Hirshfeld-Becker, D. R., Henin, A., Faraone, S. V., Dang, D., et al. (2006). A controlled longitudinal five year follow-up study of children at high and low risk for panic disorder and major depression. *Psychological Medicine, 36,* 1141–1152.

Biederman, J., Rosenbaum, J. F., Hirshfeld, D. R., Faraone, S.V., Bolduc, E. A., Gersten, M., et al. (1990). Psychiatric correlates of behavioral inhibition in young children of parents with and without psychiatric disorders. *Archives of General Psychiatry, 47,* 21–26.

Bronfenbrenner, U. (1986). Ecology of the family as a context for human development: Research perspectives. *Developmental Psychology, 22,* 723–742.

Calkins, S. D., Fox, N. A., & Marshall, T. R. (1996). Behavioral and physiological antecedents of inhibited and uninhibited behavior. *Child Development, 67,* 523–540.

Caspi, A., & Silva, P. A. (1995). Temperamental qualities at age 3 predict personality traits in young adulthood: Longitudinal evidence from a birth cohort. *Child Development, 66,* 486–498.

Cicchetti, D. (1989). Developmental psychopathology: Past, present, and future. In D. Cicchetti (Ed.), *The emergence of a discipline: The Rochester symposium on developmental psychopathology* (pp. 1–12). Hillsdale, NJ: Erlbaum.

Cooper, P. J., & Eke, M. (1999). Childhood shyness and maternal social phobia: A community study. *British Journal of Psychiatry, 174,* 439–443.

Davidson, R. (1994). Asymmetric brain function, affective style, and psychopathology: The role of early experience and plasticity. *Development and Psychopathology, 6,* 741–758.

DiLalla, L., Kagan, J., & Reznick, J. (1994). Genetic etiology of behavioral inhibition among 2-year-old children. *Infant and Behavior Development, 17,* 405–412.

Hayward, C., Killen, J., Kraemer, K., & Taylor, C. (1998). Linking self-reported childhood behavioral inhibition to adolescent social phobia. *Journal of the American Academy of Child and Adolescent Psychiatry, 37,* 1308–1316.

Heimberg, R. G., Stine, M. B., Hiripi, E., & Kessler, R. C. (2000). Trends in the prevalence of social phobia in the United States: A synthetic cohort analysis of changes over four decades. *European Journal of Psychiatry, 15,* 29–37.

Hirshfeld, D. R., Rosenbaum, J. F., Biederman, J., Bolduc, E. A., Faraone, S.V., Snidman, N., et al. (1992). Stable behavioral inhibition and its association with anxiety disorder. *Journal of the American Academy of Child and Adolescent Psychiatry, 31,* 103–111.

Hirshfeld, D. R., Rosenbaum, J. F., Fredman, S. J., & Kagan, J. (1999). Neurobiology of childhood anxiety disorders. In D. Charney, E. Nestler & B. S. Bunney (Eds.), *Neurobiological foundations of mental illness* (pp. 823–838). Oxford: Oxford University Press.

Hirshfeld-Becker, D. R., Biederman, J., Calltharp, S., Rosenbaum, E. D., & Rosenbaum, J. F. (2003). Behavioral inhibition and disinhibition as hypothesized precursors to psychopathology: Implications for pediatric bipolar disorder. *Biological Psychiatry, 53,* 985–999.

Hirshfeld-Becker, D. R., Biederman, J., Faraone, S. V., Violette, H., Wrightsman, J., & Rosenbaum, J. F. (2002). Temperamental correlates of disruptive behavior disorders in young children: Preliminary findings. *Biological Psychiatry, 50,* 563–574.

Hirshfeld-Becker, D. R., Biederman, J., Henin, A., Faraone, S. V., Davis, S., Harrington, K., et al. (2007). Behavioral inhibition in preschool children at risk is a specific predictor of middle childhood social anxiety: A five-year follow-up. *Journal of Developmental and Behavioral Pediatrics, 28,* 225–233.

Hirshfeld-Becker, D. R., Biederman, J., Henin, A., Faraone, S.V., Violette, H., Wrightsman, J., et al. (2009). *Temperamental pathways to anxiety disorder in children at risk.* Manuscript submitted for publication.

Hirshfeld-Becker, D. R., Henin, A., Biederman, J., Faraone, S. V., Micco, J. A., van Grondelle, A., et al. (2007). Clinical outcomes of laboratory-observed preschool behavioral disinhibition at five-year follow-up. *Biological Psychiatry, 62,* 565–572.

Hirshfeld-Becker, D. R., Masek, B., Henin, A., Blakely, L. R., Rettew, D. C., Dufton, L., et al. (2008). Cognitive-behavioral intervention with young anxious children. *Harvard Review of Psychiatry, 16,* 113–125.

Hofmann, S. G., & DiBartolo, P. M. (Eds.). (2001). *From social anxiety to social phobia: Multiple perspectives.* Boston: Allyn & Bacon.

Kagan, J. (1994). *Galen's prophecy: Temperament in human nature.* New York: Basic Books.

Kagan, J., Reznick, J. S., & Snidman, N. (1987). The physiology and psychology of behavioral inhibition in children. *Child Development, 58,* 1459–1473.

Kagan, J., Reznick, J. S., & Snidman, N. (1988). Biological bases of childhood shyness. *Science, 240,* 167–171.

Kessler, R. C., McGonagle, K. A., Shanyang, Z., Nelson, C. B., Hughes, M., Eshleman, S., et al. (1994). Lifetime and 12-month prevalence of DSM-III-R psychiatric disorders in the United States. *Archives of General Psychiatry, 51,* 8–19.

Lerner, R. M., Hess, L. E., & Nitz, K. (1991). A developmental perspective on psychopathology. In M. Hersen & C. G. Last (Eds.), *Handbook of child and adult psychopathology: A longitudinal perspective* (pp. 9–32). Elmsford, NY: Pergamon Press.

Lewis, M. (1990). Models of developmental psychopathology. In M. Lewis & S. M. Miller (Eds.), *Handbook of developmental psychopathology* (pp. 15–27). New York: Plenum.

Ollendick, T. H., & Cerny, J. A. (1981). *Clinical behavior therapy with children.* New York: Plenum.

Ollendick, T. H., & Hirshfeld-Becker, D. R. (2002). The developmental psychopathology of social anxiety disorder. *Biological Psychiatry, 51,* 44–58.

Ollendick, T. H., & Horsch, L. M. (2007). Fears in children and adolescents: Relations with child anxiety sensitivity, maternal overprotection, and maternal phobic anxiety. *Behavior Therapy, 38,* 402–411.

Ollendick, T. H., & March, J. S. (Eds.). (2004). *Phobic and anxiety disorders in children and adolescents: A clinician's guide to effective psychosocial and pharmacological interventions.* New York: Oxford University Press.

Ollendick, T. H., & Vasey, M. W. (1999). Developmental theory and the practice of clinical child psychology. *Journal of Clinical Child Psychology, 28,* 457–466.

Plomin, R. (1986). *Development, genetics, and psychology.* Hillsdale, NJ: Erlbaum.
Plomin, R., Emde, R., Braungart, J., Campos, J., Corley, R., Fulker, D., et al. (1993). Genetic change and continuity from fourteen to twenty months: The MacArthur Longitudinal Twin Study. *Child Development, 64,* 1354–1376.
Robinson, J. L., Kagan, J., Reznick, J. S., & Corley, R. (1992). The heritability of inhibited and uninhibited behavior: A twin study. *Developmental Psychology, 28,* 1030–1037.
Rosenbaum, J. F., Biederman, J., Bolduc, E. A., Hirshfeld, D. R., Faraone, S.V., & Kagan, J. (1992). Comorbidity of parental anxiety disorders as risk for child-onset anxiety in inhibited children. *American Journal of Psychiatry, 149,* 475–478.
Rosenbaum, J. F., Biederman, J., Gersten, M., Hirshfeld, D. R., Meminger, S. R., Herman, J. B., et al. (1988). Behavioral inhibition in children of parents with panic disorder and agoraphobia: A controlled study. *Archives of General Psychiatry, 45,* 463–470.
Rosenbaum, J., Biederman, J., Hirshfeld, D., Bolduc, E., & Chaloff, J. (1991). Behavioral inhibition in children: A possible precursor to panic disorder or social phobia. *Journal of Clinical Psychiatry, 52,* 5–9.
Rutter, M. (1985). Resilience in the face of adversity: Protective factors and resistance to psychiatric disorder. *British Journal of Psychiatry, 147,* 498–611.
Rutter, M., & Garmezy, N. (1983). Developmental psychopathology. In E. M. Hetherington (Ed.), *Socialization, personality, and social development* (pp. 775–911). New York: Wiley.
Schwartz, C., Snidman, N., & Kagan, J. (1999). Adolescent social anxiety as an outcome of inhibited temperament in childhood. *Journal of the American Academy of Child and Adolescent Psychiatry, 38,* 1008–1015.
Silverman, W. K., & Ollendick, T. H. (Eds.). (1999). *Developmental issues in the clinical treatment of children.* Boston: Allyn & Bacon.
Skinner, B. F. (1938). *The behavior of organisms.* New York: Appleton.
Sroufe, L. A., & Rutter, M. (1984). The domain of developmental psychopathology. *Child Development, 55,* 17–29.
Toth, S. L., & Cicchetti, D. (1999). Developmental psychopathology and child psychotherapy. In S. W. Russ, & T. H. Ollendick (Eds.), *Handbook of psychotherapies with children and families* (pp. 15–43). New York: Kluwer Academic/Plenum.
Vasey, M. W., & Ollendick, T. H. (2000). Anxiety. In M. Lewis & A. Sameroff (Eds.), *Handbook of developmental psychopathology* (pp. 511–529). New York: Plenum.
Wickrama, K. A. S., & Bryant, C. M. (2003). Community context of social resources and adolescent mental health. *Journal of Marriage and Family, 65,* 850–866.
Wittchen, H-U., Stein, M. B., & Kessler, R. C. (1999). Social fears and social phobia in a community sample of adolescents and young adults: Prevalence, risk factors and comorbidity. *Psychological Medicine, 29,* 309–323.

CHAPTER 7

Risk and Protective Factors for Drug Use among American Youth[1]

Kee Jeong Kim

There is a considerable body of research describing the prevalence and patterns of drug use and abuse in the United States. Although the overall use of drugs in the United States has fallen by 50 percent in the past twenty years, the past ten years have shown dramatic increase in drug use by adolescents (Johnston, O'Malley, & Bachman, 2003). In 2002, more than 54 percent of U.S. high school seniors had used an illegal drug at least once. Moreover, among adolescents ages twelve to seventeen, the average ages of first use of marijuana, cocaine, and heroin were 13.7, 14.7, and 14.4 years, respectively (Johnston et al., 2003). With growing concern that drug-related problems are endemic to society, researchers have identified a set of risk factors for the onset and prognosis of drug use among youth. The identified risk factors range from a dysfunctional family environment, deviant peer influences, to disadvantaged neighborhoods (Patterson, Reid, & Dishion, 1998).

Studies on the risk factors of drug use have informed parents, educators, and practitioners about the importance of detecting life conditions that place youth at heightened risk for drug use early on, which has resulted in several prevention programs. However, critiques point out that effectiveness of the prevention programs is somewhat attenuated because they were all developed on a premise that a singular pathway leads at-risk youth to drug use (Dishion, McCord, & Poulin, 1999). If, as the critiques claim, multiple pathways for adolescent drug use exist, then there is a need for the development of pathway-specific prevention to elevate the level of program effectiveness. In this chapter, I provide theoretical discussions about the heterogeneous pathways by specifically focusing on how drug use behaviors develop and change over time within each pathway.

I first review recent developmental theories of adolescent psychopathology that imply the existence of at least two distinctively different pathways of adolescent drug use. Second, I use my own data to theorize a third developmental pathway that extends the current theories. Then, I turn my attention to another critical limitation that exists in the current literature on youth drug use. That is, earlier studies on adolescent drug use have not fully addressed the directionality of the relationship between risk and resilient factors and drug use behaviors. I propose a transactional model that captures dynamic changes in both the conditions of risk and resilient factors and drug use. Finally, the chapter concludes with the implications of understanding the heterogeneous pathways for the delivery of prevention and intervention services.

HETEROGENEITY: THE DEVELOPMENTAL TRAJECTORIES OF DRUG USE

From the life course perspective, a trajectory refers to "a pathway or line of development over the life span" and trajectories are "long-term patterns of behavior and are marked by a sequence of transitions" (Elder, 1985, pp. 31–32). The interdependent age-graded trajectories have become an important concept for studying variation in substance use and antisocial behavior such as its onset, continuity, and discontinuity (Laub & Sampson, 1993; Warr, 1998).

There are two eminent trajectory taxonomies of antisocial behavior and substance use. Early and late onset offending patterns specified by Patterson and Yoerger (1993) and life-course-persistent/adolescence-limited patterns proposed by Moffitt (1993) share many of commonalities in regard to different correlates related to each trajectory pattern. Developmental antecedents of the early onset/life-course-persistent trajectory reside in psychopathological individual, social, and familial conditions. According to Moffitt (1993), the etiological chain for life-course-persistent offending trajectory begins as early as birth with "neuropsychological deficits" (p. 680) that affects verbal and executive functions and personality development (e.g., temperament). Poor cognitive abilities and difficult temperament are risk factors for antisocial outcomes in later childhood as well as for the disrupted parent-child relationship. Once such children enter school, they either (a) interact with other peers in a dysfunctional fashion that reflects ineffective communication experiences with parents or (b) seek out peers displaying very similar antisocial behavior. As a result, the child is more likely to miss further opportunities to practice prosocial skills and to continue to have "the life-course-persistent antisocial syndrome" (Moffitt, 1993, p. 685). Similarly, Patterson and his colleagues (1993, 1998) also view early starters as those who engage in a series of deviant behaviors including drug use during early adolescence and have serious deficits in their social skills due to social risk factors. Early starters are likely exposed to poor parenting skills and disruptive family transitions (e.g., parents' divorce), are aggressive and defiant, and are more likely to get rejected by conventional peers in schools (Patterson et al., 1993; Vuchinich, Bank, & Patterson, 1992). Lack of learned prosocial practices exposes early onset drug users to an increased risk for evolving into adult drug users. The shape of the life-course-persistent trajectory is flat linear without much slope, which indicates a substantive change in drug use because the early onset drug users remain at the high level of drug consumption throughout the years of adolescence once the drug use behavior is set in motion.

On the other hand, the late onset adolescent-limited trajectory follows an inverted U-shape developmental curve with its peak at around ages fifteen through seventeen. Antecedents for the adolescent-limited trajectory are sharply contrasted against those shared by the life-course-persistent drug users. Maturity gap, social mimicry, and deviant peers are related to onset of the late onset adolescent-limited trajectory (Moffitt, 1993; Patterson et al., 1993). When adolescents recognize a gap between their physical maturity and limited access to adult behaviors, they attempt to engage primarily in rebellious activities such as drinking, smoking, experimenting with drugs, and sexual intercourse to overcome the maturity gap (Moffitt, 1993; Piquero & Brezina, 2001). Deviant peers encourage and reinforce the rebellious activities (Patterson et al., 1993). The researchers suggest that adolescent-limited and late starters tend to mimic a few rebellious behaviors during puberty and more actively engage in the deviant behaviors during middle and late adolescence. Once they enter adulthood, however, they gradually withdraw from the deviant acts because the need to express their frustrations declines with maturity and they achieve autonomy and independence as adults (Moffitt, 1993; Piquero & Brezina, 2001).

The magnitude of the influence that the taxonomy theories have made on the field of adolescent psychopathology has been indescribably large.

For example, new statistical programs (e.g., SAS TRAJ; Jones, Nagin, & Roeder, 2001) were developed exclusively to test the theories' core conceptual inquires as to whether or not two trajectories really exist in the population. Preventive intervention researchers have begun paying attention to the notion of heterogeneity in the development pathways for drug use. Despite these notable contributions, there also have been important critiques of the two trajectory models that should not be ignored.

The most frequently challenged component in the taxonomic theories is whether the life-course-persistent trajectory truly exists. To date, there is not a single empirical research study showing the highly stable, flat, linear pattern of the life-course-persistent trajectory. Empirical studies tracing trajectories over an extended period have found that the shape of the high-rate life-course-persistent trajectory was not as linear as the taxonomic theories propose. For instance, Thornberry and Krohn (2001) chart out a bell-shaped, curvilinear trajectory among the high-rate, chronic, life-course-persistent offenders in their study. Bushway and his colleagues (2003) document much more complex patterns of behavioral changes than the taxonomic theories proposed. The high-rate, chronic, life-course-persistent trajectory identified in their study showed a cubic pattern of change in antisocial behaviors over time. At age thirteen, the chronic juvenile offenders in their study started relatively low on the level of antisocial behaviors. The rate of chronic juvenile offenders started to increase afterwards and peaked at age fifteen but declined from late adolescence through early adulthood. Their offense rate at age twenty was approximately five times lower than their peak rate. However, between ages twenty and twenty-three (their last assessment) the crime rate rose again and this age group remained higher than others did.

As illustrated in the two examples of empirical studies, changes in drug use behaviors among youth at heightened risk are not static. Rather, accompanying the developmental changes are noticeable fluctuations that taxonomic theories cannot explain. Some researchers question labeling nonlinear patterns of change as "life-course-persistent" because the nonlinear patterns were consistently identified only among youth at the greatest risk.

Another heavily debated topic is that antisocial individuals do not easily fall into two groups as the theories have proposed. There is growing speculation that a third, and perhaps a fourth, trajectory might co-exist in the population along with the two trajectories of change in antisociality.

Additional research is necessary to uncover the more complex patterns of change, continuity, and discontinuity in antisocial behavior than the previous dichotomized patterns. In the next section, I theorize a third trajectory of drug use that might reconcile the ongoing debate of two life-course truisms about antisociality: that adult drug use is almost always preceded by childhood and adolescent drug use, yet most antisocial youth end up as law-abiding adults (Thornberry & Krohn, 2001).

THEORIZING A THIRD TRAJECTORY OF DRUG USE

My departure for theorizing a third trajectory is data-driven. I observed desistance from criminal behaviors among some early onset delinquents studied in a very limited number of studies (Bushway et al., 2003; Chung, Hill, Hawkins, Gilchrist, & Nagin, 2002). Gradual and steady decline over time in some early onset juvenile offenders' crime rate is not proposed by any existing taxonomic theories. They share a commonality with life-course-persistent individuals with regard to starting out their adolescent years as prototypical at-risk youth. On the other hand, they are similar to adolescent-limited individuals in terms of withdrawing from criminal activities *before* the adolescence period is over. Although the first sign of the existence of desistor trajectory was reported in the criminology literature, change in adolescent drug use behavior has not been studied in the framework of heterogeneous pathways. To my knowledge, this would be the first attempt to chart out the desistance pattern specifically for drug use. I present a summary of the findings from a national longitudinal study investigating diverse patterns of continuity and change in adolescent drug use. The study was designed to examine drug use trajectories from early adolescence through early adulthood.

Data for theorizing the third trajectory pattern of drug use comes from the National Longitudinal Study of Adolescent Health (Add Health Study), Waves I, II, and III (1994, 1995, and 2001, respectively). The Add Health Study is the most recent, comprehensive research project of adolescents in the U.S. (Bearman, Jones, & Udry, 1997). More than 20,000 students in the seventh through twelfth grades were included in the first wave (1994) of the Add Health Study ($N = 20,745$). For 90 percent of youth, a parent (77% mothers and 23% fathers) also participated in the in-home interview during the first year of the project. The second wave was carried out one year later, and included 14,738 of the original study members. In the third wave of the study, data from 15,197 of the original 20,745 adolescents (now young adults with a mean age of twenty-one) were collected in 2001. The current investigation focuses on 1,971 focal adolescents (841 boys and 1,130 girls) who endorsed the information on their drug use for all three waves of data collection.

Every high school in the United States (U.S.) was eligible for the random sample if it included an eleventh grade and had a minimum enrollment of thirty students. The random sample was then stratified into eighty clusters by region (Northeast, Midwest, South, West), urbanicity (urban, suburban, rural), school size (125 or fewer, 126–350, 351–775, 776 or more students), school type (public, private, parochial), and ethnicity. For the first wave of data collection, an in-home sample of 20,745 adolescents was drawn consisting of a core sample from each community. Adolescents participated in in-home interviews while parents completed a questionnaire about family and relationships with focal adolescents. The Wave II in-home interviews repeated this procedure. Portions of the in-home interviews were collected using Audio-CASI (audio computer-aided self-interview). Respondents listened to questions through earphones, and their responses were recorded on a laptop computer. Focal adolescents answered four questions (marijuana, cocaine, inhalants, and other illegal drugs) related to their drug use during the past month (i.e., how many times did you use each substance?). These items were repeatedly measured at three different points in time (1994, 1995, and 2001).

Using SAS TRAJ (Jones, Nagin, & Roeder, 2001), the drug use trajectories were examined. The semi-parametric mixture model, which I applied to examine the trajectories identifies a small number of latent classes of individuals with respect to similarity in patterns or careers of drug use over age. A solution for four trajectories was the best-fitting model to the data: *non-drug users* (N = 1,238) who had virtually no drug use experience, *moderate drug-users* (N = 491) who used drugs once or twice per year, *chronic drug-users* (N = 57) whose rate of drug use was fairly constant from age thirteen through age twenty-one, and *desistors* (N = 185) who consumed the highest amount of drugs in the beginning of adolescence but gradually decreased the amount of drug use over time. The desistors' rate of drug use changed dramatically from early adolescence to middle adolescence.

Revealing the desistance pattern of drug use among adolescents, a set of questions arose. What promoted the dramatic change in the amount of drug consumption among the desistors? What kinds of protective and resilient factors did the desistors have that the life-course-persistent drug users did not? To answer these questions, the analyses proceeded by examining the means for fourteen adolescent environmental, familial, individual, and peer predictors of each drug use trajectory. The fourteen adolescent antecedents for the initiation of and continuity in drug use were entered in a multinomial regression as the independent variables (table 7.1). The findings respond to a theoretical need with regard to recognizing a group of juvenile drug users on the relatively high end of the drug use propensity continuum who are not as psychopathological as the chronic drug users and do not become adult drug users (Cohen & Vila, 1996).

At least for the early adolescence period, continuity in drug use was explained by a lack of parental involvement in the lives of the adolescents,

Table 7.1. Odds Ratios Distinguishing Desistors, Chronic Drug Users, and Moderate Drug Users from Non-Drug Users

	Chronic Drug Users	Desistors	Moderate Drug Users
Gender (1 = Male; 2 = female)	.84**	1.05*	1.01
Environmental Context			
Family economic hardship	.97	1.01	1.00
Neighborhood violence	1.66**	1.03	1.22**
Family Context			
Parent's substance use	1.29**	1.07	1.00
Parent's marital quality	.95	.86**	.99
Involved parent-adolescent conflict	.99	1.42**	1.12*
Parenting practices	.74**	.82**	.92*
Individual Characteristics			
Conduct problems	1.89**	1.96*	.98
Emotional problems	1.58**	.99	1.02
Motivations to engage in risky behaviors	1.41**	1.33**	1.11*
Self-efficacy	1.53**	1.06	.82
Educational aspirations	1.44**	1.01	1.02
Peer Context			
Deviant peers	1.02	1.00	.98
Other adults support	.93	.80**	.99

Note: Reference group: Non-drug users; *p< .05, ** p< .01.

conduct problems, and elevated motivations to engage in risky behaviors. Further continuity in drug use was warranted by experiencing more neighborhood violence and substance use by parents. However, change in drug use from the middle through late adolescence periods was revealed by the desistor group in which parent-adolescent conflicts and marital conflicts were more acute during the transition from childhood to adolescence than those in the chronic drug user group. Because all the correlates examined in the study were measured during seventh grade, the results imply that the desistor's transition from elementary school to middle school might not have been as smooth as the other youths in the sample (Coie & Jacobs, 1993). Negative family conditions may have strongly influenced the adolescents who entered middle school with insecure feelings about themselves. Desistors also reported a much higher level of emotional distress than the chronic users, which could be interpreted as a direct result of having frequent conflicts with parents and witnessing marital discords in the family.

Nonetheless, the developmental change in drug use occurred as a function of having at least one adult figure who could provide support and advice. These findings imply that if the transition from childhood to adolescence, known as a period of "storm and stress," were not smoothly progressed for some youth, they might be placed at heightened risk for drug experimentation. However, the presence of a conventional adult figure that could help them navigate the challenging period of the transition protects them from becoming chronic drug users.

Equally intriguing is the higher level of self-efficacy and educational aspirations that distinguished the chronic users from the desistors. At a glance, this particular finding appears to contradict the concept that drug use is most prevalent among anxious and insecure youth looking for an escape from poor conditions or a way to feel better about themselves. However, recent studies revealed that young people with high self-esteem and confidence were more likely to take illicit drugs than those whose self-confidence is low (e.g., Gorman & Derzon, 2002). These characteristics are not a problem and, in fact, can be powerfully used in treatment and prevention services. Future prevention and treatment services must focus on helping adolescents channel their energies in a positive direction along with redirecting self-efficacy and aspirations to succeed academically.

Due to limited information on neuropsychological, biological, cognitive, and personality factors available in the dataset utilized, the extraction of desistors in my examples does not describe the full spectrum of desistors' profiles. What needs to be underscored is that two life-course truisms held by the taxonomic theories need to be revisited by acknowledging the existence of a third trajectory. In my theorizing driven by data, the third trajectory constitutes the following characteristics.

Desistors' behavior change in drug use occurs gradually and steadily. The gradual pattern of desistance is substantively different from a keen change occurring during a very short period of time that typically is evoked by a life turning-point experience (Duncan, 2003). The most plausible antecedent for the desistance trajectory is a relatively rough transition from late childhood to adolescence among at-risk youth. What keeps them from being a chronic drug user, however, is the presence of at least one prosocial adult who can provide constructive advice and encouragement that the desistors might not directly receive from their parents or siblings. The more risk factors to which the desistors are exposed, the more difficult and perhaps longer it takes for any protective factor to act on the lives of early at-risk youth. The power of a protective factor buffering adverse impacts of multiple risk factors provides another compelling rationale for delivering prevention and intervention services that promote resilience among at-risk youth.

INTERPLAY BETWEEN ANTECEDENTS AND DRUG USE

The healthy debate about taxonomic theories has greatly advanced understanding of the heterogeneity of drug use trajectories. Far less advanced is our understanding of the specific role that the drug use behavior plays in shaping the course of any trajectory. Scholars criticize the taxonomic theories for the lack of theorizing around the interplay between risk and resilient factors and drug use over the life course. Each trajectory pattern comes with its own set of antecedents that are all considered time-fixed variables in the existing theories. However, in reality most antecedents rising from all spheres of adolescent functioning are dynamic entities. If emotionally distressed teenagers started using drugs as a way of coping, the antecedent of their drug use is emotional distress. If the drug use did not ease the emotional discomfort and rather exacerbated the emotional distress, the antecedent of the elevated emotional distress is drug use. The emotional distress is no longer a *time-fixed* antecedent for drug use.

It becomes a *time-varying* antecedent for, as well as an outcome of, drug use. In the following section, I propose a transactional model in which changes occur within the antecedents as a function of drug use, which leads to further change in drug use.

Traditionally, two competing theories guide the research on risk factors and adolescent antisocial behaviors, including substance use, social causation, and social selection. According to the social causation approach, adverse conditions in the developmental ecology increase the risk for drug use. Figure 7.1 summarizes the risk factors for drug use and temporal orders among the risk factors that have been revealed in the past several decades of research, all guided by the social causation theory. Drug use is perceived as a developmental outcome of preceded risk factors (i.e., antecedents) that exist in multiple layers of adolescent lives from family, school, peers, and neighborhood.

In contrast, the social selection theory suggests that behavioral problems reduce social competencies and, thus, increase the risk for crises in social relationships. For example, drug-using adolescents may be too mercurial to be reliable friends. The symptom would jeopardize friendship development with conventional peers and school achievement, which requires focus, energy, and the regulation of competing emotions. It is conceivable that the drug-using adolescents make friends with deviant peers not necessarily by their choice but by the only option left for them. Deviant peers are the well-established antecedent for drug use, which brings up the notion of social causation theory. I attempt to integrate the

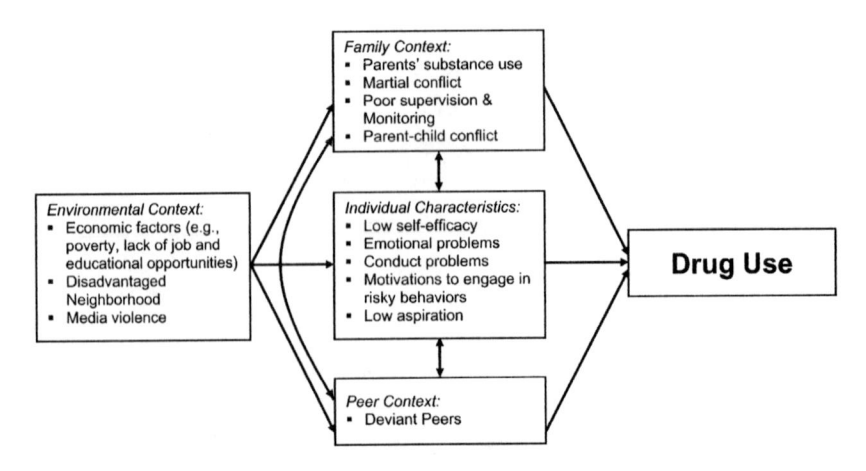

Figure 7.1. A Developmental Pathway to Adolescent Drug Use

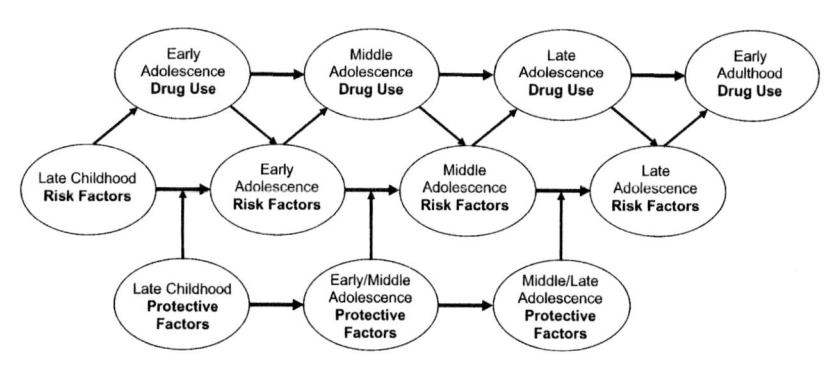

Figure 7.2. A Transactional Model of Risk, Resilience, and Drug Use

vicious self-perpetuating cycle happening in many lives of at-risk youth into a transactional model (see figure 7.2).

The transactional model derives from contemporary theory, which suggests that social stress at one point in time is predicted to increase later maladjustment, and maladjustment is expected to increase stress in a reciprocal process (Kim, 2005; Kim, Conger, Elder, & Lorenz, 2003). Thus, controlling for earlier levels of these variables, they should each explain significant change at later levels. What remains to be established, however, is how this proposed reciprocal influence between personal and social disadvantage and behavioral problems differs among desistors, adolescent-limited, and life-course-persistent drug users. Future studies testing the transactional model separately for each trajectory pattern will better inform scholars as to which, and when, resilient factors show salient influences on altering the expected relationship between risk factors and drug use. Additionally, this information will help with tailoring prevention and intervention services for individuals from different social disadvantages and strengths.

IMPLICATIONS FOR PREVENTION AND INTERVENTION SERVICES

Understanding drug use typologies and variations in drug use prognosis and psychosocial covariates by the membership is relevant not only to research but to public policies on prevention and treatment. The U.S. faces an epidemic of underage and illegal substance use. When substance use etiology, prevention, and intervention are considered, one obvious reason to study adolescents is that very rarely is substance use initiated prior to or after the second decade of life (Johnston et al., 2003). In addition, one of the most compelling reasons to focus on adolescents is that successful interventions are likely to have long-term benefits across the life span.

Traditionally, universal drug use prevention programs have two goals: to delay age of first use and to reduce the number of youth who would experiment with illicit drugs. However, this chapter clearly points out that the prevention and intervention needs of the multiple developmental trajectories are not the same. The findings provide prevention and intervention implications suggesting that the early onset deviant youths require different preventions or treatments depending on which developmental trajectory of drug use individuals follow. For both desistors and chronic drug users, inconsistent parents who do not monitor their children's activities contribute to high risk for drug use. Thus, efforts targeting parents' management practices and family norms regarding adolescent substance use are just as promising for preventing the early initiation of substance use. Parent training in improving how they monitor their children is particularly important.

In addition, short-term intervention strategies might not be optimal for curtailing drug use because it tends to persist over a long period for the majority of dependent users. Yet, some school intervention programs providing alternative activities such as recreational activities and service-related community projects tend to reduce susceptibility of substances. Other programs provide better opportunities for drug education, increase teachers' awareness of drug use, provide more drug counseling, and support law enforcement efforts to limit drugs on the school campus. Indeed, the most successful programs are contextual in nature; they include work to strengthen the relationships between families, schools, and communities.

In this chapter, I have raised awareness of one additional important parameter for consideration in constructing effective service programs. Preventions and interventions that demonstrate promise in promoting changes in drug use will not be universal or designed for the entire population of youth, but precisely tailored to the heterogeneous trajectories. The most effective interventions will attend to distinctively different underlying problems, skills deficiencies, and systemic problems or deficiencies across different trajectories.

NOTE

1. This chapter was developed using research findings from Add Health, a program project designed by J. Richard Udry, Peter S. Bearman, and Kathleen Mullan Harris, and funded by grant P01HD31921 from the National Institute of Child Health and Human Development, with cooperative funding from seventeen other agencies. Special acknowledgment is due Ronald R. Rindfuss and Barbara Entwisle for assistance in the original design. Persons interested in obtaining data files from Add Health should contact Add Health, Carolina Population Center, 123 W. Franklin Street, Chapel Hill, NC 27516-2524 (addhealth@unc.edu).

REFERENCES

Bearman, P. S., Jones, J., & Udry, J. R. (1997). The national longitudinal study of adolescent health: research design. Retrieved March 4, 2009, from http://www.cpc.unc.edu/projects/addhealth/design/wave1

Bushway, S. D., Thornberry, T. P., & Krohn, M. D. (2003). Desistance as a developmental process: A comparison of static and dynamic approaches. *Journal of Quantitative Criminology, 19*, 129–153.

Chung, I., Hill, K. G., Hawkins, J. D., Gilchrist, L. D., & Nagin, D. S. (2002). Childhood predictors of offense trajectories. *Journal of Research in Crime and Delinquency, 39*, 60–90.

Cohen, L. E., & Vila, B. J. (1996). Self-control and social-control: An exposition of the Gottfredson-Hirschi/Sampson-Laub debate. *Studies on Crime and Crime Prevention, 5* 125–150.

Coie, J. D., & Jacobs, M. R. (1993). The role of social context in the prevention of conduct disorder. *Development & Psychopathology, 5*, 263–275.

Dishion, T., McCord, J., & Poulin, F. (1999). When interventions harm: Peer groups and problem behavior. *American Psychologist, 54*, 755–764.

Duncan, G. (2003). Modeling the impacts of child care quality on children's preschool cognitive development. *Child Development, 74*, 1454–1475.

Elder, G. H., Jr. (1985). Perspectives on the life course. In G. H. Elder, Jr. (Ed.), *Life course dynamics* (pp. 23–49). Ithaca, NY: Cornell University Press.

Gorman, D. M., & Derzon, J. H. (2002). Behavioral traits and marijuana use and abuse: A meta-analysis of longitudinal studies. *Addictive Behaviors, 27*, 193–206.

Johnston, L. D., O'Malley, P. M., & Bachman, J. G. (2003). *The Monitoring the Future national survey results on adolescent drug use: Overview of key findings, 2002* (NIH Publication No. 03-5374). Bethesda, MD: National Institute on Drug Abuse.

Jones, B., Nagin, D. S., & Roeder, K. (2001). A SAS procedure based on mixture models for estimating developmental trajectories. *Sociological Methods & Research, 29*, 374–393.

Kim, K. J. (2005). Interconnected accumulation of life stresses and adolescent maladjustment. *The Prevention Researcher, 12,* 13–18.

Kim, K. J., Conger, R. D., Elder, G. H., Jr., & Lorenz, F. O. (2003). Reciprocal influences between stressful life events and adolescent internalizing and externalizing problems. *Child Development, 74,* 127–143.

Laub, J. H., & Sampson, R. J. (1993). Turning points in the life course: Why change matters to the study of crime. *Criminology, 31,* 301–325.

Moffitt, T. E. (1993). Adolescence-limited and life-course-persistent antisocial behaviors: A developmental taxonomy. *Psychological Review, 100,* 674–701.

Patterson, G. R., Reid, J. B., & Dishion, T. J. (1998). Antisocial boys. In J.M. Jenkins & K. Oatley (Eds.), *Human emotions: A reader* (pp. 330–336). Malden, MA: Blackwell.

Patterson, G. R., & Yoerger, K. (1993). Developmental models for delinquency behavior. In S. Hodgins, (Ed.), *Mental disorder and crime* (pp. 140–172). Newbury Park, CA: Sage.

Piquero, A. R., & Brezina, T. (2001). Testing Moffitt's account of adolescence-limited delinquency. *Criminology, 39,* 353–370.

Thornberry, T. P., & Krohn, M. D. (2001). The development of delinquency: An interactional perspective. In S. O. White (Ed.), *Handbook of youth and justice* (pp. 289–305). New York: Plenum.

Vuchinich, S., Bank, L., & Patterson, G. R. (1992). Parenting, peers, and the stability of antisocial behavior in preadolescent boys. *Developmental Psychology, 28,* 510–521.

Warr, M. (1998). Life-course transitions and desistance from crime. *Criminology, 36,* 183–216.

CHAPTER 8

Placing Developmental Paradigms in Context: Health and Adaptation in Late Life[1]

Karen A. Roberto

In the past two decades, research on health and illness in late life has burgeoned, generating valuable information about the issues and concerns surrounding particular conditions and the strategies used by older adults to manage chronic health problems such as arthritis, osteoporosis, diabetes, heart disease, and hypertension. This monolithic approach to the study of aging and health has generated valuable information about the issues and concerns surrounding particular conditions, and the strategies used by older adults to manage specific health problems in their daily lives. However, coping with multiple health conditions is common with advancing old age. Seventy percent of persons aged sixty-five and older have two or more co-occurring chronic diseases (Wolff, Starfield, & Anderson, 2002), and the prevalence of these conditions increases with age. Understanding the realities of the daily life of older adults with multiple health problems is paramount for advancing the study of health and aging in late life.

The literature focused on daily functioning when faced with multiple health conditions, albeit limited, suggests that older adults' concerns about their health transcend any particular condition (e.g., Penrod, Gueldner, & Poon, 2003; Schoenberg, Leach, & Edwards, 2009). In my research program on the lives of older women with chronic health conditions, we also found that older women had difficulty identifying the specific influence of one disease versus another; their problems and symptoms blended together (Roberto, Gigliotti, & Husser, 2005). The women did not view each condition as a separate force in their lives, but rather managed their health in totality by employing a variety of coping strategies. These findings challenge scholars to consider new paradigms for the study of chronic conditions in late life that looked beyond a single condition and focus on how managing multiple health concerns shape and transform the daily lives of older adults.

In this chapter, I discuss the development of a theoretical framework used in our research on the collective influence of health-related changes on daily functioning in late life. The underlying premise for this line of research was the need to move beyond the examination of illness states, and consider health and illness as processes that develop and have consequences over time. As such, older women's personal histories became an important source of *context* or unmeasured heterogeneity for understanding how experiences throughout their life course influenced their responses to health-related changes (e.g., limited mobility, diminished energy) and the adaptations they made in their daily life (George, 2003; Wadsworth, 1997). Recognizing that some level of aggregation is necessary to advance scientific inquiry, the challenge became *identifying* and *linking* antecedents of the older women's past life with their current life circumstances, personal agency (i.e., ability to act in one's own interest or in accordance with one's own desires), and health conditions in order to understand the processes (i.e., choices and adaptations) they use in their daily lives, and ultimately, the outcomes and consequences of the changes they make.

THE ADAPTATION TO CHRONIC ILLNESS PROJECT

In 2003, I began an investigation of functional, psychological, and social consequences of living with multiple health problems. The primary objective of this research was to identify management strategies used by older adults to maintain a satisfying quality of life. Initially, the Center for Survey Research at Virginia Tech conducted twenty-minute structured telephone interviews with 268 older adults residing in rural southwest Virginia that yielded descriptive information about the type and frequency of care strategies they used to manage their health problems. During the second phase of the study (2004), we conducted in-depth qualitative interviews with fifty-eight older women who reported managing multiple chronic conditions during the 2003 telephone survey (for sample details, see Roberto et al., 2005). We used both closed- and open-ended questions to gain in-depth information about the older women's daily experiences with chronic health conditions. Questions covered a range of health-related topics including: problems encountered, lifestyle changes, relations with family and friends, reliance on community supports and services, and specific strategies the women used to cope with and manage their health conditions. In 2006, we conducted qualitative interviews with thirty-six of the fifty-eight women to explore further the relationship between health-related changes and their perceptions of the quality of their daily lives. Thus, the extant literature and interviews with older women informed the theorizing and development of the theoretical framework presented in this chapter.

THEORETICAL FRAMEWORK

The complexity of health issues in later life requires guidance from multiple theories, operating at different levels of analysis. As independent frameworks, a life course perspective, the trajectory model of chronic illness management, and the life span model of selective optimization with compensation (SOC) have shaped much of my work on health and illness in late life. The assimilation of elements from these three approaches provides an expansive lens from which to consider the context of chronic illness and how health problems transform the daily lives of older women.

Life Course Perspective

Life course ideas focus on the changing contexts of lives and their consequences for human development. According to Dannefer and colleagues (Dannefer & Kelley-Moore, 2009; Dannefer & Uhlenberg, 1999) there is a distinct conceptual divide in the life course literature with research on aging and the life course focusing to a greater extent on personological influences than on sociological structures. Personological factors refer to individual characteristics (e.g., personality traits, personal choice) as well as contextual factors (e.g., biographical characteristics that stem from early life experience and contextual factors such as family life of origin) that have enduring significance over the life course. Sociological factors refer to social structures and interactions that shape life course processes (Dannefer & Uhlenberg, 1999). My own theorizing about aging, health, and life course forces incorporates elements from both these categories, taking into consideration the older women's unique personal biographies (i.e., values, beliefs, life experiences) and the social systems (e.g., family, work, community) that shaped their past, current, and future life experiences. From this perspective, aging reflects a lifetime accumulation of interacting individual and social processes that shape older women's beliefs about health and their responses to illness-related challenges and constraints.

One of the basic principles of a life course perspective is that people experience a sequence of transitions (i.e., a change in state or stage) and periods of stability throughout their lives that form distinctive trajectories in various life domains (Elder, 1998). Characteristics of trajectories include timing or age of occurrence (e.g., birth of first child), duration in a specific state (e.g., being married), sequencing or the transition to next stage of life (e.g., old age), and density or transitions in multiple life domains occurring at approximately the same time (George, 2003). In the health domain, trajectories may be punctuated by occasional transitions, but more typically include periods of relative stability and gradual change. Discussions of health trajectories usually focus on outcomes, raising questions about the illness experiences individuals bring to late life. However, it is also possible to construct trajectories of long-term social risk factors (e.g., social class) or protective factors (e.g., religious involvement) and to use such trajectories to predict responses to health-related changes.

Life course investigators also acknowledge the importance of social bonds in the trajectories of individuals. Older adults actively engage in health behaviors and social relationships that support their ways of thinking and their abilities to manage their daily lives. Specifically, the life course perspective posits the principle of *linked lives*, which emphasizes relational interconnectedness of lives (Elder, 1998). Individual lives are embedded within relationships with family and other social network members and are influenced by them. A basic premise of my research is that relationships with family, friends, and others have a significant influence on older women as they make changes and adapt to health-related challenges in their daily life (Roberto, 2004; Roberto & Husser, 2007; Roberto & Reynolds, 2002). For example, family members react and respond to the initial diagnosis of a health problem, provide short- and long-term assistance and care when necessary, and frequently interact with the health care system and may assume some responsibility for compliance with the women's health care regime (e.g., managing medication). Family members also exert normative beliefs or expectations about age-appropriate behaviors, which may have either an enabling or inhibiting effect on older women's abilities to manage their health problems. Thus, the ways in which the women restructure their lives as a result of changes in their health are often contingent upon, and some times in conflict with, the behaviors and beliefs of family members, close friends, and others in their social world. Thus, employing a life course perspective within my model helps bring attention to how individual lives are historically and socially organized and guides understanding of the way individuals think, feel, and act in late life.

Trajectory Model of Chronic Disease Management

Corbin and Strauss's (1988) trajectory model incorporates many elements of the life course perspective to provide a multidimensional framework for the study of the unfolding of a chronic illness (Robinson et al., 1993). It focuses on the active role that people play in shaping the course of their illness within the context of their everyday living situation. In this model, the term *trajectory* denotes not only the potential physiological development of an illness but also the work involved in its management and the changes in people's lives that in turn affect how they manage their illnesses. In our research, we find that the trajectory of an illness gives rise to two types of changes—change in health status that the older women have little or no control over (the illness itself) and change in daily routines either initiated by or imposed upon the women (or others) in response to their health conditions (Roberto et al., 2005).

One property of trajectories is *phases*, which correspond to the physical and psychological status of the illness (Corbin & Strauss, 1988). Four phases most relevant to my work on older women's chronic health conditions include comeback, stable, unstable, and downward phases. The *comeback* phase includes the physical and emotional recovery that takes place following an acute episode of a chronic illness such as after a fracture occurs. When in a *stable* phase there is little change in the course of the illness. In an *unstable* phase, the illness is persistently out of control as when experiencing the unpredictability of pain. A *downward* phase exists when the course of the illness is descending slowly or rapidly. Individuals do not necessarily move through the phases in a linear fashion and they often respond to their illnesses is on different levels. For example, older women often physically come back from an osteoporotic fracture but continue to struggle emotionally with the aftermath of the disease (e.g., fear of future fracture) that contributes to the changes they make in their daily lives. These changes may promote positive outcomes, such as removing clutter in the home to reduce the chances of falling in the future. Conversely, women with a fear of falling may avoid social outings, which could result in social isolation or loneliness.

Living with and managing chronic illnesses requires a considerable amount of *work*, including managing the tasks of everyday life and making social and psychological accommodations in order to compensate for illness-related change. In other words, older women institute changes in their lives to be able to manage the disruptions to daily routines and activities relative to their health conditions. The actions and experiences of older women working through these tasks can best be understood by identifying the key problems imposed upon them by their health conditions and the basic strategies used to manage these problems (Strauss, 1984). *Key problems* such as controlling symptoms and carrying out prescribed regimes may vary from woman to woman but they are to some degree persistent and relatively permanent. To manage the key problems, older women must develop and implement *basic strategies* to manage the changes in daily life brought about by changes in their health. These strategies often depend on assistance from their social network, thus requiring coordination *agents* (e.g., family members, friends, formal services, and organizations). The *consequences* or effectiveness of the strategies and arrangements depend on how well the older women and agents organize their efforts to handle the key problems. This theoretical approach contributes to my model of health and illness by focusing on the levels and types of changes that continually take place as older women make health-related adjustments in their daily lives.

Selective Optimization with Compensation Model

The selective optimization with compensation model (SOC) emerged from the life-span perspective put forth by Baltes (1987), which provides a framework for the study of constancy and change in individual beliefs and behaviors. The life-span perspective posits individual development as a *lifelong adaptive process* that is multidimensional and multidirectional; an ongoing, changing, and interacting system of gains and losses influenced by changes in life demands. This life-span framework also recognizes intra-individual variability or *plasticity* within development, which suggests that individuals have the capacity for differential behavior in response to different situations (i.e., contexts). Although plasticity denotes change, there are both explicit and latent limits on individuals' capacity for adapting to change.

Extending these principles to the study of successful aging, the meta-model of SOC (Baltes & Baltes, 1990; Marsiske, Lang, Baltes, & Baltes, 1995) describes fundamental developmental processes that underlie successful adaptation to shifts in balance between growth and decline. It builds on the assumption that throughout life, individuals encounter certain opportunity structures (e.g., education, employment, social networks) that contribute to personal resources and abilities. When confronted with declining resources (e.g., changes in health), older individuals engage in a process of selection in which existing goals are reevaluated and those that are most important and realistic are maintained. Adaptation occurs because of three interacting components: selection, optimization, and compensation.

Selection is the act of persons choosing, consciously or unconsciously, to work toward new goals or maintain what is important in their lives. Selection of goals occurs across several domains (e.g., physical, cognitive, social) and is guided by three general sets of influences: culture and individual pressures (i.e., general norms and tasks of development), social inequity and social differentiation (e.g., gender, social class), and inter-individual differences or non-normative influences (Marsiske et al., 1995). Although theoretically and conceptually meaningful, there is little empirical evidence documenting how these influences play out in the selection process. However, research suggests that there are changes in goal-orientation over the course of one's life. In late life, individuals tend to shift their goals from promoting growth and gains toward maintaining the status quo and preventing loss (Ebner, Freund, & Baltes, 2006; Freund, 2006). Recognizing this shift in priorities is particularly relevant when studying health-related adaptations, which typically require older women to make loss-based adjustment in their daily lives.

Optimization involves individual efforts aimed at maintaining, enhancing, or acquiring skills and abilities that prevent future loss or enrich resources and reserves. Optimization encompasses specific processes or mechanisms for achieving goals within a selected domain of functioning (e.g., self-care) as well as at a broader, domain-general level processes (e.g., cognitive skills) that are fundamental to a variety of other domains (e.g., intellectual functioning, social functioning). Increased adaptive fitness is the expected outcome of optimization (Marsiske et al., 1995).

Compensation refers to engaging in behaviors to counteract loss in abilities. In an effort to maintain a given level of functioning, individuals use compensatory processes that change or alter their behaviors to increase the likelihood of goal attainment. For example, to reduce the likelihood of falling, and the amount of energy needed, an individual may consolidate laundry facilities on the main floor of the house. Compensatory efforts operate through modifications at the individual and social levels, but as the example suggests, older adults also may make modifications to their physical environment (Baltes, Neumann, & Zank, 1994).

Research guided by the SOC model primarily addresses either motivational-volitional processes (e.g., active life management; intentional self-development) or sensorimotor-cognitive functioning (Riediger, Li, & Lindenberger, 2006). Although researchers acknowledge the significance of social context as individuals make changes in their daily lives or routines, both lines of research emphasize the importance of individual goal selection and personal resources for engaging in the SOC process. Our approach for understanding the women's daily selections, their strategies for optimizing their skills and abilities, and the ways in which they compensated for health-related changes is to situate the SOC model within the broader context of their life course.

A Contextualized SOC Model

Integrating constructs from the life course perspective and the trajectory model of chronic illness with the SOC model furthers the theoretical unfolding of the ways in which older women adapt to changes in their abilities brought about because of their health conditions. Contextualizing the SOC model (figure 8.1) required consideration of three emergent and interacting layers influenced by broader life-course elements (e.g., social location). The outermost layer represents the women's *personal biography*, which recognizes what the women have come to *value* in their life. The middle layer describes *resources* accumulated and *obstacles* faced throughout their lives, and the innermost layer, where we place the *SOC* elements, represents their current situation, functional abilities, and the adaptations they are making in response to changes in their health. Dot-

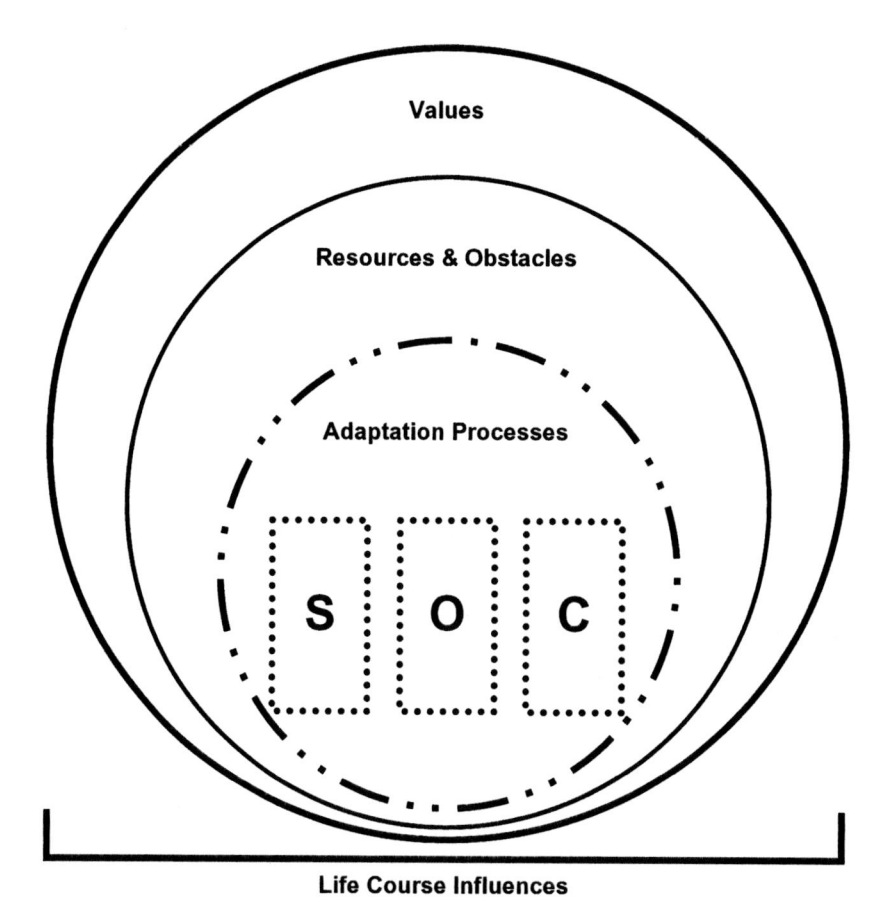

Figure 8.1. Contextualized SOC Model (Roberto & Husser, 2007)

ted lines around the SOC boxes symbolize the potential for the women to make changes to their adaptation strategies, while the perforated line between the inner and middle layers of the figure illustrates the process of negotiation that occurs between the women's adaptation strategies and their resources and obstacles. Lastly, SOC boxes are influenced by the outer layer (i.e., values) as the women's personal biographies affect the selection process. Embedding the individualized SOC processes in the center of the women's lives specifically acknowledges the importance of personal and external factors in our model, including individual (e.g., values, personality characteristics) and circumstantial elements (e.g., access to resources) that affect the processes by which they make daily health-related adaptations. Thus, by situating the SOC processes in the broader context of the women's life course and illness trajectory, we expand the utility and comprehension of the SOC processes as a framework for examining adaptation to health-related changes in daily life.

Figure 8.2 further explains and elaborates on the original elements of this framework and includes an additional component for consideration—the consequences or outcomes of the adaptation process. The first set of factors, which combines the outer and middle layer of the first figure (values, resources, and obstacles), are the antecedents of adaptation processes. First, from the representations of the women's cumulative histories or personal biographies, are values that underlie and influence their life trajectories. Based on the research literature and our own data analyses, we conceptualized four important intrinsic personal beliefs or values evident throughout the women's lives. *Engagement* describes a desire to be socially connected to important people, be it family, friends, or individuals representing larger community entities such as the church or civic organizations. Although the relevance of these social relationships may wax and wane over time, relationship stories are integral to how older women make meaning of their lives. *Independence* refers to the importance women place on being able to do things for themselves. They want to maintain their autonomy, to live life on their own, without having to rely or be dependent on others. Explanations for desired independence vary; for some women it is an issue of self-concept and self-esteem, while for others it is a respect for other people's time. *Continuity* refers to the maintenance of a sense of identity that is

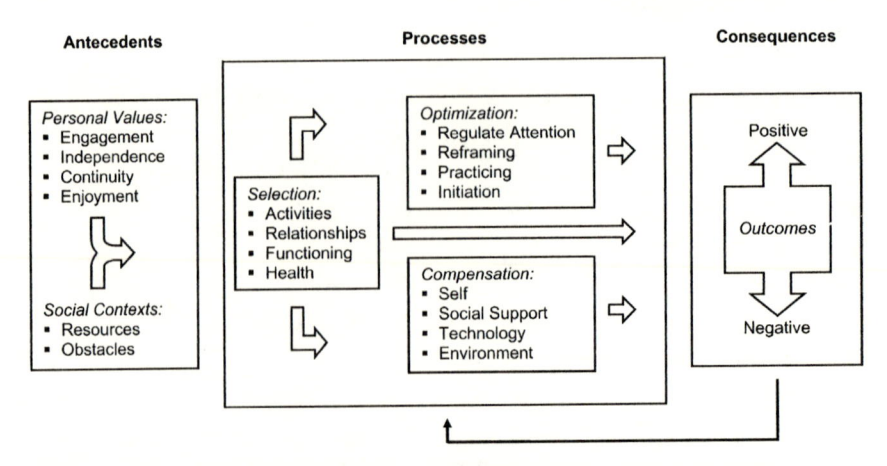

Figure 8.2. Antecedents, Processes, and Consequences of Health Changes in Late Life

congruent with the women's perceptions of their past self, activities, and traditions. Continuity oftentimes is expressed as a characteristic or personality trait, but it is also evident in coping and behavior patterns as well as descriptions of lifelong activities influenced by family or community culture. *Enjoyment* describes an overall sense of joy or gratitude for life. Both explicit and implicit throughout their interviews, the women spoke about loving life and being happy with and grateful for their experiences.

This first set of factors also includes social contexts, which are an accumulation of individual and social influences evident in the women's lives, identified in our model as *resources* and *obstacles*. *Resources* include tangible and non-tangible elements that facilitate adaptation and coping, for example mobility, education, finances, faith, positive attitudes toward life, family, friends, and neighbors. *Obstacles* represent barriers or challenges that impede adaptation processes, such as specific health-related limitations (e.g., pain, intolerance to medication), stressful life events (e.g., death of a family member or loved one; loss of a valued skill or possession), cultural views and expectations (e.g., beliefs about aging, gender roles), and relationships (e.g., overbearing adult children). From the older women's interviews, and the inferences we made from their descriptions of their lives and relationships, we conceive resources and obstacles as depending on the complex interaction of individual, temporal, and societal influences that shaped and reshaped their life experiences. For example, interviews with two women with diabetes with the same monthly income revealed that one believed she could not afford to buy special food (finances = obstacles) whereas the other was pleased such food items were available for her purchase (finances = resources). Furthermore, we observed that for some women, a resource could simultaneously act as an obstacle that enhanced or impeded optimal adaptation and well-being, as in situations where women described with pride the assistance they received from their children, yet concomitantly expressed some frustration. One woman noted how grateful she was that her adult son helped create a safer environment in her home (e.g., installed railings in and outside the house to help prevent falling), but harbored resentment because instrumental support was the only kind of support she received from him. She yearned for a social visit from her son that was motivated by desire to spend time with her, not because of a task or emergency. While her son's handy work supported her physical well-being, her emotional well-being suffered from their apparent lack of closeness.

Together, this first set of factors influences when older women will engage in SOC processes. Taken from the innermost layer of figure 8.1, the individual components of SOC shape (middle box in figure 8.2) the women's daily functioning. We identified four goals, representing physical, psychological, and social domains of daily life that the women commonly *selected* as being important in this phase of their lives. Selections resulted from a combination of loss-based and elective changes. The women described participating in *meaningful activities* associated with pleasure, a sense of identity, creativity, or social connections, sustaining *meaningful relationships* with significant members in their social network that provided a sense of connection, instrumental support, or opportunities for positive interactions, maintaining *daily functioning* and behaviors that promoted and supported independence, and sustaining or improving *health* by partaking in behaviors beneficial to their physical and mental health.

Selections were guided by personal values sustained throughout the women's life course and are influenced by individual and social resources and obstacles that required them to negotiate between what they valued and their immediate goals. These interacting layers influenced not only selection, but also optimization and compensation. *Optimization* strategies used by the women involved regulating the amount of attention given to health problems, reframing beliefs and behaviors about what is important or how to carry out a specific task, practicing skills and abilities in order to retain or enhance functioning, and intentionally initiating interactions to actively pursue and engage in the selection. Their *compensation* strategies included altering behavior (self), seeking out and relying on others (social support), using technology and assistive devices, and changing the environment.

Finally, an alluded to, but a virtually unstudied component of our theoretical model is an indication of whether the selected goals and use of optimization and compensation strategies result in the desired *outcome*—optimal aging via the regulation of health-related loss. Findings throughout the health and aging literature suggest numerous antecedent and process variables, including those proposed in our framework, which may contribute to as well as hinder positive outcomes for older adults (Aldwin, Park, & Spiro, 2007). Although our qualitative data suggests that women who achieve their goals have a more positive outlook about themselves and their lives in general, we have yet to examine directly this aspect of the model.

HEALTH ADAPTATIONS IN CONTEXT: A CASE ILLUSTRATION

To illustrate our theorizing about older women's responses to chronic illness and diminishing abilities, I draw upon the narrative of seventy-nine-year-old Rhonda, who reported having congestive heart disease, osteoporosis, arthritis, asthma, and pernicious anemia. She was one of the fifty-eight women who participated in qualitative interviews in 2004; she was also interviewed in 2006 as the health and adaption study continued.

Values

Throughout her life, Rhonda valued engagement, independence, and found enjoyment in her life. She has two children and two stepchildren and said that they were "always a close family." She took pleasure in raising her children and taking care of her husband. She maintained numerous close friendships throughout her life. For eleven years, she worked for the town treasurer. She loved to "see all the people when they came in to pay their bills and talking to them and helping them in any way I could." Now, in her later years, she remarked that she "loves going to the seniors program" where she can "visit with everybody," and play Rook (card game). Rhonda also spends time every day calling at least two other older adults she knows who are homebound and talking on the telephone or sending e-mail to friends and relatives. Being independent also was clearly important to Rhonda as she told the interviewer repeatedly that she would do anything to remain on her own, living in her own home for as long as possible. "That matters to me to be able to stay at home and live by myself and look at the river." In addition, Rhonda was extremely positive; she described her life during both interviews as one full of joy. "I don't cry or feel sorry for myself or wish I was no longer living. I have never done that. I love living, I love life." She compared her enjoyment of life to her father's, who she described as "jolly right up to the end."

Resources

Rhonda graduated from high school, lives in a rural community, and described herself as "easy going." During the interview, she focused more on resources than obstacles throughout her life. She always enjoyed close and emotionally satisfying family and community relationships.

Currently, family members provided her instrumental and informational support. Her neighbors also were helpful. They brought her mail in from the roadside box to her front door, ran errands for her, and provided her with at least one hot meal per week. Rhonda reported always having a strong faith, an accepting disposition, and positive attitude toward life. She said she just "does not let things get her down." For example, she indicated that she has a high tolerance for pain and told the interviewer, "I just tough it out."

Obstacles

Rhonda is a widow and lives alone on a limited income. Her second husband died in 1996. Her primary obstacle is the pain she experiences throughout her body, which she attributes to arthritis and osteoporosis. It prohibited her from going to the senior center as often as she would like and driving long distances required for visits with family members. Rhonda also reported not sleeping well because of the pain. She is allergic to most medications. At the time of the first interview, she described herself as physically weak and needed to use a wheelchair to maneuver around her home; by 2006 she had regained some of her stamina and used a walker during the day and when she went out, but kept her wheelchair for getting around during the night.

Selections

In applying the SOC component of our theoretical framework, we take a selection rather than a deficit perspective. That is, selections are the starting point for understanding not only the older women's current goals, but how they achieve these goals. As Elder (1998) suggests, "the constructivist role of the individual in making a life course [is] coupled with recognition that all choices and initiatives are constrained, more or less" (p. 978). Although the personal and social antecedents converge (overlapping arrows in Table 2) and have a collective influence on the women's current goals, we contend that their personal biographies (i.e., what they have come to value in life) have a greater influence on their selections, whereas their resources and obstacles tend to more heavily influence their optimization and compensation strategies. It is important to note some selections may not require optimizing and compensating behaviors; thus selections can lead directly to outcomes. However, most often, one or the other kind of strategy (either optimization or compensation) is necessary to engage in the selected activities, behaviors, or relationships. Interviews with Rhonda revealed that she strived to satisfy three primary goals or selections in her daily life that required changing the way she was used to managing her life.

Meaningful Activities. Rhonda enjoyed playing Rook at the senior center. When her pain became intense and increased the amount of effort it took her to get to the center, she compensated by reducing her playing time to one day per week. When asked if it was the playing of Rook or socializing with others that motivated her attendance, she responded, "playing the Rook." She laughed as she explained that she started going to the center for the socializing, but "developed a bad habit of playing Rook." Rhonda also indentifies herself as a genealogist. When she had to forgo her writing due to pain, she replaced some of the time she spent writing with other independent activities such as watching television, listening to the radio, and reading. In 2006, Rhonda's pain had subsided enough so that she played Rook two days for about a half a day and returned to her genealogy and writing.

Meaningful relationships. Being able to stay in contact with her family members and friends was also important for Rhonda. Although she could no longer drive long distances to visit them, she compensated by initiating contact with her children and many of her grandchildren through telephone calls and e-mail. When her pain became worse, she found she could not spend as much time on the computer. Thus, her pain became an obstacle to communicating with her family and friends, as well as keeping up with her own writing. She compensated by limiting her time on the computer, using it not to write for her own pleasure, but to maintain her social connections, thus optimizing her relationships as opposed to her genealogy work. During her 2006 interview, Rhonda commented that her children visited her often and were always helping her. Although she did not like to take money from them, her appreciation and satisfaction was evident as she described how her son-in-law "hid" a ten-dollar bill in her coffee cup and under the bread for her to find after the family left.

Daily Functioning. As previously noted, Rhonda valued her independence and being able to manage her own home and household chores has allowed her remain independent. She described herself as very task-oriented. "I plan little things to do every day and by the end of the day, one way or another, I achieve them. I am pretty tough . . . if I set my mind to do something I will do it." Rhonda optimized her ability to do her housework by continuing to vacuum and mop the floors from her wheelchair, thus maintaining skills and abilities to prevent future loss. She also regulated the amount of attention she gave to household tasks, stating, "I am not a fastidious housekeeper like I used to be." For example, she explained that she no longer washed her dishes every day. "I don't have too many so I just rinse them off and put them in a pan and then one day I get up and do dishes." To compensate for her physical limitations, she reduced the size of her living space by moving her bedroom and computer room to the first floor of her home (i.e., no longer goes upstairs) and used a lightweight duster with pivot handle, which made it easier for her to clean from her wheelchair. When her pain limited her functioning, twice she hired someone to help clean. During both interviews, Rhonda discussed accepting assistance from her family and friends. When her children and grandchildren visit, they replenish her food pantry, clean the house, take her trash to the landfill, plant flowers, and so forth. Her neighbor gets her mail for her every day and puts wood for the stove in the box outside of her door when needed. Collectively, making compensations allowed her to maintain her independence and stay in the home she loves overlooking the river.

Outcomes

During both interviews, Rhonda rated her quality of life (poor, fair, good, or excellent), as good. In 2006, we asked her to talk about the quality of her life, particularly in relationship to changes in her health. Rhonda explained that she was not as frustrated by what she can no longer do as she once was. "I am contented, sort of. It doesn't bother me because I guess I know I can't and I think well, I'll do just what I can and be happy." Thus, it appeared that Rhonda's health-related changes allowed her to successfully maintain her independence, and remain engaged in activities and relationships that sustained, and perhaps enhanced, her quality of life.

Although we have not quantified this component of the model, I theorize that if the processes individuals such as Rhonda use to achieve their selections do not have positive results, they would need to reassess their selections or change the strategies they use to reach their desired outcomes. For example, Rhonda could decide that a desired goal was not achievable, and modify or drop it from her list of selections or she could change the strategies she uses to optimize her current abilities or compensate for the declines in her functional abilities related to her health conditions. Regardless of what type of change occurs, personal values and social contexts continually influence the choices made and processes employed.

FUTURE DIRECTIONS FOR RESEARCH AND INTERVENTION

In this chapter, I have outlined a model to study adaptation to health-related changes in late life. The framework places individual-level theorizing about adaptation to the accumulation of functional changes resulting from multiple chronic health conditions within the broader context of older women's life experiences, trajectories, and relationships. Placed within a life course perspective, the basic premise underlying the framework is that individuals are active agents in the construction of their lives. It recognizes intrinsic characteristics and the opportunities and challenges that shaped and continue to shape the essence of the older women and the importance they place on various aspects of their lives. They make choices within the opportunities and constraints related to their family background, stage in life course, structural arrangements, and historical conditions. From my work, primary antecedents are the value placed on relationships and independence as well as the individual (e.g., positive attitude) and social (e.g., informal and formal support) resources women have in their lives. Together, these antecedents influence the processes used to achieve important daily goals when older women are faced with the realities of declining health. In this model pivotal processes are *selecting*, which places priority on the most important activities in the women's lives, and *optimizing* and *compensating*, which involve changing their perception about what or how they could achieve a selection, and accepting assistance in order to achieve selected goals. These processes represent both cognitive and behavioral change. Ultimately, the framework takes into consideration the complex ways that personal and social characteristics generate distinctive pathways between health-related adaptations and positive or negative outcomes.

This integrative framework has several strengths that make it a particularly relevant model for the study of health and adaptation in late life. First, it is a dynamic model whose conceptual constructs link biological, psychological, and social variables. Second, as defined, the constructs take into consideration, rather than statistically account for, the nuances of life course influences. These processes characterize or underlie the vulnerability and resilience exhibited by older women as they adapted to health-related changes in their daily lives. Its constructs are flexible and lend themselves to individual expression that provides for a more holistic understanding of adaptation to multiple health problems in late life.

In concert with these theoretical inferences, the framework has important methodological implications for future investigations of health adaptation processes and outcomes in later life. First, because several of the contextual elements identified in our theoretical model are still at the conceptual stage, they present several measurement challenges. We need greater precision in how we operationally define and assess their relationship to health-related changes experienced by older adults. For example, how do we best classify the myriad of factors identified during the interviews with the women that could eventually constitute a standardized instrument to measure contextual variables? Second, the difficulty of fully integrating life course perspective into the study of adaptation to illness is the lack of data covering longer periods. As an interim step, our current research relies on retrospective accounts of the influences on the women's lives to understand the processes that characterized their individual pathways of vulnerability and resilience to health-related changes (George, 2003). To further understanding of the pathways by which individual and social factors affect health behaviors and adaptation strategies requires the use of longitudinal investigations. Third, although we relied on data derived from the perspective of the older women, their lives are linked with members of their social network. Expectations, and the changes and challenges in both the lives of older adults and those with whom they interact, merge to influence the dynamics of their relationships. Securing a deeper understanding of this interdependence and the multi-directional influences of social relationships in light of health-related adaptations requires that future researchers study relationships as cohesive units collecting data from dyads, triads, families, and so forth, conducting relationship level analyses, and interpreting the findings within the context of the relationships (Roberto & Husser, 2007). Fourth, because the study sample was comprised of only women, we cannot ignore the influence of this gendered lens on the development of our theoretical model. For example, all of the women in our sample selected meaningful relationships as one of their current goals, and in some cases, relationships were the only selection identified. The research literature suggests that the social relationships of men and women differ; thus, we do not know if the same selection patterns would hold true for older men. Future application of the model with more diverse samples that intentionally consider gender and other life course forces such as race, ethnicity, cohort membership, cultural scripts, and social systems will help further refine the model.

The framework also has practical relevance for health care professionals and service providers, thereby increasing its utility in the development of prevention strategies to better equip older women to cope with health-related changes and better interventions when older individuals experience health-related adversity. Awareness of older women's life histories and values, in conjunction with knowledge of their available resources and current challenges, can provide health care and other professionals important insights into the ways in which older women may most successfully manage their health problems. By recognizing these powerful influences, practitioners can tailor interventions to the individual. In addition, taking into consideration personal relevance and social forces not only helps bring focus to the older women's current goals (selections), but also to the process of letting go of what they can no longer do. The simultaneous recognition of gain and loss is an important aspect of adaptive agency—individual expression is allowed, common underlying influences and processes are identified, and a more holistic understanding of the consequences of changing health in late life results. Intervention strategies informed by this type of information may have a greater chance of success than those that suggest a one-size-fit all approach. Thus, a flexible and more inclusive framework will help prevent the implementation of intervention strategies that run counter to what is meaningful in the older women's lives or constitute a hardship.

As life expectancy continues to increase, understanding all aspects of health and illness will become even more central to the quality of life of America's elderly population. Although researchers may choose different entry points in the study of aging and health, understanding the complexities of individuals' lives calls for the use of multidimensional theoretical frameworks. The model put forth in this chapter aims to further understanding of how individual aging and the events, behaviors, and relationships of earlier life stages shape health-related adaptation strategies and the consequences of their use on maintaining or enhancing well-being in late life.

NOTES

1. This research was supported in part by the Cooperative State Research, Education, and Extension Service, U.S. Department of Agriculture, under Project No. VA-135688 of the Virginia Agricultural Experiment Station.

2. Acknowledgement and great appreciation is given to Erica Husser for her work on all phases of the adaption to chronic illness project and the development of the theoretical framework.

REFERENCES

Aldwin, C. M., Park, C. L., & Spiro, A. III. (Eds.) (2007). *Handbook of health psychology and aging.* New York: Guilford.

Baltes, P. B. (1987). Theoretical propositions of life-span developmental psychology: On the dynamics between growth and decline. *Developmental Psychology, 23,* 611–626.

Baltes, P. B., & Baltes, M. M. (1990). Psychological perspectives on successful aging: The model of selective optimization with compensation. In P. B. Baltes & M. M. Baltes (Eds.), *Successful aging: Perspectives from the behavioral sciences* (pp. 1–34). New York: Cambridge University Press.

Baltes, P. B., Neumann, E. M., & Zank, S. (1994). Maintenance and rehabilitation of independence in old age: An intervention program for staff. *Psychology and Aging, 9,* 179–188.

Corbin, J., & Strauss, A. (1988). *Unending work and care: Managing chronic illness at home.* San Francisco: Jossey-Bass.

Dannefer, D., & Kelley-Moore, J. A. (2009). Theorizing the life course: New twists in the paths. In V. Bengtson, D. Gans, N. M. Putney, & M. Silverstein (Eds.), *Handbook of theories of aging* (2nd ed., pp. 389–412). New York: Springer.

Dannefer, D., & Uhlenberg, P. (1999). Paths of the life course: A typology. In V. Bengtson & K. W. Schaie (Eds.), *Handbook of theories of aging* (pp. 306–326). New York: Springer.

Ebner, N., Freund, A., & Baltes, P. (2006). Developmental changes in personal goal orientation from young to late adulthood: From striving for gains to maintenance and prevention of losses. *Psychology and Aging, 21,* 66–68.

Elder, G. (1998). The life course and human development. In R. M. Lerner (Ed.), *Handbook of child psychology: Vol. 1. Theoretical models of human development* (5th ed., pp. 939–991). New York: Wiley.

Freund, A. M. (2006). Age-differential motivational consequences of optimization versus compensation in younger and older adults. *Psychology and Aging, 21,* 240–252.

George, L. K. (2003). What life-course perspectives offer the study of aging and health. In R. Settersten (Ed.), *Invitation to the life course: Toward new understandings of later life* (pp. 161–190). Amitville, NY: Baywood.

Marsiske, M., Lang, F. R., Baltes, P. B., & Baltes, M. M. (1995). Selective optimization with compensation: Life-span perspectives on successful human development. In R. A.

Dixon & L. Backman (Eds.), *Compensating for psychological deficits and declines: Managing losses and promoting gains* (pp. 35–79). Mahway, NJ: Erlbaum.

Penrod, J., Gueldner, S. H., & Poon, L. W. (2003). Managing multiple chronic health conditions in everyday life. In L. W. Poon, S. H. Gueldner, & B. M. Sprouse (Eds.), *Successful aging and adaptation with chronic disease* (pp. 181–208). New York: Springer.

Riediger, M., Li, S. C., & Lindenberger, U. (2006). Selection, optimization, and compensation as developmental mechanisms of adaptive resource allocation: Review and preview. In J. Birren & K.W. Schaie (Eds.), *Handbook of the psychology of aging* (6th ed., pp. 289–313). New York: Academic Press.

Roberto, K. A. (2004). Care practices and quality of life of rural old women with osteoporosis. *Journal of the American Medical Women's Association, 59*, 295–301.

Roberto, K. A., Gigliotti, C. M., & Husser, E. K. (2005). Rural older women's experiences with chronic health problems: Daily challenges and care practices. *Health Care for Women International, 26,* 672–692.

Roberto, K. A., & Husser, E. K. (2007). Social relationships: Resources and obstacles to older women's health adaptations and well-being. In T. J. Owens & J. J. Suitor (Eds.), *Advances in life course research, Volume 12: Interpersonal relations across the life course* (pp. 383–410). New York: Elsevier Science.

Roberto, K. A., & Reynolds, S. (2002). Older women's experiences with chronic pain: Daily challenges and self-care practices. *Journal of Women & Aging, 14*(3/4), 5–23.

Robinson, L. A., Bevil, C., Arcangelo, V., Reifsnyder, J., Rothman, N., & Smeltzer, S. (1993). Operationalizing the Corbin & Strauss Trajectory Model for elderly clients with chronic illness. *Scholarly Inquiry for Nursing Practice: An International Journal, 7,* 253–264.

Schoenberg, N. E., Leach, C., & Edwards, W. (2009). "It's a toss up between my hearing, my heart, and my hip:" Prioritizing and accommodating multiple morbidities by vulnerable older adults. *Journal of Healthcare for the Poor and Underserved, 20,* 134–151.

Strauss, A. (1984). *Chronic illness and the quality of life* (2nd ed.). St. Louis: The C.V. Mosby Company.

Wadsworth, M. E. J. (1997). Health inequalities in the life course perspective. *Social Science and Medicine, 44,* 859–869.

Wolff, J. L., Starfield, B., & Anderson G. (2002). Prevalence, expenditures, and complications of multiple chronic conditions in the elderly. *Archives of Internal Medicine, 162,* 2269–2276.

Part III

FAMILIES, RELATIONSHIPS, AND TRANSITIONS

CHAPTER 9

Dialectics and Transactional Models: Conceptualizing Antecedents, Processes, and Consequences of Change in Parent-Child Relationships[1]

Leon Kuczynski, Robyn Pitman, and Monique B. Mitchell

Contemporary research on parent-child relations reflects a curious gap between theory and practice. Assumptions about the process and consequences of socialization have radically changed since the unidirectional theories that dominated the field prior to the 1970s (Kuczynski, 2003). Dynamic concepts such as bidirectional causality, contextual specificity, and the active agency of children receive wide endorsement at the theoretical level. However such ideas are not implemented to a great extent in empirical research. Researchers more often than not acknowledge bidirectional causality in discussion sections of their reports but fail to actually implement bidirectionality in their research questions and designs. Indeed, textbooks, empirical studies, and popular opinion continue to favor views of parental influence as linear and deterministic (Collins, Maccoby, Steinberg, Hetherington, & Bornstein, 2000).

Implementing dynamic family models of socialization is difficult because many basic concepts such as agency, bidirectionality, and context in parent-child relationships have been implicit, under-conceptualized, or conceptualized in piecemeal fashion (Kuczynski, 2003). It is difficult to take seriously the importance of bidirectional influence between parents and children when it is also assumed that parents have more agency and power in relationships or that children are passive and powerless. Likewise, it is difficult to take seriously the importance of the parent-child relationship as a context for understanding parent-child dynamics when researchers study parents and children as if they are individuals who exist independently of each other. Moreover, conceptions of positive outcomes such as compliance (e.g., Kuczynski & Hildebrandt,

1997) and intergenerational transmission of values (e.g., Kuczynski, Marshall, & Schell, 1997) are fundamentally linear and deterministic. Researchers cannot fully explore qualitative change or novel dynamics emerging from interactions between the generations through research designs and measures built on assumptions of unidirectional influence and continuity. In order to implement a vigorous program of research on dynamic processes in parent-child socialization, therefore, we must renovate a whole system of underlying assumptions.

The purpose of this chapter is to explore how reformulating conceptions of context, antecedents, and change supports the study of dynamic parent-child socialization processes. To achieve this aim, we use ideas from longstanding dialectical and transactional models of human development. We discuss the overarching theoretical frameworks of social relational theory (Kuczynski & Parkin, 2007), dialectical causality, and transactional models as a context for our theorizing on dynamic processes in parent-child relationships. In combination, these theories highlight human agency, the embeddedness of agency in relational contexts, and a focus on qualitative change.

After exploring these core concepts, we present three sections that theorize a dialectical/transactional perspective on contexts, antecedents, and change, respectively. We argue that context is best understood as a process of meaning-making where situations and events are both constructed and acted upon by human agents. We use the metaphor of contradiction to explore the antecedents of change. Specifically, we expand on the idea of contradiction by highlighting the processes of ambivalence and ambiguity in creating opportunities for change. In the final section, we focus on the nature of qualitative change from a dialectical perspective. In contrast to behavioral and mechanistic models that emphasize linear causation and continuity, dialectics focus distinctively on qualitative change or the generation of novelty. Qualitative change represents the generation of new meanings, new ways of thinking and acting, or new life course trajectories. We will illustrate these concepts with excerpts from interviews we have collected using transactional frameworks. Our goal is to demonstrate the usefulness of conceptual tools provided by transactional and dialectical theory for guiding future research on dynamic processes in parent-child relationships and interactions.

THE THEORETICAL CONTEXT OF THEORIZING

The overarching framework of social relational theory (Kuczynski & Parkin, 2007) shaped our theorizing in this chapter. Social relational theory is an open-ended interdisciplinary framework for envisioning dynamic processes and outcomes in socialization and parent-child relationships. In this chapter, we focus on two key assumptions of this perspective: human agency and dialectics. Social relational theory assumes that both parents and children are equal agents with inherent capacities for initiating action, interpreting their environments, and resisting threats to autonomy. This perspective leads to an empirical interest in what individuals do, think, and experience as they engage in interactions with each other and events in their lives. It guides researchers to ask questions of parents and children in a parallel manner, paying equal attention to the child-to-parent and parent-to-child directions of influence. Therefore, the same basic understanding of agency should guide studies designed to explore the social strategies, goals, motives, and interpretive activities of both parents and children. Furthermore, the investigation of both parents and children should include similar agentic categories when considering their social strategies, goals, motives, and interpretive activities (Kuczynski, 2003). Other perspectives, such as symbolic interactionism, share social relational theory's focus on human agency. However, a second important assumption of social relational theory is a dialectical conception of bidirectional causality, inspiring transactional models of development and additional ideas concerning the interrelatedness of agency, context, and change.

Dialectics is a meta-theory about the inherent holistic and dynamic nature of all phenomena. This framework asserts that all phenomena and every process consist of an opposing system of forces that actively relate to produce continuous qualitative change. In essence, dialectics asserts that individuals and their social or physical environments only cause this qualitative change through interaction. Individuals and their environments are dynamically related aspects of a system that perpetually interact with one another. These interactions produce constant change, and each new outcome sets in motion the beginning of a new process of contradiction and further change.

According to a dialectical perspective, human development is clearly a more complicated business than understood from behavioral or information processing perspectives. These unidirectional approaches oversimplify the process of human development by relating antecedents directly to consequences. Because of this complex characterization of human development, comprehensively implementing the whole of dialectics in one study is a daunting task. Therefore, researchers use the term *transaction* to translate dialectical ideas into process models that are amenable to empirical research. Using various transactional models, researchers have expanded on the implications of dialectics in several areas that include describing environmental phenomena (Altman & Rogoff, 1987), investigating human development (Sameroff, 1975), exploring processes of individuals' engagement with potentially stressful environments (Lazarus & Folkman, 1984), and the dynamics in parent-child social interactions and relationships (Kuczynski & Parkin, 2007). These scholars may differ to the extent that they focus on dialectical principles of holism, contradiction, and qualitative change. However, they all emphasize the importance of individual interpretations of events, social interactions, and the mutual influence between individuals and their environments. Our own approach in this chapter is integrative in order to illustrate the potential applications of dialectical transactional models for theorizing context, antecedents, and change.

THEORIZING CONTEXT: TRANSACTIONS BETWEEN PERSON AND ENVIRONMENT

Dialectical and transactional theory leads researchers to examine context from the perspective of the human agent. In contrast to the common practice of considering only the influence of contexts on individuals, it also considers how agents influence their social and ecological contexts. Individuals are not only constrained by contexts, but also act to change contexts and make use of the opportunities contexts afford them. In other words, the assumption of human agency implies a constructivist view of context (Wapner & Demick, 2002). With respect to parent-child social interactions, this means that parents and children serve as environmental contexts for each other. They are not merely physical entities to each other, but mutually embody meanings and representations that evolve as they interpret and evaluate one another's behavior. As formulated in social relational theory, bi-directional influence comes about as parents and children interpret or construct meanings from each other's behaviors and the events in their lives. Parents and young or adult children constantly anticipate, resist, negotiate, and accommodate each other's perspectives during social interactions (Kuczynski & Parkin, 2007). In our theorizing to date, we consider two levels of context: 1) the parent-child relationship context and 2) the micro transactional context.

Parent-Child Relationship Contexts

For parents and children the most proximal overarching context is the parent-child relationship (Kuczynski, 2003). Parents and children are individuals as well as dyads connected by an involuntary, interdependent relationship that emerges and endures over time. Dialectically speaking, the relationship is a whole that is more than the sum of its parts. Moreover, the relationship context is itself a cognitive representation based on a history of accumulative interactions of each dyad member. Over time, this emergent relationship subsequently creates a context for the dyad's future interactions (Hinde, 1979). Numerous phenomena stemming from the relationship context affect the way parents and children interact in the present. These include (a) predictions based on their relationship history, (b) future-oriented socialization and relationship goals for a continued relationship, and (c) vulnerabilities stemming from the mutual needs of both parents and children (Lollis & Kuczynski, 1997). The parent-child relationship both constrains and enables the agency of parents and children, making them both receptive and vulnerable to each other's influence (Kuczynski, 2003). The major implication is that the parent-child relationship is an overarching context that influences how parents and children interpret and respond to each other during their transactions with each other.

Transactional Contexts

Transactions are conceptualized as the micro system of individuals' meaning-making as they engage with their environment. A transactional perspective can be contrasted with a social interactional perspective because the latter approach eschews cognitions and focuses on behavioral reactivity and shaping between isolated elements in a social interaction (Kuczynski & Parkin, 2007). Our view of transaction is an integration of several previous treatments of transaction. Sameroff's (1975) transactional model of human development emphasizes the importance of parents' and children's continually changing representations of each other over time, but does not break down the processes that may be involved in such transactions. An important direction offered by Lazarus and Folkman's (1984) model of stress and coping is the focus on cognitive appraisals that shape individuals' decision-making in response to stressful events. In this model, new relational meaning emerges because of each individual's cognitive evaluation process. Each person appraises the environment as benign, irrelevant, or stressful, basing their appraisal on personal commitments and beliefs. Only events evaluated as stressful stimulate qualitative changes in coping responses. Mitchell (2008) suggests that two primary cognitive processes, interpretation and evaluation, determine whether transactions between individuals and their contexts lead to qualitative change in their inner lives and interpersonal relationships. In dialectical terms, a key process involved in the antecedents of potential change is the perception of contradiction in the transaction.

THEORIZING THE ANTECEDENTS OF CHANGE: CONTRADICTION

Dialectical researchers use the metaphor of contradiction as a guide for conceptualizing the antecedents of change. Any system will have aspects that are shared or congruent as well as aspects that are contradictory and dissonant. For instance, parents and children, as agents, have separate and potentially conflicting needs, perspectives, and goals. However they are also continually embedded as agents within the unity and interdependence of their shared relationship. A dialectical analysis focuses on the contradictory aspects of systems because the tension that emerges from contradiction provides opportunities for change whereas harmony and consensus serve to maintain stability and continuity (Riegel, 1976). The dialectical tensions are potentially generative because they entail points of uncertainty. They provide opportunities for individuals to create new meanings that temporarily resolve the contradiction, sending them on new trajectories for action and understanding. In our transactional perspective, we suggest that contradictions must be both evaluated as perturbing or stressful, and acted upon rather than ignored in order to precipitate actual change.

Generally, dialectical researchers have emphasized direct forms of contradiction. For example, Kuczynski and Parkin (2009) explore the role of parent-child *conflict* and parents' and children's experiences of *violated expectations* regarding each other's behavior as potential instigators of change in parent-child interactions and their understandings of each other. However, our metaphor of contradiction also includes other events that elicit dialectical tension and potentially give rise to qualitative change. Two forms of contradiction that have been relatively unexplored in this respect are the states of *ambivalence* and *ambiguity*. Ambivalence and ambiguity are recurring phenomenon of daily experience that engender uncertainty and thus provide opportunities for individuals to create new interpretations that may launch them on new trajectories (Valsiner, 2006a).

Ambivalence

Ambivalence describes the complex psychological processes having to do with individuals' frequent experience of events, emotions, and meanings that simultaneously pull the individual in different directions through positive and negative emotions, evaluations, or opposing directions for action (Lüscher & Pillemer, 1998). The parental role involves diverse conflicting functions such as providing authority, care, and security, while at the same time seeking intimacy and long-term connection with children (Harach & Kuczynski, 2005). The process of everyday child rearing provides many occasions of ambivalence as parents are torn between allowing exploration and guarding against danger, seeking obedience and allowing autonomy, being engaged but not overinvolved, promoting interdependence but not at the cost of independence (Holden & Ritchie, 1988). To illustrate parental ambivalence we provide an example from our interview data where a mother expresses her concerns about how to interpret her twelve-year-old son's reports of being bullied at school and her uncertainty about how she can address this issue. Ambivalence is apparent in her description of frustration of feeling pulled between the different ways she could address her son's perceptions of being bullied, the "what ifs" of her choices to respond, and the effect her decision may have on her son.

> It's frustrating . . . because you are not always sure how much is his perception and how much he has let it fester and he has gone over it and over

it until the point where everyone else can do no wrong—Oh sorry, he can do no wrong and everyone else has just been picking on him and picking on him so you are then caught in the middle trying to decide whether it is something that has been blown out of proportion or something that you need to, you know, really focus in on and help him work through. And social interactions with classmates becomes huge, and you are not sure if it's someone who looked at him wrong and he is taking it to be a huge deal, or something that has been going on for weeks and turns into a bullying thing that you should actually take some response to—so it is very frustrating to know what your reaction should be.

Children also experience ambivalence in their relationships with parents. For example, in a recent study of Vietnamese youth undergoing acculturation in Canada (Boiger, Kuczynski, Le, & Osland, 2008) participants responded to questions regarding perceptions of their parents' attempts to pass on indigenous Vietnamese values in the context of competing modern cultural values. Although the example involves a particular cultural group, it illustrates the general process of children's active interpretation and evaluation of parental messages as they internalize them (Kuczynski, Marshall, & Schell, 1997).

The children evaluated their parents' values and childrearing strategies as positive, negative, and ambivalent. An example of a positive evaluation from a child was, "So as I get older and I look back, I appreciate everything that they've done for me, simply because it's out of love." An example of a negative evaluation from a child was, "They didn't care, um plain and simple like that. They were the parents and they knew what was best, and you had to adhere to that or else you weren't really their child and they would treat you as such."

Furthermore, positive and negative evaluations also demonstrated the effect that the parents had on children's perception of themselves. An example of a positive evaluation made by a child was, "I'm glad she's like that. Because, you know like I said, to motivate me right" while an example of a negative evaluation made by a child was, "It's very difficult to aim very high and never achieve what they want. I think it's very depressing sometimes, it plays a big negative role on your confidence." Children also made evaluations regarding a perceived similarity between themselves and their parents. An example of a positive evaluation made by a child was, "I guess they have the right to feel that way, I would feel that way towards my children too." An example of a negative evaluation made by a child was, "There are a lot of things that they've done which I know I would never do to my kids."

Much more often than giving a straightforward positive or negative evaluation, the children engaged in ambivalent evaluation. The ambivalent evaluations included scenarios in which children (a) partially disagreed with parents, critiquing parents' various ideas, (b) accepted parental ideas but not their child-rearing strategies, and (c) described experiences of conflicted love. In the first example, children qualified agreement with their parents by partially rejecting their parents' values. These statements took the following form: "I think, in some ways, they are right, but um, you know, obviously their way of thinking is too traditional, and it's too closed minded." In the second type of scenario, when children were critical of their parents, yet understood the reasons for their parents' beliefs, their ambivalent evaluations took the following shape: "So I disagree with a lot of the teachings, but I can understand the fact that they didn't grow up here and they're adjusting as much as I am." Some children accepted parental goals but not their parents' means of pursuing them. An example of this type of response is "Back when I was in high school though, the way that he, I mean he has the right motivation, but the way he used to help me is not the best way to help somebody." Other children felt strong compassion for their parents yet found it impossible to meet some of their expectations. An example of this sort of evaluation is "I'm being logical. But inside, deep down inside, I do feel that this is like the greatest sin in the world to be saying to your family, who the hell are you, why do I have to be there for you." This last type of ambivalent evaluation is probably the most representative of the common understanding of ambivalence in parent-child relations, where children feel torn between valuing their relationships with their parents and valuing new possibilities for autonomy.

Ambiguity

Lazarus and Folkman (1984) define ambiguity as a "lack of situational clarity." However, the lack of clarity, its implications for a person's well being, and the potential for qualitative change are not intrinsic properties of situations, but rather products of the individual's interpretive process (Mitchell, 2008). According to Mitchell, individuals experience ambiguity in transactions where they perceive minimal or conflicting cues in the environment. Their ambiguous feelings inhibit them from processing and evaluating the event's potential to impose upon their beliefs, commitments, and well being.

In socio-cultural perspectives, individuals faced with ambiguity continually employ meaning-making processes in order to cope with their dynamically changing contexts.

> Every next immediate moment in the life of an organism is ambiguous as a step between the already known and the still unknown. This state is the normal state of affairs during which an unexpected and unpredicted new phenomenon may emerge (Valsiner, 2006a, p.118).

As in the case of ambivalence, the phenomenon of ambiguity has received minimal attention despite its ubiquitous presence and importance in a theory of change. In our research, we were attentive to the presence of ambiguity in the spontaneous accounts of parents and children. The following example illustrates a mother's state of ambiguity with regard to her twelve-year-old son's inner thoughts and feelings.

> *Interviewer*: How much do you think you know about both his behavior away from home and also inner thoughts and feelings that he has?
>
> *Mother*: Inner thoughts and feelings probably only about 40 percent—he's one to be the emotional volcano so everything is fine and then you head up at night to sobs of all the horrible things that have happened and you can't really discuss it at that time of the night because we are tired and it's bedtime so he tends to really bottle things in and he is hard to read. . . . he will say "fine" if he isn't willing to discuss it so he is a tough one to crack. . . . and he's worked himself up to the world hates me kind of thing.

In the next example, a thirteen-year-old girl responded to questions about changes in her daily routines. Her responses focused on her relationship with her sister and revealed the lack of clarity she had regarding changes in the nature of their transactions.

> Like when we're here it's just like she'll walk through the door and be like "hey" or whatever and I'll be like "hello" and then that's about it. . . . that's all we do. . . . Like when we were little we used to have to kiss each other goodnight. Like we'd do everything together and then when she got older it was just really weird for me. Like it was kind of hard because we

used to play games in the morning so we'd have all our beanie babies and just play games but. . . . she stopped wanting to do it and I didn't really understand why. . . . Cause I'm a four-year-old and she's an eight-year-old and I'm like "c'mon play with me" and she's like "no I don't want to." So then we kind of started moving apart.

Ambiguity also plays an important role in major life transitions. In her study of children's experiences of the transition into foster care, Mitchell (2008) found an association between the intensity of children's stress appraisals and their ambiguous interpretations of events. Children with higher levels of stress often indicated a lack of clarity about what would happen to them once placed into care, what their home would be like, who would be caring for them, if their basic needs would be met, and if they would ever see their loved ones again.

By highlighting the processes of ambiguity and ambivalence as potential antecedents of change, we have illuminated new grounds for future research. There is disagreement, however, regarding how ambivalence and ambiguity relate to each other. Weigert (1991), for example, has suggested that the main distinction between these processes is that ambiguity is something an individual *knows* (cognition) while ambivalence is something an individual *feels* (emotion). Other researchers have adopted a more encompassing definition of these constructs (e.g., Lettke & Klein, 2004; Valsiner, 2006a) and have encouraged further exploration of their conceptualization and measurement. However, there is agreement that ambivalence and ambiguity are independent constructs, although they may sometimes co-occur or give rise to one another (Lettke & Klein, 2004). Future research warrants exploration of the implications of various naturally occurring combinations of ambiguity and ambivalence for qualitative change. It is also important to determine under what circumstances ambivalence and ambiguity instigate changes in individuals. Research to date has not progressed beyond identifying the presence of ambivalence and ambiguity in the parent-child relationship. Next, scholars must demonstrate the links between the meanings that individuals construct from these experiences and subsequent changes in their thoughts and actions. The choices that parents and children make when confronted with emotional and cognitive uncertainty within their transactions may determine the likelihood of change. When confronted with uncertainty individuals could choose to either ignore or manage their uncertainty, maintaining their prior state of understanding and, therefore, stability following a transaction. In this case, uncertainty would remain unresolved, at least temporarily. Choosing to confront ambivalence and ambiguity, on the other hand, opens the possibility for new meaning-making. New meanings may emerge from processes such as self-reflection and problem solving. These meanings can then instigate qualitative change, not only at the representational level, but also at the level of action.

THEORIZING CHANGE: NOVELTY

A defining feature of dialectics is its distinctive focus on qualitative change or the emergence of novelty. Dialectical causality implies a continuous process of change in a changing context. The language of dialectical research is replete with concepts such as transformation, working models, changed representations, bifurcations, phase shifts, and turning points. These concepts represent the dialectical metaphor of temporary *synthesis*, the idea that aspects of a system continually combine to create novel adaptive or maladaptive states of becoming. Sameroff's (1975) transactional model of development depicts parent and child engaged in continual transformation as each partner responds to the emerging characteristics of the other. "The child alters his [her] environment and in turn is altered by the changed world he [she] has created" (Sameroff, 1975, p. 281). In a dialectical view, outcomes are always in process. A conception of an outcome as "mission accomplished" or a story book ending such as "and they lived happily ever after" is incompatible with a dialectical perspective, which would anticipate continual change after a battle or the beginning of a marriage.

An important challenge for future research is to empirically translate theoretical ideas on qualitative change. Developmental and psychological literature recognizes many ideas regarding what qualitative change looks like (Kuczynski, Lollis, & Koguchi, 2003). The qualitative transformation that takes place, as individuals adapt to one another or respond to environmental events, can be either transitory or enduring. Classic concepts such as *accommodation* and *second order change* attempt to capture radical change in cognitive understanding and patterns of family interaction. Research on *automatic* and *effortful processing* suggests that qualitative changes from habitual scripted responding to more considered thoughtful responding with respect to the environment occurs when individuals encounter unexpected information. The idea of *co-construction* in the socio-cultural literature implies that novel meanings emerge as individuals interpret and re-communicate messages to each other during social interaction. As proposed earlier, ambiguous experiences can be conceptualized as choice points that may launch individuals on new trajectories. All of these ideas have been under-used in empirical research.

We must replace outdated unidirectional conceptions of potential outcomes to capture more realistically the complex qualitative change that occurs when antecedents transform into outcomes. For example, iconic deterministic conceptions such as *compliance* and *intergenerational transmission* imply an exact match between the wishes or values of parents and the resulting behavior of children. Kuczynski and Hildebrandt (1997) argue, though, that the concepts of *accommodation* and *negotiation* provide a better depiction of children's compliance with parental wishes. These concepts more fully reflect a synthesis of parent and child goals. Similarly, the child's indiscriminate internalization of parental values, as implied by intergenerational transmission, is inadequate. A child's process of internalizing parental values can be better captured by *working models* of values. These constructions convey the active, recurrent interpretations and evaluations of competing messages from parents and other sources of information within the child's environment (Kuczynski et al., 1997). The purpose of applying these more expansive concepts is to infuse ideas of agency and syntheses into deterministic conceptions of the socialization process.

A second challenge to researchers is the development of conceptual lenses to enable identification and description of the transactions associated with qualitative change. Transactions involving qualitative change in representation occur at micro and macro levels of analysis. Sameroff (2009) suggests that qualitative change is ubiquitous in everyday life, occurring whenever an individual is induced by events to think or act differently or change their representation of an event. For example, an unexpected answer ("I feel like crap.") to a conventional greeting ("How are you?") may instigate a moment of non-routine meaning-making and a more considered social interaction.

Parents and children frequently make decisions about how to respond to perturbing events or discoveries regarding each other's daily behaviors. These events may cause a qualitative change in the goals and strategies used during social interactions. A well-researched example concerns the situational specificity of parental use of unelaborated power assertion versus reasoning in responses to children's transgressions (Kuczynski, 1984). When mothers interpret a situation as requiring no more than immediate compliance, they use the strategy of mild power assertion such as unexplained commands, suggestions, and prohibitions. However, when mothers interpret the child's behavior as a transgression involving a safety issue or a moral offense, they qualitatively change their strategies. In these situations, they employ more nuanced responses to behaviors, including the strategic use of warmth, explanation, and reasoning. In an experimental demonstration, Kuczynski (1984) manipulated mothers' perceptions so that, rather than require immediate, observable compliance from their children, they pursued a more enduring compliance that would persist even in their absence. A changed representation of the same context produced differences in the parents' way of interacting, which subsequently induced long-term as opposed to immediate compliance in the children's behavior.

At a macro level, individuals can readily recall critical events in their lives that had important consequences for positive and negative trajectories in their lives and identity formation (Holland, this volume). Such events have the potential to play a role in life transitions, which are life altering qualitative shifts in an individual's inner life and interpersonal world (Cowan, 1991). Life course research has illustrated how change can occur because of normative or non-normative transitions that transpire at various developmental stages during the lifespan. Divorce, life-threatening illnesses, death, career changes, entry into college, marriage, and becoming a parent are just a few of the many events that elicit transitions and evoke qualitative change over time. Although such transitions may appear to occur gradually over time, it may be useful to consider transitions in terms of a series of discrete new syntheses that take place as individuals adapt to the new realities in their lives. Integrating the concepts of transitions (Cowan, 1991) and transactions (Lazarus & Folkman, 1984), Mitchell (2008) conceptualizes a transition as a series of transactions that build on successive qualitative shifts in an individual's inner life and interpersonal relationships. In her work on children's transitions into foster care, Mitchell demonstrated that children's experiences of their initial transition into foster care could be segmented into two separate transactions:

the apprehension transaction and the foster home placement transaction. Events such as notification of the need for placement into care, a child's transfer and placement into a foster home, and the loss and formation of relationships all entailed new and ambiguous experiences. The ambiguity of these transactions resulted from children's interpretations of minimal or conflicting cues in the environment and precipitated stressful appraisals and coping strategies to assist with emotional upheaval. Mitchell (2008) concludes that the transition into foster care resulted in a series of transactions that produced significant qualitative shifts in children's assumptive worlds and major relationships.

Divorce is another experience of a macro transition resulting from a series of micro transactions. Events such as learning about parents' decision for divorce, child relocation, parental relocation, and altered family routines, rules, and responsibilities each may throw the family system, and each person's representations, into a state of perturbation. Following these events, old ways of thinking and acting are no longer useful. Therefore, the period following such transactions is an opportune time for researchers to look for changed representations regarding the meaning of marriage, family relationships, self, and others.

Although it seems fruitful to segment life course transitions into a series of discrete transactions that enter the awareness of the individual, this is less easy to do when considering developmental change where parents gradually adjust their behavior to gradual changes in the child's behavior. In the case of developmental change another dialectical metaphor—quantitative change incrementally leading to a turning point that catalyzes qualitative change—may be useful. Incremental change leading to qualitative change may occur both at an individual level and at the level of dyadic parent-child relationships. Change in one's thinking or understanding of the context unfolds over time until retrospectively one can recognize that a significant qualitative shift has occurred.

We found many examples of such large retrospectively recognized changes in the acculturation study of Vietnamese youth (Boiger et al., 2008). In response to a question regarding how they may have changed after living in Canada, youth never reported fully adopting the ideas of their parents or the new culture in which they lived. Rather, their reports indicated that they had constructed a new model of values and cultural identity: a qualitative synthesis of the various influences to which they were exposed. One youth described his integration of parental and new cultural values as follows:

> My views are a little different than my parents. Okay, my parents like the way Vietnamese families' functions; they're really traditional, so they believe in the traditional beliefs and values, and I mean mutual, I think they are, I think it's something that at least Asian people should follow. Yeah, I don't think I would be as strict as my parents though, or as traditional, but I would still want to preserve some of the point that I think is important, not all of it.

Another youth described the forging of a new bi-cultural identity out of the diverse ideas communicated by his parents and the surrounding culture:

> Um, I think that um there's a lot of things in the Vietnamese culture that I think are better than the Canadian culture. And, that I would, and those, values, I would actually, you know, value and make it my own value, something to live by. I think that I've got a good mix of both, and that um, there's a lot of things about the Canadian culture that I like and I appreciate and that I go by. And um it's, there's pros and cons with both cultures and I just try to pick the best that are best for me from both cultures and I try to, you know, live by a set of mixed cultures.

In dyadic parent-child relationships, there are changes in the quality and expression of the relationship throughout childhood, adolescence, and adulthood. For instance, during early and middle childhood there are changes in both the frequency with which children choose to interact with parents and the expression of affection in the relationship. Such changes may be reflected in the parent's changed representations of the relationship. In the following example, a mother reflects on changes in experiences of intimacy and closeness with her twelve-year-old son.

> We used to always read before going to bed and that has kind of stopped but that used to be a really good way to kind of snuggle in and read and talk and move into other discussions but now that he is older and goes to bed and reads on his own for a while and says you know when the lights are out—that's kind of gone.

What is important to note from this example is the change in the mother's characterization of her son's bedtime routine. She is able to compare previous bedtime transactions with her son to her son's current routine, one that no longer includes her or the sharing of those every day moments together. It is unclear whether this retrospectively recognized change is the product of a series of qualitative shifts attributable to specific transactions or whether change occurred incrementally over time, for instance varying between intimacy and rejection of intimacy. However, the lost bedtime routine with her child is an example of qualitative change. The mother must now accept that she and her son's previous patterns of interaction, and her associated feelings of closeness, are no longer a part of their transactions.

Our final example comes from the perspective of a thirteen-year-old girl discussing her new status of self-sufficiency and responsibility.

> Yeah, my mom also said the other day, cause there's this store just down here and they have newspapers and stuff, so I was riding my bike over there and she was like "I'm starting to realize that I don't care where you go" like she knew I went there. I was just like "I'm going to go to the store to get a newspaper" but she's not like "oh make sure you do this and make sure you do this and call me when you get there" 'cause it's just like right down the street. But she's not watching me to make sure I'm okay out on the patio and stuff. She's just like "yeah." I'm just kind of amazed that I'm not. Just last year they decided, you know, if you want to go somewhere like downtown just call us and you can go. Just in the summer. So it's changed a lot, I've gotten lots more responsibility and they trust me way more than they did.

What is important to note is that change appears to have occurred for both the child and the parent. As both engaged in a conversation over an everyday occurrence (i.e., going to the store) both the child and the parent experienced a realization that the parent no longer needs to enforce as many boundaries or assert the same level of oversight over the child's activities. For the child, the point of change is her realization that a previous rule has changed and that she has more freedom and also responsibility for regulating her own behavior. For the parent, however, change appeared to have an incremental path to a turning point as she realized that she no longer cared about monitoring her child's whereabouts as closely as before.

THEORIZING: OUTCOME IN PROCESS

In a dialectical perspective, outcomes always are in process; so it must be with conclusions. Our theorizing in this chapter occurs within a holistic conception of the methodology cycle (Valsiner, 2006b). We regard methodology as the whole process of knowledge construction that involves not only the researcher's decision to test theory but also to use theory and construct theory with the goal of understanding phenomena. We are not alone in finding inspiration in dialectical and transactional models of development. Dialectical perspectives have long provided theoreticians with an alternative to mechanistic worldviews and their linear associations between antecedents and consequences. Moreover, dialectical perspectives encourage an improved understanding of the processes of change. A purpose of dialectically oriented research is to shed light on the complexity of individual functioning in real-life situations. A dialectical perspective, therefore, plays an important counterpart to the limiting unidirectional models that have dominated psychological research.

Our approach was to take the idea of dialectics seriously, mining for key ideas to help scholars conceptualize context, antecedents, and transformative change. We expanded on existing ideas regarding individuals' transactions with their environments and highlighted a variety of interpretive processes relatively neglected in research on change. These included interpretive processes related to both individuals' perceptions of context and their evaluations of the significance of events in their daily lives. In particular, we illustrated the potential importance of ambiguity and ambivalence. These concepts are part of the frontier of new conceptions regarding individuals' engagement with their environments. Lastly, we provided suggestions for using transaction to identify causes of qualitative shifts in the process of change. Consistent with the dialectical nature of theorizing, we are aware of the temporary nature of our syntheses and invite engagement with these ideas in anticipation of new syntheses to come.

NOTE

1. This chapter was supported by a grant to the first author from the Social Sciences and Humanities Research Council of Canada.

REFERENCES

Altman, L., & Rogoff, B. (1987). World views in psychology: Trait, interactional, organismic, and transactional perspectives. In D. Stokols & I. Altman (Eds.), *Handbook of environmental psychology* (Vol. 1, pp. 1–40). New York: Wiley.

Boiger, M., Kuczynski, L., Le, A., & Osland, I. (2008, November 6). Bicultural ambivalence: Family acculturation of Vietnamese youth in Canada. Paper presented at the On New Shores Conference, Guelph.

Collins, W. A., Maccoby, E. E., Steinberg, L., Hetherington, E. M., & Bornstein, M. H. (2000). Contemporary research on parenting: The case for nature and nurture. *American Psychologist, 55*, 218–232.

Cowan, P. A. (1991). Individual and family life transitions: A proposal for a new definition. In P. A. Cowan & M. Hetherington (Eds.), *Family transitions* (pp. 3–30). Hillsdale, NJ: Erlbaum.

Harach, L., & Kuczynski, L. (2005). Construction and maintenance of parent-child relationships: Bidirectional contributions from the perspective of parents. *Infant and Child Development, 14*, 327–343.

Hinde, R. A. (1979). *Toward understanding relationships.* London: Academic Press.

Holden, G. W., & Ritchie, K. L. (1988). Child rearing and the dialectics of parental intelligence. In J. Valsiner (Ed.), *Child development within culturally structured environments: Parental cognition and adult-child interaction* (pp. 30–59). Norwood, NJ: Ablex.

Kuczynski, L. (1984). Socialization goals and mother-child interaction: Strategies for long-term and short-term compliance. *Developmental Psychology, 20*, 1061–1073.

Kuczynski, L. (2003). Beyond bidirectionality: Bilateral conceptual frameworks for understanding dynamics in parent-child relations. In L. Kuczynski (Ed.), *Handbook of dynamics in parent-child relations* (pp. 1–24). Thousand Oaks, CA: Sage.

Kuczynski, L., & Hildebrandt, N. (1997). Models of conformity and resistance in socialization theory. In J. E. Grusec & L. Kuczynski (Eds.), *Parenting and the internalization of values: A handbook of contemporary theory* (pp. 227–256). Hoboken, NJ: Wiley.

Kuczynski, L., Lollis, S., & Koguchi, T. (2003). Reconstructing common sense: Metaphors of bidirectionality in parent-child relations. In L Kuczynski (Ed.), *Handbook of dynamics in parent-child relations* (pp. 421–438). Thousand Oaks CA: Sage.

Kuczynski, L., Marshall, S., & Schell, K. (1997). Value socialization in a bidirectional context. In J. E. Grusec & L. Kuczynski (Eds.), *Parenting and the internalization of values: A handbook of contemporary theory* (pp. 23–50). New York: Wiley.

Kuczynski, L., & Parkin, C. M. (2007). Agency and bidirectionality in socialization: Interactions, transactions, and relational dialectics. In J. E. Grusec & P. Hastings (Eds.), *Handbook of socialization: Theory and research* (pp. 259–283). New York: Guilford.

Kuczynski, L., & Parkin, M. (2009). Pursuing a dialectical perspective on transaction: A social relational theory of micro family processes. In A. Sameroff (Ed.), *Transactional processes in development* (pp. 247–268). Washington, DC: American Psychological Association.

Lazarus, R. S., & Folkman, S. (1984). *Stress, appraisal, and coping*. New York: Springer.

Lettke, F., & Klein, D. M. (2004). Methodological issues in assessing ambivalences in intergenerational relations. *Contemporary Perspectives in Family Research, 4*, 85–113.

Lollis, S., & Kuczynski, L. (1997). Beyond one hand clapping: Seeing bidirectionality in parent-child relations. *Journal of Social and Personal Relationships, 14*, 441–461.

Lüscher, K., & Pillemer, K. (1998). Intergenerational ambivalence: A new approach to the study of parent-child relations in later life. *Journal of Marriage and the Family, 60*, 413–425.

Mitchell, M. B. (2008). The transitioning into care project: Honouring children's lived experience of the foster care transition. Unpublished doctoral dissertation, The University of Guelph.

Reigel, K. F. (1976). The dialectics of human development. *American Psychologist, 10*, 689–700.

Sameroff, A. (1975). Transactional models of early social relations. *Human Development, 18*, 65–79.

Sameroff, A. (2009). The transactional model. In A. Sameroff (Ed.), *Transactional processes in development* (pp. 3–22). Washington, DC: American Psychological Association.

Valsiner, J. (2006a). Ambivalence under scrutiny: Returning to the future. *Estudios de Psicologia, 27*, 117–130.

Valsiner, J. (2006b). Dangerous curves in knowledge construction in psychology: Fragmentation of methodology. *Theory and Psychology, 16*, 597–612.

Wapner, S., & Demick, J. (2002). The increasing context of context in the study of environment behavior relations. In R. B. Bechtel & A. Churchman (Eds.), *Handbook of environmental psychology* (pp. 3–14). New York: Wiley.

Weigert, A. J. (1991). *Mixed emotions: Certain steps toward understanding ambivalence*. Albany: State University of New York Press.

CHAPTER 10

The Dynamic Cultural Context of Emotion Socialization[1]

Julie C. Dunsmore and Amy G. Halberstadt

Emotional skills play a key role in children's future social and career success, and, indeed, in their physical and mental health (Halberstadt, Denham, & Dunsmore, 2001; Saarni, 1999). Parents and culture play important roles in children's development of emotional skills (Ellsworth, 1994; Halberstadt, 1991). In recent years, developmental scientists have begun to focus on understanding how parental emotion socialization operates within cultural contexts to influence children's development of emotional skills. The next frontier is to understand *dynamic* aspects of emotion socialization processes within cultural contexts, that is, to address how associations between parental emotional socialization, cultural context, and children's developing emotional skills may change across time. We begin this exploration here.

First, we discuss definitions of culture and of change. We then compare and contrast four heuristic models that address culture in relation to parents' emotion socialization and children's socioemotional outcomes, with particular emphasis on within-nation cultures formed by ethnicity and social class. Through integration of these models, we theorize three different ways through which change is especially pertinent to emotion socialization within cultural context. Next, we delineate needed advances in the measurement and investigation of cultural context as instantiated by ethnicity and class and address how these measurement issues relate to investigation of change. We conclude with recommendations for addressing the dynamic process of emotion socialization within cultural context in future research.

DEFINITIONS

Culture

Culture refers to shared values, beliefs, and customs that are transmitted intergenerationally (Cole & Tan, 2007; Hofstede, 2001; Parke & Buriel, 2006). Nationality is often used as a proxy for culture in comparative studies, and, within nations, race or ethnicity and social class are sometimes used as proxies for culture. Though these characteristics may relate to culture, they do not necessarily cohere and may at times confound rather than reflect an individual's cultural location (Cole & Tan, 2007; Parke & Buriel, 2006). Because culture comprises group beliefs and customs, culture is also not synonymous with an individual's identity. Hofstede (2001) notes, "culture is to a human collectivity what personality is to an individual" (p. 10). In this chapter, we address ethnicity, social class, and their intersection as factors that may relate to cultural beliefs and identity within broader societal groupings.

Change

Change is a concept that can be understood in many ways. With regard to emotion socialization, a fundamental question in extant research has to do with the consequences of emotion socialization practices for children's development of emotional skills, based on children's age or maturation and the timing of those practices. The concept of change becomes more complex when cultural context is considered. Because of variations in beliefs about and values for emotion-related behaviors, culture impacts which socialization processes are used and are most effective at different timepoints during development. Thus, cultural norms and practices are likely influences on parental socialization practices and children's developmental outcomes. In this chapter, we propose three ways of conceptualizing change that we believe are especially pertinent to generating a dynamic understanding of emotion socialization within cultural context.

CULTURE AND EMOTION SOCIALIZATION: COMPARISON OF CONCEPTUAL MODELS

In table 10.1, we provide a comparison of four conceptual models that address culture and emotion socialization, at least through implication. All

Table 10.1. Conceptual Models Addressing Influences of Culture on Parental Emotion Socialization

	Emotion Socialization Antecedents and Mechanisms (Eisenberg et al., 1998)	Minority Children's Developmental Competencies (Garcia Coll et al., 1996)	Socialization of Emotion-Related Schemas (Dunsmore & Halberstadt, 1997)	Cultural Socialization of Emotion (Cole & Tan, 2007)
Purpose of model	Provide framework identifying emotion socialization mechanisms and their processes, outcomes, and moderators	Redress marginalization of class, culture, ethnicity, and race in conceptual models of child development, family socialization part of model	Propose process through which emotion socialization affects children's developing schemas about emotions, self, and world	Identify essential components in framework for understanding interplay of culture and emotion socialization
Discussion of culture	Often use term subculture, connoting focus on smaller, more homogenous groups within nations; SES mentioned within culture	Adaptive culture is defined as shared goals, beliefs, and customs that are separate from those of dominant culture; both historical influences and current contexts shape adaptive culture; race, ethnicity, and class are central as (a) aspects of family social position, (b) influences on family resources and socialization goals, and (c) relevant to child developmental competencies	Cultural appraisals of emotion-related situations, expectations about emotional experience and expression, and definitions of self and others noted as relevant to emotion socialization; race/ethnicity included both as child characteristic and aspect of culture; class included within culture	Defined as shared principles that guide shared customs transmitted intergenerationally; individual members of a culture vary in extent to which they endorse those principles and practices; emphasize cultural views of acceptable behavior, socialization goals, and ideas about how to achieve socialization goals

(continued)

Table 10.1. (continued)

	Emotion Socialization Antecedents and Mechanisms (Eisenberg et al., 1998)	Minority Children's Developmental Competencies (Garcia Coll et al., 1996)	Socialization of Emotion-Related Schemas (Dunsmore & Halberstadt, 1997)	Cultural Socialization of Emotion (Cole & Tan, 2007)
Discussion of change	Child age or skill influences parent emotion socialization; myriad situational influences act on parent emotion socialization choices	Historical change influences adaptive culture; family social position may change across the lifespan and thereby influence the adaptive culture experienced by the child; variation in child maturational timing and phenotypic characteristics associated with maturation may elicit differential socialization responses within the adaptive culture	Child age or skill influences parent emotion socialization; situational influences mentioned	Child age or skill influences parent emotion socialization
Proposed or implied pathways linking culture to parents' emotion socialization behaviors	Both direct and indirect pathways; direct pathways include cultural display rules and values that influence parents' expressiveness and reactions to children's emotions; indirect pathways include cultural	Adaptive culture influenced by way that social stratification (combination of social position, prejudice/oppression, and segregation) affects the support families experience in their communities; adaptive culture proposed	Moderating pathways proposed—fit between cultural patterns of and beliefs about emotional expressiveness and child emotionality emphasized as influence on family beliefs and expressiveness; fit between all emphasized	Pathways are not illustrated, but examples emphasize moderating pathways, different influences on socialization behaviors depending on fit between cultural goals, interpretation of

	influences on parents' individual beliefs and socialization goals, which then influence socialization behaviors	to directly affect family socialization; emotion socialization not directly addressed, but family beliefs, values, goals, and practices included in family socialization	as influence on child's developing schemas; parent beliefs also noted as mediator between culture and emotion socialization practices	children's behaviors, immediate pressures of the situational context
Proposed or implied pathways linking change to parents' emotion socialization behaviors	Direct pathways proposed linking (a) child age or developmental skills and (b) situational factors to parents' emotion socialization choices	Both direct and indirect pathways; some moderation implied in mention that effect of child maturation-related phenotypic characteristics on socialization practices may vary according to culture-specific beliefs	Direct pathway proposed linking child age or developmental skills to parents' emotion socialization choices; moderating pathway proposed through which cultural beliefs about emotions and child maturation and learning in regard to emotion regulation skills influences emotion socialization	Direct pathway implied linking child age or developmental skills to parents' emotion socialization goals and practices; note cultural differences in content of emotional skills yet universal developmental sequence for achieving those skills; dynamic nature of culture highlighted

of these models address change in the fundamental sense described above, through focus on the consequences for children of parental socialization practices depending on children's age or developmental skills.

EMOTION SOCIALIZATION ANTECEDENTS AND MECHANISMS

Eisenberg, Cumberland, and Spinrad (1998), and Eisenberg, Spinrad, and Cumberland (1998) developed a heuristic model of emotion socialization mechanisms in order to guide research on emotion socialization processes and outcomes. Though they do not explicitly define culture, the authors use examples that address national differences as well as examples that address within-nation differences, and often use the term *sub-culture*, which connotes smaller, more homogenous groups within nations. Descriptions of effects of socioeconomic status on parents' emotion socialization are included as examples of culture. Culture is included as both a direct influence on parents' emotion socialization behaviors and as an indirect influence, affecting parents' emotion socialization behaviors by influencing parents' own individual beliefs and socialization goals. Thus, Eisenberg and colleagues' conceptualization of the role of culture in emotion socialization seems consistent with mediational pathways.

With regard to change, Eisenberg and colleagues (Eisenberg, Cumberland et al., 1998; Eisenberg, Spinrad et al., 1998) propose a direct pathway linking child age or developmental skills to parents' emotion socialization choices. Though more ephemeral situational factors are also listed as influences on parents' emotion socialization choices, discussion of change in emotion socialization is primarily framed as a consequence of change in children's skills and parents' age-based expectations. Thus, in regard to how the concept of change relates to culture and emotion socialization, their conceptualization again seems to emphasize both direct and indirect linear pathways.

Minority Children's Developmental Competencies

To rectify the long-standing marginalization and biased treatment of class, culture, ethnicity, and race in developmental models, Garcia Coll et al. (1996) created a model of minority children's development of competencies that thoroughly centralizes these issues. Adaptive culture is a critical component of their model, defined by the goals, beliefs, and practices shared within a community of color that are distinct from those of the dominant culture. Both historical and current community contexts affect adaptive culture. Race, ethnicity, and class permeate the model, first as aspects of the family's social position that may be associated with experiences of discrimination, oppression, and segregation; next as influences on resources available to the family and on family socialization goals; finally as linked to the developmental competencies that are relevant for the child. Although Garcia Coll et al. do not directly address emotion socialization, emotion socialization is consistent with their description of family socialization. They proposed that adaptive culture directly influences family socialization.

Garcia Coll et al. (1996) also address change on multiple levels. First, they note that historical change in institutionalized and implicit systems of oppression influence adaptive culture. Second, they note that family social position may change across a child's lifetime and thereby influence adaptive culture. Third, they note that children's own change, not only in skills but also in phenotypic characteristics related to child maturation, may elicit different socialization responses depending on the adaptive culture. The first two levels are consistent with linear pathways of change in adaptive culture and emotion socialization, both direct and mediated. The third, however, hints at a moderating pathway through which the effect of children's physical maturation on emotion socialization may vary depending on cultural context.

Socialization of Emotion-Related Schemas

In earlier work we focused on mechanisms through which family emotional expressiveness, one key aspect of emotion socialization, might operate to influence children's construction of schemas about emotions, their sense of self, and their social world (Dunsmore & Halberstadt, 1997). We proposed culture as a critical influence that both affects the family's style of emotional expressiveness and alters the meaning communicated by the family's emotional expressiveness to the child. In our model, we noted race and ethnicity as cultural characteristics that may influence how others in children's social worlds respond to them and how children self-define their own identities, thus creating different lenses with which to view behavior. We also delineated specific aspects of cultural beliefs and practices that we considered particularly relevant for emotion socialization: cultural appraisal patterns, display rules and ideas about appropriate emotional experience, and ways of thinking about oneself and others (e.g., emphasis on independence or interdependence). Like Eisenberg, Cumberland et al. (1998) and Eisenberg, Spinrad et al. (1998), we discussed parental beliefs about emotions as potential mediators between culture and parental emotion socialization behaviors. However, we also emphasized moderating pathways linking culture to emotion socialization in our discussion of the fit between aspects of culture and other factors, such as child characteristics or parental beliefs.

Regarding change, we noted age-related parental expectations and child skills as influences on parents' emotion socialization choices. In addition to this direct pathway, we considered moderating pathways formed by fit between cultural beliefs and children's emotion-related skills and between cultural beliefs and children's speed in acquiring those emotion-related skills.

Cultural Socialization of Emotion

Finally, we turn to Cole and Tan's (2007) framework for understanding the interconnections between culture and emotion socialization. Cole and Tan define culture as shared principles that guide shared customs transmitted intergenerationally, though individual members of a culture may vary in the extent to which they subscribe to those shared principles and customs. Cultural views of appropriate and desirable behavior, socialization goals for encouraging desired behavior, and perspectives about the achievement of socialization goals are critical for understanding emotion socialization behaviors. Cole and Tan provide many examples of different influences of culture on emotion socialization according to fit between aspects of cultural principles and customs and between culture and other influences on socialization behavior, such as child characteristics. Thus, we interpret their model as consistent with moderating pathways linking culture and emotion socialization. Cole and Tan also emphasize the interplay between socialization goals and more proximal family or situational pressures on emotion socialization practices.

Cole and Tan (2007) discuss change in two ways. First, like Garcia Coll and colleagues (1996), they note the consequences of change in cultural context for emotion socialization goals and practices. Second, as in the other three models, they suggest linear pathways linking change in child age and developmental skills to change in parents' emotion socialization. Cole and Tan emphasize that extant research supports cultural differences in the *content* of emotional skills but that the *sequence* of developing emotional skills appears similar across cultures.

Integration of Conceptual Models

In our integration of these conceptual models, we first focus on the *structure* of proposed pathways. This is important because links connecting culture and emotion socialization at the theoretical level direct researchers' choices for measurement and analysis of change. We then turn to the models' shared reliance on the socioecological approach.

Structure. Whether proposing direct or indirect linkages between culture and emotion socialization, Eisenberg, Cumberland et al. (1998), Eisenberg, Spinrad et al. (1998), and Garcia Coll et al. (1996) conceptualize linear pathways. In contrast, both Dunsmore and Halberstadt (1997) and Cole and Tan (2007) emphasize moderating pathways, whether through interactions between culture and other influences on emotion socialization or among different aspects of culture. In our recent work on parents' beliefs about children's emotions, we have tested interrelations among different aspects of cultural context (ethnicity, indices of class) and parents' beliefs about emotions as predictors of emotion socialization practices with African-American, European-American, and Lumbee Native American parents, comparing moderation and mediation models. Conceptualizing beliefs as having varying influences on parental behavior, depending on ethnicity or education, is a very different framework for thinking about cultural context compared with the linear linkages in mediational models. We remain drawn to the idea of *good fit* between parents' beliefs about emotions and other sociodemographic indices of their cultural context, which would suggest moderating effects. However, our data instead support only linear pathways, with emotion socialization beliefs serving as mediating mechanisms through which the cultural context influences socialization behaviors.

Regarding the concept of change, all four models recognize the importance of child maturation and learning as antecedents for change in parental emotion socialization. Garcia Coll et al. (1996) and Cole and Tan (2007) also discuss change over time in the cultural context itself.

Whereas Eisenberg and colleagues (Eisenberg, Cumberland et al., 1998; Eisenberg, Spinrad et al., 1998), and Cole and Tan conceptualize only linear pathways related to change, Garcia Coll et al. and Dunsmore and Halberstadt (1997) include moderating pathways through which change in one factor interacts with other factors to affect emotion socialization.

These differences in structural conceptualizations are critical for measurement, analysis, and interpretation of the dynamic interrelations between culture and emotion socialization processes, and for application of research findings to clinical and education practice and policy. If pathways are largely linear, then research needs to focus on identifying mechanisms mediating relations between cultural context and emotion socialization across the lifespan, and practice and policy may focus on impacting those mediating mechanisms. If pathways are largely interactional, then research needs to focus on examining combinations of aspects of cultural context with other factors across the lifespan, and practice and policy may focus on communicating and supporting the import of these niches for development. In both cases, more nuanced measurement of the cultural context will be necessary for the field to progress.

Socioecological approach. Despite different emphases of these models, all share several aspects of the socioecological approach (Rothbaum & Trommsdorff, 2007). First, all acknowledge children's active role in evoking and shaping parent socialization behaviors. This is evident in the linear pathways linking change in child age and developmental skills to change in emotion socialization in all four models. Second, all discuss emotion socialization and culture as taking place within nested settings, embedded in multiple layers of systems that may be differentially influential and that may change over time. Finally, all emphasize the critical role played by parents' and children's interpretations of the *meaning* of each others' behavior. For example, it is not the child's emotional expression *per se* that elicits parent responses; it is the parent's perception that the emotional expression is appropriate or inappropriate given the current situation and its antecedents, the child's developmental level and rate of development, and cultural norms that influence the response. Likewise, it is not the parent's reaction *per se* that leads the child to continue or discontinue his or her emotional expression; it is the child's gleaning of meaningful information about social norms, his or her relationship with the parent, and the situational costs and benefits of the emotional expression at that point in time. In the next section we extend these aspects of the socioecological approach to propose three ways through which change influences emotion socialization within cultural context.

CONCEPTUALIZING CHANGE IN RELATION TO CULTURAL CONTEXT

Cultural Beliefs about Human Development

Beliefs about human developmental processes may vary across cultural contexts in ways that influence emotion socialization. We highlight two types of beliefs about human developmental processes in particular. First, cultural variation exists in beliefs about when children are developmentally ready for emotion socialization (Halberstadt, 1991; Hyson & Lee, 1996). When parents believe children are not yet developmentally ready for emotion socialization, they are unlikely to engage in active emotion socialization and may instead attempt to protect their children from emotion-laden situations. Thus, change in child age or attainment of skills (such as language) may serve as a stimulus variable marking developmental readiness and thereby eliciting differential emotion socialization patterns.

Second, cultural variation in implicit theories about human development may influence emotion socialization. Incremental theorists believe that emotion-related traits and skills can change over time, whereas entity theorists believe that emotion-related traits and skills are stable and do not change. In cultural contexts emphasizing incremental theories of emotional development, parents may be alert for changes in children's maturation and learning and for situational learning opportunities for emotion socialization, for example by taking advantage of conflicts to teach about negative emotions. In cultural contexts that emphasize entity theories of emotional development, however, parents may be less sensitive to changes in children's maturation and learning and may consider emotion-laden situations as events to be avoided rather than opportunities for learning important skills (Kammrath & Dweck, 2006).

Change in Cultural Context

The cultural context itself may change over time in ways that influence and are influenced by emotion socialization. We note three ways this may happen. First, historical change in the cultural context may occur. Examples may include economic or political forces that influence emotion-related experiences; world events that transform emotion-related schemas; or generational shifts in emotion display rules. Second, families may shift cultural contexts. This may happen through physical relocation or other changes in life circumstances, through changing social relationships, and/or through transformation in family values or beliefs. Third, the meaning of the cultural context and thereby its relations with emotion socialization may change as children—and parents—grow in perspective-taking skills, accumulate life experience, and come to new understandings of their cultural context and its influence.

Time as a Culturally Embedded Phenomenon

Finally, conceptualization, experience, and allocation of time may differ across cultures in ways that influence emotion socialization. Here we suggest three ways in which this may happen; this is an area ripe for future research. First, some cultures experience time as a commodity more than other cultures. The process and content of emotion socialization may be more goal-driven in a cultural context in which time is considered a resource not to be wasted, and more relationship- and insight-driven in a cultural context in which time is considered simply part of the natural environment or of little consequence.

Second, some cultures include many more transitions for children than other cultures, at both shorter and longer points in the time scale. For example, in the United States, middle-class children in urban settings tend to have many daily transitions (e.g., getting to school, school itself, multiple after-school activities, and additional evening activities). Children in other cultural contexts, however, may have many fewer transitions (e.g., getting to school, school itself, and only one or two activities outside of the family home per week). Some cultures mark transformational points in children's lives through rituals or ceremonies, such as bar or bat mitzvah, quinceanera, or various school graduations, whereas other cultures do not. Because beliefs about children's maturation are often associated with these transition points, they may result in different patterns of emotion socialization, and different patterns of emotion socialization may be associated with better or worse adjustment to the transitions.

Third, cultures may experience the passing of time in qualitatively differently ways. Many cultures understand time to follow a linear, ratio scale with only forward progression. Cultures with this understanding of time may emphasize the progression of past to present to future. However, this understanding of time is not universal. For example, some Native American traditions consider the cyclicity of time of far greater importance than the linear passing of time. The meanings embraced in emotion socialization processes may be very different if the future is part of the present, and the past is of equal importance to the future. Although the concept of non-linear time may be challenging to those accustomed to linearity, assessing understandings of time may well be a critical aspect of measuring the cultural context. We address other aspects of measuring the dynamic cultural context next.

MEASURING DYNAMIC CULTURAL CONTEXT

In combination, all of the models we reviewed call for far more sophisticated approaches to the measurement of cultural context to take into account the multiple layers of systems. Greater nuance is needed to draw meaningful inferences about universal and culturally-specific patterns of emotion socialization within nations and across ethnicities and social class. This is particularly necessary in order to develop a dynamic rather than static understanding of emotion socialization within cultural context. We provide four general suggestions for *best practices* in measuring the cultural context. We begin with the study conceptualization and operationalization, grouping the first two suggestions. We then turn to indices of the cultural context, grouping the next two suggestions. We next make suggestions specific to measurement of ethnicity and class, and consider the three concepts of change discussed above.

Dialogue with Cultural Informants

Ethnocentrism is a common problem in cross-cultural research, in which the dominant group is, whether deliberately or unintentionally, considered as the norm against which other groups are compared. Consultation with members of the cultural group under study is necessary to select and create measures that value participants' diversity (Cole & Tan, 2007; Garcia Coll et al., 1996). Constructs proposed to be measured by researchers who are not participants in the culture can be examined, refined, and re-interpreted through dialogue with cultural members.

Second, it is important to ensure that the same construct is being measured across cultural contexts. Thoughtful consideration of the operationalization of the construct is the first step. When administering interviews or questionnaires, careful translation and back-translation of materials is essential. In our own work, even when working with groups whose native language is the same as ours, we have found it useful to ask cultural informants to paraphrase items from *researcher-ese* to their own words in order to ensure that we communicate the intended meaning of the items. When quantitative self-report instruments are used, establishment of configural invariance (similar factor structures across groups) and metric invariance (similar item loadings on each factor across groups) is necessary to ensure that the same underlying construct is being measured (Vanderberg & Lance, 2000).

The overarching solution to the challenges of measuring cultural context is to know as much as possible about the cultural group before formulating hypotheses. Description of what parents and children are actually doing, at what time points and at what pace, with input from the cultural group, is always the first step. At the same time, this active engagement in the research process may transform the processes under investigation through participants' reflection on their own practices and assumptions.

Regarding the three concepts of change discussed above, seeking cultural informants' advice is likewise critical. First, it is important to measure cultural and individual views of developmental process. Second, it is important to measure indices of the cultural context over time rather than assuming continuity. Third, it is important to find out how time operates within the cultural context. All of this information is necessary for development of hypotheses; selection of measurement points, instruments, and procedures; and interpretation of results.

Use Multiple Indices

Perhaps the most basic consideration in measuring the cultural context is to do just that: measure multiple indices of the cultural context. A common pitfall is to assume cultural context based on a single index or a phenotype that is stereotypically associated with a cultural group (Cole & Tan, 2007; Parke & Buriel, 2006). Using multiple indices rather than single proxy variables may assist in de-confounding influences of cultural group from other potential influences also related to the proxy variable.

A second common pitfall is the insufficient consideration of within-group heterogeneity and across-group similarity. Some indices might involve differences within groups (e.g., collectivist cultures may have greater diversity in collectivist thinking among more educated groups compared to less educated groups). It is also important to consider across-group similarity (e.g., wealth might have similar impact across different cultures). Again, when using a single proxy variable to measure culture, it is difficult to determine what difference (or similarity) really means. By measuring several constructs, we may identify more proximal causes for differences.

Ethnicity

Ethnicity suggests common values, beliefs, and behaviors that emerge from a shared history, nationality, or ancestry (Hill, Murry, & Anderson, 2005). One way to investigate ethnicity as a form of cultural context is to measure the degree to which individuals (a) experience their ethnic identity, as one of their many identities, as central to who they are; (b) take pride in their ethnic identity; and (c) value the goal of assimilation into mainstream culture (Sellers, Smith, Shelton, Rowley, & Chavous, 1998). A second way to investigate ethnicity as a form of cultural context relates to the issue of minority status, and the usual concomitant of lived experiences of racism. Many parents with children of minority status consider it important to help their children prepare for and negotiate perceived or actual experiences of racism (Garcia Coll et al., 1996). This may include socialization about the expression and regulation of emotion.

Third, ethnicity may be related to the value the individual's community places on individualism (independence) and/or collectivism (interdependence). This distinction is one of the most commonly studied in cultural psychology (Cole & Tan, 2007; Rothbaum & Trommsdorff, 2007), and is relevant to the measurement of ethnicity as a form of cultural context because ethnic minority families often include interdependence as one of their socialization goals for their children (Parke & Buriel, 2006). Traditionally, scholars viewed individualism and collectivism as two ends of a single bipolar dimension. We know now, however, that parents from both individualistic and collectivistic cultures endorse both independent and interdependent goals for their children (Leyendecker, Harwood, Lamb, & Schoelmerich, 2002; Tamis-LeMonda, Wang, Koutsouvanou, & Albright, 2002).

In addition, multiple forms of independence and interdependence may exist, and different forms of independence and interdependence emphasized within individualistic compared with collectivistic societies (Rothbaum & Trommsdorff, 2007). For example, Yamagishi and Yamagishi (1994) distinguish between trust and assurance, which are two distinct aspects of relatedness or interdependence. They characterize trust as confidence in the trustee's own good intentions, whereas assurance is characterized by confidence that the structure surrounding the relationship benefits the trustee who behaves in a way that benefits the trustor. Kusserow suggests variations within individualism. Hard offensive individualism stresses children's achievement and aspirations for future success. Hard defensive individualism emphasizes promoting children's resilience and skill at protecting themselves from threats. Soft individualism focuses on cultivating children's unique qualities and protecting children's self-esteem (Kusserow, 2004). These types of individualism may well vary by ethnicity or by class, which is sometimes confounded with ethnicity.

Class

Reflective of prestige, power, and economic well-being, researchers typically measure social class through three indices: education, income, and occupational status. Using all three indices together provides better measurement of social class because each indicates a different form of resources (Conger & Dogan, 2007). Each, however, is confounded with ethnicity in the United States. Assessing families' socioeconomic status at the parental and neighborhood levels may more clearly illuminate what *class* differences mean and contribute in terms of emotion socialization practices. An additional family-level index of class is net wealth, which may provide a better sense of the financial buffers that families experience and a more accurate assessment of economic parity across ethnicities (Darity & Nicholson, 2005). Income inequality within the family's community may be a better predictor of family outcomes than traditional measures of economic status (Pickett & Wilkinson, 2007). Neighborhood conditions, assessed through measures of violence and crime, perceived school quality, neighborhood income, and person to household space density (Duncan & Magnuson, 2003) may also be important to families' emotion socialization practices.

Change

The first way in which concepts of change are related to these measurement issues is that beliefs about human developmental processes may be associated with indices of ethnicity and class. Second, change over time in family social position or residence may influence emotion socialization; historical change in the cultural context that influences family experiences with oppression may also influence emotion socialization. Early childhood is the time of greatest change in social class (Parke & Buriel, 2006). Parents' assimilation and adherence to individualistic and collectivistic goals may also change over time.

Third and finally, family status on indices of ethnicity and class may be differentially salient in different situations and at different ages. For example, in our work with Lumbee Native Americans, we hear anecdotal reports that ethnic identity is less salient in K–12 school years, when Lumbee children are the majority group in their schools despite being members of a minority group within the larger culture. However, upon transition from high school to work settings, the military, or college, in which Lumbee are no longer the majority group, ethnic identity becomes more salient. As another example, parents' endorsement of soft individualism may be more common when children are younger, whereas their endorsement of hard offensive individualism may become more salient as children progress in school and are in a position to develop skills and credentials to reach their aspirations.

DIRECTIONS FOR FUTURE RESEARCH

Expanded measurement of the cultural context in future research might benefit by developing dimensions in addition to individualism/collectivism to characterize cultures on a broad level. For example, Hofstede (2001) has identified four other dimensions besides individualism/collectivism. These include power distance (the extent to which the society is hierarchically organized), uncertainty avoidance (feeling threatened by ambiguous situations), masculinity/femininity (distinct or overlapping gender roles), and long-term versus short-term orientation (promotion of future rewards).

It is also important to consider socializers beyond parents. Extended family may be differentially important across ethnicities, and division of labor for emotion socialization may be differentially shared among mothers, fathers, and other family members. School and peer contexts may be differently valued across cultural contexts. Access and value placed on cultural artifacts that communicate meanings of emotions, such as media and books, may also differ across cultural contexts.

In this chapter, we have given careful consideration to the *dynamic* aspect of the cultural context for emotion socialization through theoretical consideration of concepts of change. Better understanding of how cultural context influences beliefs about developmental processes is necessary to identify outcomes associated with children's development of emotional competence across cultural contexts. Better understanding of how cultural contexts themselves change is necessary to develop effective intervention and prevention strategies to promote children's emotional competence. In addition, better understanding of how time is conceptualized across cultural contexts is necessary to develop culturally-sensitive criteria for emotional competence.

In conclusion, research on the dynamic cultural context of emotion socialization will thrive by embracing the tension between within-culture and across-culture approaches. It is important to describe cultural niches thoroughly, and at the same time to recognize that measures and constructs appropriate for one niche may not generalize to other cultural niches. It is important to identify universal principles through which emotion socialization operates, yet culturally meaningful constructions of these principles may not exist or may be so broad as to be meaningless. Most likely, the cultural story is complex, with some overlap when relevant constructs are consistent across cultures and some differentiation when relevant constructs vary across cultures. We believe that a multifaceted approach to measuring cultural contexts, encompassing both sociodemographic indices and psychological constructs relevant to socialization goals, and fully incorporating consideration of multiple concepts of change, can fruitfully bridge within-culture and across-culture approaches to illuminate emotion socialization processes.

NOTE

1. Funding was provided by R03 53572 from NICHD and by an AdvanceVT Seed Grant. We express appreciation to Alfred J. Bryant, Jr. for his comments on an earlier version of this manuscript and Karen Beale for sharing her consideration of class.

REFERENCES

Cole, P. M., & Tan, P. Z. (2007). Emotion socialization from a cultural perspective. In J. E. Grusec & P. D. Hastings (Eds.), *Handbook of socialization: Theory and research* (pp. 516–542). New York: Guilford.

Conger, R. D., & Dogan, S. J. (2007). Social class and socialization in families. In J. E. Grusec & P. D. Hastings (Eds.), *Handbook of socialization: Theory and research* (pp. 433–460). New York: Guilford.

Darity, Jr., W., & Nicholson, M. J. (2005). Racial wealth inequality and the Black family. In V. C. McLoyd, N. E. Hill, & K. A. Dodge (Eds.), *African American family life: Ecological and cultural diversity* (pp. 78–85). New York: Guilford.

Duncan, G. J., & Magnuson, K. A. (2003). Off with Hollingshead: Socioeconomic resources, parenting, and child development. In M. H. Bornstein & R. H. Bradley (Eds.), *Socioeconomic status, parenting, and child development* (pp. 83–106). Mahwah, NJ: Erlbaum.

Dunsmore, J. C., & Halberstadt, A. G. (1997). How does family emotional expressiveness affect children's schemas? *New Directions for Child Development, 77*, 45–66.

Eisenberg, N., Cumberland, A., & Spinrad, T. L. (1998). Parental socialization of emotion. *Psychological Inquiry, 9*, 241–273.

Eisenberg, N., Spinrad, T. L., & Cumberland, A. (1998). The socialization of emotion: Reply to commentaries. *Psychological Inquiry, 9*, 317–333.

Ellsworth, P. C. (1994). Sense, culture, and sensibility. In S. Kitayama & H. R. Markus (Eds.), *Emotion and culture: Empirical studies of mutual influence* (pp. 23–50). Washington, D.C.: American Psychological Association.

Garcia Coll, C., Crnic, K., Lamberty, G., Wasik, B. H., Jenkins, R., Garcia, H. V., et al. (1996). An integrative model for the study of developmental competencies in minority children. *Child Development, 67*, 1891–1914.

Halberstadt, A. G. (1991). Toward an ecology of expressiveness: Family socialization in particular and a model in general. In R. S. Feldman & B. Rimé (Eds.), *Fundamentals of nonverbal behavior* (pp. 106–160). New York: Cambridge University Press.

Halberstadt, A. G., Denham, S. A., & Dunsmore, J. C. (2001). Affective social competence. *Social Development, 10*, 79–119.

Hill, N. E., Murry, V. M., & Anderson, V. D. (2005). Sociocultural contexts of African American families. In V. C. McLoyd, N. E. Hill, & K. A. Dodge (Eds.), *African American family life: Ecological and cultural diversity* (pp. 21–44). New York: Guilford.

Hofstede, G. (2001). *Culture's consequences: Comparing values, behaviors, institutions and organizations across nations.* Thousand Oaks, CA: Sage.

Hyson, M. C., & Lee, K. M. (1996). Assessing early childhood teachers' beliefs about emotions: Content, contexts, and implications for practice. *Early Education and Development, 7*, 59–78.

Kammrath, L. K., & Dweck, C. (2006). Voicing conflict: Preferred conflict strategies among incremental and entity theorists. *Personality and Social Psychology Bulletin, 32*, 1497–1508.

Kusserow, A. (2004). *American individualisms: Child rearing and social class in three neighborhoods.* New York: Global Publishing at St. Martin's Press.

Leyendecker, B., Harwood, R. L., Lamb, M. E., & Scholmerich, A. (2002). Mothers' socialization goals and evaluations of desirable and undesirable everyday situations in two diverse cultural groups. *International Journal of Behavioral Development, 26*, 248–258.

Parke, R. D., & Buriel, R. (2006). Socialization in the family: Ethnic and ecological perspectives. In W. Damon, R. M. Lerner (Series Eds.), & N. Eisenberg (Vol. Ed.), *Handbook of child psychology: Vol. 3, Social, emotional, and personality development* (6th ed, pp. 429–504). Hoboken, NJ: Wiley.

Pickett, K. E., & Wilkinson, R. G. (2007). Child well-being and income inequality in rich societies: Ecological cross sectional study. *British Medical Journal, 335*, 1080–1084.

Rothbaum, F., & Trommsdorff, G. (2007). Do roots and wings complement or oppose one another? The socialization of relatedness and autonomy in cultural context. In J. E. Grusec & P. D. Hastings (Eds.), *Handbook of socialization: Theory and research* (pp. 461–489). New York: Guilford.

Saarni, C. (1999). *The development of emotional competence.* New York: Cambridge University Press.

Sellers, R. M., Smith, M. A., Shelton, J. N., Rowley, S. A. J. & Chavous, T. M. (1998). Multidimensional model of racial identity: A reconceptualization of African American racial identity. *Personality and Social Psychology Review, 2*, 18–39.

Tamis-LeMonda, C. S., Wang, S., Koutsouvanou, E., & Albright, M. (2002). Childrearing values in Greece, Taiwan, and the United States. *Parenting: Science and Practice, 2*, 185–208.

Vanderberg, R. J., & Lance, C. E. (2000). A review and synthesis of the measurement in variance literature: Suggestions, practices, and recommendations for organizational research. *Organizational Research Methods, 3*, 4–70.

Yamagishi, T., & Yamagishi, M. (1994). Trust and commitment in the United States and Japan. *Motivation and Emotion, 18*, 129–166.

CHAPTER 11

Transformation and Change: Parenting in Chinese Societies[1]

Susan S. Chuang

As researchers have scrutinized current ways of thinking about normative family functioning, they have brought into question traditional notions of family ranging from family structure (i.e., single vs. two parents) to parenting roles (i.e., gendered roles of fathers as breadwinners and mothers as caregivers), and their underlying assumption of universality. In reassessing family dynamics, many researchers have strived to be more inclusive of ethnic diversity in their work. As part of this transformation, research on fathering has gained prominence among social and behavioral scientists. For example, over the past several decades, understanding of the roles and responsibilities between mothers and fathers has changed. Normative parental roles are no longer viewed as a stark dichotomy (maternal caregiver and paternal breadwinner), but rather, seen as ranging from traditional roles to more egalitarian relationships, with fathers engaging in child caregiving and household chores and mothers contributing to the household income. A number of factors contribute to the transformation of parenting dynamics and roles including societal changes (e.g., increased numbers of mothers entering the workforce) and the inclusion of culturally diverse families as a focus of study.

In conjunction with the attention on parenting, the role of culture and family functioning has become the forefront of many research agendas (Chuang & Gielen, 2009; Chuang & Moreno, 2008; Chuang & Tamis-LeMonda, 2009). In my work, I view *culture* as a set of shared values, beliefs, and practices, which include the dynamically structured relationships affecting the course of development. Culture is not an *objective* reality, but rather it is a shared understanding among individuals, affecting their attitudes, judgments, emotions, and practices. In this sense, culture is not static but fluid and dynamic, dependent upon societal and group factors (Super & Harkness, 2002).

In order for social and behavioral scientists to capture the variations and nuances of a particular group, they need to modify or expand their conceptual approaches. In addition, modification of methodological strategies will allow researchers to gain greater specificity in their focus and study designs, which will provide a more accurate portrayal of family functioning and processes within a cultural context. Researchers must examine specific ethnic groups on their own terms rather than limiting their focus on comparative research (Chuang, 2006; Moreno, 1991; Phinney & Landin, 1998). Such specificity provides a framework to investigate the impact of cultural factors on particular issues and to examine whether current conceptualizations of parenting, which are nested within a Westernized framework, are culturally relevant and applicable to minority groups.

In this chapter, I will examine social and cultural changes in Chinese societies, as well as Chinese families who have migrated to other countries and the extent to which current research reflects these changes. I rely on emerging research, albeit limited, on Chinese families, and fathers in particular, to illustrate how culture has influenced researchers' views and theories on parenting. I begin with a brief overview of the demographic trends of Chinese populations in both China and other migrating countries (i.e., Canada, United States), followed by a discussion on the role of culture in parenting, with a focus on contemporary views on fathering. Next, I will illustrate how, through recent economic and political changes, these factors are antecedents of change in fathering and family functioning. I conclude the chapter with a discussion of future directions on theorizing and posit how these directions can guide community professionals and social policy makers to create programs and policies that are relevant and culturally sensitive to the populations at hand.

DEMOGRAPHIC TRENDS AMONG CHINESE SOCIETIES

Most of our knowledge about families, whether it be about parenting, fathering, or family functioning, has been primarily developed by a Westernized perspective, based on European American families. Only recently have researchers become more inclusive in their sampling strategies to include varying ethnic minority families. Researchers have been particularly interested in Asian families because these societies appear to be qualitatively different from Westernized societies. In addition, Asian societies have shared a long history of between-country interactions and have common cultural heritages. However, each country's experiences of the influences of modernization, economic growth, and globalization are unique and country-specific. Thus, how family roles, relationships, and child socialization have changed has gained considerable interest among social scientists.

Although the population of Chinese societies far exceeds other Asian societies (e.g., Japanese, Korean), current understanding of Chinese families is limited. China accounts for 20 percent of the world's population with over 1.28 billion people (Shwalb et al., 2002). Recent population trends also reveal that substantial numbers of Chinese families are immigrating to other countries including Canada and the United States. Currently, Asians are one of the fastest growing groups in both these countries. For example, from 2001 to 2006, 1.1 million immigrants arrived in Canada, of which 58.3 percent were born in Asian countries, including the Middle East. Immigrants from the People's Republic of China accounted for 14 percent of the recent immigrant population. Overall, the general immigrant population rose from 17.9 percent in 2001 to 19.8 percent in 2006, the highest increase in severnty-five years (Statistics Canada, 2006).

Because the general immigration population in North America has significant implications for individual immigrant groups, researchers need to situate these trends of Chinese newcomers within the broader immigrant context. A closer look at the immigration patterns reveals a radical shift over the last century in terms of ethno-profiles. For example, the growth and diversity in the 1960s were the result of changes of the *Immigration Act* of 1952, which resulted in the development of immigration policies based on the principles of family reunification and labor market contribution. Thus, Canada accepted into the country individuals from all nations if they met the immigration regulations. Because of these policy changes, immigrants came from many countries with diverse cultural backgrounds. For example, before 1971, the majority of Canadian immigrants were of European origin (81%). Now, the population has become increasingly more multi-ethnic and multi-cultural with representation of over 200 ethnic groups, with 57 percent of newcomers from Asian countries. Moreover, newcomers, on average, have higher birth rates than native,

Caucasian families (Statistics Canada, 2006). Thus, the immigrant population and their children are growing at a faster rate than are their native Canadian counterparts.

These patterns of immigration are similar in the United States. For example, in 2000, over 2.4 million Chinese people lived in the United States. Placed in a broader context, the last decade revealed a foreign-born population increase of 11.1 percent from 7.9 percent of the total population. In 2000, only 14 percent of children in immigrant families were of European or Canadian descent. Rather, the majority of families (86%) emigrated from Latin America (62%), Asia (22%), or Africa (2%). In terms of birth rate, births in immigrant families increased to 47 percent compared to 7 percent for U.S.-born parents. To date, one in five children is from an immigrant family (Hernandez, Denton, & MacCartney, 2008).

Such increases in the Chinese population in China, and especially in receiving countries such as Canada and the United States, provide researchers access with an opportunity to systematically and comprehensively examine family functioning and relationships among Chinese families. Also, as increasing numbers of Asians go through the educational systems, the media and the public at large have developed stereotypic views that Asian American children are the *model minority*, being academically successful in various venues (e.g., elementary to college, higher scores on standardized achievement tests). These views have also spurred many researchers to examine the roles of parents in their children's educational achievement to further understand the cultural context (Chao & Tseng, 2002).

CULTURE AND PARENTING

The role of culture in parenting has a long history, stemming from classical works of anthropologists who placed an emphasis on child socialization and parenting within a cultural model (Chao & Tseng, 2002). The notion of culture has influenced the study of human development, with a growing number of theorists and scholars invoking culture to explain a variety of phenomena. One of the most influential scholars is Triandis (1995) and his worldviews on cultural orientations of countries. Triandis argues that the culture of a country can be classified, based on interpersonal and intergroup behaviors. He proposed two general worldview models:

individualistic (I) and collectivistic (C) orientations. An *individualistic* orientation framed the individual as separate from others with the focus on attaining personal goals such as independence and self-expression. Countries viewed as individualistic were Westernized countries such as Canada and the United States. Conversely, a *collectivistic* orientation promoted the maintenance of common beliefs, attitudes, and practices as defined by the group, and the importance of interdependence (cooperation) among group members.

Triandis (1995) characterizes Asian countries such as China, Japan, and Korea as collectivistic, due in part to the cultural history of Confucianism. Briefly, Confucianism is grounded in the basic tenets of the common good and social harmony over individual interests. Social responsibilities are designated by clear lines of authority. Respect for the status of others and the subordination of the self for the good of the collective is deemed necessary if peace and riches are to follow. Consequently, the collective group is the ultimate measure for approval or rejection of behavior.

The family represents one type of collective group. A cornerstone of Confucianism is *filial piety*. Filial piety refers to the principle that one behaves in a manner that will bring honor and not disgrace to the family name. Children are to be devoted and obedient to their parents (Chao & Tseng, 2002). Therefore, filial piety justifies adult authority over children and authority for elders over members of younger generations. Thus, filial piety serves as a building principle that governs the general behavioral patterns of socialization. It provides specific rules of intergenerational conduct applicable throughout life.

Confucian teachings also provide the framework for the roles and functions of each member of the family. Confucianism defines the role of a father as *yi jia zhi zhu* or *master of the family*. Fathers possess the most powerful position in the family, controlling the financial resources and making the important decisions about the family and children. Clearly stated in the doctrine are gendered familial roles such as men should not speak about issues *inside* the home while women should not speak about issues *outside* the home. Thus, fathers are to be aloof and distant in the family setting. Moreover, and based on the traditional Chinese adage, *strict father, kind mother,* fathers assume the role of a stern disciplinarian and are not encouraged to engage in emotional indulgence with their children (Shwalb et al., 2002).

This dichotomous (individualistic/collectivistic) perspective provided a framework for social and developmental researchers to conduct comparative research and to explore family functioning among Asian societies. Although useful as an initial step toward understanding cultural differences in family processes, the I/C framework fell short in accounting for sociocultural variability and the fluidity of culture across time. The result was an oversimplified and stereotyped characterization of family processes as either collectivistic *or* individualistic. As Kagitiçibasi (1980) warns, "There is a danger that Individualism/Collectivism is too readily used as an explanation for every behavioral variation between so-called individualistic and collectivistic cultures—an all-purpose contrast. If Individualism/Collectivism is used to explain everything, it may explain nothing" (p. 9).

Unfortunately, many researchers did not heed Kagitiçibasi's (1980) warning. Thus, much of the current knowledge about Chinese families is bounded within the I/C framework where researchers' over-reliance on general descriptions are based on Confucianism to characterize parent-child interactions and socialization processes. In traditional Chinese society, the primary socialization goal was to encourage and train children to develop attitudes and behaviors that were in line with Confucian teachings (e.g., interdependence, obedience to authority). Many researchers focused primarily on parental control and parental assertiveness. Consistent findings revealed that compared to Western parents, Chinese parents were more likely to use parental control and assertiveness, and were less responsive and affectionate to their children (Chen & Chen, in press). However, parental control and restrictiveness have consistently been associated with negative child outcomes, such as poor academic performance among Western families. In this area of research, parents who facilitated their children's independence fared better than those children whose parents were more controlling. The findings were robust and held by many researchers as *universal*. However, studies of Chinese families showed a positive association between parental control and children's higher academic achievement (Chao & Tseng, 2002). Moreover, with the changing social environment of a market-oriented society, these traditional Chinese parenting practices and strategies may not be compatible with contemporary families. Thus, some researchers such as Chao (1995) as well as my own work (Chuang, 2006) moved beyond the I/C framework, drawing upon more process-oriented parenting and socialization models, and at the same time, reassessing these models to increase their cultural relevance. This approach is best exemplified by Chao's (1995) work on parenting beliefs. While utilizing the parenting styles model as a foundation for her work, Chao rejected its implied universality by explicitly examining the cultural meanings of these parenting constructs. Through in-depth interviews, she revealed that although European American mothers focused on their children's individuality, self-expression, and separateness from parents, this was not the case for Chinese origin families. Rather, Chinese mothers strived for promoting their children's self-reliance, such as self-care, allowing the parents to engage in other duties. Thus, independence as defined by Western families was not the goal for Chinese families. Supporting some of Chao's findings, my own research found that Chinese mothers encouraged their children to make decisions and have opinions to promote self-reliance but also to promote their children's individuality and self-expression (Chuang, 2006). The results stress the relevancy of culture-specific nuances of constructs, which may hold different meanings for parents and thus, lead to different parenting and socialization processes for children (Chen & Chen, in press).

This integrative and critical approach, one that questions standard meanings and seeks cultural relevancy, extends beyond global measures, and provides a framework for identifying distinct processes of various groups. This is preferred to the adherence of static models, which may inadvertently add credence to overgeneralizations of and support to stereotypic characterizations of certain ethnic groups.

Contemporary Views on Fathering

Over the last four decades, there has been growing interest in the role of fathers and their impact on children. Interestingly, fathering research has taken a different line of inquiry than traditional work on parenting. Initially, the major lines of fathering focused on the *good dad* vs. *bad dad* dichotomy. A good dad was a provider who could financially support his family as opposed to the bad dad (or *deadbeat dad)* who had limited or no financial resources. Thus, the fathers' primary role was *breadwinning*. Unfortunately, this excluded investigation of other paternal roles of fathers (i.e., child caregiver).

It was not until the 1970s that researchers began to re-conceptualize the roles of fathers to reflect a more accurate portrayal of contemporary fatherhood. This re-conceptualization was greatly influenced by the era of the feminist movement, along with society's view that fathers need to be positive role models for their children (Lamb, 2004). These shifts directed researchers to explore paternal behaviors with a particular focus on *what* fathers should do. Lamb, Pleck, Charnov, and LeVine's (1987) conceptualization of fathering was the first model that clearly delineated a multidimensional framework that allowed researchers to explore the levels of father involvement and the effects on their children's lives. Their model included three dimensions: (a) paternal engagement, which included direct interaction with the child including caretaking and play; (b) accessibility or availability to the child (within earshot distance of the child); and (c) responsibility for the child (e.g., making doctor appointments) (Lamb, 2004). This model gained prominence and dominated the field with little attention paid to other aspects of fathering. Moreover, as with the parenting research, investigations of fathering among other ethnic minority families has lagged behind, providing an incomplete picture with respect to fathers' roles. Especially among Chinese families, the research is sparse and at times, contradictory.

This is particularly the case with respect to the role of Confucianism. For example, an early observational study of urban Chinese families found that fathers spent very little time caring for young children, especially infants. Consequently, mothers viewed their husbands as incompetent caretakers of children. One woman stated that, if "a man held an infant, he might become confused and drop it" (p. 349). These findings provide support that Confucianism is still influential on family functioning (Jankowiak, 1992).

Recent findings seem to suggest that the role of Confucianism in the family has diminished. In a population survey by the Chinese National Bureau of Statistics (2001), 77 percent of men believed that men should do half of the domestic work. Only one-half of the men and women believed that men and women should maintain the traditional parent-role differentiation where men's roles should be primarily outside of the home while women should primarily be responsible for activities inside of the home. Fathers also reported higher levels of familial responsibilities and involvement in their children's lives. Thus, in contrast to Confucianism, Chinese fathers were more egalitarian in their approach to family relations.

Once again, this discrepancy may be due to an over-reliance on global measures at the expense of a more detailed and contextually situated approach. In an attempt to theorize about fathering, moving beyond what fathers do (behavioral assessments), I positioned my research to examine the *processes* and *conceptualization* of fathering. For example, my colleague and I (Chuang & Su, 2008) interviewed first-generation Chinese-Canadian and Chinese fathers from mainland China about their daily activities with their toddlers. Instead of using pre-designed global measures, we used a multi-method approach that allowed us to examine various aspects of fathering. First, we used in-depth interviews, which is one of the first studies to tap into fathers' conceptions and definitions of their parental roles in the family. Thus, fathers were not restricted to pre-conceived, pre-determined roles based on European American findings about fathering. Rather, fathers' responses were representative of their own perceived roles and values within their cultural context. Their responses revealed that fathers conceptualized their role as multi-dimensional. Fathers' descriptions of their role were not only economic provider, but also included child caregiver, playmate, educator/trainer, and household caretaker.

In conjunction with the interviews, we assessed fathers' levels of involvement using time diaries, a two-day, twenty-four-hour account of all of their social activities with their toddlers and families (Chuang & Su, 2008). Fathers reported a variety of behaviors, including playing with and caring for their children, and engaging in housework. This second methodology of fathers recalling their social interactions with their families provides insight into family dynamics and child interactions. For example, Chinese-Canadian and Chinese fathers spent an average of forty-five minutes during workdays taking care of their children whereas American fathers generally spent thirty-two minutes with their young children. Moreover, these fathers, regardless of country, also engaged in household chores.

In summary, over time, the field of fathering, as well as parenting, has slowly transformed. As researchers began examining the role of culture on family functioning, the inquiry of universalism and context-dependency *pushed* the field forward. Placing families within their cultural contexts has challenged researchers to rethink and re-define global constructs, and to assess critically their methodological strategies. Moreover, there have been other significant changes at the societal level that have altered fathering, thus transforming the meanings and expectations of fatherhood.

ECONOMIC AND POLITICAL CHANGES

Although inclusive and process oriented conceptualizations and methodological techniques are crucial in understanding familial and paternal processes among Chinese and Chinese-origin families, more macro, social, and cultural events may have a profound impact on family functioning. Thus, scholars must take these social and historical events into account as they design and implement their research studies. To illustrate, I argue that two significant societal factors, the transformation of China's economic structure (including increased numbers of women entering the workforce) and the one-child policy, served as antecedents of family change.

Economic Changes. For thousands of years, China has been an agricultural society where resources were limited and most people lived under poverty conditions. It was not until the early 1980s that China's economy exploded. Full-scale reforms targeted various cities and geographic locations, systematically creating a competitive market economy. In less than twenty years, there was a dominance of state-owned enterprises, and significant growth of both domestic and foreign private and joint ventures. This economic movement was so successful that China is now the fourth largest economy in the world, with a growth rate of about 10 percent per year.

To succeed in a competitive world, the traditional parenting attitudes and practices of promoting interdependence, obedience, and cooperation, were no longer compatible. Rather, the primary goals and strategies for parents to ensure the success of their children shifted to emphasize individual initiative, competitiveness, assertiveness, and self-reliance. In addition, schools have transformed, with educational goals, policies, and practices designed to promote and support children's assertive and independent skills. Children are now encouraged to engage in public debates and to propose their preferences for extracurricular activities. Thus, the market-oriented society has instigated change in parents' socialization goals and strategies for their children and so these findings of independence and self-reliance among parents' practices and beliefs accurately portray contemporary families. Chen and Chen's (in press) research on Chinese parents of school-aged children in two cohorts, 1998 and 2002, provides evidence of this change. They found that the 2002 cohort parents reported more warmth and less power assertion over their children than those in the 1998 cohort. However, there were no differences on their encouragement of academic achievement. Their results suggest that parents' beliefs and attitudes toward their children's socioemotional well-being and their views of their relationships have qualitatively changed in accordance with the changing societal environment.

This shift in the economy has also given rise to an increased number of women entering the workforce. As women entered the workforce in mass numbers, it significantly altered family functioning and the parental roles such as division of household labor. As mentioned earlier, the survey illustrated a shift in conceptual views of gendered roles, with a move *away* from traditional obligations as prescribed by Confucius to a more egalitarian approach that expects fathers' involvement in completing household tasks. Specifically, the survey findings revealed that 77% of Chinese men believed that parents should equally share domestic work (Chinese National Bureau of Statistics, 2001). My preliminary findings on immigrant Chinese fathers also revealed that regardless of their wives' financial contributions to the family, fathers were highly involved in both household chores and caregiving duties.

Social Change. Alongside the economic boom, the one-child policy was instituted in the late 1970s where previously, family sizes were usually large, consisting of three to four generations. Now, the *four-two-one* structure (four grandparents, two parents, one child) is the common family composition in urban families. Because of this change in family structure, researchers have noticed a rise in paternal indulgence, where fathers now seem to *spoil* their children. Unintentionally, the one-child policy may have created a so-called Westernized parenting approach—becoming more *child-centered*, especially among the well-educated population (Shwalb et al., 2004). However, this policy, in conjunction with the gender equality laws, and women's increased participation in the workforce, also may have had some influence on the increased rise in divorce rates among Chinese couples. Since the inception of the one-child policy (from 1990 to 2000), there was an increase in divorces among Chinese couples of 50 percent, from 800,000 to 1.2 million (Shwalb et al., 2004).

These economic and social changes have inevitably transformed family dynamics and parenting processes as well as socioemotional functioning. However, few researchers have explicitly explored how these macro-level factors (institutional and community) have influenced and transformed individuals and families. The dynamic nature of parenting necessitates gathering of information from multiple informants as each individual influences, and is influenced by others (Chen & Chen, in press).

THE IMMIGRATION AND ACCULTURATION PROCESS

With the dramatic influx of newcomers in North America, scholars have been increasingly interested in the ways in which immigrants change and adapt to their host country. For my purposes here, *acculturation*, defined as the process of cultural and psychological changes that individuals face because of contact with a new culture, is a major influence on parenting and fathering. Specifically, immigrants bring with them their cultural values, beliefs, and behaviors from their country of origin as they engage and negotiate a new sociocultural terrain. Thus, regardless of the degree to which parents acculturate to their new environment, acculturation is inevitably an antecedent of change. With the complexities of the acculturative process of moving from one country to another, each individual acculturates at a different rate, facing their own challenges and barriers. All families go through changes as they leave behind their native country and re-establish themselves in the receiving country. Currently, the examination of acculturation and Chinese fathering is extremely limited. As Qin (2009) reports, shortly after immigrating to the United States Chinese fathers experience many challenges, including the difficulties of adjusting to a new country. This was especially true of fathers who lost their employment status after migration. These economic difficulties, in turn, created greater challenges to their behavioral and psychological involvement with their children. Moreover, as fathers' roles in the family changed negatively (e.g., loss of employment), fathers' levels of stress and feelings of alienation increased. As a result, adolescents often expressed a sense of emotional disconnect from their parents as they themselves adjusted to a new cultural context.

My recent research on acculturative influences among Chinese fathers from mainland China and immigrant Chinese fathers revealed that Confucianism is less influential on Chinese fathers, regardless of country (China, Canada) as most of the fathers conceptualized their roles as more multi-faceted (Chuang & Su, 2008). However, immigrant Chinese fathers were more likely to consider their children's interest when making child care decisions than were Chinese fathers. Also, newcomer fathers were less authoritarian (e.g., controlling, restrictive) and more authoritative (e.g., promoting independence) than were fathers in China (Chuang & Su, 2009). These findings suggest that conceptions of family roles change as a function of being exposed to the host culture; thus, reinforcing the need for fathering to be understood within the sociocultural context. Given this dynamic process, the study of how fathers, specifically, and families, in general, negotiate and balance their values and beliefs as they navigate a new country requires continued investigation.

TRANSFORMING VIEWS AND ASSUMPTIONS ABOUT CULTURE

Over the past few decades, researchers, educators, and policymakers have come to understand the importance fathers play in their children's lives. The heightened interest in the multidimensional roles associated with fathering (e.g., economic provider, nurturer) has resulted in research on ethnic and immigrant fathers gaining a considerable amount of momentum. Scholars are slowly recognizing the importance of defining *parenting* within its cultural context as cultural principles guide mothers' as well as fathers' parenting practices, beliefs, and child socialization strategies. Thus, culture should be the medium from which to explain family functioning, rather than treating culture as a *peripheral variable*. With the multitude of variations of families' sociocultural position, socioeconomic status, and immigrant backgrounds, researchers will need to use and refine theoretical and methodological frameworks that will accurately capture the nuances and complexities of families. However, disentangling these factors is not simple; thus, no one theory can exclusively address the various complexities and dynamic processes of parenting, family functioning, and culture.

I concur with others who have stressed the importance of addressing sociocultural processes in all aspects of the research agenda, including the conceptual framework and hypotheses of the study, the ethnic appropriateness of the informants, the use of culturally sensitive and relevant methodological strategies, and the interpretation of the findings within a cultural context (Quintana et al, 2006). Subsequently, future research on immigrant families must incorporate both qualitative and quantitative methodologies and the use of a multi-informant approach to tap into the dynamics and ever-changing social relationships among various family members. These strategies will assist researchers to better theorize about fathering at a richer and deeper level, and thus, position understanding of parenting within family and cultural processes.

Unfortunately, most theoretical models (i.e., family systems theories, ecological theories) fall short in capturing the variability inherent in understanding culture and family processes between groups and across time, and inadvertently imply a level of sociocultural stability that is unwarranted. To capture the influence of culture on parenting, and fathering in particular, researchers need to use a more *critical ecological* approach to family functioning, one that more fully accounts for ongoing transitions in context and meaning among and between groups over time.

To understand fathering among ethnic minority and immigrant families, researchers need to work in partnership with other stakeholders including community service providers and policymakers. Collaborating with others who have first-hand experience with parents and families will ensure that the research focus is relevant, applicable, and tangible to the community at-large. With these common goals of building knowledge of positive fathering and family functioning, the information gathered can guide the development of prevention and intervention programs and services. Greater attention to the intersection of social, cultural, and economic factors will afford greater insight into strategies for addressing potential challenges and issues facing parents as their social environment changes over time, and ultimately, improve the lives of families.

NOTE

1. The author appreciates and thanks Robert Moreno for his insightful comments and support on this chapter.

REFERENCES

Chao, R. K. (1995). Chinese and European American cultural models of the self reflected in mothers' child-rearing beliefs. *Ethos, 23*, 328–354.

Chao, R., & Tseng, V. (2002). Parenting of Asians. In M. H. Bornstein (Ed.), *Handbook of parenting: Vol. 4, Social conditions and applied parenting* (2nd ed., pp. 59–93). Mahwah, NJ: Erlbaum.

Chen, X., & Chen, H. (in press). Child's socioemotional functioning and adjustment in the changing Chinese society. In R. K. Silbereisen & X. Chen (Eds.), *Social change and human development: Concepts and results.* London, UK: Sage.

Chinese National Bureau of Statistics. (2001). Fifth Bulletin of national population census (no. 1). Retrieved on April 2, 2009 from http://www.stats.gov.cn/tjgb/rkpcgb/

Chuang, S. S. (2006). Taiwanese-Canadian mothers' beliefs about personal freedom for their young children. *Social Development, 15*, 520–536.

Chuang, S. S., & Gielen, U. P. (Eds.) (2009). On new shores: Family dynamics and relationships among immigrant families [Special issue]. *Journal of Family Psychology, 23* (3).

Chuang, S. S., & Moreno, R. P. (Eds.) (2008). *On new shores: Understanding immigrant fathers in North America*. Lanham, MD: Lexington Books.

Chuang, S. S., & Su, Y. (2009). Says who? Decision-making and conflicts among Chinese-Canadian and Mainland Chinese parents of young children. *Sex Roles, 60*, 527–588.

Chuang, S. S., & Su, Y. (2008). Transcending Confucian teachings on fathering: A sign of the times or acculturation? In S. S. Chuang & R. P. Moreno (Eds.), *On new shores: Understanding immigrant fathers in North America* (pp. 129–150). Lanham, MD: Lexington Books.

Chuang, S. S., & Tamis-LeMonda, C. S. (Eds.) (2009). From shore to shore: Understanding fathers, mothers, and children in North America [Special issue]. *Sex Roles, 60* (7/8).

Hernandez, D. J., Denton, N. A., & MacCartney, S. E. (2008). Immigrant fathers: A demographic portrait. In S. S. Chuang & R. P. Moreno (Eds.), *On new shores: Understanding immigrant fathers in North America* (pp. 47–103). Lanham, MD: Lexington Books.

Jankowiak, W. (1992). Father-child relations in urban China. In B. S. Hewlett (Ed.), *Father-child relations: Cultural and biosocial contexts* (pp. 345–363). New York: Aldine De Gruyter.

Kagitçibasi, C. (1980). Individualism and collectivism. In J. W. Berry, M. H. Segall, & C. Kagitçibasi (Eds.), *Handbook of cross-cultural psychology. Vol. 3. Social behavior and applications* (pp. 1-50). Needham Heights, MA: Allyn and Bacon.

Lamb, M. E. (2004). *The role of the father in child development* (4th ed.). Hoboken, NJ: Wiley.

Lamb, M. E., Pleck, J. H., Charnov, E. L., & Levine, J. A. (1987). A biosocial perspective on paternal behavior and involvement. In J. B. Lancaster, J. Altman, A. S. Rossi, & L. R. Shorroa (Eds.), *Parenting across the lifespan: Biosocial dimensions* (pp. 111–142). New York: Aldine De Gruyter.

Moreno, R. P. (1991). Maternal teaching of preschool age children in minority and low status families: A critical review. *Early Childhood Research Quarterly, 6*, 395–410.

Phinney, J. S., & Landin, J. (1998). Research paradigms for studying ethnic minority families within and across groups. In V. C. McLoyd & L. Steinberg (Eds.), *Studying minority adolescents: Conceptual, methodological, and theoretical issues* (pp. 89–109). Mahwah, NJ: Erlbaum.

Qin, D. (2009). Gendered processes of adaptation: Understanding parent–child relations in Chinese immigrant families. *Sex Roles, 60*(7/8), 467–481.

Quintana, S. M., Aboud, F. E., Chao, R. K., Contreras-Grau, J., Cross, W. E., Hudley, C, et al. (2006). Race, ethnicity, and culture in child development: Contemporary research and future directions. *Child Development, 77*, 1129–1141.

Shwalb, D. W., Nakazawa, J., Yamamoto, T., & Hyun, J.-H. (2004). Fathering in Japanese, Chinese, and Korean cultures: A review of the research literature. In M. E. Lamb (Ed.), *The role of the father in child development* (4th ed., pp. 146–181). New York: Wiley.

Statistics Canada. (2006). *The Daily: 2006 Census: Immigration, citizenship, language, mobility and migration.* Retrieved April 8, 2009 from http://www.statcan.ca/Daily/English/071204/d071204a.htm

Super, S., & Harkness, C. M. (2002). Culture and parenting. In M. H. Bornstein (Ed.), *Handbook of parenting: Vol. 4. Social conditions and applied parenting* (2nd ed., pp. 59–93). Mahwah, NJ: Erlbaum.

Tamis-LeMonda, C. S. (2004). Conceptualizing fathers' roles: Playmates and more. *Human Development, 47,* 220–227.

Triandis, H. C. (1995). *Individualism and collectivism.* Boulder, CO: Westview Press.

CHAPTER 12

Becoming a Parent Again:
An Exploration of Transformation Among Grandparents Raising Grandchildren

Megan L. Dolbin-MacNab

For a growing number of Americans, contemporary grandparenthood involves assuming responsibility for parenting and meeting the basic needs of one or more grandchildren. In the United States, there are approximately 2.4 million grandparents raising grandchildren (Simmons & Dye, 2003). Typically, grandparents raise their grandchildren because the grandchild's parents are unable to fulfill their parenting responsibilities. This could result from a number of interconnected issues such as substance abuse, child abuse and neglect, teen pregnancy, military deployment, incarceration, HIV/AIDS, physical and mental illness, divorce, and death. Other factors that encourage the formation of grandparent-headed families include cultural traditions of familism, particularly among African-American and Latino grandparents (Goodman & Silverstein, 2006), and policies that require or encourage foster care placement with relatives.

Although the phenomenon of grandparents raising grandchildren reflects a structural change within a larger family system, assuming parenting responsibilities also transforms grandparents' lives. For instance, the added financial demands of caring for a grandchild may make it difficult for grandparents, who are often on fixed or limited incomes, to afford necessities such as housing, food, or health care. Socially, acquiring parenting and childcare responsibilities may limit grandparents' freedom, alter their retirement plans, and compromise their ability to participate in leisure and social activities. Relationally, grandparents may struggle with needing to assume the role of parent rather than traditional grandparent. These are just a few examples of the many changes experienced by custodial grandparents. For a more detailed discussion of how raising a grandchild transforms grandparents' lives see Hayslip and Kaminski (2005).

VARIED PATHWAYS: CONSEQUENCES OF CHANGE

Although grandparents as surrogate parents has been a component of family life for centuries, in the last fifteen years, grandparents' needs have gained considerable public attention. Much of this attention, which has resulted in the proliferation of community-based support services and the development of legislation to assist custodial grandparents, stems from evidence that grandparents struggle with the changes and demands that accompany raising a grandchild. More specifically, a growing body of literature suggests that, as result of the demands of caring for a grandchild and the associated lifestyle changes, grandparents are likely to experience negative consequences such as compromised physical and mental health. By considering these negative consequences over time, it is possible to conceptualize grandparents in terms of their overall trajectories of change or patterns of adjustment.

Physical and Mental Health Outcomes

Physically, compared to noncaregiving grandparents, grandparents raising grandchildren report worse overall health, lower satisfaction with their health status, and more limitations in activities of daily living (Minkler & Fuller-Thomson, 1999). Additionally, because of the stress associated with raising a grandchild, grandparents may engage in dangerous health behaviors such as increased smoking, obesity, and alcohol consumption as well as decreased physical activity (Hughes, Waite, LaPierre, & Luo, 2007). Unfortunately, due to the demands of parenting a grandchild, it is likely that some grandparents would also be negligent in obtaining health care, which may further exacerbate existing acute and chronic illnesses (Hayslip & Kaminski, 2005).

Psychologically, grandparents describe symptoms of psychological distress related to the demands and lifestyle changes associated with raising a grandchild. Specifically, grandparents report high rates of depression and personal distress (Minkler, Fuller-Thomson, Miller, & Driver, 1997), particularly when their grandchildren have behavioral problems (Hayslip, Shore, Henderson, & Lambert, 1998). Other relevant psychological outcomes for custodial grandparents include poor role satisfaction and meaning (Hayslip et al., 1998), anxiety, and parenting stress (Hayslip & Kaminski, 2005). Regardless of the particular indicator of psychological distress, there appears to be consistent and clear evidence that, across diverse samples of grandparents, raising a grandchild is associated with compromised mental health.

Based on the existing literature, it would seem that the consequences of raising a grandchild are primarily negative. The dominant discourse on grandparents raising grandchildren supports this conclusion; it tends to portray grandparents as socially isolated, depressed, unhealthy, and overwhelmed. Although this narrative may accurately reflect many grandparents' realities, the experience of raising a grandchild appears much more nuanced. For example, although parenting is a source of stress for many grandparents (Hayslip & Kaminski, 2005), others describe it as being easier and more enjoyable the second time around (Dolbin-MacNab, 2006). Similarly, while there are grandparents who experience depression and poor mental health, others report savoring the close relationship they develop with their grandchild, feeling a greater sense of purpose, and being more productive (Dolbin-MacNab & Keiley, 2006; Hayslip & Kaminski, 2005). Furthermore, findings that raising a grandchild is associated with compromised physical health (e.g., Minkler & Fuller-Thomson, 1999) are being tempered by evidence that some grandparents' health is unaffected or improved and that health outcomes may have little to do with the caregiving itself (Hughes et al., 2007). Those grandparents who experience health problems appear to be those who are raising grandchildren with neither parent present in the home, those with few resources, and those with other vulnerabilities related to race, gender, class, and preexisting health conditions (Hughes et al., 2007). Finally, although some grandparents describe a sense of frustration related to the loss of their role as traditional grandparent (Kolomer & McCallion, 2005), others embrace their unique relationship with their grandchild (Hayslip & Kaminski, 2005). As these examples suggest, there is significant variability in how grandparents experience their roles and responsibilities.

Outcomes Over Time: Change Trajectories

Given these variations in grandparents' responses to the lifestyle and role changes associated with raising a grandchild, it is likely that grandparents' overall trajectories of adjustment (i.e., physical and mental health outcomes) would show similar diversity. I propose three possible trajectories of change over time: adaptation, stagnation, and deterioration. With *adaptation*, grandparents are able to successfully respond to the changes associated with caring for a grandchild and, as a result, experience few negative consequences. They might even experience some positive outcomes because of their altered family structure and responsibilities. Even if these grandparents struggle initially, over time, their physical and mental well-being remains intact or improves. Grandparents experiencing *stagnation* seem as if they are handling the demands of raising a grandchild. However, because these grandparents are surviving by managing from day to day, they exist in a tenuous situation where a crisis or an accumulation of stressors could quickly result in significant negative outcomes. Finally, *deterioration* captures grandparents who are unable to respond successfully to the demands and changes associated with raising a grandchild. As a result, they exist in crisis mode and experience significant declines in their physical and mental health. Because it is likely that these grandparents will eventually reach a point where they can no longer tolerate the negative consequences of raising a grandchild, they may send the grandchild to the foster care system, return the grandchild to his or her parent(s), or give up on parenting while still providing for the grandchild's most basic needs.

There is little doubt that raising a grandchild is a life-altering experience with the potential for positive and negative physical and psychological consequences. However, in order to advance the understanding of grandparents raising grandchildren, there needs to be intentional theorizing about why some grandparents are able to adapt, while others stagnate or deteriorate. As a family therapist, I have met both types of grandparents; the grandmother who returned her grandchildren to the foster care system because she was so depressed versus the grandmother who started taking computer classes in order to provide herself and her granddaughter with a better life. In these cases and others, theorizing is needed about which specific aspects of grandparents' contexts are significant in determining whether they are positively or negatively transformed by raising a grandchild as well as their overall trajectories of change over time. Also needed is exploration of the mechanisms or processes through which these changes occur.

In response to these needs, the remaining portion of this chapter presents an empirically-based and theoretically-informed exploration of how grandparents are transformed by raising their grandchildren. The goals of this exploration are to (a) offer insight into antecedents of both the positive and negative consequences of raising a grandchild, (b) demonstrate the complexity of these antecedents and grandparents' environments, and (c) explore change processes (i.e., how antecedents actually result in consequences). This exploration is also intended to provide a framework for developing interventions and policies that are responsive to the needs of grandparents and their grandchildren. Although this exploration does not address grandchildren's experiences, living with grandparents is likely to transform grandchildren as well. For a more detailed discussion of grandchildren's experiences see Dolbin-MacNab and Keiley (2009).

EXPLAINING DIVERSE CONSEQUENCES: ANTECEDENTS OF GRANDPARENT CHANGE

Understanding why grandparents are positively versus negatively changed by the experience of raising a grandchild requires attention to numerous intrapersonal, interpersonal, and sociodemographic antecedents of change. Taken together, these antecedents comprise the grandparent's context. This definition of context is informed by ecological system theory (Bronfenbrenner, 1979), which postulates that individuals and their environments (or context) are interdependent. The environment includes multiple nested layers, which range from an individual's immediate environment (microsystem) to the broader sociocultural context (macrosystem). According to ecological systems theory, individuals have varying opportunities and limitations, depending on the quality of their proximal and distal environments (Bronfenbrenner, 1979). Those individuals with more opportunities have greater freedom and control in how they respond and adapt to environmental demands. For custodial grandparents, the opportunities versus limitations within their broader context are likely to be central in determining whether raising a grandchild results in positive or negative transformation.

In addition to ecological systems theory, this conceptualization of grandparent context and the antecedents of grandparent change is informed by intersectionality, which purports that "cultural patterns of oppression are not only interrelated but are bound together and influenced by the intersectional systems of society, such as race, gender, class, and ethnicity" (Collins, 2000, p. 42). Thus, some grandparents may occupy social identities (e.g., being female, poor, and a minority) that collectively increase their risk of oppression and amplify their vulnerability to negative outcomes associated with raising a grandchild.

There are three groups of antecedents proposed to be significant in determining how the experience of raising a grandchild transforms grandparents. These include intrapersonal, interpersonal, and sociodemographic antecedents. *Intrapersonal antecedents* comprise cognitive and affective processes internal to the grandparent such as cognitive appraisal and coping (Lazarus & Folkman, 1984), intergenerational ambivalence (Lüscher & Pillemer, 1998), and role timing or conflict (Landry-Meyer & Newman, 2004). The *interpersonal antecedents* consist of factors reflecting grandparents' family and social relationships. These include characteristics of the grandchild and parenting responsibilities, dynamics within the extended family system, and social support. Finally, the *sociodemographic antecedents* capture grandparents' social location and include social identities such as race and ethnicity, financial resources, gender, and age.

Conceptually, the proposed groups of antecedents are interdependent. As such, all of the antecedents may be influential in determining whether the experience of raising a grandchild results in positive or negative transformation for grandparents. However, as discussed later in the chapter, I conjecture that the intrapersonal antecedents of cognitive appraisals and coping are the primary processes through which some grandparents adapt to raising a grandchild while others stagnate or deteriorate. In this sense, cognitive appraisals and coping may moderate the impact of the other antecedents on indicators of grandparent adjustment such as physical and mental health.

Intrapersonal Antecedents

Cognitive appraisal and coping. In Lazarus and Folkman's (1984) conceptualization of stress and coping, stress develops when the demands from individuals' environments exceed their resources and threaten their well-being. Cognitive appraisals and coping are processes that mediate the impact of stress on individual outcomes (Lazarus & Folkman, 1984). In terms of cognitive appraisals, primary appraisals represent whether an individual interprets a stressor as being irrelevant, benign-positive, or stressful. Individuals can also perceive stressful events as a challenge, a threat, or a harm/loss. Secondary appraisals exist alongside primary appraisals and constitute an individual's assessment of the resources that are available to cope with the stressor(s). As an associated process, coping is the cognitive and behavioral means by which an individual responds to a stressful event (Lazarus & Folkman, 1984). Thus, coping is a dynamic process that intersects with cognitive appraisals to eliminate or modify the problem creating distress and to regulate emotional distress and maintain emotional equilibrium (Lazarus & Folkman, 1984).

The quality of grandparents' cognitive appraisals is likely to be significant in determining whether raising a grandchild positively or negatively changes them. That is, grandparents who appraise their situation as benign-positive may be more likely to respond positively to the changes and demands associated with caring for their grandchildren. In contrast, grandparents who appraise their situation as a threat to their well-being or a loss (e.g., a loss of their freedom or the loss of their traditional grandparent role) may be at increased risk for negative consequences such as poor physical health, depression, or anxiety. Unfortunately, given that grandparents report a multitude of stressors and difficult lifestyle and role changes, it appears that many grandparents have a tendency toward negative appraisals.

Grandparents' approaches to coping are also likely to shape how they experience changes associated with raising a grandchild. For example, task coping strategies such as confronting a problem, using self-control, and accepting responsibility have been associated with reduced grandparent stress and parental distress (Ross & Aday, 2006). In contrast, analyses of some of my recent data reveal that high levels of emotion coping have been linked to poor grandparent mental and physical health. Although much more research on grandparent coping is needed, like cognitive appraisals, how grandparents cope with the demands of raising a grandchild may be a powerful determinant of whether their experience results in a positive or negative transformation.

Psychological ambivalence. Psychological ambivalence, which is most acute during status and life course transitions, is a subjective experience that emphasizes contradictory cognitions, emotions, and motivations directed toward another person, such as a parent or caregiver (Lüscher & Pillemer, 1998). Individuals experience these contradictory thoughts and feelings simultaneously and their ambivalence stems from power imbalances, conflicting norms or role expectations, autonomy versus dependence needs, and co-existing family conflict and solidarity. Although ambivalence can never be permanently resolved, interaction patterns within families represent "the expression of ambivalences" and "efforts to manage and negotiate these fundamental ambivalences" (Lüscher & Pillemer, p. 414). When linked with grandparents' appraisals and coping strategies, these efforts can result in family harmony or conflict.

Grandparents raising grandchildren are particularly likely to experience ambivalence. Letiecq, Bailey, and Dahlen (2008) note that ambivalence can result from grandparents' desire to assist their grandchildren and adult children while preserving their own retirement plans and lifestyles. Ambivalence can also stem from a desire to be a traditional grandparent, yet being in the position of parent. Similarly, ambivalence can explain why some grandparents describe parenting their grandchildren as a satisfying *second chance* (Hayslip & Kaminski, 2005) while also reporting compromised physical health (Minkler & Fuller-Thomson, 1999), depression (Minkler et al., 1997), and poor role meaning and role satisfaction (Hayslip et al., 1998).

How grandparents manage their ambivalences is likely to be central in determining whether they are positively or negatively transformed because of raising a grandchild. Although all grandparents may experience some ambivalence, those who experience high levels of ambivalence may find their situations to be more stressful or difficult to manage, putting them at increased risk for compromised physical or mental health. In addition, when grandparents are highly ambivalent, they may be more likely to interpret their situations negatively and find it difficult to employ effective coping strategies, placing them at additional risk. Finally, if grandparents' ambivalence is negatively influencing their interactions with friends and family, stress may accumulate and overwhelm grandparents' resources for coping with the demands and changes associated with raising a grandchild. As researchers have not examined these linkages empirically, the influence of ambivalence on grandparents' adjustment and responses to the changes stemming from raising a grandchild remains a fruitful area for investigation.

Role timing and conflict. Grandparents raising grandchildren are parenting at a time in their lives when most of their peers are not. Due to the inability to complete tasks traditionally associated with middle or later adulthood, fulfilling an *off time* role has been associated with feelings of psychological distress and loss (Landry-Meyer & Newman, 2004). Because grandparents occupy both the roles of grandparent and primary caregiver with their grandchildren (Hayslip et al., 1998), they may also experience role conflict and struggle to reconcile their desire to be indulgent grandparents with their perception that their grandchildren need firm parenting (Landry-Meyer & Newman, 2004).

Although empirical studies have not made a clear association between role timing, role conflict, and grandparent outcomes, it makes theoretical sense that these concepts would have a powerful influence on how raising a grandchild changes grandparents. For example, grandparents who are *off time* (e.g., grandparents who are older, who have not parented for an extended period, or who have already spent some time in a retirement lifestyle) may be overwhelmed by the demands of caregiving and the changes in their day-to-day lives, resulting in an increased risk for negative outcomes. Similarly, grandparents who had functioned as traditional grandparents for some time before transitioning to the role of primary caregiver may experience amplified role conflict. In contrast, grandparents who were very involved with their grandchildren prior to assuming caregiving responsibilities or grandparents who have never really left the parenting role may experience few changes associated with raising a grandchild. The nature of grandparents' cognitive appraisals (i.e., positive versus negative) and the intensity of their ambivalence may further amplify or suppress feelings of role conflict. Regardless, it appears that grandparents who have difficulty reconciling conflicting roles are the ones most at risk for being negatively transformed by the experience of raising a grandchild.

Interpersonal Antecedents

Grandchild factors and parenting. Regardless of their previous degree of involvement, transitioning from the role of grandparent to parent represents a significant change in terms of grandparents' lifestyles, commitments, and resources. Because of these changes, the demands associated with parenting are likely to be central in determining whether grandparents experience positive or negative outcomes. In fact, there is mounting evidence that parenting demands and characteristics of the grandchild intersect to create stress that eventually results in negative physical and psychological consequences for grandparents.

Due to their histories of abuse and neglect, children raised by grandparents often experience physical, emotional, and behavioral problems (Hayslip et al., 1998). These difficulties, which may manifest themselves in terms of hyperactivity, defiance, distrust, or an inability to form emotional bonds, can make parenting extremely challenging. Grandparents, particularly those who have not parented for some time, may find it difficult to respond effectively to their grandchildren's unique needs and behavioral problems. Grandparents may experience additional parenting stress when their expectations related to discipline or child development do not align with current cultural conceptions of parenting. Over time, the accumulation of stress associated with parenting a difficult grandchild may result in compromised grandparent well-being. In fact, raising a grandchild with significant emotional, physical, or behavioral problems has been associated with pychological distress, depression, and poor role satisfaction and role meaning (Hayslip et al., 1998).

Even if grandchildren do not have behavioral or health problems, parenting is a demanding activity that requires a high degree of emotional and physical involvement. For older grandparents and grandparents who have not parented for an extended period, the daily demands and lifestyle changes associated with parenting may be exhausting and overwhelming. Furthermore, since ideas about appropriate parenting behavior evolve with time, grandparents may find that their previous parenting strategies are no longer effective or considered appropriate by the professionals with whom they come into contact. This can create additional stress, as human service professionals may ask grandparents to revisit their parenting skills, despite the fact that some grandparents see themselves as wiser and better parents the second time around (Dolbin-MacNab, 2006). Additionally, the environment in which grandparents are raising their grandchildren may be a source of stress; grandparents often worry about how to manage the negative influence of peers and society (e.g., drugs, violence, and sex) on their grandchildren. Similarly, single grandmothers may face the added stress of providing male role models for their grandchildren and managing the load of parenting on their own. Although not all grandparents find their parenting responsibilities to be stressful (Dolbin-MacNab, 2006), those that do may be particularly at risk for developing physical and mental health problems, especially if their stress exceeds their coping resources and they are not engaging in adequate self-care.

Extended family system dynamics. When a grandparent becomes a surrogate parent for a grandchild, relationships within the entire family system are changed. For instance, the grandparent and the grandchild's parent may find their relationship strained or permanently damaged because of the circumstances that brought the grandchild into the grandparent's care. Grandparents must balance maintaining a relationship with their adult child while still protecting the grandchild from further disruption or harm. Having to strike this balance or coming to the realization that one's child is not capable of being an effective parent can be particularly devastating and guilt-inducing for grandparents. Furthermore, if grandparents choose to maintain a relationship with their adult child, in many cases, they must cope with manipulation, deceit, and broken promises. Grandparents may also find themselves caught in the middle of the relationship between the adult child and the grandchild. In fact, a major source of stress reported by grandparents is handling their grandchildren's hurt and disappointment in relation to their parents. Managing this relationship can escalate grandparents' ambivalent feelings and may erode their sense of well-being.

Other family dynamics could have a positive or negative influence on grandparents' lifestyles and personal adjustment. For instance, grandparents' relationships with their other adult children could be a source of support or tension. Some adult children may provide emotional and instrumental support to the grandparent, for the purpose of assisting the grandparent in adjusting to the demands and lifestyle changes associated with raising a grandchild. However, other adult children may resent the grandparent for investing so much energy into one portion of the family or blame their sibling for burdening the grandparent. These feelings of resentment may result in family conflict, cut-offs, or relational distance.

When grandparents experience burden because of their parenting responsibilities, strained financial resources, and feelings of ambivalence or role conflict, the added stress of family conflict may overwhelm their ability to cope and negatively influence their physical and mental health. Family systems theory, which postulates that families are composed of interdependent individuals and subsystems that form patterns of interaction in order to maintain equilibrium in the larger family system (Cox & Paley, 2003), helps to further explain this potential linkage. When confronted with normative or non-normative events such as a grandparent raising a grandchild, families adapt and reorganize to create new patterns of interaction and restore equilibrium (Cox & Paley, 2003). When individuals and families are not able to restore equilibrium or reorganize around problematic patterns of interaction, systemic or individual pathology can develop. Some of the relational changes that occur when a grandparent raises a grandchild may exceed a family's ability to adapt and regaining a sense of normalcy or equilibrium may be difficult. When this occurs, the family will not only have difficultly functioning effectively, but the grandparent may be at increased risk for being negatively impacted by raising a grandchild.

Social support. When examining the question of why some grandparents respond positively to raising a grandchild while others respond negatively, researchers and practitioners frequently name social support as an explanatory factor or antecedent. Higher levels of social support may buffer grandparents from negative consequences such as poor physical health, anxiety, and depression. Social support for grandparents raising grandchildren includes the availability of emotional or instrumental support from friends, family members, and other individuals, as well as grandparents' perceptions of the size and availability of their social support networks.

Generally, social support appears to be protective for custodial grandparents. Adequate social support reduces the negative impact of stressors such as grandchild health difficulties, grandchild behavior problems, and parenting hassles on grandparents' physical and mental health, as well as their life satisfaction (Gerard, Landry-Meyer, & Roe, 2006). Unfortunately, many grandparents become isolated from and lose the support of their peers because of the changes associated with raising a grandchild (e.g., increased childcare responsibilities, limited time and energy, and scarce financial resources). These grandparents, who may not have developed alternative social connections to rely on for assistance, may find themselves and their resources becoming overwhelmed—placing them at particular risk for negative outcomes.

Sociodemographic Antecedents

It is beyond the scope of this chapter to review every demographic factor that might influence the transformation of custodial grandparents. However, a number of grandparents' social identities may be particularly relevant to whether the changes they experience are positive or negative. As suggested by the notion of intersectionality (Collins, 2000), these social identities can be described as being interdependent, in that vulnerability or oppression associated with one characteristic (e.g., class) may be tied to another (e.g., race or ethnicity).

Race and ethnicity. Although grandparents raising grandchildren exist in all racial groups, African-Americans are more likely than their Latino or White counterparts to be raising their grandchildren (Simmons & Dye, 2003). Differences in prevalence may be due to variations in cultural traditions regarding family. For example, because of strong traditions of shared parenting and extended families, some scholars have described African-American grandmothers as "guardians of the generations" (Goodman & Silverstein, 2006, p. 1607). Similarly, a sense of familism has been associated with Latino grandparents' willingness to raise their grandchildren, especially during times of crisis and migration (Goodman & Silverstein, 2006). In contrast, white grandparents often have relationships with their grandchildren that do not involve significant childcare or being a disciplinarian or authority figure (Goodman & Silverstein, 2006). As such, assuming parenting responsibilities is not a normative part of many white grandparents' experiences.

Although some researchers use cultural traditions to explain why racial minority grandparents raising grandchildren should experience fewer negative outcomes, empirical data do not support this linkage. In fact, data suggest that African-American grandparents raising grandchildren experience higher rates of depression than their noncaregiving African-American peers, while custodial Latino grandparents report lower well-being than their coparenting Latino peers (Goodman & Silverstein, 2006). That said, in racially diverse samples, white grandparents raising grandchildren still display the highest levels of burden and negative mood. Thus, although cultural traditions may predispose certain grandparents to a more positive or negative perspective, they are likely to be insufficient in buffering grandparents from the stressors and demands associated with raising a grandchild. Additionally, cultural norms may be shifting or oversimplified in that grandparents who are willing to be involved with their grandchildren and believe in the importance of familism may not necessarily be as enthusiastic about becoming solely responsible for their grandchildren's daily care.

Financial resources. Because many custodial grandparents are on fixed or limited incomes, the added expense of raising a grandchild can have a dramatic impact on grandparents' financial standing. Estimates suggest that approximately 20 percent of grandparents raising grandchildren are living in poverty (Simmons & Dye, 2003). However, many more may have difficulty affording housing, food, health care, and other necessities. Even if grandparents can cover the costs of daily living, extras such as leisure activities may be beyond their reach.

Although the link between having adequate financial resources and how raising a grandchild transforms grandparents has not been investigated in depth, grandparents often name financial concerns as one of their biggest sources of stress. If grandparents are experiencing high levels of stress related to financial difficulties, it follows that prolonged or acute financial strain could result in grandparents experiencing elevated levels of anxiety and depression. Furthermore, if grandparents must make difficult choices about where to spend their financial resources, it is possible that some would put the needs of their grandchildren ahead of their own needs for self-care, mental health treatment, or preventative health care. Over time, this could result in those grandparents who are most financially stressed developing negative outcomes because of assuming responsibility for the care of a grandchild.

Gender. The vast majority of grandparents raising grandchildren are female (Simmons & Dye, 2003). The predominance of women as surrogate parents for their grandchildren is not surprising given gender differences in mortality rates and cultural expectations about women as caregivers and parents. These cultural expectations may result in grandmothers feeling obligated to assume responsibility for their grandchildren, even if it is not in their best interest or becomes detrimental to their physical and mental health. Moreover, gender may intersect with other social identities, such as race, class, and marital status, to further influence grandmothers' overall level of risk and resilience (Collins, 2000).

Because the emphasis in the literature has been on grandmothers, knowledge about changes experienced by grandfathers raising grandchildren remains limited (Kolomer & McCallion, 2005). However, emerging research suggests that they experience a loss of freedom and concerns about health problems. Grandfathers also need to adjust to parenting responsibilities and may feel a sense of regret related to "losing the opportunity to spoil their grandchildren like other grandparents" (Kolomer & McCallion, 2005, p. 290). It seems probable that grandfathers' experiences result, in part, from conflict between the roles of parent and grandparent as well as ambivalence about raising a grandchild at a time in their lives when they should be retired or indulging their grandchildren.

Grandfathers' experiences may also reflect shifting cultural conceptions of fatherhood. For example, some grandfathers may have been relatively uninvolved or distant with their own children. Although they may desire to be more involved with their grandchildren, some of these grandfathers may lack the knowledge, skills, and confidence to take a more active parenting role. Whatever the reason, it is notable that grandfathers do not report clinically significant levels of depression resulting from raising grandchildren (Kolomer & McCallion, 2005). This could reflect cultural conceptions about acceptable forms of male emotional expression. It could also be due, in part, to the fact that most custodial grandfathers are married and can share the responsibilities and strain of caregiving with their highly involved female spouses.

Age-related health issues. While there is wide variation in the age of grandparents raising grandchildren, older grandparents may be more likely to experience negative transformation. For example, the physical and emotional demands of parenting may result in older grandparents overexerting themselves, engaging in less preventive care, and neglecting protective health behaviors. Together, these behaviors may result in older grandparents exacerbating existing health problems, developing new health problems, and failing to obtain treatment. Similarly, limitations in activities of daily living, as well as acute and chronic health problems, may compromise older grandparents' sense of competence and ability to cope with the demands of caregiving. When this occurs, grandparents may display physical or mental health difficulties.

FROM ANTECEDENTS TO CONSEQUENCES: CHANGE PROCESSES

Although the previous discussion demonstrates how multiple contexts can influence how grandparents respond to the changes that accompany raising a grandchild, what is needed is an explanation of *how* it is that these specific antecedents result in a given consequence or trajectory of change. To this end, this portion of the chapter explores the *Accumulation of Risk Model* (Garbarino, 1992) and the *Double ABCX Model of Adjustment and Adaptation* (McCubbin & Patterson, 1983) as potential processes or mechanisms of change.

Accumulation of Risk

The accumulation of risk model proposes that when risk factors accumulate, without compensatory protective factors, pathology (or negative consequences) will develop (Garbarino, 1992). For custodial grandparents, risk factors may accumulate in two ways. First, due to changes associated with raising a grandchild, grandparents may add new risk factors to their context. For example, the strain of a change in financial status or the addition of parenting stress may overwhelm a grandparents' already fragile existence and result in negative outcomes. Second, risk can accumulate when existing stressful antecedents of change increase in severity or duration. An illustration of this process would be the grandmother whose existing diabetes becomes out-of-control when the demands of parenting interfere with her blood sugar monitoring and preventive health care. Regardless of how grandparents' risk accumulates, it is the balance (or imbalance) of risk versus protective factors that is likely to be central in determining whether grandparents are positively or negatively changed by the experience of raising a grandchild. That is, grandparents with more stressful antecedents of change may be most at risk for poor physical or mental health consequences as well as stagnation or deterioration over time.

Double ABCX Model

Although the accumulation of risk model explains why some grandparents experience positive versus negative transformation because of raising a grandchild, it still does not address the *mechanism* by which a buildup of risk factors results in pathology. The Double ABCX model offers insight into one possible mechanism. According to the model, the impact of accumulating stressors (A) on an outcome (X) is influenced by adaptive resources and supports (B) and by the meaning or definition of the stressor (C) (McCubbin & Patterson, 1983). The model also includes a temporal component, in that any outcome (X) results from a circular process that is ongoing and informed by past responses to stressors (McCubbin & Patterson, 1983). Outcomes resulting from this model of stress and coping range from bonadaptation to maladaptation (McCubbin & Patterson, 1983). Bonadaptation is associated with positive adjustment and occurs when there is balance between the accumulation of stressors and the individual's ability to respond to those stressors. In contrast, maladaptation is the physical or psychological dysfunction that results from an imbalance in demands and the ability to respond to those demands.

Based on the Double ABCX model, it appears that the intrapersonal antecedents of grandparent change may be pivotal in explaining why an accumulation of risk factors results in negative consequences such as poor physical or mental health. That is, perhaps the cognitive and affective processes of appraising a situation, coping with a stressor, resolving role conflict, and negotiating ambivalence moderate or mediate the influence of the other interpersonal and sociodemographic antecedents on grandparent outcomes. To illustrate, becoming primarily responsible for the care of her granddaughter, a grandmother may experience the accumulating stressors (A) of limited financial resources, parenting stress, conflict with her adult children, and increased cigarette use. To manage these stressors, the grandmother may access adaptive resources or supports (B) such as joining a support group or doing daily devotionals. If this grandmother appraises the situation (C) as a loss or is highly ambivalent, her efforts to address her accumulating stress may not be sufficient to prevent negative outcomes (X) such as depression or lung problems. In contrast, if this grandmother feels that she can manage being both grandparent and parent and views her changed circumstance as a challenge to overcome, then her strategies for coping (B) with accumulating stress (A) may prevent her from developing negative outcomes (X). Or, she could even experience bonadaptation in the form of a sense of personal satisfaction and increased vitality. Regardless of the exact outcome, the Double ABCX model suggests that understanding how grandparents are transformed because of raising a grandchild may be closely linked to how they interpret and cope with their situation, within the context of their interpersonal relationships, social locations, and past experiences.

IMPLICATIONS FOR PROFESSIONAL PRACTICE

This exploration of the antecedents, processes, and consequences of change associated with raising a grandchild has numerous practice implications. In the realm of intervention and prevention programming, practitioners must do more to acknowledge that grandparents will vary in terms of their ability to adapt successfully to the demands of raising a grandchild. Therefore, community-based programs must avoid a *one size fits all* approach and tailor their services based on grandparents' particular contexts and change trajectories. For example, grandparents who are adapting to raising a grandchild might benefit from enrichment activities, advanced instruction related to parenting, or opportunities to mentor struggling grandparents. In contrast, grandparents who are stagnating or deteriorating may need instrumental assistance, intensive parenting education, or training in effective coping and cognitive reappraisals. Grandparents may view programs that are not able to respond to variations in their trajectories (particularly those grandparents who are adapting reasonably well to their caregiving responsibilities) as too depressing or too problem-focused. If this occurs, higher functioning grandparents might avoid seeking services that could otherwise be beneficial to them.

Programs must also move beyond standard (or convenient) approaches to practice and explore new avenues for improving grandparent physical and mental health. For instance, a *one-stop shopping* approach would allow practitioners to address multiple antecedents of negative change while also overcoming common barriers to service utilization: lack of service awareness, difficulty managing multiple services, and service fatigue. Services provided as part of this approach could include low-cost medical care, affordable psychotherapy, tutoring for grandchildren, legal aid, parent education, and support groups. Those grandparents who are experiencing a significant number of risk factors might also benefit from intensive crisis intervention services and home-visiting programs. Regardless of the exact model of program delivery, in order to make a difference in grandparent outcomes, programs must address all of the domains within grandparents' contexts. Program staff and administrators must also work creatively to reach grandparents and engage them in their services.

In the realm of policy, grandparents could benefit from policies that reward the contributions they are making to society by keeping children out of an already burdened foster care system. For example, as having a legal relationship to one's grandchild has been linked to grandparent role clarity and adjustment (Landry-Meyer & Newman, 2004), barriers to grandparents gaining legal custody or guardianship could be removed. Similarly, larger foster parent payments and child-only TANF grants could partially ameliorate that stress associated with limited financial resources. Policies that are beneficial to all vulnerable families could also benefit grandparents. Some of these include affordable prescription medicine, health care, and high-quality childcare. With the support of these and other policies, grandparents may experience less stress, which would decrease the odds that they would experience negative transformation because of raising a grandchild.

Finally, if communities want to prevent negative transformation among grandparents raising grandchildren, they must shift their perceptions and expand their capacity. Society often sees grandparents raising grandchildren as an indication of family decline and failure. Communities must challenge these perceptions and replace them with the notion that, regardless of their degree of success, grandparents are providing an invaluable service to society and their families. Once perceptions shift, especially among those in power, communities can then work toward building their capacity to respond to the needs of grandparents and their families. Community capacity building would need to occur on all levels within the community. Of particular importance is including grandparents in the process of building capacity. Grandparents should be empowered to advocate for themselves by participating in social action and other grassroots efforts. It is only when communities and grandparents work in concert that the negative consequences associated with raising a grandchild can be minimized.

REFERENCES

Bronfenbrenner, U. (1979). *The ecology of human development: Experiments by nature and design.* Cambridge, MA: Harvard University Press.

Collins, P. H. (2000). *Black feminist thought: Knowledge, consciousness, and the politics of empowerment* (2nd ed.). New York: Routledge.

Cox, M., & Paley, B. (2003). Understanding families as systems. *Current Directions in Psychological Science, 12,* 193–196.

Dolbin-MacNab, M. L. (2006). Just like raising your own? Grandmothers' perceptions of parenting a second time around. *Family Relations, 55,* 564–575.

Dolbin-MacNab, M. L., & Keiley, M. K. (2006). A systemic examination of grandparents' emotional closeness with their custodial grandchildren. *Research in Human Development, 3,* 59–71.

Dolbin-MacNab, M. L., & Keiley, M. K. (2009). Navigating interdependence: How adolescents raised solely by grandparents experience their family relationships. *Family Relations, 58,* 162–175.

Garbarino, J. (1992). *Children and families in the social environment.* New York: Aldine De Gruyter.

Gerard, J. M., Landry-Meyer, L., & Roe, J. G. (2006). Grandparents raising grandchildren: The role of social support in coping with caregiving challenges. *International Journal of Aging and Human Development, 62*, 359–383.

Goodman, C. C., & Silverstein, M. (2006). Grandmothers raising grandchildren: Ethnic and racial differences in well-being among custodial and coparenting families. *Journal of Family Issues, 27*, 1605–1626.

Hayslip, B., & Kaminski, P. L. (2005). Grandparents raising their grandchildren. *Marriage and Family Review, 37*, 147–169.

Hayslip, B., Shore, R. J., Henderson, C. E., & Lambert, P. L. (1998). Custodial grandparenting and the impact of grandchildren with problems on role satisfaction and role meaning. *Journal of Gerontology: Social Sciences, 53B*, S164–S173.

Hughes, M. E., Waite, L. J., LaPierre, T. A., & Luo, Y. (2007). All in the family: The impact of caring for grandchildren on grandparents' health. *Journal of Gerontology: Social Sciences, 62B*, S108–S119.

Kolomer, S. R., & McCallion, P. (2005). Depression and caregiver mastery in grandfathers caring for their grandchildren. *International Journal of Aging and Human Development, 60*, 283–294.

Landry-Meyer, L., & Newman, B. M. (2004). An exploration of the grandparent caregiver role. *Journal of Family Issues, 25*, 1005–1025.

Lazarus, R. R., & Folkman, S. (1984). *Stress, appraisal, and coping*. New York: Springer.

Letiecq, B. L., Bailey, S. J., & Dahlen, P. (2008). Ambivalence and coping among custodial grandparents. In B. Hayslip & P. Kaminski (Eds.), *Parenting the custodial grandchild* (pp. 3–15). New York: Springer.

Lüscher, K., & Pillemer, K. (1998). Intergenerational ambivalence: A new approach to the study of parent-child relations in later life. *Journal of Marriage and the Family, 60*, 413–425.

McCubbin, H. I., & Patterson, J. M. (1983). The family stress process: The double ABCX model of adjustment and adaptation. *Marriage and Family Review, 6*, 7–37.

Minkler, M., & Fuller-Thomson, E. (1999). The health of grandparents raising grandchildren: Results of a national study. *American Journal of Public Health, 89*, 1384–1389.

Minkler, M., Fuller-Thomson, E., Miller, D., & Driver, D. (1997). Depression in grandparents raising grandchildren: Results of a national longitudinal study. *Archives of Family Medicine, 6*, 445–452.

Ross, M. E. T., & Aday, L. (2006). Stress and coping in African-American grandparents who are raising their grandchildren. *Journal of Family Issues, 27*, 912–932.

Simmons, T., & Dye, J. L. (2003). *Grandparents living with grandchildren: 2000*. Retrieved April 20, 2006, from http://www.census.gov/prod/2003pubs/C2kbr-31.pdf

CHAPTER 13

Exploring Processes of Family Stress and Adaptation: An Expanded Model

Angela J. Huebner

I was having these panic attacks, but then I didn't know what it was. My heart just racing and palpitating constantly all the time, and I couldn't sit still, I couldn't sleep, I couldn't eat, I couldn't do anything, so I'm running to the doctor, hospital thinking I'm having a heart attack, "Well, Ms. X, you're fine, everything is fine, dadadadada." But in my mind everything wasn't fine.

—GWOT, National Guard wife after fifteen month separation; Huebner 2006

The worst time is when the phone rings because you don't know who is calling. They could be calling, telling you that he got shot or something.

—GWOT, thirteen-year-old son of Army Soldier; Huebner, Mancini, Wilcox, Glass, & Glass, 2007

Deployment of a family member to an active war zone is inherently fraught with stress as the chance for injury or death is real. For this reason, military deployments provide a useful real-life laboratory within which to explore the processes of transformation that families undergo as they experience stressful, unpredictable, potentially life-threatening situations, and the processes or mechanisms associated with both positive and negative adaptation. It is important for researchers and interventionists to understand how this stress affects families and to explore what differentiates those families that cope well from those that do not. Previous research suggests that the stressor itself, the available resources, and the meaning attributed to the stressor are predictive of overall adaptation (McCubbin,

Thompson, & McCubbin, 1996). Little is known however, about *how* these factors coalesce to influence adaptation—the process through which they interact. Furthermore, even less is known about how to intervene *within the process* when adaptation goes awry.

This chapter begins with a description of the context of interest: military deployment. I then introduce concepts borrowed from other theoretical traditions and practices as potential explanations for understanding and influencing transformation and change in adaptation among families. The resulting synthesized model incorporates specific ideas about how transformation and change occur in families under stress. The chapter ends with suggestions about how this model can inform interventions for families under stress.

MILITARY DEPLOYMENT

There are approximately 200,000 United States troops deployed to active theaters of war in Iraq and Afghanistan (Reuters, 2007; Whitlock, 2008). Over the course of the seven-year Global War on Terrorism (GWOT), about 1.5 million American service members have spent time serving in Iraq; most have completed multiple deployments—20,000 having been deployed *five or more times* (Olson, 2007). Recent figures issued by the Department of Defense (2009) state that nearly 5,000 United States (U.S.) service members have died in theater.

About 40 percent of U.S. service members are married with children (Office of the Deputy Under Secretary of Defense, 2005). This translates into literally thousands of family members who have or who are experiencing the effects of military deployment. The term *military deployment* is usually discussed as a cycle that includes pre-deployment (the service member is getting ready to deploy—often includes time away from home in training), deployment (the service member is actually engaged in theater), reunion (the service member returns home), and redeployment (when the cycle begins again). Military deployments in the current GWOT have lacted between twelve-eighteen months. This duration, coupled with the practice of multiple deployments means that military families are constantly experiencing or anticipating separation from a loved one. Additionally, it is important to note that only about one-third of military families actually reside on a military installation (Booth et al.,

2007). In other words, most of the military families experiencing deployment are living in civilian communities, potentially in neighborhoods where they are the only ones experiencing such separation, thus limiting opportunities for support.

Existing research on the effects of military deployment substantiates the notion that such separations can be stressful for families. Negative consequences, as reported by soldiers, include time away from family, missing important events, and deterioration in marital relationships (McLeland & Sutton, 2005; Newby et al., 2005). Spouses of deployed service members report feeling poorly prepared for the separation; others report poor coping during the separation (Caliber Associates, 2003; Orthner & Rose, 2006). A recent study revealed that rates of child maltreatment in military families increase during pre-deployment and return from military deployment (Gibbs, Martin, Kupper, & Johnson, 2007). Finally, adolescents in the midst of parental deployment to an active war zone reported feelings of uncertainty and loss, role confusion, symptoms of depression, changes in daily routines, and increased relationship conflict (Huebner et al., 2007).

THEORETICAL FRAMEWORKS

The theoretical starting point for my exploration of the mechanisms of transformation and change among families experiencing military deployments is the *Double ABCX Model of Adjustment and Adaptation* (McCubbin & Patterson, 1983). This model is well-suited as a starting point for this task because it delineates the factors thought to be associated with adjustment. The model falls short however, in suggesting *how* these factors operate to influence change, both at the individual and family level. Throughout this chapter, I will suggest ways in which this could occur. Additionally, I will add thoughts about how to intervene if the resulting adaptation is less than optimal.

In the Double ABCX model, "A" refers to the stressor, "B" refers to existing resources, "C" refers to the perception of "A," and "X" refers to the crisis. The "double" title refers to the pile-up of stressors that can occur. As illustrated in figure 13.1, for my purpose, the observable stressor (A) is the deployment of a spouse or parent. The pileup of stressors (the "double" part of the model) can encompass multiple deployments or

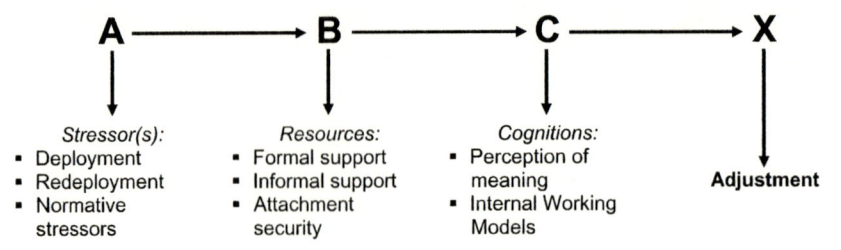

```
A ─────────► B ─────────► C ─────────► X
│            │            │            │
▼            ▼            ▼            ▼
Stressor(s):    Resources:       Cognitions:
• Deployment    • Formal support  • Perception of
• Redeployment  • Informal support  meaning      Adjustment
• Normative     • Attachment      • Internal Working
  stressors       security          Models
```

Figure 13.1. Expanded Double ABCX Model of Adjustment for Deployment

deployments in combination with other normative developmental stressors. It is important to note that normative stressors encompass a range of lifespan issues such as stage of marriage, developmental level of children, and aging parents. In the context of military deployment, I conceptualize the "B" or *resource* factor as formal and informal support systems. In an effort to delineate mechanisms of transformation, I am introducing the notion of attachment security as a specific type of resource, one that is indicative of how adaptation and change occur. Briefly, attachment security refers to the bond one has with significant others. This bond becomes activated (i.e., a potential source of support) when one perceives a threat (e.g., separation from a loved one). The "C" factor refers to the perceptions and cognitions that at-home parents and children have about their situations, including the deployment (A) itself as well as the available resources. Within the "C" factor of perceptions and cognitions, I am highlighting the concept of *internal working models*. It is my contention that internal working models are the mechanism largely responsible for determining how one perceives the stressful event and resources. Internal working models are hypothesized to be mental representations or schemas of self and others that form through early experience in relationships. They form the template for how the individual assumes the relationship or scenario will unfold, thus functioning to guide responses to various situations and relationships (Bretherton, 1985). Within the double ABCX model, I suggest that these internal working models influence how the stressor is perceived (as stressful or not), the perception of the availability of resources (e.g., attachment security), and thus one's willingness or ability to access them. In this model, "X" represents level of adaptation or adjustment to stressors. This can include indicators of family coping and overall wellness.

In summary, I propose the concepts of attachment security and internal working models as the mechanisms driving transformation and change—defined as adaptation or the "X" factor—in the double ABCX model of stress and coping. Attachment security represents a major source of support ("B"); internal working models influence one's perception ("C") of the actual availability and effectiveness of that support. A review of attachment theory is in order for a more comprehensive understanding of attachment security and internal working models.

ATTACHMENT, ATTACHMENT SECURITY, AND INTERNAL WORKING MODELS

One of the main assumptions of attachment theory is that human beings form close interpersonal relationships (attachment bonds) with others in an effort (consciously or unconsciously) to ensure their survival (Bowlby, 1969). Attachment bonds, as evidenced in the relationship between the caregiver and the individual, serve three main functions (Ainsworth, Blehar, Waters, & Wall, 1978). First, they keep the individual close to his or her caregiver. Second, they provide a sense of relationship security (secure base or resource) from which the individual can explore his or her world. Third, and of particular interest in the context of deployment separation, attachment bonds provide comfort in times of stress. Attachment patterns or styles range on a continuum from *secure* to *insecure* based on the way the individual copes with stress, separation, or loss in their intimate relationships (Ainsworth et al., 1978).

Early studies of infants lead to several conclusions about these attachment patterns (Ainsworth et al., 1978). For example, securely attached infants demonstrate little distress when the caregiver leaves, secure in the knowledge that he or she will return. Further, securely attached infants seek out their caregiver in times of stress or fear, secure in the knowledge that the caregivers will provide comfort. Insecure attachments tend to fall into one of two types: ambivalent or avoidant. Infants with ambivalent attachments become very distressed upon separation, due in part to the fact that they cannot consistently depend on their caregivers to return after separation nor to provide comfort in times of fear. Infants with avoidance attachments tend to avoid their caregivers, showing no preference for them over a stranger; they do not seek out the caregiver in times of stress, rather they avoid the caregiver. It is important to note that these attachment patterns are indicative of the type of interactions experienced between caregivers and infants at home. According to Ainsworth et al., caregivers who are emotionally expressive, and available to the infant's bids for attention tend to have infants with secure attachments. Caregivers who exhibited little sensitivity to their infants, ignoring bids for attention and then interfering inappropriately when attention is not being sought, are more likely to have infants with insecure attachment styles. Finally, those caregivers who stifle emotional expression and avoid or limit physical contact are more likely to have infants with avoidant attachment styles.

Similar attachment patterns and associated behaviors occur in adulthood (Simpson & Rholes, 1998). For example, a securely attached adult can easily become comfortable in a close relationship, experiencing it as a consistent place of support and comfort, especially in times of stress. The insecurely attached individual struggles in a close relationship, not experiencing it as a consistent place of support and comfort. Underlying these patterns are different types of internal working models. The securely attached individual believes that his or her needs can be met through close relationships, and that he or she matters and is worthy of support from significant others. Insecurely attached individuals desire close relationships and want their needs to be met but, because of prior experience, do not believe this can happen. This belief translates into the idea that close relationships are not worth the effort or are not to be trusted, thus not a source of support.

These patterns of attachment are of interest because there is a clear relationship between early attachment styles and adaptation and adjustment later in life. In early childhood, secure attachment is associated with more harmonious relations with parents, better social skills with peers in the pre-school years, higher levels of empathy, and greater self-esteem and self-confidence (Thompson, 1999). Among adolescents, insecure attachment is associated with internalized distress such as depression, anxiety, guilt, unhappiness, or suicidality; secure attachment has been associated with less emotional distress and significantly lower levels of engagement in aggressive and delinquent behaviors (Johnson & Whiffen, 2003). Among adults, secure attachments have been positively associated with relationship satisfaction (Johnson & Whiffen); attachment style is linked to differences in coping strategies (Mikulincer, Florian, & Weller, 1993) and perception of support (Collins & Feeney, 2004).

Although limited, empirical studies specifically exploring families in the context of war provide support for hypothesized links between attachment and adjustment within a family system. In one of the few studies that employed an attachment framework to review existing research on wartime separation, Vormbrock (1993) concludes that at-home spouses evidence similar distress responses as do children to separation from attachment figures. In their study of wives of deployed service members during Operation Desert Storm, Medway, Davis, Cafferty, Chappell, and O'Hearn (1995) find that wives with less attachment security felt greater distress after the deployment of their husbands; they also found a positive relationship between mothers' distress and children's problem behaviors. Findings from our 2005 study conducted with adolescents having a deployed parent in the current GWOT suggest that the non-deployed parent (i.e., the at-home spouse) has a pivotal influence on the adjustment of other family members, such that more positive parent adaptation leads to better child outcomes (Huebner & Mancini, 2005). Other studies conducted in the context of previous military conflicts also echo this finding (e.g., Jensen, Martin, & Watanabe, 1996; Medway et al., 1995). The reverse seems to be the case as well. A study of National Guard and Reserve spouses conducted during Operation Desert Shield/Storm concluded that problems children experienced because of the deployment negatively affected the at-home parent's well-being (Rosenberg, 1992).

According to Bowlby (1969), internal working models are the underlying mechanism through which manifestations of different attachment styles occur. Internal working models begin formation at birth. During the early years, the infant's brain is wired via interaction with others. Based on experiences with primary caretakers, the infant learns what to expect in various situations. For example, the infant may learn that when he or she cries, an adult appears to help ease the distress, thus reinforcing the idea that the child has agency in the environment, such that others respond positively and soothingly when he or she cries. In other words, this experience builds or reinforces the infant's internal working model of close relationships as a source of support. Alternatively, if the caregiver is not responsive, the infant learns that he or she has no effect on the environment, thus reinforcing the belief that action is futile. In other words, this experience builds the internal working model of close relationships as a source of no support. With repeated experience, these internal working models—mental representations or schemas of self and others—become the templates for figuring out how the world works, functioning to help individuals safely navigate their environments, including relationships with others (Bretherton, 1985). Internal working models do this by acting as filters dictating which aspects of an experience are given attention, which are ignored, how information is interpreted, and even what is remembered (Piertromonaco & Feldman Barrett, 2000). This input filtering effect of internal working models has received empirical support. For example, Collins and Feeney (2004) examine appraisals of available informal social support among individuals with various attachment styles. In a laboratory-induced stressful situation in which the type of social support given was *identical*, insecurely attached individuals perceived negative social support from their partner while secure individuals perceived support that was more positive.

It is important to note that theory and empirical research suggest that internal working models increase in specificity with age and relational experience, and are relationship specific such that different internal working models may operate in different relationship contexts (Collins & Read, 1994). With respect to the double ABCX model of family stress and coping, I propose that internal working models are the mechanisms most strongly influencing how stressful experiences are processed and interpreted and what behaviors result from this interpretation. For example, in the context of deployment, if a spouse has insecure attachment security, she may not perceive her spouse's attempts of support as positive, as he tries to comfort her about the deployment separation. This insecure attachment most likely developed from her early experiences of not receiving support as a child. With repeated experience and time, this translated into her belief that she is not worthy of comfort nor can she provide it. This belief (solidified in her internal working model about support relationships) may keep her from attending a family readiness group meeting of other spouses with deployed service members (e.g., "They can't help me"), thus inhibiting her ability to access available support that might actually be useful in her own adaptation to the deployment.

Attachment styles seem to be remarkably stable over the lifespan (e.g., Franley, 2002). Bowlby explains this continuity by suggesting that individuals master a variety of mechanisms, which serve to protect the integrity of the internal working model (Bretherton & Munholland,

1999). This makes sense given their function of helping the individual to filter information. If the mechanisms were not stable, they would not provide a function template. Examples of these mechanisms include defensive exclusion (e.g., disregarding inputs such as thoughts, feelings, or perceptions that might overwhelm or be inconsistent with the activated internal working model), diversion of attention (e.g., focusing away from one's own attachment needs), and misattribution (e.g., changing the input or story).

It is important to note however, that stability does not equate with fixed or unchangeable. Bowlby suggests that the stability of the attachment relationship depends a great deal on the stability of the caretaking environment, an idea that has received empirical support. For example, Waters, Hamilton, and Weinfield (2000) present evidence from three longitudinal studies suggesting a relationship between discontinuity in attachment security and the experience of negative life events. More specifically, they suggest that it is not just negative events per se that are disruptive—rather it is the experience of negative life events that alter the caregiver's ability to be responsive. Negative life events include loss of parent, parental divorce, life-threatening illness of a parent or child, parental psychiatric disorder, and physical or sexual abuse by a family member. As applied to the context of military families, these findings provide further support for the idea that attachment security is vulnerable during the stressful period of deployment.

MECHANISMS OF CHANGE

In sum, these findings point to an expanded process model of stress and coping. Previous applications of the double ABCX model have not explicitly investigated attachment security as a resource nor have they explored the role of internal working models in influencing cognition that may influence perception or use of resources. Given the empirically supported significant impact of attachment security on positive adaptation, this seems an appropriate addition to the model.

I propose that within the double ABCX model, the *process* of change or adaptation originates in interplay between the "B" and "C" factors. Recall that the "C" factor refers to how one perceives and makes meaning about the stressor event (A) and resources (B). Consistent with the evidence previously presented, it seems likely that internal working models are the actual mechanisms that dictate (via their filtering function) what enters into cognition, and the meaning that is attributed to the perception (e.g., "This deployment separation is scary and I can't cope." versus "This deployment separation is a challenge to be dealt with."). The "C" factor also dictates what the individual perceives as helpful resources (B) and, perhaps even more importantly, his or her ability to access those resources. By expanding the model in this way, I am not suggesting that resources outside of attachment security are unimportant; rather I am suggesting that attachment security and internal working models affect the individual's ability or willingness to access other resources that could aid in adaptation.

Although thus far I have discussed the process of adaptation occurring in the ABCX model at the individual level, it is important to note that the process of adaptation is occurring for all the family members in the system simultaneously. Family systems theory (Whitchurch & Constantine, 1993) provides a framework for exploring how different subsystems interact with each other in turn influencing adaptability and change to the whole system (e.g., spousal subsystem interacting with parent-child subsystem to influence adaptation). Figure 13.2 refers to the hypothesized relationship among the attachment subsystems and their link to family adaptation. Specifically, I theorize that attachment between the spouses is

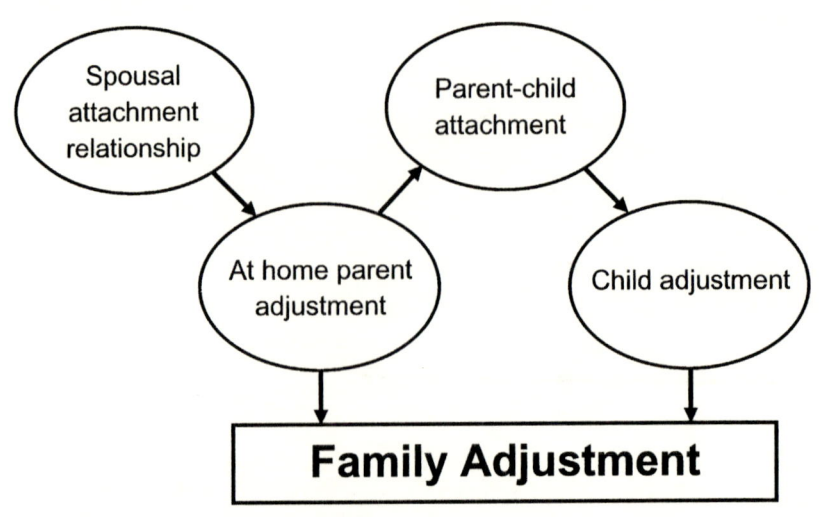

Figure 13.2. Model of Relationships among Attachments

a potential resource that will influence the at-home parent's adjustment—either positively or negatively. This adjustment will in turn influence the at-home parent's ability to maintain a secure attachment to the child. In turn, this parent-child attachment (considered a potential resource in the child's adjustment) relates to the child's overall adjustment. Conversely, child adjustment may also influence parent-child attachment. Thus, both at-home parent adjustment and child adjustment will contribute to overall family adjustment.

Preliminary data from a pilot study I conducted in Virginia with spouses of deployed service members supports this process model. Briefly, participants in this pilot study were five wives who were currently or had recently experienced their husband's deployment to an active war zone. All had school-age children. Interview questions focused on three areas: participants' relationship with their husband (spousal attachment), their relationship with their children (parent-child attachment), and overall adjustment (mother's and children's). Analyses revealed that those wives with secure spousal attachments evidenced better overall individual coping, more maternal sensitivity (an indicator of secure parent-child attachment), and better child adjustment compared to those wives with insecure spousal attachments (Huebner & Powell, 2007).

APPLICATION OF THE EXPANDED DOUBLE ABCX MODEL OF ADAPTATION

The presented process model provides a lens on the processes related to adaptation among families in stressful conditions. Knowing *how* the process works is the first step in helping families achieve optimal adaption. Knowing *how to intervene in the process* is equally important in cases in which adaptation is not going well. To this end, this chapter concludes with a discussion of the implications of this model for influencing family adaption in the context of military deployment: interventions at the individual level and those at the community level.

First, if internal working models are indeed pivotal in family adaptation, interventions designed to change ineffective internal working models seem in order. If ineffective internal working models (i.e., those models contributing to suboptimal adaptation) are changed (e.g., to promote security of attachment), then one's perception of resources and one's ability to access resources would change. Additionally, changes in internal working models are hypothesized to lead to changes in one's repertoire of coping skills, thus leading to changes in adaptation and adjustment. A variety of clinical techniques have been used to access and transform internal working models, most falling within the realm of cognitive behavioral therapy.

Mindfulness is a type of cognitive behavioral therapy, but one with a specific focus. Therapists have incorporated mindfulness practice into a variety of clinical techniques designed to decrease negative adaptation including depression, anxiety, eating disorders, and life dissatisfaction (for a review see Melbourne Academic Mindfulness Interest Group, 2006). Mindfulness is a way of relating to our experiences with deep attention and awareness. The concept of attention is particularly relevant when considered in the context of potential transformation of internal working models. Recall that according to attachment theory, internal working models are "protected" from change via several defensive mechanisms, including defensive exclusion, diversion of attention, and misattribution. The act of awareness in mindfulness can bring these defenses to consciousness. Mindfulness practices encourage a neutral, non-judgmental, or curious stance toward the defenses; such a stance helps to keep the defense process at the conscious level—defensive or judgmental stances seem to function to push the defenses back to the unconscious level (Brach, 2004). This conscious attention and curiosity then serve to diffuse the defenses, allowing access to the particular internal working model of interest. The idea is that if the attachment system is not secure, mindfulness could precipitate earned attachment security (i.e., changing the attachment system from insecure to secure) via changes in the internal working model related to that particular attachment relationship.

As applied to the context of family adjustment during military deployment, this model suggests that changes in the internal working model (via therapy) about one's attachment security could lead to changes in cognitive appraisals about the situation. For example, a wife with an insecure attachment style may be more likely to interpret lack of communication from her deployed husband as rejection (e.g., "My husband hasn't called me because he doesn't really love me. If he did, he would know how difficult this is for me and be in better contact. I can't count on him. Maybe I should just leave him."). This sense of distress or preoccupation with the marital relationship may inhibit her ability to demonstrate maternal sensitivity to her child in turn fostering an insecure attachment system in the child. Unchecked, this pattern has the potential to set into motion the host of negative outcomes related to insecure attachment outlined earlier. If attachment security can be altered (via changes in this particular internal working model about the spousal relationship), then the cognitive appraisal or meaning about the lack of communication could change (e.g., "My husband hasn't called but I'm sure there is a good reason. Maybe I should check with other wives in his unit to see if they have heard from their husbands. Maybe it's just an issue of access to the phone. I'm sure he'll call as soon as he is able."). This approach could potentially alleviate her preoccupation with the marital relationship, thus allowing her to be more intentional about fostering a secure attachment with her child. Together this familial attachment system sets the stage for positive adaptation to the stress of the military deployment.

Second, if accessed, community level interventions or programs could also be a helpful source of support. Many such programs are already in existence throughout the military. Examples include marriage enrichment programs, psycho-educational and informational classes about the deployment cycle, family readiness groups that provide support for spouses, and youth activity programs designed to enhance youth's coping skills and social support networks. It is important to note that while such programs do exist for military families, they are not mandated nor are they implemented consistently across locations. Anecdotal evidence suggests wide variation in how frequently families access such programs. Resources are only resources if they are utilized.

I propose that that expanded double ABCX model provides one explanation for why families do not access programs as well as ways to increase utilization. According to this model, attachment security status and internal working models may account for family members' inability to perceive the resources as actual resources that may be helpful for them. For this reason, it is not sufficient for service providers to only offer resources and programs and expect families to use them. Instead, service providers must be intentional about getting family members to attend. This intentionality could include personal invitations for participation and removal of obstacles for attendance (e.g., providing meals, childcare, transportation), all with an intent of forming personal relationships (attachments), which make it *safe* for family members to take in new information. In other words, service providers need to be aware that information about their services is being filtered and that one way of circumventing the filter is through the formation of personal relationships that help to increase family members' earned attachment security (i.e. shifting their attachment from insecure to secure) thus changing family members' perception and ability to actually utilize the support programs that are already there. In the end, utilization of support will lead to better family outcomes.

In summary, I have proposed an expanded version of the ABCX model of family adaptation—one that incorporates processes thought to mediate family adaptation. I suggest that this process occurs in the context of multiple attachment relationships—the spousal relationship and the parent-child relationship. Individuals' internal working model influences their perception of the stressor event and resources. Such influence is important given that it determines what characteristics of the situation garner attention and which are ignored. In short, it influences whether one responds to the stressor with a spirit of curiosity and challenge or in the spirit of hopelessness and defeat. This response is important because it determines the quality of adaptation. In the context of military families, clinicians and service providers should be intentional about their exploration of attachment systems within such families so that secure attachments can be fostered at multiple levels (individual, couple, parent-child), thus increasing the likelihood of positive adaptation or coping.

REFERENCES

Ainsworth, M., Blehar, M., Waters, E., & Wall, S. (1978). *Patterns of attachment: A psychological study of the strange situation.* New York: Wiley.

Booth, B., Segal, M., Bell, D., Martin, J., Ender, M., Rohall, D., & Nelson, J. (2007). What we know about Army families: 2007 update. *Prepared for the Family and Morale, Welfare and Recreation Command.* Fairfax, VA: Caliber Associates.

Bowlby, J. (1969). *Attachment and loss: Volume 1. Attachment.* New York: Basic Books.

Brach, T. (2004). Radical acceptance: *Embracing your life with the heart of a Buddha.* New York: Bantam Books.

Bretherton, I. (1985). Attachment theory: Retrospect and prospect. *Monographs of the Society for Research on Child Development, 50,* 3–35.

Bretherton, I., & Munholland, K. (1999). Internal working models and attachment relationships: A construct revisited. In J. Cassidy & P. Shaver (Eds.), *Handbook of attachment: Theory, research, and clinical applications* (pp. 89–114). New York: Guilford.

Caliber Associates. (2003). *Survey of spouses of activated National Guard and Reserve component members*. Fairfax, VA: Author.

Collins, N., & Feeney, B. (2004). Working models of attachment shape perceptions of social support: Evidence from experimental and observational studies. *Journal of Personality and Social Psychology, 87*, 363–383.

Collins, N., & Read, S. (1994). Cognitive representations of attachment: The structure and function of working models. In K. Bartholomew & D. Perlman (Eds.), *Advances in personal relationships: Vol. 5. Attachment processes in adulthood* (pp. 53–90). London: Jessica Kingsley.

Department of Defense. (2009). *Defenselink Casualty Report*. Retrieved March 10, 2009, from http://www.defenselink.mil/news/casualty.pdf

Franley, C. R. (2002). Attachment stability from infancy to adulthood: Meta-analysis and dynamic modeling of developmental mechanisms. *Personality and Social Psychology Review, 6*, 123–151.

Huebner, A. (2006). [Examining the effects of military deployment on at-home parent and child adjustment]. Unpublished raw data.

Huebner, A., & Mancini, J. (2005). *Adjustments among adolescents in military families when a parent is deployed*. Final report to the Military Family Research Institute and Department of Defense Quality of Life Office. Department of Human Development, Virginia Polytechnic Institute and State University. Retrieved on August 12, 2008, from http://www.unirel.vt.edu/news/Huebner_Mancini_teens_study.pdf

Huebner, A., Mancini, J., Wilcox, R., Grass, S., & Grass, G. (2007). Parental deployment and youth in military families: Exploring uncertainty and ambiguous loss. *Family Relations, 56*, 111–121.

Huebner, A., & Powell, C. (2007, November). *Exploring attachment and family adjustment during deployment: "When momma ain't happy, ain't nobody happy."* Poster presented at the 69th Annual Conference of National Council on Family Relations, Pittsburgh, PA.

Jensen, P. S., Martin, D., & Watanabe, H. (1996). Children's response to separation during Operation Desert Storm. *Journal of the American Academy of Child and Adolescent Psychiatry, 35*, 433–441.

Johnson, S., & Whiffen, V. (2003). *Attachment processes in couple and family therapy*. New York: Guilford.

McCubbin, H., & Patterson, J. (1983). The family stress process: The double ABCX model of adjustment and adaptation. In H. I, McCubbin, M. B. Sussman, & J. M. Patterson (Eds.), *Social stress and the family: Advances and developments in family stress research and theory* (pp. 7–37). New York: The Haworth Press.

McCubbin, H., Thompson, A. I., & McCubbin, M. A. (1996). *Family assessment: Resiliency, coping and adaptation*. Madison: University of Wisconsin Press.

McLeland, K., & Sutton, G. (2005). Military service, marital status, and men's relationship satisfaction. *Individual Differences Research, 3*, 177–182.

Medway, F. J., Davis, K. E., Cafferty, T. P., Chappell, K. D., & O'Hearn, R. E. (1995). Family disruption and adult attachment correlates of spouse and child reactions to separation and reunion due to Operation Desert Storm. *Journal of Social and Clinical Psychology, 14*, 97–118.

Melbourne Academic Mindfulness Interest Group (2006). Mindfulness-based psychotherapies: A review of conceptual foundations, empirical evidence and practical considerations. *Australian and New Zeland Journal of Psychiatry, 40,* 285–294.

Mikulincer, M., Florian,V., & Weller, A. (1993). Attachment styles, coping strategies, and posttraumatic psycholgical distress: The impact of the Gulf War in Israel. *Journal of Personality and Social Psychology, 64,* 817–826.

Newby, J., McCarroll, J., Ursano, R., Fan, Z., Shigemura, J., & Tucker-Harris, Y. (2005). Positive and negative consequences of military deployment. *Military Medicine, 170,* 815–819.

Office of the Deputy Under Secretary of Defense. (2005). *2005 Demographics: Profile of the Military Community.* Retrieved on Jan 2, 2007, from Department of Defense: http://cs.itc.dod.mil/files/content/AllPublic/Workspaces/DoDITC-CS-Public/PDF/MHF/QOL%20Resources/Reports/Combined%20Final%20Demographics%20Report.pdf

Olson, S. (2007, August 29). Extending tours, stressing troops. *In These Times.* Retrieved April 4, 2008, from www.inthesetimes.com/main/print/3295/

Orthner, D., & Rose, R. (2006). *Deployment and separation adjustment among Army civilian spouses.* Washington, DC: Army Research Institute for the Behavioral and Social Sciences.

Pietromonaco, P., & Feldman Barrett, L. (2000). The internal working models concept: What do we really know about the self in relation to others? *Review of General Psychology, 4,* 155–175.

Reuters, M. R. (2007, November 24). U. S. to reduce Iraq troop levels by 5,000. *Washington Post.* Retrieved November 26, 2007, from http://www.washingtonpost.com/

Rosenberg, F. (1992). *Spouses of Reservists and National Guardsman: A survey of the effects of Desert Shield/Storm.* Fort Detrick, Frederick, MD: Walter Reed Army Institute of Research.

Simpson, J., & Rholes, S. (1998). *Attachment theory and close relationships.* New York: Guilford.

Thompson, R. (1999). Early attachment and later development. In J. Cassidy & P. Shaver (Eds.), *Handbook of attachment: Theory, research and clinical applications* (pp. 265–286). New York: Guilford.

Vormbrock, J. (1993). Attachment theory as applied to wartime and job-related marital separation. *Psychological Bulletin, 114,* 122–144.

Waters, E., Hamilton, C., & Weinfield, N. (2000). The stability of attachment security from infancy to adolescent and early adulthood: General introduction. *Child Development, 71,* 678–683.

Whitchurch, G., & Constantine, L. (1993). Systems theory. In P. Boss, W. Doherty, R. LaRossa, W. Shumm, & S. Steinmetz (Eds.), *Sourcebook of family theories and methods: A contextual approach* (pp. 325–352). New York: Plenum.

Whitlock, C. (2008, February 2). Germany rebuffs U.S. on troops in Afghanistan. *Washington Post.* Retrieved April 3, 2008, from http://www.washingtonpost.com

SOCIETY, SYSTEMS, AND INTERVENTIONS

CHAPTER 14

Community Resilience: A Social Organization Theory of Action and Change

Jay A. Mancini and Gary L. Bowen

Human beings are innately social. They organize themselves into social groups that range in size from dyads to large collectives of individuals that interact to accomplish individual and collective results. For the purposes of our discussion, we refer to these social groups as communities, which vary in their structure, function, and accomplishments over time. As systems, these communities are open and dynamic and must change and evolve to achieve their results and to remain viable to their citizens. Behavioral and social scientists have applied the concept of resilience to describe the ability to maintain, regain, or establish favorable outcomes in the face of adversity or challenge. Building the capacity of communities either to improve normative everyday life or to respond effectively to crisis events has emerged as a high priority among professionals across many disciplines, including family science, sociology, psychology, social work, and education.

Our primary interest is to identify the protective processes that buffer communities against risk exposure, support adaptive community functioning in the context of events or situations that threaten the well-being of the community and its members, and promote adaptive community functioning. The source of community risks can be either internal (e.g., rapid increase in the population) or external (e.g., natural disaster). In our approach, these protective processes are aspects of social organization, which communities can address and promote. We place high value on the potential merits of community networks for building the capacity of communities to effectively prepare for and respond to risks. Moreover, we place a premium on positive effects that can accrue from the intersection of formal and informal networks. An underlying assumption in community support efforts is that the collective efforts of community members or of groups within the larger community increase the odds that communities can adapt and change in the face of hardship and challenge and generate order, safety, and material and social resources and opportunities for their members. We assume that communities already possess the raw material necessary for resilience in the form of people, groups, and organizations. Thus, our capacity building/social action approach is strengths-based and asset-oriented (Kretzmann & McKnight, 1993).

Our efforts to understand community resilience began in earnest in the late 1990's, and were initially focused on the operation of formal and informal support systems in the United States military (Bowen & Martin, 1998). That multiple-year initiative continues to the present, and includes basic and applied research accessing qualitative and quantitative methods (e.g., Bowen, Martin, & Mancini, 1999; Bowen, Mancini, Martin, Ware, & Nelson, 2003), and applications to diverse community and social problems (e.g., Bowen, Bowen, Richman, & Woolley, 2002; Kiefer, Mancini, Morrow, Gladwin, & Stewart, 2008). Change, transformation, and contextual influences have always been part of our thinking; however, our indicators were most often tacit rather than intentional and explicit.

This chapter extracts and elevates dimensions of our thinking that are centered on change. We also reflect on contexts that must be accounted for in order to understand change. The concept of social organization is central to our understanding of community resilience. A first step in disentangling the many aspects of social organization is to discuss the nature of communities and the natural ways they frame individual and family life that have implications for prevention and intervention.

CONCEPTUALIZING COMMUNITIES AS CONTEXTS

Much of our work blends basic and applied social science, including translational dimensions. Consequently, we conduct research and provide consultation with direct relevance to prevention and intervention. Communities are *places*, *targets*, and *forces* for prevention (Mancini, Nelson, Bowen, & Martin, 2006). Taking this tripartite view on communities ultimately uncovers intervention or leverage points for change and transformation (a direct discussion of leverage points occurs later in this chapter).

First, communities are *places* for prevention. The term *place* suggests location in a physical and geographical sense, including boundaries and demarcations. Prevention efforts need to account for boundaries because they signify resources (e.g., agencies, organizations, and close-knit groups) and deficits. If we consider community in a variety of ways that speak to boundaries or ways collections of individuals and families are organized (e.g., geographic, geopolitical, and social/emotional), we open up the roadmap available to preventionists, program developers, and others, including community members themselves, who are committed to improving communities. An ecology of the community emerges that peels back the layers of the community and shows sources of influence on people and their situations. This ecology captures the range of relationships between individuals and their social and physical environment, most importantly including relationships, connections, and networks (discussed later in the chapter). The *place* approach to communities focuses attention on avenues into communities and pushes preventionists to explore the multitude of ways community members are organized within physical boundaries of interaction.

Second, communities are *targets* for prevention and intervention activities. We will later discuss the community capacity concept, comprised of shared responsibility and collective competence. Community capacity aspects of social organization focus on the development of informal social networks to enhance community life and move communities closer to achieving their desired results, including community resilience. This approach leads toward identifying and targeting community norms, beliefs, and expectations as they apply to specific issues (e.g., prevention of intimate partner violence, improving neighborhood safety, or promoting school success), which is a primary consideration in furthering change. The idea of target also brings an image of concentric circles and layers, and suggests a roadmap for further understanding communities and their many facets, including their socio-demographic features. Some community-level socio-demographic features, like the proportion of community members mired in poverty, are risk markers for community hardship and challenge.

Third, communities are *forces* for prevention. This third way of framing communities from a prevention and intervention viewpoint attaches force, power, and influence to community members and their families in a collective way. Communities can be mobilized, that is, enabled to shift conditions that influence community members. Our social organization approach aims to facilitate the mobilization of community members to enact change, and to be in the lead on change rather than to be led toward change or, for that matter, mired in the status quo. Conceptualizing communities as *places*, *targets*, and *forces* for prevention takes them from being viewed as passive and impersonal locations that only have descriptive value to a conceptualization that provides resources for articulating a roadmap for transformation and change. In our framework, we position dimensions of communities to point toward resilience; such positioning opens up a focus on an important, strengths-oriented view of communities and aligns with a capacity-building agenda.

COMMUNITY RESILIENCE

Our theorizing to date has always located the discussion of communities within a results framework (Orthner & Bowen, 2004). Though theorizing about results per se is not our current focus, in brief, the idea is to place high value on pinpointing desired results at a community level that are measureable and aligned with prevention and intervention activities. We discovered through working with communities that keeping the focus on desired results (e.g., high school graduation rates) provided a much clearer roadmap than approaches centered primarily on particular activities (e.g., school assignment policies). We are taking the opportunity in this chapter to pivot the discussion on community resilience specifically as a desired result.

Communities, like the members and families that inhabit them, are dynamic rather than static. As living systems, they face opportunities, as well as challenges—some expected and some unexpected. At any one point in time, communities face a unique combination of situations and events, demands and hardships, and resources and opportunities in the context of contemporary circumstances, historical events and actions, and an unfolding future.

Community resilience is the ability of communities to cope and adapt in the context of challenge and adversity in ways that promote the successful achievement of desired community results. This definition of community resilience aligns with the widely accepted definition of resilience articulated by Luthar, Cicchetti, and Becker (2000, p. 543): "a dynamic process encompassing positive adaptation within the context of significant adversity." At any one time, communities may face any number of hardships and challenges that require collective attention and management.

It is important to add several caveats to our discussion of community resilience. First, the determination of resilience requires attention to at least three time points: baseline, that is, gauging the status quo of community results before the adversity or challenge (time 1), post adversity or challenge, that is, capturing the consequences of challenge or adversity on the community (time 2), and assessing the results of community actions in response to the challenge or adversity (time 3 or follow-up). Because community resilience is fluid, formal and systematic approaches to understanding it must allow that fluidity to be captured. Resilient communities are able to maintain, regain, or establish an expected or satisfactory range of functioning over time in the context of adversity or challenge. Importantly, communities can use adversity and challenge to achieve resilience. Second, what constitutes a successful level of community functioning varies across place, time, and circumstance. In other words, resilience has upper and lower limits; however, the line of demarcation between resilience and non-resilience is not fixed and what constitutes resilience is considered within a narrow or broad band of functioning. Third, community resilience is assessed indirectly by examining the degree to which the community achieves results consistent with the ability of the community to maintain order and stability and to address the needs of its members. Communities that achieve a satisfactory level of performance at any one time are resilient.

The examination of community resilience requires attention to the protective processes that account for the ability of communities to demonstrate resilience in the context of challenge and adversity. Some years ago, we began considering social organization as an umbrella framework that provides guidance for understanding these protective processes, and that suggests leverage points for prevention and intervention to strengthen communities and to promote their resilience.

ELEMENTS OF SOCIAL ORGANIZATION

The organizing term we have used for several years to encapsulate our approach to community resilience and change is *social organization*

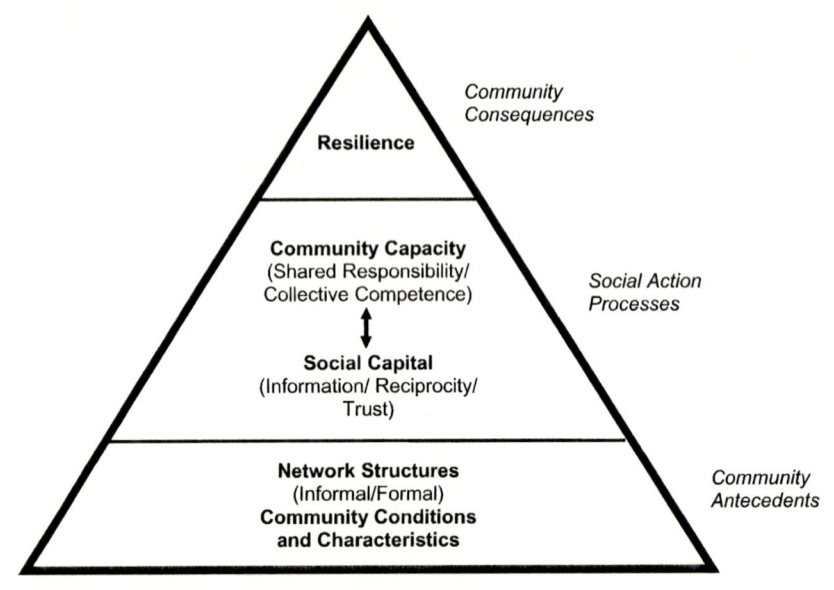

```
                    /\
                   /  \
                  /    \  Community
                 /Resil-\ Consequences
                /  ience \
               /----------\
              / Community  \
             /  Capacity    \
            / (Shared Resp./ \  Social Action
           / Collective Comp.)\ Processes
          /        ↕           \
         /    Social Capital    \
        /   (Information/        \
       /    Reciprocity/Trust)    \
      /----------------------------\
     /      Network Structures      \
    /        (Informal/Formal)       \ Community
   /       Community Conditions       \ Antecedents
  /          and Characteristics       \
 /--------------------------------------\
```

Figure 14.1. *Social Organization and Change*

(Bowen, Mancini, & Martin, 2005; Mancini, Martin, & Bowen, 2003; Bowen, Martin, Mancini, & Nelson, 2000). Previously, we used the term community capacity as the broad rubric for our theorizing on change and community contexts, however, it became apparent that community capacity is one component of social organization. Social organization is a broader and more encompassing concept that captures a broader array of protective processes that are associated with community resilience. In figure 14.1 we have placed the elements of our social organization model into a pyramid, with the base containing antecedent network structures and broad-based community conditions and characteristics (e.g., community as place, target, and force for prevention activities), the mid-section identifying primary social action processes of community capacity and social capital, and the top section including the community results associated with resilience.

Social organization describes the "collection of values, norms, processes, and behavior patterns within a community that organize, facilitate, and constrain interactions among community members" (Mancini, Martin, & Bowen, 2003, p. 319). According to Mancini, Bowen, and Martin (2005), social organization is the:

process by which communities achieve their desired results . . . Social organization includes networks of people, the exchanges and reciprocity that transpire in relationships, accepted standards and norms of social support, and social controls that regulate behavior and interaction (p. 572).

Our work is greatly influenced by our colleagues who have also been working with social organization theorizing (Cantillon, Davidson, & Schweitzer, 2003; Chaskin, Brown, Venkatesh, & Vidal, 2001; Furstenberg & Hughes, 1997; Janowitz, 1991; Sampson, 1991; Sampson, Morenoff, & Gannon-Rowley, 2002; Small, 2002). However, as we have noted elsewhere (Mancini, Bowen, & Martin, 2005), unlike most of our colleagues, we seek to emancipate social organization thinking from studies of disorganization, crime, and delinquency. Very often in the literature social organization and social disorganization are positioned at opposite ends of a continuum. Typically theorists and researchers begin by invoking social organization as a concept and then quickly replace it with social disorganization and investigations of individual problem behavior and community disadvantage. It seems to us that by keeping the lens on social organization several advantages emerge. First, how communities are framed does not quickly slide into a social problems mindset but rather helps with being intentional about capacity-building and resilience (Kretzmann & McKnight, 1993). Second, from a research perspective, the investigation of communities is less about "good" and "bad" and more about degrees of community preparedness for addressing adversity and challenge.

In our theorizing we mainly discuss networks, social capital, and community capacity, although we are aware that there are other potentially relevant dimensions of social organization, including explicit attention to shared and diverse community leadership (The Harwood Group, 1999). We postulate that these main elements in our thinking are interrelated and reciprocal, but we have only conducted partial tests of our model (Bowen, Mancini, Martin, Ware, & Nelson, 2003; Bowen, Martin, Mancini, & Nelson, 2001; Mancini, Bowen, Ware, & Martin, 2007). We begin with a discussion of networks because in many respects the work of building community capacity and moving toward resilience mainly occurs within networks.

Networks

We speak of informal networks, formal networks, and network effect levels (how networks coalesce and interface). These networks and their effect level are structural elements in our conceptualization of social organization. Consequently, they are included in Figure 14.1 as community antecedents. However, we do not see them as static and fixed. We do see them as capable of change and transformation, structural elements which can be developed, aligned, and strengthened through systematic attention and effort. Though networks provide a framework, they remain malleable. Consequently, networks appear under the larger social organization umbrella. Change in communities does not occur in the absence of networks because networks represent the "upper limit" for potential support and mobilization. Consequently, these networks are necessary but not sufficient for social action.

Informal networks are those relationships with extended family members, friends, neighbors, work colleagues, and informal support groups, which are, in effect, mainly voluntary relationships characterized by mutual exchanges and reciprocal responsibility. On average, individuals have a great deal of choice in the development and maintenance of their informal networks, and network linkages may be maintained in face-to-face interactions and by electronic means (e.g., telephone, e-mail). Formal networks are associated with agencies and organizations, in which there is an element of obligation (e.g., job descriptions and associated expectations). In a community, social service agencies, hospitals, schools, employers and the like are principal formal organization networks of social care. Networks are primary community entities through which much of community life is enacted. Interaction occurs through networks, and may be between friends and neighbors or between community members and service providers. We assume that most individuals in communities are part of multiple networks, and that a minority of community members are entirely isolated from network participation or effects.

In many respects community resilience is all about relationships, and relationships are all about connections, and connections are all about networks. From a prevention and intervention perspective, focusing on the relationships that community members have, and the connections they have with one another as a result, as well as the larger and broader interface of relationships and connections, establishes the foundation of community strengths and change. Ultimately, informal networks are what changes communities, that is, people themselves are the drivers and enactors of change. Consequently, we have argued in earlier work (Mancini,

Bowen, & Martin, 2005) that a primary function of formal networks is to enhance informal networks.

A substantial literature exists on social support that is beyond the scope of this discussion. However, it is worth briefly mentioning primary functions of informal network relationships and connections. Their primary functions include (Cohen, Underwood, & Gottlieb, 2000, p. 89): *emotional* (to assist individuals and families in dealing with despair and worry), *instrumental* (to assist in accomplishing practical tasks), *informational* (to facilitate achieving better decisions), *companionate* (to spend time together, in effect, developing a context for support), and *validation* (to support individuals and families to feel more worthwhile, competent, and hopeful). An examination of these network functions supports discussions of how informal networks can be strengthened by formal networks, which is a foundational argument we have long promulgated. Because we contend that meaningful changes in communities depend on informal networks, marshaling resources and systems to build those relationships, connections, and networks becomes a primary element of our social action approach, including the development and encouragement of community responsibility and leadership.

Formal networks are significant in forwarding change because of their mission of providing support programs and services; they provide an expertise that complements the energy found in informal networks. From our perspective, formal networks are stronger when they are diverse and comprehensive, when outreach becomes a primary activity, and when particular entities in a community formal system collaborate, thereby avoiding "silo" approaches to community support. Leverage points for change are opened wider under these conditions. Of particular importance in our thinking about formal networks is their role in supporting informal networks. In our consultation activities we emphasize the idea that formal systems should, in part, gauge their success by how well they establish a community network of support and how well informal networks are functioning in their community as a result of their efforts. In terms of positioning communities to make positive changes, informal networks contribute the power of interpersonal relationships to the mix, and formal organizations contribute specialized expertise (e.g., educators, community organizers, and health care professionals). Formal networks must be careful not to overfunction—to assume responsibility for tasks that informal networks can perform. When this happens, formal networks may grow at the expense of informal networks and actually constrain the kinds of exchanges that provide the basis for forming and maintaining informal networks.

A final and most significant note about networks involves their intersections. Though we do not formally discuss methods of partnership and collaboration within and between organizations, the idea of nexus and intersection at a conceptual level is prominent. Small and Supple (2001) have discussed levels of network effects. First-order effects occur within a homogeneous network, such as in a single agency or among friends. Efforts to deal with an issue or problem are contained within the single network. Putnam (2000) discusses the idea of "bonding" that occurs within a network, and its importance for enacting change. Organizations that are of many minds may have difficulty galvanizing themselves to meaningful action. Second-order effects occur among similar networks, such as between a family service agency and a community health center, or among contiguous neighborhoods. While the assets to enact change are expanded, they still are homogeneous, according to our split of formal and informal networks. Third-order effects are derived from dissimilar networks, such as partnerships between community agencies and neighborhood groups, which expand Putnam's idea of "bridging" from the individual to the community level. When there is agreement across disparate groups about desired community change, the resource base for mobilizing a community dramatically increases, as well as the probability for buffering challenge or adversity and for achieving desired community results.

When dissimilar networks focus on common issues, the odds increase of making positive differences in communities. It is within these networks that social capital develops and that community capacity evolves. In other words, networks provide the framework for social action because it is through networks that community members develop relationships and feel connected to one another. The optimal configuration and intersection of networks for achieving community resilience likely vary depending on the combination of adversities and challenges that the community faces. In some cases, formal networks may need to assume greater leadership and involvement than at other times, such as the case with the current economic crisis that communities are facing across the United States. In other cases, informal networks may need to be mobilized and activated, such as reaching out in rural communities to the families of members of the National Guard and Reserve who are deployed to war zones.

Social Capital: Information, Reciprocity, and Trust

We include social capital in our conceptualization of community social organization because of its contribution to understanding, in part, what occurs within and between networks. We recognize that social capital has its champions (Putnam, 2000) and its detractors. For example, Arneil's (2006) critique centers on historical perspectives on the development of social capital, and the trajectory of change in American civil society; she argues for a more diverse perspective. Edwards (2009) argues convincingly that social capital thinking is insufficient for fully understanding situations faced by collectivities.

We define social capital as the aggregate of resources that arise from reciprocal social relationships in formal and informal networks. The resources fuel the community's ability to achieve desired results through collective action. This definition is consistent with what Woolcock and Narayan (2000) labeled the "networks view" of social capital. Information and its exchange between network members are at the core of social capital, as are the reciprocity (transaction) that occurs via interaction and the trust that emanates from successful exchanges. Social capital is seen in the actions and results of civic and social advocacy groups, local faith communities, and other community-based membership groups. Yet, social capital is not fully fungible—forms and types of social capital may vary in their implications for building community capacity and achieving community resilience in the face of specific types of adversity or positive challenge. For example, the successful reintegration of war veterans back into their civilian communities after service or discharge may depend more on the availability of mental health resources and services from the Veterans Health Administration than the operation of the local police and fire department. However, the local police and fire department are likely to be far more instrumental in helping the community deal with wild fires that are sweeping through the local community. In agreement with Putnam (1993), because it both emerges from and supports actions and interactions within and between formal and informal networks, we contend that the supply of social capital in a community increases with its use.

Community Capacity: Shared Responsibility and Collective Competence

The degree to which people in the community demonstrate a sense of *shared responsibility* for the general welfare of the community and its individual members, and demonstrate *collective competence* by taking advantage of opportunities for addressing community needs and confronting situations that threaten the safety and well-being of community members, are the two elements of community capacity. As noted above, social capital provides the *social energy* for community capacity, which is generated from the actions and interactions within and between formal and informal networks. In return, the demonstration of community capacity fuels the development of social capital—a reciprocal relationship.

Our definition of community capacity differs from that of Chaskin and colleagues (2001) who associate capacity with available resources (e.g., human capital, organizational resources, and social capital). It is closer to Sampson's (2003) concept of collective efficacy, which focuses attention on community members' shared beliefs that result in action to meet a community goal, although our view of community capacity is considered a generalized group orientation that arises over time rather than a belief relative to specific adversities or challenges.

Several nuances of our definition of community capacity require further specification. First, there is concern (sentiment) expressed both for the community in general and for parts of the community. That is, individuals as well as collections of individuals within communities value and are invested in the well-being of others. Second, capacity occurs in degrees, rather than being present or not. If lined up along a continuum of preparedness to effectively deal with adversity or challenge, communities' abilities would vary rather than be purely present or absent. Third, capacity is derived more from the accumulated experiences of community members as a collective than from conformity to external authority. In other words, capacity does not result from a mandate but develops over time by people's responses to challenges. Finally, we view collective competence as bespeaking action. Action clearly goes beyond the expression of positive sentiments; it is the implementation of those sentiments. Communities described as collectively competent seize opportunities for improvement or recovery rather than only being reactive to risks. These actions occur in terms of normative everyday life situations in addition to situations of threat or crisis.

A point that distinguishes our approach is the emphasis on *demonstrating* capacity rather than only discussing capacity-related sentiments or resources. In our scheme, community capacity is anchored in taking action that produces observable results associated with community resilience. Rather than being fixed, the capacity that a community possesses is fluid. Consequently, intentional actions within and between formal and informal networks can enhance the level of community capacity.

We have recently discussed the descriptive and heuristic value of moving from a two-dimensional model of community capacity to a two-dimensional model with typological features. Of course, the logical typology is the simplest way to capture this expansion of the model. First, we dichotomize both shared responsibility and collective competence into low and high levels with high having more positive connotation. Then, we cross the two dimensions, which results in four community capacity types (see figure 14.2). We label these types for descriptive purposes only.

From a community capacity point of view, communities with both high shared responsibility and high collective competence would be communities more likely to demonstrate community resilience. We would consider these communities as *synergetic communities*. On the opposite side of the functioning continuum, we would place communities with low shared responsibility and low collective competence, which we would consider *disengaged communities*.

The last two community capacity types are high on one dimension and low on the second dimension. *Relational communities* would be high on shared responsibility but low on collective competence. In essence, these are communities with good intentions but which experience difficulty in making things happen. In some cases, these communities may lack the necessary leadership to be able to leverage positive sentiments into action. Last, *able communities* are those with low shared responsibility but high collective competence. These communities may have the ability to pull together and respond to crises but lack the sense of common identity, shared experiences, and relationships necessary for handling the more common and day-to-day challenges of community living.

The relative proportion of communities that would fit into these four cells is unknown, although we imagine a smaller proportion of communities would fit the *able* designation. We believe that a sense of shared responsibility is a necessary and prerequisite condition for demonstrating collective competence. Of course, the question of threshold points of

Shared Responsibility

	High	Low
High (Collective Competence)	*Synergetic Community:* High in both shared responsibility and collective competence	*Able Community:* Low in shared responsibility, high in collective competence
Low (Collective Competence)	*Relational Community:* High in shared responsibility, low in collective competence	*Disengaged Community:* Low in both shared responsibility and collective competence

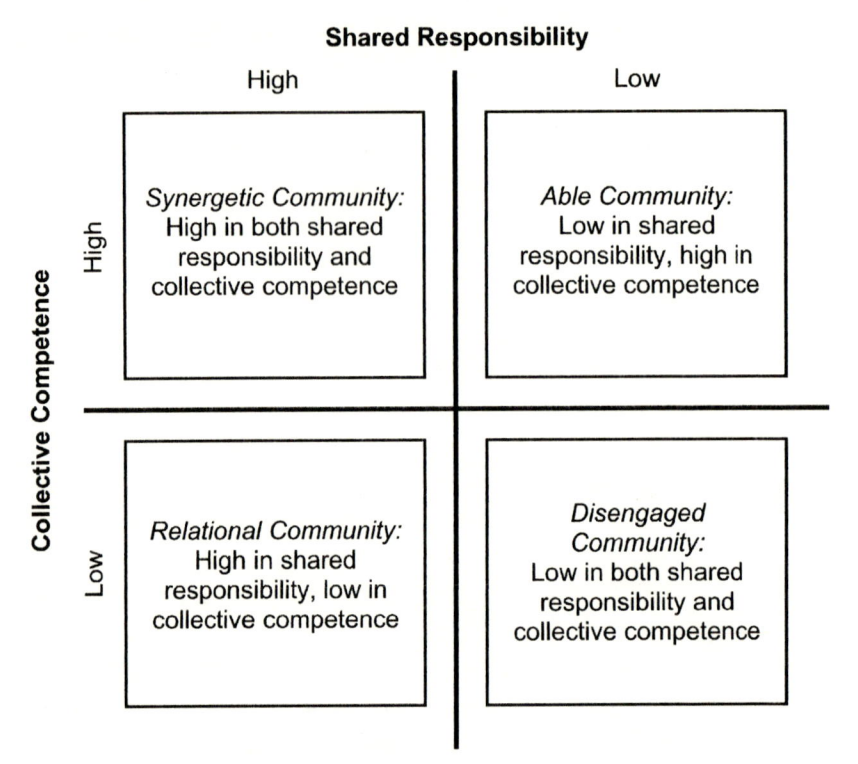

Figure 14.2. *Community Capacity Typology*

shared responsibility looms large, as well as the context of different situations and combinations of adversity and challenge (see figure 14.1). We think that each of these community types have different implications for intervention and prevention activities. These activities lie in the nature and operation of formal and informal networks in the community, and the specific types and levels of community leadership within these networks that may be necessary for guiding each of these communities in the context of adversity and challenge.

LEVERAGE POINTS, TRANSFORMATION, AND CHANGE

The social organization, community capacity-building approach is a social action and change framework. It is undergirded by applied research and program development work in building community capacity in support of military families (Bowen, Orthner, Martin, & Mancini, 2001; Heubner,

Mancini, Bowen, & Orthner, 2009). Leverage points are associated with all parts of the social organization framework—spots where prevention and intervention activities are aligned well with the framework. The assumption is that collective activities increase the potential for changing the status quo in a community, the usual way of doing business or the common state of affairs. Particular leverage points become clearer as communities identify desired results and take stock of their limitations and assets that have to be accounted for in considering community change.

As mentioned earlier, the most likely leverage points in communities are associated with networks, both formal and informal. This is so because networks are visible, vibrant, and where most people connect with each other and with formal systems. In particular, the discussion of network effects levels draws out how multiple networks become agents of community change. Preparing vulnerable populations to exhibit greater resilience during a time of natural or man-made disaster is an example (Kiefer et al., 2008). Disaster preparedness requires an extensive set of advance activities for communities to respond well when a disaster is actually experienced. Support systems must a priori be established so that, for example, faith-based community organizations know how to best contact their more vulnerable members. Community residents must know their neighbors well enough to look after them when a crisis is looming (for example, in the case of an anticipated hurricane, to encourage community members to take advantage of shelters or listen to evacuation orders, rather than remain in their dwellings). Governmental and emergency management organizations must know where higher proportions of vulnerable community members live, so that evacuation resources can be targeted. Throughout the disaster preparedness and recovery process shared responsibility and collective competence processes are important, the former mobilizing community member's recognition of the well-being of others in the community, and the latter mobilizing actions that make life-saving differences in communities.

In this social organization framework the information aspect of social capital is highlighted, and identified as exchanges within social relationships, especially as individuals coalesce around common and desired results. Information becomes a powerful element in the process of community members connecting, especially if its companion, reciprocity, becomes the norm.

Change is also associated with community capacity itself, if capacity is seen as requisite to community members coming together around shared goals and making decisions to take action. Consequently, as a leverage point, building community capacity becomes a focus on assessing levels of shared responsibility and collective competence among community members (research on sense of community in effect does this exactly). If people are in contiguity by virtue of being part of the same networks, and if interaction and transaction occurs in those networks that builds trust and bonds of reciprocal obligation, then odds of shared responsibility increase, which increase the odds of demonstrating collective competence.

Although we present the four-fold typology of community capacity (figure 14.2) as a preliminary and untested heuristic, each type has implications for social action. For example, strong and diverse leadership as discussed by The Harwood Group (1999) may be most important to jump start *relational* communities. In that case, the desired result is to harness positive sentiments (i.e., sense of shared responsibility) with community resources that previously have not been mobilized to action around a community need. Conversely, with both high shared responsibility and high collective competence, *synergetic* communities may need community leadership to delegate more than direct. *Able* communities may need leaders capable of building a sense of community among community members through creating opportunities for interaction and shared experiences. The most difficult challenge is among *disengaged* communities, where shared responsibility and collective competence are low. In such cases, the primary challenge is to develop opportunities for community members to be less isolated from one another, which is a task for formal networks, according to our approach. These communities may require community leadership to play a combination of roles, including supporting, coaching, and directing (cf., Blanchard, Zigarmi, & Zigarmi, 1985, for a discussion of situational leadership).

IMPLICATIONS OF SOCIAL ORGANIZATION THEORY FOR THEORIZING

Ultimately, this social organization and community capacity-building framework is presented as a roadmap for supporting prevention and intervention efforts on behalf of communities. Its origins were in the field laboratory of building support programs for vulnerable families. Thus far, it appears that using a social organization approach stimulates thought and action on any number of significant community-level issues and problems, including community health and community response to disasters.

There are a range of implications for prevention science, all of which reflect social organization as a theory of change (Mancini, Huebner, McCollum, & Marek, 2005; Weiss, 1995). A theory of change framework is perhaps the foundation to fully articulating the elements that bring about change in a community. Prevention science as a discipline focuses on expectations of change, and the trail that change and transformation follow. Social organization is a change framework, and capacity-building is its keystone. What people know, with whom they interact, who they ultimately trust, their level of regard for others, and collaboration with others around important community matters are at the core of social organization, and all of these elements reflect leverage points for community resilience. Consequently, social organization provides leads on change linkages (theory of change). However, further empirical work is required to specify those linkages. For example, what are the mechanisms that link networks with community capacity (shared responsibility and collective competence)? Does social capital mediate the relationship between networks and community, as we proposed earlier? Although in several places we discuss the issue of community leadership, this component has not yet formally entered the model. We believe that we are on the cusp in proposing community leadership as a social action process. As work continues, our framework questions centered on linkages will be prominent because an essential requirement of a theory of change is the specification of linkages.

A core proposition in our theory of change framework is the relationship between formal and informal networks. An important program function of formal networks is to build informal networks. That is, to intentionally develop programs that provide opportunity for community members to build connections that can thrive well beyond the bounds of a formal program. But how are informal network functions enhanced by activities of formal networks? In program development circles there are concerns about aligning activities with results, a goal being that professionals can discern exactly the relationship between causes and effects, as well as what moderates and mediates them.

In a theory of change there needs to be clarity about what the force is that pushes change. Very often, vagary exists around understanding the exact nature of an intervention or prevention effort. It is an ongoing challenge to know the elements of the intervention that make a difference. Because of its identification of networks as prime movers in community change and resilience, social organization provides direction on what makes a difference in change (e.g., the interface between networks and social capital regarding information, reciprocity, and trust). Yet in this mix, we recognize there are moderators and mediators that we have not yet identified. For example, how do the relationships between networks, social capital, and community capacity vary depending on the socio-demographic and physical structure of the community? Several years ago, our empirical work accounted for certain mediators and moderators affecting family adaptation among military families (Bowen, Mancini, Martin, Ware, & Nelson, 2003), so we are attuned to needing to further explore them.

A related element to understanding the intervention—what it is that pushes change—concerns understanding how the structure of an intervention or prevention effort differs from its processes. Confusing configurations with functions may lead to misspecification of what works to influence community change. For example, within a particular program, is change furthered by a curriculum, program delivery mode, community readiness, program leader attributes, interaction among program participants, severity of community problems, or assets already in the community? A theory of change approach has a complete taxonomy of the elements from A to Z, and elevates the many assumptions that are behind them.

In our theory of change there is a definable end point we generically term a *result*. In this chapter, we have identified community resilience as a primary desired result. Because the social organization framework includes a *results* element, and is tied into a results management approach to program planning, it potentially facilitates communities identifying exactly what should change. What should change is anchored by two questions. The first is, "Are you satisfied with the status quo?" The status quo question is the gateway for beginning the discussion of desired changes to promote community resilience. In our consulting work, we ask this question after reviewing community-level information with community members. The related question is, "What do you want to see at the end of the day?" The end of the day question moves the discussion toward considering desired results, differences, and changes. This theory highlights the importance of clearly articulated results, in effect providing guidance for indicators of positive change as well. From a program perspective, there is a tendency to provide programs that on the surface seem that they should make some positive difference (or at the least not make anything worse) but fail to align those program efforts with desired results. In the light of day, very often program efforts are misaligned with what communities want changed or transformed to promote community resilience.

We present social organization as a framework for partitioning aspects of community life, as an umbrella for showing the relationship between those elements, and as a social action approach that directly relates to prevention and intervention programs. It is a framework to elevate the significance of networks in communities, and to make community capacity building as a pivot point. A community that maintains, regains, or establishes favorable community results over time despite adversity (clear crises) or positive challenges (more normative, everyday life events) is considered resilient. In sum, building community capacity is building protective processes that can come into play as needed by a community in its efforts to maintain, regain, or establish resilience. Value systems are part of a social organization approach, and include prevailing values about what is important in community life (therefore what related goals should be established), and the norms that accompany those values. While resilience itself may be difficult to translate into a specific desired result, focusing on elements of community capacity-building processes provides relatively more concrete touch points.

REFERENCES

Arneil, B. (2006). *Diverse communities: The problem with social capital.* New York: Cambridge University Press.

Blanchard, K., Zigarmi, P., & Zigarmi, D. (1985). *Leadership and the one minute manager.* New York: Blanchard Management Corporation.

Bowen, G. L., Bowen, N. K., Richman, J. M., & Woolley, M. E. (2002). Reducing school violence: A social capacity perspective. In L. A. Rapp-Paglicci, A. R. Roberts, & J. S. Wodarski (Eds.), *Handbook of violence* (pp. 303–325). New York: Wiley.

Bowen, G. L., Mancini, J. A., Martin, J. A., Ware, W. B., & Nelson, J. P. (2003). Promoting the adaptation of military families: An empirical test of a community practice model. *Family Relations, 52,* 33–52.

Bowen, G. L., & Martin, J. A. (1998). Community capacity: A core component of the 21st century military community. *Military Family Issues: The Research Digest, 2*(3), 1–4.

Bowen, G. L., Martin, J. A., & Mancini, J. A. (1999). *Communities in Blue for the 21st century.* Fairfax, VA: Caliber Associates.

Bowen, G. L., Martin, J. A., Mancini, J. A., & Nelson, J. P. (2000). Community capacity: Antecedents and consequences. *Journal of Community Practice, 8,* 1–21.

Bowen, G. L., Martin, J. A., Mancini, J. A., & Nelson, J. P. (2001). Civic engagement and sense of community in the military. *Journal of Community Practice, 9,* 71–93.

Bowen, G. L., Orthner, D. K., Martin, J. A., & Mancini, J. A. (2001). *Building community capacity: A manual for U.S. Air Force Family Support Centers.* Chapel Hill, NC: A Better Image Printing.

Cantillon, D., Davidson, W. S., & Schweitzer, J. H. (2003). Measuring community social organization: Sense of community as a mediator in social disorganization theory. *Journal of Criminal Justice, 31,* 321–339.

Chaskin, R. J., Brown, P., Venkatesh, S., & Vidal, A. (2001). *Building community capacity.* New York: Aldine De Gruyter.

Cohen, S., Underwood, L. G., & Gottlieb, B. H. (Eds.), (2000). *Social support measurement and intervention: A guide for health and social scientists.* New York: Oxford University Press.

Edwards, R. (2009). The dynamics of families, social capital and social change: A critical case study. In J. A. Mancini & K. A. Roberto (Eds.), *Pathways of human development: Explorations of change* (pp. 267–289). Lanham, MD: Lexington Books.

Furstenberg, F. F., & Hughes, M. E. (1997). The influence of neighborhoods on children's development: A theoretical perspective and a research agenda. In J. Brooks-Gunn, G. J. Duncan, & J. L. Aber (Eds.), *Neighborhood poverty (Vol. 2): Policy implications in studying neighborhoods* (pp. 23–47). New York: Russell Sage Foundation.

Huebner, A. J., Mancini, J. A., Bowen, G. L., & Orthner, D. K. (2009). Shadowed by war: Building community capacity to support military families. *Family Relations, 58,* 216–228.

Janowitz, M. (1991). *On social organization and social control.* Chicago: University of Chicago Press.

Kiefer, J. J., Mancini, J. A., Morrow, B. H., Gladwin, H., & Stewart, T. A. (2008). *Providing access to resilience-enhancing technologies for disadvantaged communities and vulnerable populations.* Oak Ridge, TN: Community & Regional Resilience Initiative, Oak Ridge National Laboratory. Retrieved April 10, 2009 from http://www.isce.vt.edu/files/Kiefer,Mancini,%20Morrow,%20Gladwin,%20&%20Stewart,%202008.pdf

Kretzmann, J. P., & McKnight, J. L. (1993). *Building communities from the inside out.* Chicago: ACTA.

Luthar, S. S., Cicchetti, D., & Becker, B. (2000). The construct of resilience: A critical evaluation and guidelines for future work. *Child Development, 71,* 543–562.

Mancini, J. A., Bowen, G. L., & Martin, J. A. (2005). Community social organization: A conceptual linchpin in examining families in the context of communities. *Family Relations, 54,* 570–582.

Mancini, J. A., Bowen, G. L., Ware, W. B., & Martin, J. A. (June, 2007). *Engagement, participation, and community efficacy: Insights into social organization.* Paper presented at the Hawaii International Meeting on the Social Sciences, Honolulu, HI.

Mancini, J. A., Huebner, A. J., McCollum, E. E., & Marek, L. I. (2005). Program evaluation science and family therapy. In D. H. Sprenkle & F. P. Piercy (Eds.), *Research methods in family therapy* (2nd ed.) (pp. 272–293). New York: Guilford.

Mancini, J. A., Martin, J. A., & Bowen, G. L. (2003). Community capacity. In T. P. Gullotta & M. Bloom (Eds.), *Encyclopedia of primary prevention and health promotion* (pp. 319–330). New York: Kluwer Academic/Plenum.

Mancini, J. A., Nelson, J. P., Bowen, G. L., & Martin, J. A. (2006). Preventing intimate partner violence: A community capacity approach. *Aggression, Maltreatment, and Trauma, 13*(3/4), 203–227.

Orthner, D. K., & Bowen, G. L. (2004). Strengthening practice through results management. In A. R. Roberts & K. Yeager (Eds.), *Handbook of practice based research* (pp. 897–904). New York: Oxford University Press.

Putnam, R. D. (2000). *Bowling alone.* New York: Simon & Schuster.

Sampson, R. J. (1991). Linking the micro-and macrolevel dimensions of community social organization. *Social Forces, 70,* 43–64.

Sampson, R. J. (2003). The neighborhood context of well-being. *Perspectives on Biology and Medicine, 46* (3 supplement), 553–564.

Sampson, R. J., Morenoff, J. D., & Gannon-Rowley, T. (2002). Assessing neighborhood effects: Social processes and new directions in research. *Annual Review of Sociology, 28,* 443–478.

Small, M. L. (2002). Culture, cohorts, and social organization theory: Understanding local participation in a Latino housing project. *American Journal of Sociology, 108,* 1–54.

Small, S., & Supple, A. (2001). Communities as systems: Is a community more than the sum of its parts? In A. Booth & A. C. Crouter (Eds.), *Does it take a village? Community effects on children, adolescents, and families* (pp. 161–74). Mahwah, NJ: Erlbaum.

The Harwood Group (1999). *Community rhythms: Five stages of community life.* Bethesda, MD: The Harwood Group and the Charles Stewart Mott Foundation.

Weiss, C. H. (1995). Nothing as practical as good theory: Exploring theory-based evaluation for comprehensive community initiatives for children and families. In J. P. Connell, A. C. Kubisch, L. B. Schorr, & C. H. Weiss (Eds.), *New approaches to evaluating community initiatives: Concepts, methods, and contexts* (pp. 65–92). Washington, DC: Aspen Institute.

Woolcock, M., & Narayan, D. (2000). Social capital: Implications for development theory, research, and policy. *The World Bank Research Observer, 15,* 225–249.

CHAPTER 15

The Dynamics of Families, Social Capital, and Social Change: A Critical Case Study

Rosalind Edwards

In mainstream thinking, social capital—basically, who we know and what we do for each other—is posed, tautologically, both as a problem: there is less beneficial social capital in society than there used to be; and as a solution: the remedy for this problem is to develop social capital. I argue that, ultimately, social capital is not enough. It is not enough conceptually, and it is not enough empirically. That is, the dominant conception of social capital is problematic, with its in-built static and formulaic ideas about the social fabric, which cannot capture the intricate dynamics of people's relationships within and between families. There are major shortcomings in the way social capital theories and their operationalization understand the values people hold, the social resources that people access and generate, the actions people take, and shifts in society over time. Social capital does not explain people's everyday, lived experience. Whatever its form, it cannot bring about social change; rather social capital involves the differential exercise of power and helps to maintain inequalities.

In this chapter, I discuss how particular ideas about family and social change are embedded in thinking about social capital and the methodology of its investigation. My intent is to provide a warning about the uncritical adoption of ideas about the nature of social change. I begin my critical case study of understanding and studying social change with a brief introduction to different conceptions of social capital, addressing why it has become so popular as a way to promote social change. I then move on to review ideas about the links between families, social capital, and social change. As implied by my use of the term *critical*, my perspective highlights the way that mainstream theories of social capital reproduce and reify particular forms of family and community life, inherently marginalizing and obscuring other aspects of social capital's generation, access, use, and effects. In particular, I am concerned with the implications of and for social divisions that shape society; that is, the substantial material and cultural cleavages and resultant inequalities between groups of people. The main hierarchies and disparities of power and resources addressed here are generational (age), gender, class, and racial/ethnic positions—any or all of which can intersect with one another. I show how these power dynamics determine the ways in which social capital reproduces social inequalities rather than changing or overcoming them. From this perspective, the implications of thinking about the relationship between families, social capital, and social change lead away from a predefined and prescriptive theory toward a consideration of epistemology and methodology. The final part of this chapter is thus devoted to a discussion of how investigators can know about whether and in what ways the social world is changing.

SOCIAL CAPITAL: WHAT AND WHY

What is Social Capital?

Social capital is a key concept in policy making and in academic debates internationally. Different theorists emphasize slightly different constituent features, but generally, as a concept social capital refers to the way that people connect through social networks and common values within these networks including trust and reciprocity. Together these networks and values are said to constitute a resource that equates to a kind of capital. It can be invested and accumulated, frittered away through injudicious spending, provide little yield, or indeed, it can be completely the wrong sort of currency.

Particular forms of social capital theorizing have become dominant and influential in policy making. James Coleman's body of work (e.g., 1990) explores the relationship between social and human capitals, paying particular attention to the parental role in children's educational achievement. His ideas have become part of orthodox thinking in the field of education policy and practice. Robert Putnam's work (e.g., 2000) has been concerned with social capital as a "public good" that is embodied in civic engagement and has implications for democratic and economic prosperity. Policy makers concerned with a variety of aspects of *social exclusion* have taken up his arguments. Pierre Bourdieu (1997/1986) theorizes social capital as interdependent with other capital resources, in particular economic capital, but his ideas have had less of an impact on policy framing than Coleman's and Putnam's. Nonetheless, his ideas remain influential in critical strands of academic analysis, such as Diane Reay's (1998) study of mothers' involvement in their children's primary schooling.

Why the Interest in Social Capital?

A range of reasons have been put forward as to why the concept of social capital has come so rapidly to the fore in recent years. Schuller, Baron, and Field (2000) have reviewed many of these explanations. They listed a *politico-psycho-anthropological* explanation in which social capital arguments resonate personally with the experiences of those in the heart of intellectual and political debates. Other reasons for the rise of social capital ideas they reviewed include concerns about the excesses of individualism, and the notion that ideas live in cycles with social capital as a revival or rebranding of longstanding themes. Schuller and colleagues place primary emphasis on "a growing concern to revalorize social relationships in political discourse; to reintroduce a normative dimension into sociological analysis; to develop concepts which reflect the complexity and inter-relatedness of the real world" (p. 2).

Another explanation for the interest in social capital relates to conceptions of contemporary society as undergoing radical social change, producing a strong impulse to instill certainty. Contemporary life is marked by a pervasive sense of concern about the condition of society, and uncertainty about what will be encountered in the future—a *risk society* (Beck, 1992). Social capital offers a particular sort of explanation of, and remedy for dealing with, perceived changes in the way people live, work, and relate to each other. In particular, the idea provides intellectuals and politicians concerned with what they regard as the disintegration of families and communities from the mid-twentieth century an opportunity to take action that will redeem society (Arneil, 2006). A preoccupation with the supposed demise of families and communities has a long history, as do the concerns about social cohesion and social order encompassed in social capital ideas (e.g., Edwards, 2008). Brought together, these assessments of the condition of families and social capital are a good example of the adage *old wine in new bottles*.

Arguably, the career of the concept of social capital has been more policy-driven than theory-driven, in large part related to the shift toward a *third way* policy paradigm, between right and left, between pro-market approaches and monopolistic state services. Key themes of this third way include an emphasis on civil society, an expectation that people should take personal responsibility for planning and meeting their own needs and bettering themselves, and a concomitant stress on their choices as consumers of welfare provision. Ideas about reduced stocks of social capital, and about the need to repair them in order to counteract damaging changes in families and communities, are part of this policy paradigm (Franklin, 2007).

Several commentators have pointed out that the social capital theorists favored in policy development tend to give primacy to the economic or political effects or outcomes of family and social relationships, bolstered by the use of the term *capital* (reviewed in Franklin, 2007). This imposes an implicit functionalist economic rationality on social life. Simultaneously, a view of society as *prior to* and *causative of* the production of the economy takes attention away from economic and social injustice, and redirects attention to families and culture as the focus of policy intervention. Consequently, Britain has witnessed an explicit focus on parenting as a designated area of policy intervention, with mothering and fathering posed as having consequences for society rather than the reverse. There has been a shift from concerns about material poverty toward a more communitarian focus on moral poverty and cultural pathology. This has resulted in a policy emphasis on inculcating approved norms and values in the practice of parenting. Inequality and disadvantage have become associated with parents' inadequate management of themselves and their children. In this paradigm, policy makers believe that lack of resources are a symptom rather than a cause of disadvantage (Gillies, 2008).

Coleman, Putnam, and other mainstream social capital theorists thus point toward a comfortable way forward. They provide a link between ordered families, ordered communities, and an ordered society through shared values. Next, I describe how both *the family,* in the so-called traditional nuclear form, and high stocks of social capital are based on shared values and trust. Both are fundamental and strong bases for social cohesion, yet also easily eroded.

FAMILIES, SOCIAL CAPITAL, AND SOCIAL CHANGE

New Right and conservative thinking sees *the family* as both a norm and an ideal, but as under threat. Social change is happening—for the worse. In particular, the *breakdown* of the *traditional* nuclear family with breadwinner father and homemaker mother, and the concomitant rise of a range of diverse family forms (e.g., single mother, cohabitation, dual-earner, living apart together [LAT], step-families, same-sex relationships) are regarded as bringing social fragmentation and disorder in their wake (e.g., Davies, 1993; Dennis, 1993; Morgan, 1995; Murray, 1994). Mothers place their own needs above those of their children and husbands, facilitated by their entry into the labor market or the availability of welfare support, both of which enable them to live independently. In this view, the family requires protection from state intervention, especially in the form of welfare benefits that undermine family responsibility, and/or it requires encouragement and support in the form of pro-family policy.

This normative, conservative family ideology has manifested in dominant forms of social capital theorizing represented by Coleman and Putnam, who profess this functionalist assessment of the condition of contemporary family life and negative direction of social change. Such theorists view social capital as the glue that holds society together. As with the family, they contend that social capital is eroding. Indeed, they place family change at the root of this *social capital lost* story, with particular forms of intergenerational and gender relations implicated. In this way, academics and policy makers who advocate a middle ground between conservative and liberal politics, the third way described earlier, actually reproduce very conservative, rather than progressive, notions of family life.

Intergenerational Socialization

The socialization of children is a key, but under-acknowledged issue in social capital thinking. Coleman identified social capital as a resource within the family that inheres in the structure of intergenerational relationships between parents and children. In his model, parental interest and support enables children to increase their human capital (e.g., educational achievement). The more children that parents have, the more diluted the attention. For Coleman, the process of social capital building within families integrally links to social capital as a community resource, embedding parents and children in close neighborhood relationships. Together, parent-child relations and social ties outside of families create a dense social structure of cohesive norms, extensive trust, and obligations, which Coleman called *intergenerational closure*. Putnam (2000) also drew in the socialization of children when he argued that "good families have a ripple effect by increasing the pool of good peers" (p. 314), which he said proved effective against youth crime and drug and alcohol abuse in neighborhoods.

Bourdieu (1997/1986) also focused on generational socialization within families in his thinking about social capital. He viewed social capital as "made up of social obligations (connections) . . . [it] is the aggregate of the actual or potential resources which are linked to the possession of a durable network of more or less institutionalized relationships of mutual acquaintance and recognition" (pp. 47–51). People derive social capital from their membership in a family and other social groups. Bourdieu pointed out that social capital has to be developed continuously, rather than merely being constituted in "the geneological definition of kinship relations" (p. 52). Material and symbolic exchanges that produce obligations and mutual recognition of group (family) membership accumulate over time and are transmitted across generations. Drawing on Bourdieu's ideas, for example, Pat Allatt (1993) demonstrated how elite middle class parents used their social networks on behalf of their children to transfer privilege and are ensure advancement. This process implicitly taught their children the value of social connections: how to use social capital and how to create their own social capital. Allatt remarked, "This is a critical transfer, since such aspects of social capital have to be recreated with each new generation" (p. 143).

Bourdieu's arguments thus were quite different from those made by Coleman and Putnam. Although he similarly saw social capital as deriving from family relationships, he regarded its type and content as inevitably shaped by the material, cultural, and symbolic status of the individual and family concerned. People have packages of capitals that work together in different ways. Those who have more or less equivalent economic or cultural capitals, for example, will obtain an unequal return on them according to the nature of the social capital available to them and the extent to which they are able to access and use it. For Bourdieu, social capital is ubiquitous and interacts with other capitals in multiple synchronic ways. Rather than undergoing a deterioration instigated by features of contemporary family life that fracture the "proper" socialization of children, social capital is continually transmitted and accumulated to reproduce social inequality. This is not a case of social capital lost, but a representation of continuity in the various uses of social capital to reinforce disparities of power and resources.

Gender Relations

Changes in family life are posed as key in the social capital lost story. Again in contrast to Bourdieu's ideas about ubiquity, in Coleman's (1990) view changing family structures, specifically increases in single mothers, absent fathers, and mothers working outside the home, have led to a deficit in social capital, as have geographical mobility and migration. The rise of youth-oriented media and leisure activities, and a focus on children's rights, leads to a generational divide and further undermines parent-led norms in children's socialization. In addition, according to these arguments the existence of welfare state benefits and services promotes free-rider norms, negating parental and community trust-based obligations. Putnam (2000) identified similar culprits in his portrayal of decreasing levels of social capital in society, even though he focused primarily on civic engagement through membership of self-sustaining voluntary associations in social capital building. Features of contemporary family life that Putnam considered as causing social capital decline included women's rising labor market participation and dual-earner households, a decline in marriage, increased television viewing (posed as a major culprit), and an exodus of middle class and respectable working-class families from particular neighborhoods that erodes the social capital of those left behind in the ghetto. Generally, in Putnam's view, an older, civically active generation is being replaced with a younger one whose *stocks* of social capital are much reduced.

As with thinking on the family, the dominant *breakdown* versions of social capital regard it as in need of protection and encouragement. Coleman is ambivalent about state intervention in this respect, posing substitute forms of organizational social capital building as a policy dilemma. Putnam, though, regards intervention to regenerate social capital as the central challenge for social policy to meet, including the promotion of family-friendly and community-congenial workplaces and youth volunteering schemes. Indeed, he poses social capital as a correlate of egalitarian policies; it is social capital building that will deal with material inequalities.

Within the dominant portrayal of the foundations of social capital, "traditional" nuclear families are key, accompanied by gender relations in which married fathers are breadwinners, and their wives are homemakers dedicated to the care and socialization of their (joint biological) children as well as community activity. Other family forms characterized as "non-traditional families" set up a false dichotomy. Such families do not conform to the longstanding gender and generational order that underpins a stable, social capital rich society, but, in the social capital lost story of social change, are changing norms in negative ways.

However, I argue that mainstream social capital theorists' reification of the nuclear, functional family form, and their preoccupation with destructive social change driven by changes in families and communities, obscure and marginalize the ways that social capital can operate in different ways in different circumstances for different social groups. To do this I draw on findings from a five-year program of research concerned with families and social capital that I directed[1], as well as other empirical work. This allows me to illustrate a grounded understanding of change and, as crucially, gives a sense of continuity in how access to, and the effects of, a range of resources can reinforce inequalities.

MARGINALIZED IN THE MAINSTREAM

Children and Older Adults

As Ginny Morrow (1999) shows in her influential consideration of social capital, the mainstream models put forward by Coleman and Putnam marginalize conceptions of children as active participants in shaping the nature of family life and caring relationships, and in generating social capital for themselves, parents, siblings, and other family members. As exemplified in Coleman's ideas about intergenerational closure discussed above, socialization is a one-way street. Children are conceived of as passive *tabula rasa* recipients, drawing on traditional psychologically based models that construct childhood as a condition of *becoming* in terms of their future capacities, not their *being* in the here and now.

Empirical projects in our program of research on families and social capital[2], however, show how both as siblings and as friends, children and young people shape and generate social capital for each other, encouraging and sanctioning behavior in the wider community just as much as parents do. Sister and brother relationships, for example, were highly implicated in children and young people's sense of community belonging and marginalization, and in their access to social capital. Our projects also revealed the networking and exchanges that go on within minority cultural enclaves for young people in particular. Their sense of a shared racial and ethnic diasporic identity despite involuntary or voluntary geographical dispersal provided them with resources to draw upon. As part of this shared identity, their transnational links sustained family life and other relationships across national borders after migration. African-Caribbean young people, for example, used these aspects of their social capital to respond to social exclusion, racial inequality, and marginality in British society. The generation and use of social capital also applied to young people's engagement in some niche globalized youth leisure culture. In Northern Ireland, for example, this youth leisure culture offered the possibility of transcending the sectarian divide in ways that institutional efforts at integrated and cross-community initiatives found difficult.

The oldest generation can be equally ignored in mainstream social capital theorizing and measurement as theorists use this demographic to act as a foil for the comparison between the contemporary generation and the oldest generation's past practices. Yet, their current activities also have social capital implications. Examples of these activities from our research include older people's practical and emotional support of each other and younger generations. For example, older minority ethnic people's participation in cultural rituals and celebrations maintained their connections to their family in their country of origin and provided them with social and cultural resources.

Gender, Race, and Class

What is also missing in the Coleman and Putnam inspired family and social capital lost picture, are issues of power and conflict—a dynamic to which Bourdieu's ideas draw attention. The divisive and oppressive side of the same family and gender relations, such as an unequal division of labor and domestic abuse, is ignored (Arneil, 2006). Social capital theories also obscure the complexity and ambivalence of family life in general. Indeed, particular class and ethnic groups are implicitly found in the description of family structures posited as deficient in social capital. Images of working class families are conjured up in Coleman's reference to low social capital *family deficiencies*: "poor, uneducated *and* disorganized, structurally weakened or broken by the personal disorganization of the parent or parents" (1988, pp. 385–386, original emphasis). And, in the United Kingdom (UK), as well as the United States (U.S.), single motherhood is a common family form among the African-Caribbean population, while larger families (more children than average) are more common among Bangladeshi and Pakistani minority ethnic groups. Both Black mothers and White middle class mothers are implicated in the idea that dual-earner families undermine the social capital generation, because, at least in the UK, it is these groups who are most likely to be undertaking substantial paid work. Yet, measured social capital is high in institutionalized welfare states, such as those in Scandinavia, where gender and income equality are guiding principles, including mothers' integration into the paid labor force (Stolle, 2002).

Several projects in our research program found that social capital in parenting is a highly gendered resource. Family connections and their associated social capital were organized and maintained predominantly by and between women, whether these networks were occurring locally, transnationally, or across generations. However, alongside this, gendered and cultural expectations can place oppressive constraints on people's social behavior. Our project on British-Italian families, for example, found that gendered cultural expectations placed constraints on individuals' social behavior. As feminists (e.g., O'Neill & Gidengil, 2006) have pointed out, women are central producers of social capital through their gendered social positioning as family and community carers and networkers. Yet, this very social positioning, and consequent social capital generation, is in itself problematic in reinforcing a gendered division of labor. Mainstream social capital theories have their roots in longstanding economic and political assumptions about public and private spheres and often neglect the sorts of social capital informally generated and used by mothers, children, and young people, especially from working class and minority ethnic backgrounds.

ECONOMIC AND MORAL RATIONALITY—
PUBLIC AND PRIVATE SPHERES

Mainstream social capital theorizing tends toward explanations that position society as producing the economy, thus providing non-economic solutions to social problems. Yet, at the same time, dominant perspectives on social capital are imbued with economic rationality in their understandings of how people are motivated to act. Indeed, Coleman explicitly sought to combine economic rationality and social organization theories in his body of work: he uses rational exchange and cost-benefit analyses to theorize about patterns of obligation, investment, and repayment that supposedly produce a structural moral rationality in the form of cohesive norms and sanctions.

For Coleman, parents invest in their children as the next generation who will in turn support them in later life. They invest by being physically present, giving attention to children, and developing an intense relationship that involves talk about personal matters and expectations of educational achievement. Likewise, Bourdieu's ideas about social capital work also run the danger of falling into this economic rationality mold. In his model, parents invest in their children for the continuance of the family's economic interests across generations – although generally he is critical of understandings of human behavior that see it as intrinsically rational or utilitarian, since this takes no account of social divisions, cultural environment, and historical circumstances. In the wider community too, people are understood to be doing things for each other on the basis that, in due course, they will benefit from the cost of their helpful effort—an assumption of economic rationality. In this model, state-provided welfare benefits and services undermine such economic rationality by producing free-rider norms, while women's economic independence through the labor market and notions of children's rights undermine ideas of gender complementarity and intergenerational obligations, as noted earlier.

Rationality Misattribution

I argued earlier in this chapter that the popularity of social capital thinking is a manifestation of a (theoretical, economic, social, and political) desire for certainty in a perceived risk society. For similar reasons, economic rationality is also a feature of theorizing and policy making concerning a whole range of aspects of family life, prioritizing individual utility maximization and in particular perceived economic costs and benefits (Carling, Duncan, & Edwards, 2002). Such thinking understands economic self-interest as at the root of, for example, partnership choices, gendered divisions of labor, employment behavior, decisions to become a parent, and child care choices. For some commentators then, the economic rationality and consumer culture of late capitalism have invaded the domestic sphere, corrupting the way in which family relationships are understood and experienced (Sennett, 1998).

In contrast to this gloomy picture, another explanatory strand of work in the area of family studies shows that prioritizing economic rationality misattributes both the reasoning and values of individuals embedded in social networks. This more considered work places social ties and moral responsibilities at center stage, with people building identities and reputations as a certain sort of person. Adults and children use these moral identities and reputations in negotiating relations with others (Duncan & Edwards, 1999; Finch & Mason, 1993; Smart & Neale, 1999). Social divisions such as gender, social class, and ethnicity are important identities in that they prescribe norms for acting in particular social and local circumstances. This major strand of theorization poses family life as deeply moral; an important aspect of understanding that is not captured in mainstream social capital thinking, which assumes that human beings use an exchange or rationality framework to make decisions.

Amoral Families?

Assumptions of economic rationality, combined with the suppositions about oppositions between the private and the public or social discussed below, mean that social capital theorizing often places family-based social capital as outside of morality, as *amoral*. The basis of this claim is rooted in a political science perspective. In liberal democratic political theory, *generalized trust* is valued because it is disinterested and impartial. This form of trust is posed as *moral* in conventional political science terms because it extends beyond particularistic group attachments such as family, to members of other social groups in the civic sphere. Trust within socially integrated groups such as families, however, does involve particularistic attachment and is termed "amoral familialism" (Woolcock,

1998, pp. 171–72). Putnam (1993), for example, contrasts the civically vibrant horizontal networks of northern Italy, where *moral generalized trust* was generated through people coming together in credit associations, singing societies, and so on, with the less economically prosperous *amoral familialism* of southern Italy with its legacy of exclusive group loyalties. Yet, as noted earlier, mainstream social capital theorists also argue that it is families that socialize children to trust and other (moral) bases of social capital.

The absence of an understanding of family life as deeply moral is the result of a political perspective that removes family from conceptions of what constitutes *the social* and *citizenship*, separating it off as the private sphere (McCarthy & Edwards, 2002). Morality, from this particular political science perspective, is only applicable within the public domain through the collective civic engagement of independent, autonomous individuals.

Gender and Generation

Again, there are gendered and generational implications to this focus on the public. First, a particular understanding of individuals who come together in the civic sphere is invoked, implicitly based on typical male experience, that is, the atomized subject of liberal political philosophy. Thus, it is far easier for men to appear to fit its requirements. Least able to fit in are children, who are the prototypes for forms of *dependency* and institutionalized as dependent in families, education systems, social security systems, and so on. This construction of the individual who is active in the public, civic sphere hides more relational notions of interdependence and connection highlighted by some feminists (McCarthy & Edwards, 2002).

Second, historically, women and children have been marginalized from the public sphere on multiple levels: physically, normatively, politically, and conceptually. As Barbara Arneil (2006) perceptively pointed out, Putnam and other social capital lost proponents ignored the historical subordination of women and other cultural minorities that was prevalent during the first half of the twentieth century, the era that they point to as social capital rich. Rather than losing social capital since then, Arneil highlighted the continual struggles in the U.S. to move from discrimination toward social justice. Longstanding gender divisions resulted in mothers taking responsibility for children's emotional and practical care and upbringing. They do not benefit from family as a social capital resource for public sphere engagement in the same way as men, for example in terms of family connections easing the path to financial and political power (O'Neill & Gidengil, 2006). Further, mothers may be involved in informal and small-scale networks of association that are not acknowledged by the dominant social capital focus on more formal, organized civic society, such as child care networks, liaison with health visitors, and so on (Stolle, 2002). Indeed, they may use this social capital to help them balance employment and family life, rather than mothers' employment being part of the destruction of societal social capital. To sum up, in dominant social capital terms, unless the activities of mothers and children are conducted within recognized civic engagement, they remain absent or amoral despite their posited key significance to social capital building.

WHO'S BONDING, WHO'S BRIDGING?

The networking and exchanges involved in social capital raise complex issues of identity and affiliation in what scholars refer to as its *bonding* and *bridging* forms. As I will argue, material inequalities are reproduced in the types of social capital that people generate and access, rather than transcending them.

Coleman's work on social capital was largely concerned with advocating a social world characterized by a bonding social capital based on ties between adults and children living in the same sort of (nuclear) family. As described earlier, children are socialized into a homogenous set of values and participate in communities made up of networks of these families who share the same values. Bourdieu also was concerned with what, in effect, is bonding social capital within and across generations. For him, people derive their social capital from the obligations and mutual recognition involved in their family, class, and other social group connections. Bourdieu was more concerned with exclusionary practices around bonding that create and sustain inequalities, while Coleman saw bonding social capital largely as an unmitigated good.

Other social capital theorists are concerned with bridging across social difference rather than an analysis of how those divisions are accumulated, transmitted, and maintained. Putnam (2000) described the bonding form of social capital as based on homogeneous ties of trust and reciprocity between *people like us*, reinforcing exclusive identities, and restricted to enabling people simply to get by. In his view, bonding capital seldom generates rich social capital used more widely in a society. Outward-looking, cooperative, bridging social capital enables people to get ahead in life and fosters social inclusion (notably incarnate in voluntary associations). Nonetheless, Putnam saw a link between the two posited forms of social capital: the more bonding in a society in terms of stable nuclear families, the more bridging across class and ethnicity outside of those families that will occur.

Data from our program of research, however, revealed that there is a need to move beyond narrow conceptions of amounts of, and distinctions between, bonding and bridging social capital based on fixed sociodemographic characteristics such as identity. As Anthias (2007) points out in relation to ethnic ties, this is potentially essentialist.

> One major problem lies in denoting a fixed boundary between bonds existing *within* a group, and bridges which exist *between* groups. The definitional elements here have the danger of becoming essentialist in as much as the boundaries between bonding and bridging may be flexible and changing, depending on context and meaning (p. 791).

Importantly, people's conceptions of their affiliations are fluid and complex. One example from our work is that children's and young people's understandings of who is a sibling go well beyond the technical facts of biological ties and co-residence, and focus on the quality of relationship and the social nature of the tie. Another example is the shifting affiliation for some young African-Caribbean people. Their sense of identity can change as being from, say, a particular or several islands in the Caribbean, or the Caribbean as a whole, or black, or from London, or a particular area of London, according to circumstances. Furthermore, generally for transnational families, networks flow across national boundaries as well as across and within generations, which may represent bonding and bridging social capital at the same time.

This flexibility around identifications and affiliations for individuals depending on the context in which they are relating to others raises the crucial methodological question of who constructs and judges homogeneity and heterogeneity? Who evaluates whether someone is like or different from another person and on what basis? I will return to this point about the problems of researching social capital, and the implications for assertions of social change, later.

GETTING BY AND GETTING ON

Bonding social capital is about being embedded in dense and intensive networks of family and friends, as confirmed in our research. Its strengths are that it is solidarity-based, and provides the obligation and commitment-based practical help and emotional support to people that enable reciprocal day-to-day survival. But, it also has drawbacks. Bonding social capital subjects relationships to pressures of intense hopes and emotions. Broken expectations can lead to conflict and guilt, and it is unlikely to provide any wider benefits beyond the everyday negotiation of disadvantage.

Our research showed that, in contrast, bridging social capital is concerned with individuals instrumentally building relationships that preserve and accumulate relative social advantage. The strengths of this form of social capital are that it is aspirational in terms of social mobility, and ensures maintenance of and access to further resources. Importantly, though, bridging social capital also has drawbacks. It involves people in considerable worries about status maintenance, like which school they are going to send their children to, or whether they are moving in the right networks to get the right sort of job. Crucially, it is also concerned with neutralizing or offsetting ongoing obligations, for example by buying-in help. It disengages from the ongoing solidarity-based trustful obligations and reciprocity that are key components of social capital, and is more concerned with individualized investments and yields. This bridging form of social capital is most evident among middle class people in our studies, or people from working class, low income, and minority backgrounds really aspiring to *get out to get on*.

In our research, for example, we charted the ways that middle class parents with access to resources such as money, high status social contacts, and legitimated cultural knowledge drew on these capitals to advance the life chances of their children. Such procurement of advantage involved attachment to dispersed and less bonded social groups. In contrast, working class parents often used their resources to help their children negotiate disadvantage and challenges through reciprocal day-to-day survival support networks. These sorts of processes are at the heart of the unequal workings of social capital.

Another example is our longitudinal study of young people's transitions to adulthood, where young working class people living in deprived areas can pursue quite different trajectories in terms of their involvement in reciprocal relationships and affiliations within their local neighborhood. Those who value success and want to get on in life have to get out of their local community, both emotionally and later on physically. Others may value "getting on" but are not prepared or able to cut themselves off in this way (see Holland, this volume). Following the logic of the get out to get on process, eventually a change in location and values may mean that bridging social capital across diverse characteristics can transform into an exclusive bonding social capital based on shared lifestyles. Those who are upwardly mobile, for example, embed themselves in the aspired networks and norms, perhaps even drawing up the ladder behind them.

Delving into the processes underlying the different forms of social capital illuminates how the bridging form of social capital involves an orientation to accumulating resources for instrumental ends. The everyday practices involved in bridging thus contain the seeds of social capital's own destruction, in terms of avoiding and undermining extensive trust, reciprocity, and obligations. It is ideas about the prevalence of individualized, obligation-limited social fracture that are the very reasons why policy makers believe that there is a deficit of social capital and a need to generate it nationally and in local communities, especially in its bridging form.

Third way social policies, between market and state, which turn to the development of social capital in the civic sphere as a solution to perceived contemporary ills, draw on a conception of social inclusion that is linked to social mobility, combined with ideas around the economic competitiveness of individuals, families, communities and the nation. Policies are then concerned with providing the rights and conditions for individuals, families, and communities to become socially mobile and take advantage of economic competitiveness. In other words, and ironically, policies and practice-based initiatives that promote social mobility can further embed social divisions and resource inequalities, and thus can be at odds with initiatives to promote social cohesion and build social capital.

Currently, some scholars pose repairing and enhancing social capital as the way forward in dealing with concerns about social changes in families and communities. Adoption of social capital as a guiding policy concept has over-ridden more politically challenging concepts and agendas such as poverty, social inequality, and racism. As should be clear from my previous discussion, Coleman's model points to supporting and encouraging the nuclear family form, with its so-called traditional relations between the genders and generations. The welfare state needs to be rolled back so that it does not supplant the functions of the *welfare family* that promote social capital. Putnam's ideas champion a policy focus on civil society, and more communal and voluntary aspects of association, congruent with a third way approach.

As such, social capital as an ameliorative policy aim is essentially depoliticized and behaviorist, pointing toward the small-scale, local, and civic rather than structural conditions. Yet, a grounded and critical perspective on the dynamics of families and social capital reveals that an emphasis on social capital building at the expense of wider issues of social justice can further embed the inequalities resulting from social divisions. Therefore, we need a policy focus on redistribution, and recognition that the economy and the social have consequences for people's family and community lives (rather than vice versa).

IMPLICATIONS FOR THE CONSTRUCTIONS OF THE OBJECTS OF SOCIAL CAPITAL AND SOCIAL CHANGE

If as social capital theorists claim there has been negative social change related to changes in the family, then the epistemology and methodology that form the basis for social capital assessments become an important and legitimate focus of attention. In other words, it is important to reflect upon how this knowledge about the state and trajectory of families and social capital is constructed and investigated.

One of the notable features of both Coleman's and Putnam's theorizing is that the mechanics of social capital are quite specific, even formulaic, and this makes them easily amenable to empirical investigation and quantification, particularly through the use of surveys. Indeed, building on debates about the definition of social capital, a substantial part of debate within the field is devoted to the measurement of social capital (see exchange between Devine & Roberts, 2003 & van Deth, 2003). Following Coleman leads to a focus on family form, educational qualifications, and school type, while following Putnam means investigating levels of trust and voluntary association involvement. Whatever their adherence, the formulaic nature of mainstream ideas about the mechanics of social capital means that social capital researchers tend to adopt proxy indicators of social capital from pre-existing large-scale, and perhaps longitudinal, datasets. This reliance on makeshift rather than tailored measures often obscures or misleads more than it reveals or illuminates (Furstenberg, 2006).

In contrast, Bourdieu and Wacquant (1992) treat theoretical concepts as "polymorphic, supple and adaptive, rather than defined, calibrated and used rigidly" (p. 23). Thus, capitals, including social capital, are not objects but metaphors for how society works. As opposed to objects delineating prescriptions about what to investigate, they provide researchers with a set of conceptual tools that are good for thinking; a starting point for making sense of the social world. Bourdieu's approach to social knowledge involves critical reflection not merely on the power dynamics of the practices of those who are the substantive objects of research, such as members of families and communities, but *equally* on the broader context of power relations that embrace social science and social researchers. Indeed, Bourdieu alerts us to a *logic of research* that highlights the *construction of the object*. This is an epistemological and methodological point of rupture within researchers' understanding of how research should proceed. At this point, investigators must recognize that unless they themselves construct the objects of their research, they are dealing with objects pre-constructed within narrow approaches that reflect the underlying assumptions of the powerful in society, and thereby reproduce their interests.

Another part of the construction of the object is the process that suggests which methods to pursue in empirical investigation, rather than letting the research question guide the choice of method used. For example, the focus or emphases within statistical presentation of trends and changes in family forms and household types construct particular arguments. The categories involved become socially significant, with important consequences, including policy development, for how we perceive the condition and trajectory of family life in contemporary society. Such categories then come to explain every aspect of family lives and change when, in reality, as taxonomic groups, particular family forms may not be the most important explanatory factor. Gender, or social class, for example, may be primary. Scholars in the social capital field have raised this issue as well. Ponthieux has argued that the rush to measurement and push toward international harmonization of indicators unthinkingly creates "de facto new statistical objects . . . once they exist, indicators acquire in some ways a life of their own" (pp. 1–9). Baron (2004) has commented that indicative measures of social capital used in the British Government's Social Capital Question Bank initiative implicitly inscribe the (ideal typical) "good" social capitalist as a particular sort of person. He empirically demonstrates how the construction of the survey questions and available responses are heavily inflected with age, class, ethnicity, area, employment, nation, and gender, celebrating "the economic, cultural and social life of certain, already powerful, elements of British society" (p.13).

Another telling critique of the formulaic theorization and consequent measurement of social capital, made by Portes (1998) is that it is tautological. In the capitals metaphor, social capital is a *process* of investment, accumulation, conversion, and so on; and in Bourdieu's conceptualization, conferring and legitimizing power and differentiation. Yet, in a circulatory logic, what researchers often investigate and measure are outcomes of social capital, with those collective or individual outcomes then treated as if they were evidence of the existence of social capital and extrapolated social change. A sense of process is an element of understanding that is muted within the dominant social capital field in terms of invoking families and examining social capital itself. Social capital debates that implicate families potentially subject them to the double jeopardy of objectification through unreflexive categorical presentations that take on a life of their own from both fields.

The arguments above are not a position against quantitative approaches, but rather a call for more reflexivity about the construction of explanatory categories and indicative variables. In other words, researchers need to consider thoughtfully the way they are constructing knowledge about social change. Understanding the underlying suppositions and preconstructions of what to measure, explore and investigate, and assess about the nature of society and families invoked by them, encourages a quizzical approach to the dominant construction of social capital and of families, and how they are said to be part of social change. Importantly, reflexivity opens up the ability to identify some social capital processes, marginalized and obfuscated in mainstream thinking. Just as importantly, it also leads to the conclusion that what social researchers understand to be the case is not separate from how they come to understand it. Thus, in the face of any assertions about social change and prescriptions about the detail of the mechanisms by which families, social capital, or any aspect of the social world works, it is important to reflect on what is being constructed and in whose interests. Overall then, this critical case study calls for an understanding of the relationship between families, social capital, and social change. Indeed, any ideas about the nature of society, social change, and what to do about them should be grounded in epistemological and methodological reflexivity and vigilance.

NOTES

1. The Families & Social Capital programme of research was funded by the United Kingdom's Economic and Social Research Council between 2002 and 2007, under award reference number M570255001. The program involved ten core empirical projects and a similar number of additional, associated research studies. The core projects in particular looked at various aspects of the inter-relationship between the dynamics of family change and processes of social capital in different circumstances and localities. They covered the life course, from children and young people, through parents, to older people, looked at issues of race/ethnicity, social class and gender, and encompassed local, national and transnational contexts. The range of methods we used included secondary analysis of quantitative data, primary surveys, in-depth interviews, group discussions, participant observation, visual techniques, and reviews of policy, theoretical, and research literature. For a full report of the program see www.lsbu.ac.uk/families/ESRC_Group_report.pdf . For current research projects of the Families & Social Capital Research Group visit www.lsbu.ac.uk/families.

2. Further details and references to published literature for all the findings discussed in this chapter are provided in the final report on our program of research (see link provided above).

REFERENCES

Allatt, P. (1993). Becoming privileged: The role of family processes. In I. Bates and G. Riseborough (Eds.), *Youth and inequality* (pp. 139–159). Buckingham: Open University Press.

Anthias, F. (2007). Ethnic ties: Social capital and the question of mobilizability. *The Sociological Review*, 55, 788–805.

Arneil, B. (2006). *Diverse communities: The problem with social capital.* New York: Cambridge University Press.

Baron, S. (2004). Social capital in British politics and policy making. In J. Franklin (Ed.), *Politics, trust and networks: Social capital in critical perspective* (pp. 5–16). Families & Social Capital ESRC Research Group Working Paper No. 7. London South Bank University. Retrieved January, 4, 2004, from http://www.lsbu.ac.uk/families/workingpapers/familieswp7.pdf

Beck, U. (1992). *Risk society: Towards a new modernity.* London: Sage.

Bourdieu, P. (1997/1986). The forms of capital. In A. H. Halsey, H. Lauder, P. Brown, & A. S. Wells (Eds.), *Education: Culture, economy, society* (pp. 46–58). Oxford: Oxford University Press.

Bourdieu, P., & Wacquant, L. (1992). *An invitation to reflexive sociology.* Cambridge: Polity.

Carling, A., Duncan, S., & Edwards, R. (Eds.) (2002). *Analysing families: Morality and rationality in policy and practice.* London: Routledge.

Coleman, J. S. (1988). The creation and destruction of social capital: Implications for the law. *Notre Dame Journal of Law, Ethics and Public Policy, 3*, 375–404.

Coleman, J. S. (1990). *Foundations of social theory.* London: Harvard University Press.

Davies, J. (Ed.) (1993). *The family: Is it just another lifestyle choice?* London: Institute of Economic Affairs.

Dennis, N. (1993). *Rising crime and the dismembered family.* London: Institute of Economic Affairs.

Devine, F., & Roberts, J. M. (2003). Alternative approaches to researching social capital: A comment on van Deth's "Measuring social capital." *International Journal of Social Research Methodology, 6*, 93–99.

Duncan, S., & Edwards, R. (1999). *Lone mothers, paid work and gendered moral rationalities.* Basingstoke: Macmillan.

Edwards, R. (Ed.) (2008). *Researching families and communities: Social and generational change.* Abingdon: Routledge.

Finch, J., & Mason, J. (1993). *Negotiating family responsibilities.* London: Routledge.

Franklin, J. (2007). *Social capital: Between harmony and dissonance*, Families & Social Capital ESRC Research Group Working Paper No. 22. London South Bank University. Retrieved January 2, 2007, from http://www.lsbu.ac.uk/families/workingpapers/familieswp22.pdf

Furstenberg, F. (2006). Banking on families: How families generate and distribute social capital. In R. Edwards, J. Franklin, & J. Holland (Eds.), *Assessing social capital: Concept, policy and practice* (pp. 95–110). Newcastle: Cambridge Scholars Press.

Gillies, V. (2008). Childrearing, class and the new politics of parenting. *Sociology Compass, 2*, 1079–1095.

McCarthy, J. R., & Edwards, R. (2002). The individual in public and private: The significance of mothers and children. In A. Carling, S. Duncan, & R. Edwards (Eds.), *Analysing families: Morality and rationality in policy and practice* (pp. 199–217). London: Routledge.

Morgan, P. (1995). *Farewell to the family: Public policy and family breakdown in Britain and the USA.* London: Institute of Economic Affairs.

Morrow, V. (1999). Conceptualising social capital in relation to the wellbeing of children and young people: A critical review. *Sociological Review, 47*, 744–765.

Murray, C. (1994). *Underclass: The crisis deepens.* London: Institute of Economic Affairs.

O'Neill, B., & Gidengil, E. (Eds.). (2006). *Gender and social capital.* London: Routledge.

Ponthieux, S. (2002, November 4–6). *The measurement of social capital: A new turn or a dead end.* Paper presented to the SIENA Group conference on Social Statistics, ONS/OECD.

Portes, A. (1998). Social capital: Its origins and applications in modern sociology. *Annual Review of Sociology, 24*, 1–4.

Putnam, R. D. (1993). *Making democracy work: Civic traditions in modern Italy.* Princeton: Princeton University Press.

Putnam, R. D. (2000). *Bowling alone: The collapse and revival of American community.* New York: Simon and Schuster.

Reay, D. (1998). *Class work: Mothers' involvement in their children's primary schooling.* London: UCL Press.

Schuller, T., Baron, S., & Field, J. (2000). Social capital: A review and critique. In S. Baron, J. Field, & T. Schuller (Eds.), *Social capital: Critical perspectives* (pp. 1–38). Oxford: Oxford University Press.

Sennett, R. (1998). *The corrosion of character: The personal consequences of work in the new capitalism.* New York: Norton.

Smart, C., & Neale, B. (1999). *Family fragments?* Cambridge: Polity.

Stolle, D. (with Lewis, J.) (2002). Social capital—an emerging concept. In B. Hobson, J. Lewis, & B. Siim (Eds.), *Contested concepts in gender and social politics* (pp. 195–230). Cheltenham: Edward Elgar.

van Deth, J. (2003). Measuring social capital: Orthodoxies and continuing controversies. *International Journal of Social Research Methodology, 6*, 79–92.

Woolcock, M. (1998). Social capital and economic development: Towards a theoretical synthesis and policy framework. *Theory and Society, 27*, 151–208.

CHAPTER 16

Psychosocial Impact of Illness: A Transformative Experience

Michèle Preyde

Universally, almost everyone will experience a significant medical illness personally or within the family at one point or another. Advancements in medicine have resulted in a growing number of people who survive major illnesses, and this brings comfort. However, the experience of illness is considerably stressful. Supportive care in hospital settings has been a relatively recent adjunct to medical care. There are several varied theories informing psychosocial intervention, including theories of stress and adaptation, social support, cognition and behavior, and social learning (e.g., self-efficacy). How best to provide psychosocial care is still unknown. Much progress has been made in the development of hospital-based psychosocial intervention, for example, addressing informational needs has resulted in improved functioning. However, there is a need for enhanced theoretical understanding with respect to therapeutic change for decreasing distress arising from uncertainty. Several systematic literature reviews revealed a lack of consensus on the definitive theoretical foundation on which to base effective psychosocial intervention. There are inconsistent results across the board and the limitation in advancing theoretical confirmation at this point stems from problems in research design and implementation. The success of psychosocial research in hospital settings is vulnerable due to the lack of support from the organizational culture within hospitals, and medical professionals who are often the gatekeepers for psychosocial care. It might be prudent to develop an understanding of the problems stemming from organizational factors in order to address them. What, then, might be an effective means for organizational change to optimize psychosocial intervention delivery and research?

There are two questions raised in this chapter. Many of the problems arising from patients' experience of illness, concern, worry, or thoughts. The theoretical mechanisms of action for interventions often include knowledge and cognitive appraisal. However, much of the distress for patients stems from not knowing the future, the course the disease will take, and the implications for living. Strategies for stress management currently include attempts at increasing a sense of personal control. Could improving acceptance of or tolerance for the unknown be beneficial? I propose that application of a theory of acceptance that employs cognitive reappraisal, and in particular training to increase acceptance or tolerance of not knowing one's personal outcomes may prove beneficial in hospital-based psychosocial care. Hospital-based psychosocial interventions are designed to help patients and their families cope will illness, but are often delivered in hospital environments that are frequently characterized by high levels of stress. Currently, the hospital context appears to be rife with problems arising from the organizational culture that is affecting psychosocial clinical research, and thus the development of an evidence-base for practice. In particular, medical personnel are experiencing critical levels of emotional distress, and often do not see the emotional distress patients experience. In the absence of actual changes in patients' health status or organizational health, can reappraisal diminish psychological distress? That is, what lessons learned from research in psychosocial intervention at the individual patient level are applicable at the organizational level? Can interventions, based on a theory of acceptance help patients cope with the uncertainty of their illness trajectory, and professionals deal with a stressful hospital environment? In this chapter, I conceptualize change as the process of adaptation to stress, which is occurring on two levels: the individual patient and the hospital environment.

HISTORICAL CONTEXT: TRANSFORMATION WITHIN THE HOSPITAL SETTING

There have been tremendous conceptual shifts in health care. In the Victorian era, professionals including physicians served as moral philosophers, attempting to ensure that patients' use of their bodies was *moral* (Haller, 1981). The conceptual shift, for example, from a person possessed by demons to a person with an illness had enormous implications for personal well-being. Another example is the view of illness as an imbalance of humor requiring bleeding or purging shifting to an understanding of bacterial infections. There was a time when the medical community considered people with mental retardation *feeble-minded*, and viewed this feeble-mindedness as the root of social ills. These transformations in conceptualizing illness have not only had profound consequences on research and treatment options, but also on the relationship between the practitioner and the patient.

Knowledge in medicine is rapidly changing. A recent transformation within health and mental health settings has fostered a culture of knowledge such that scientific-based approaches have replaced unsystematic (and biased) practices (Brown, Crawford, & Hicks, 2003). This has been the case for medical treatments, but not the distress associated with medical illness where in some places a philosophy prevails: do not ask patients if they are experiencing distress when the resources to effectively deal with it are lacking. At first glance, this thinking seems to defy logic for those learned in psychosocial care, but on further reflection one may ask what benefit would come of uncovering a problem without having the ability to address it. In fact, psychological distress often goes unnoticed by medical professionals (Sollner et al., 2001). Furthermore, medical professionals themselves often experience critical levels of distress. In fact, stress and burnout are quite common among hospital personnel (Sherman, Edwards, Simonton, & Mehta, 2006), have implications for patient well being (Vahey, Aiken, Sloan, Clarke, & Vargas, 2004), and may contribute to an ill hospital-environment. Although space prohibits my addressing these personal and interpersonal factors, they too may be affected by organizational culture.

Thus, advancements in psychosocial care have been slow to follow advances in medicine. There appears to be great difficulty in establishing an evidence-base for psychosocial intervention developed to address distress in patients. Only recently has the focus of hospital-based interventions included psychological distress associated with illness. Although there is some development of knowledge, the theoretical foundation for the evidence-base of psychosocial intervention is not well established. Consistent with ecological theory, efforts to develop the evidence base have been hampered by hospital environment factors. One key factor is the medical professional experience of *distress*, the very target for change in psychosocial intervention for patients.

TRANSFORMATIVE EXPERIENCES: THE TRANSFORMATIVE POWER OF ILLNESS

Illness is an antecedent of change. The experience of physical (or mental) illness can be distressing for individuals and their family members. The psychosocial impact of physical illness, and the psychosocial interventions designed to alleviate or help alleviate various challenges (e.g., coping with distress) have been the focus of much research. Objectives of this research include developing an understanding of people's experience of illness and the challenges associated with managing illness symptoms and outcomes, identifying people more prone to have problems coping, designing interventions for those in need of psychosocial care, testing for intervention effectiveness, and examining the intervention's mechanism of action. Treatment for physical illness occurs in environments where professionals aspire to use sound research evidence to decide on a course of treatment. A strong evidence base should also inform the basis for the psychosocial interventions available to help people cope with these illnesses, but this foundation of research is less established relative to medicine; in fact, some consider it woefully behind in demonstrating effectiveness. Thus, one main research goal is to contribute to the evidence-base of the effectiveness of psychosocial interventions designed to help people cope with illness. The therapeutic change would be improved coping capacities. Evidence is not static, but continually evolves through new evidence and refinement of existing evidence through the translation of knowledge derived from research.

At the individual level, the impact of illness is stressful for patients. According to Lazarus and Folkman's (1984) *Theory of Stress and Coping*, stress develops from the interaction between the individual and the environment. Cognitive appraisal of emotional experiences develops from the ongoing transactions with the environment and evaluation of these transactions (Lazarus, 1984). Individuals experience stress when the demand from the environment exceeds their coping capacity. Coping refers to the cognitive and behavioral efforts people make in attempts to master, reduce, or tolerate the demands produced by stress. Two major functions of coping are emotional (distress) regulation and the management of the stress (problem). Cognitive appraisal of health status by patients may be particularly important and has implications for adjustment. Adjustment, then, depends, in part, on the individual's interpretation of the stressors or of the individual's coping resources, options, and constraints.

Two processes, cognitive appraisal and coping, are mediators of stress and adaptation outcomes. Primary cognitive appraisals are judgments about the person-environment transaction, considered irrelevant, benign, positive, or stressful. Stressful appraisals consist of harm, loss, threat, or challenge. Personal (e.g., beliefs) and situational (e.g., familiarity of event) factors shape the primary appraisal. Secondary appraisal refers to the evaluation of coping resources and options. Lazarus & Folkman (1984) portray coping as the processes of cognitive and behavioral efforts in attempts of managing specific demands appraised as taxing or exceeding resources. It is process-oriented as opposed to trait dependent. In this sense, coping is a process that changes as a function of continuous appraisals of the dynamic and reciprocal person-environment relationship. The reappraisal influences subsequent coping efforts. Thus, the coping process can lead to change. Folkman and Lazarus describe eight ways of coping:

1. confrontive (aggressive efforts to change the situation)
2. distancing (detaching self)
3. self-control (regulate feelings and actions)
4. seeking social support (including informational, tangible, and emotional support),
5. accepting responsibility (acknowledging one's role and effort to correct)
6. escape-avoidance (wishful thinking and behaviors to avoid problem)
7. planful problem solving (deliberate efforts to change the situation including analytic efforts to solve the problem)
8. positive reappraisal (create positive meaning)

The effectiveness of any particular coping strategy depends on the context, such that one strategy (e.g., denial) may be maladaptive in one context but may be adaptive in another (e.g., immediately following trauma; Horowitz, 1986). Coping with the stress of illness (i.e., an antecedent), then, can be viewed as a perpetual process of change and the consequences of such coping efforts as neutral, adaptive, or maladaptive.

People experiencing illness employ varied coping strategies, and for some the coping strategies employed were those used in their pre-illness lives. No one particular pattern of coping has been determined to be best for relieving psychological distress (De Faye, Wilson, Chater, Viola, & Hall, 2006). Interventions are generally based on conceptual models of coping to enhance coping with distress. The cognitive-appraisal approach to coping is based on the mental processes or perceptions that individuals have of their illness experiences (distress). For therapeutic change to occur, individuals modify existing perceptions, or create new ones by comparing new information with existing cognitions. This reorganization of perception can be adaptive or maladaptive, the nature of which depends on the perception of the stress (event), the characteristic mode of response, and the strength of need. Influences on the speed and ease of reorganization include the rigidity and precision of the original cognitive structure and the characteristics of the individual, such as personality, and the meaning that is developed. Problem-focused coping efforts tend to be used in changeable situations while emotion-focused coping tends to be used in situations not amenable to change. The effectiveness of problem-focused coping efforts mainly depends on the success of emotion-focused efforts. Negative emotions (e.g., fear) that accompany appraisals need to be regulated if they are to be kept from interfering with problem-focused forms of coping (Folkman, 1984). One of the most important components of effective coping is the awareness of when to appraise the stress as uncontrollable and focus on emotional regulation or tolerance and acceptance. Cognitive appraisal or reappraisal may be one of the most important mediators of any psychosocial intervention for therapeutic change.

INTERVENTION EFFECTIVENESS: CHANGING COPING CAPACITIES

People respond in a variety of ways to illness, and many factors affect the way people respond. For example, at the individual-level the capacity for coping, one's genetic predisposition, and illness characteristics such as severity and stigma, affect the way people respond to or deal with illness. Interpersonally, positive support may come from family members, or people in one's network could have neutral or even detrimental effects on the way a person copes with illness. Examples at the contextual level include a wide range of influences such as the availability and accessibility of high quality medical or mental health treatment, and the influence of the organizational culture within settings.

In terms of medical illness, there is some good evidence that hospital-based psychosocial intervention can help *some* people with medical illness cope. However, this research requires some fine-tuning, such as clarifying for whom is what type of psychosocial intervention most effective and efficient. Psychosocial intervention encompasses a wide range of services including tangible support (e.g., money), counseling, informational and educational support (e.g., specific to the type of cancer, financial resources available), family concerns (e.g., strained relationships), emotional distress, reassurance, referral (e.g., home care), and symptom management (e.g., dealing with pain). In meta-analyses and systematic reviews (e.g., Meyer & Mark, 1995; Preyde, MacAulay, & Dingwall, 2009; Preyde & Synnott, in press) of hospital-based psychosocial interventions for a variety of conditions, researchers have not found significant differences between categories of intervention. That is, of the different types of intervention, chiefly, cognitive-behavioral, informational, counseling, social support, or a group of miscellaneous or unusual interventions (e.g., music therapy), not one therapeutic approach has been determined to be superior based on the research evidence.

Informational interventions are widely available in most hospital settings and are consistent with principles of informed decision-making. Successfully employed informational and educational efforts reduce distress associated with symptoms of disease or symptoms of treatment; however, dealing with emotional distress from worry or uncertainty can be another matter. That is, some patients with access to informational or psychoeducational interventions still report clinical levels of psychological distress.

COMMON THEORETICAL FOUNDATIONS FOR HOSPITAL-BASED PSYCHOSOCIAL INTERVENTION

Two theoretical foundations informing psychosocial interventions are cognitive-behavioral and social support (including emotional support) theories. For both theoretical perspectives, cognitive appraisal has much to do with the success of the intervention in decreasing psychological distress. Interventions based on social support theory have been found to be effective for addressing distress in hospital patients or family members (e.g., Campbell, Phaneuf, & Deane, 2004; Preyde & Ardal, 2003). Social support, a richly complex term, represents a function of one's social environment as well as one's personality, namely social competence and appraisal (Barrera, 1986; Heller & Lakey, 1985; Pierce, Lakey, Sarason, Sarason & Joseph, 1997). Social support includes structural components such as the size of one's social network, and functional components such as emotional, instrumental, cognitive, and companionship support. Researchers often use perceived social support scales to measure this mediator, yet perceived social support also is an indication of one's personality, social competence, and appraisal tendencies. Personality influences perceived social support through reactive, evocative, or proactive social interaction, and in how one appraises the support. The effectiveness of social support, then, is partially determined by study participants' perception of support, and partially determined by participants' personal characteristics, such as their personality, and their perceptions of the personal characteristics of the support giver. It might be considered advantageous to offer social support intervention to individuals who are able to appraise support favorably, and feel valued, connected, understood, and validated by the support giver. Of importance is the perception of empathy; efforts to provide support that is not perceived as empathic may be ineffective or even harmful (Heller & Rook, 1997). Social support can influence appraisals of the illness experience and the successfulness of coping efforts. In fact, cognitive appraisal and coping are two of the most influential personal factors affecting patients' psychological adjustment (Jenkins & Pargament, 1988).

A THEORY OF ACCEPTANCE TO ADDRESS UNCERTAINTY OF PERSONAL OUTCOMES

There are a number of hospital-based interventions for reducing distress based on cognitive-behavioral theories. In psychosocial oncology (Preyde & Synnott, in press), interventions include problem-solving and coping skills training, stress management, cognitive adaptation including distraction, and relaxation. Many of these strategies can be effective for dealing with symptoms of the disease or treatment; however, dealing with uncertainty (Mishel, 1997) and disease-related worry (e.g., Hirai et al., 2008) has recently emerged as a separate issue. Few interventions specifically focus on cognitive reappraisal. Where reappraisal is used as a mechanism for change, the focus is on reappraising one's coping abilities. That is, the theoretical underpinnings of psychosocial intervention to date involve increasing self-efficacy and a sense of personal control. However, the individual often has no control over the course of disease; thus attempting to increase personal control may be counter-productive. Oncologists may be able to give patients a sense of their likelihood for going into remission or relapsing; however, how any one individual will progress is unpredictable. Not knowing one's personal outcomes is distressing and challenges coping capacities. I propose that it also interferes with many aspects of the person's life including the maintenance of healthy family and social relationships, perceptions of the self, and adjustment. Thus, addressing uncertainty in psychosocial intervention is crucial, and the best strategy may be helping people to accept the fact that they are not going to know their own personal outcomes or future, to build tolerance for this lack of knowledge, and focus on positive aspects of life. Because uncertainty is stressful (it can resemble post-traumatic stress disorder), strategies must be employed to address symptoms of distress (e.g., prevent or redirect intrusive thoughts). That is, it may be worthwhile to apply a theory of acceptance in psychosocial intervention and test building tolerance for the unknown as the mechanism for therapeutic change.

Within the drive for evidence-based practice is the opportunity to examine how the intervention might exert its effect, often referred to as the mechanism of action. Admittedly, for many patients the level of physical health has a direct effect on psychosocial well-being and coping. That is, the psychosocial impact fluctuates with the severity of the physical illness or the perceived severity and the severity of symptoms. This among other factors, need to be controlled or accounted for when examining intervention effects. The *active ingredients* of psychosocial interventions can be very difficult to isolate and evaluate. One central mechanism of action for interventions designed to alleviate psychological distress concerns cognitive appraisals, such as illness appraisals (Lazarus & Folkman, 1984). That is, the psychosocial intervention appears to have exerted its effect by changing the way people think about their illness or their family members' illness, or their coping abilities and may have less to do with the actual health status. The research to date on psychosocial, hospital-based intervention is considered limited in a variety of ways. Most intervention trials lack a theoretical framework (Campbell et al., 2004), many suffer from poor methodological quality (Preyde & Synnott, in press), and in particular, there are problems in accrual (Gotay, 1991). Barriers (Goodwin et al., 2000) to the successful conduct of psychosocial intervention research include elements of the hospital environment, such as support from medical and allied health staff. Interestingly, the health professionals delivering medical care are often themselves experiencing psychological distress (Sherman et al., 2006; Sutinen, Kivimaki, Elovainio, & Virtanen, 2002) stemming from the organizational culture. There is some evidence to suggest that the distress experienced by health professionals and the organizational culture can strongly influence professional practice and patient outcomes. While much research to date has focused on the psychosocial interventions designed to alleviate distress in patients and family members, it might also prove useful with medical staff.

INDIVIDUAL TO ORGANIZATIONAL

There are parallel efforts in medicine and supportive care to address illness and the psychosocial impact of illness. Yet, the hospital environment can be a bad place for sick people; that is, it can sometimes be difficult for patients to improve in a hospital environment that seems to be ailing. It is important to understand the nuances of organizational culture and transformation, and their effect on human health and development. Only recently have researchers begun to explore the influence of the organizational settings of hospitals on practice.

Hospital environments are vulnerable to broader societal changes. Hospital environments are often characterized by the intersection of several stressful situations, such as understaffing, overworked personnel, competition with other hospitals for scarce resources both in terms of dollars and human resources (e.g., doctor shortages), and constantly dealing with medical crises. In Canada, hospital environments can be considered victims of ill thought-out government initiatives such as cost-cutting initiatives (e.g., limiting enrollment into medical school, reducing nursing staff, reducing length of stay) that had devastating effects on the environment and culture within hospitals.

ORGANIZATIONAL CULTURE WITHIN THE CONTEXT OF THE HOSPITAL ENVIRONMENT

Organizational culture refers to a system of shared beliefs and values within organizations that guides behavior (Schein, 1990). This culture can have a significant influence on the performance of the organization and that of its members. Observable culture is comprised of methods passed on to new members, including family ceremonies or personal rituals. External sources can influence organizational culture; however, there can be many internal problems affecting the quality of the culture, such as modes of communication, differentiation of power and status, and the standards for rewards and punishments. A culture of distress often characterizes perceptions of the hospital environment. Changing the hospital culture is difficult, but possible.

One of the main theories important for understanding the organizational environment in hospital settings is equity theory. Equity theory (Walster, Walster, & Bershcield, 1978) is a general model for understanding human interactional behavior. According to this theory, people understand fairness to be the equitable distribution of rewards proportional to contribution or need. Individuals perceive equity when they consider what they received as proportional to what they put into the interaction. They make subjective evaluations of their situations and optimal interactions are those perceived as equitable. Perceptions of inequity lead to distress. Theoretically, the notions of equity or fairness are relevant to understanding hospital environments. For example, Sutinen and colleagues (2002) found low organizational fairness to be associated with psychological distress in hospital physicians. There are many environmental factors associated with the presence of distress in hospital environments in general and medical professional staff in particular, especially resource issues. In the current fiscal environment, the absence of any resources, the factors fostering distress, are not likely to change.

The purpose of developing psychosocial care was to 'treat' the psychosocial problems patients face while in the hospital and sometimes beyond (e.g., clinicians may recognize the need for child protection services and refer the case to community agencies at discharge). It is often reserved for the most challenging, disadvantaged, and vulnerable patients. Medical professionals working within the hospital environment impede access to and research in psychosocial care (Goodwin et al., 2000). In many

Canadian hospitals, especially in regional and satellite (community) hospitals, there are insufficient resources to permit screening for psychosocial distress in patients. Social workers and other allied health professionals who provide psychosocial care rely on referral from medical staff, many of whom often cannot see or detect the distress in patients (Sollner et al., 2001). Furthermore, providing medical professionals with information on each patient's psychological well-being has shown to be ineffective (Boyes, Newell, Girgis, McElduff, & Sanson-Fisher, 2006). As aforementioned, these medical personnel may be dealing themselves with critical levels of stress, perceived inequities, dissatisfaction, ill effects of poor decision making, and potentially personal mental health issues and a negative working environment. It might be a small wonder that they cannot see the distress in patients (some would pin it on the reliance on the medical model that reduces patients to a single medical condition). Furthermore, it has been noted that enrollment into psychosocial research in hospital settings often hinges on referral from medical staff, and this referral can be less than optimal (Goodwin, et al., 2000). Why it is so is cause for speculation. One would expect to find professionals in hospital settings trained to employ evidence-based practice to be supportive of such efforts to build evidence in psychosocial care. Ironically, that support seems to be lacking. A dilemma is that not only can the organizational culture have a negative influence on medical practice, but it might also hamper efforts to address psychosocial problems that patients may also be experiencing. I postulate that the distress experienced by medical and health personnel is the barrier or reason for their lack of referral of patients to psychosocial care or research. In other words, the distress experienced by medical staff prevents them from seeing or attending to the distress in patients, and from referring distressed patients to psychosocial care and research. The distress in medical staff often arises from the organizational culture of the hospital environment.

Changing an organizational culture is not an easy undertaking, and often requires many aspects of the organization to change concurrently (Robbins & Langton, 2001). My position or theory is that an organizational culture is created and maintained by individuals and their thought processes. One's beliefs of what an organizational culture is developed from his or her cognitive processes. Presumably, by changing cognitive processes, beliefs will change. In few studies have interventions been tested that attempt to target negative organizational culture in hospital settings. This body of research is still in the phase of developing an understanding of the organizational factors that affect patient outcomes. Nonetheless, Anderzen and Arnetz (2005) report favorable results with an intervention designed to improve the organizational culture through increased knowledge of psychosocial work indicators and a structured method for implementing changes based on this knowledge. Similarly, an intervention designed to reduce feelings of inequity was successful for reducing burnout for direct-care professionals working with individuals with mental disability (van Dierendonck, Schaefeli, & Buunk, 1998). While in both interventions the mechanism by which change was to occur involved cognition, it is uncertain if any of these efforts can address the psychological distress experienced by medical professionals. It may be possible to develop interventions that address distress in medical staff by changing their perceptions to optimize patient and hospital personnel outcomes. It is conceivable that fostering acceptance of distress may improve the medical staff's ability to deal with distress. It is conceivable that applying this theory of acceptance in the hospital could build tolerance for distress and may improve organizational well being and that of hospital staff and patients.

CONSEQUENCES OF THERAPEUTIC CHANGE

The changes people with illness experience can be complex. There are many changes internal to the patient such as change in status, identity, stresses and coping, and meaning of life. Changes interpersonally can include changes with roles, responsibilities, and relationships with family members. For many people, a flurry of change fluctuates with acuity of illness and the severity of symptoms or side effects. Medical treatments used in an attempt to ameliorate the illness sometimes create new problems. Nonetheless, the experience of illness is distressing for many people and their families and friends. Employing psychosocial interventions for the distress experienced by patients can bring about therapeutic change evidenced by enhanced coping with symptoms and ameliorating the distress associated with the illness. Although increasing patients' knowledge of their disease and symptoms addresses some of their concerns, many people still experience emotional distress stemming from not knowing what they will personally be experiencing. Increasing a sense of personal control has shown to have some merit; however, people often have little control over the progression of some diseases. I contend that building acceptance of and tolerance for embracing uncertainty would be an effective mechanism for change as evidenced by consequences of therapeutic change such as decreased emotional distress. These psychosocial interventions and processes are taking place in hospital settings, which are complex organizations. Barriers to successful psychosocial intervention delivery and the conduct of research include hospital personnel and the organizational culture. Often conceived of as a separate entity, organizational culture is really a fabrication by an individual or groupthink. One wonders if stress management for hospital personnel could improve the organizational culture and facilitate the delivery and conduct of research of hospital-based psychosocial intervention. The consequences would be improved quality of work life for hospital personnel and the quality of life for people experiencing major medical illness. Illness is a significant issue worldwide that can deeply affect human relationships and development. An application of a theory of acceptance may permit a transformative experience with beneficial health outcomes.

REFERENCES

Anderzen, I., & Arnetz, B. B. (2005). The impact of a prospective survey-based workplace intervention program on employee health, biologic stress markers, and organizational productivity. *Journal of Occupational and Environmental Medicine, 47*, 671–682.

Barrera, M. (1986). Distinctions between social support concepts, measures, and models. *American Journal of Community Psychology, 14*, 413–455.

Boyes, A., Newell, S., Girgis, A., McElduff, P., & Sanson-Fisher, R. (2006). Does routine assessment and real-time feedback improve cancer patients' psychosocial well-being? *European Journal of Cancer Care, 15*, 163–171.

Brown, B., Crawford, P., & Hicks, C. (2003). *Evidence-based research: Dilemmas and debates in health care*. Berkshire, UK: Open University Press.

Campbell, H. S., Phaneuf, M. R., & Deane, K. (2004). Cancer peer support programs: Do they work? *Patient Education and Counseling, 55*, 3–15.

De Faye, B. J., Wilson, K. G., Chater, S., Viola, R. A., & Hall, P. (2006). Stress and coping with advanced cancer. *Palliative Support Care, 4*, 239–249.

Folkman, S. (1984). Personal control and stress and coping processes: A theoretical analysis. *Journal of Personality and Social Psychology, 46*, 839–852.

Goodwin, P. J., Leszcz, M., Quirt, G., Koopmans, J., Arnold, A., Dohan, E., et al. (2000). Lessons learned from enrollment in the BEST study—A multicentre randomized trial of group psychosocial support in metastatic breast cancer. *Journal of Clinical Epidemiology, 53,* 47–55.

Gotay, C. C. (1991). Accrual to cancer clinical trials: Directions from the research literature. *Social Science & Medicine 33,* 569–577.

Haller, J. S., Jr. (1981). *American medicine in transition, 1840–1910.* Champaign, IL: University of Illinois Press.

Heller, K., & Lakey, B. (1985). Social support and adjustment to cancer: Reconciling descriptive, correlational, and intervention research. *Health Psychology, 15,* 135–148.

Heller, K., & Rook, K. S. (1997). Theoretical functions of social ties and support interventions. In S. Duck (Ed.), *Handbook of personal relationships* (2nd ed., pp. 102–145). New York: Wiley.

Hirai, K., Shiozaki, M., Motooka, H., Araie, H., Koyama, A., & Uchitomi, Y. (2008). Discrimination between worry and anxiety among cancer patients: Development of a brief cancer-related worry inventory. *Psychooncology, 17,* 1172–1179.

Horowitz, M. J. (1986). *Stress response syndromes.* New York: Jason Aronson.

Jenkins, R. A., & Pargament, K. I. (1988). Cognitive appraisals in cancer patients. *Social Science and Medicine, 26,* 625–633.

Lazarus, R. S. (1984). On the primacy of cognition. *American Psychologist, 39,* 124–129.

Lazarus, R. S., & Folkman, S. (1984). *Stress, appraisal and coping.* New York: Springer.

Meyer, T. J., & Mark, M. M. (1995). Effects of psychosocial interventions with adult cancer patients: A meta-analysis of randomized experiments. *Health Psychology, 14,* 101–108.

Mishel, M. H. (1997). Uncertainty in acute illness. *Annual Review of Nursing Research, 15,* 57–80.

Pierce, G. R., Lakey, B., Sarason, I. G., Sarason, B., & Joseph, H. (1997). Personality and social support processes: A conceptual overview. In G. R. Pierce, B. Lakey, I. G. Sarason, & B. R. Sarason (Eds.), *Sourcebook for social support and personality* (pp. 3–18). New York: Plenum.

Preyde, M., & Ardal, F. (2003). The effectiveness of the parent buddy program for mothers of very preterm hospitalized infants: A cohort study with control group comparison. *Canadian Medical Association Journal, 168,* 969–973.

Preyde, M., MacAulay, C., & Dingwall, T. (2009). Discharge planning from hospital to home for elderly patients: A systematic review. *Journal of Evidence-based Social Work, 6,* 198–216.

Preyde, M., & Synnott, E. (in press). Psychosocial intervention for adults with cancer: A meta-analysis. *Journal of Evidence-based Social Work.*

Robbins, S., & Langton, N. (2001). *Organizational behaviour—Concepts, controversies, applications.* Toronto, ON: Pearson Education Canada.

Schein, E. (1990). Organizational culture. *American Psychologist, 45,* 109–119.

Sherman, A. C., Edwards, D., Simonton, S., & Mehta, P. (2006). Caregiver stress and burnout in an oncology unity. *Palliative and Supportive Care, 4,* 65–81.

Sollner, W., DeVries, A., Steixner, E., Lukas, P., Sprinzl, G., & Rumpold, G. (2001). How successful are oncologists in identifying patient distress, perceived social support, and need for psychosocial counselling? *British Journal of Cancer, 84,* 179–185.

Sutinen, R., Kivimaki, M., Elovainio, M., & Virtanen, M. (2002). Organizational fairness and psychological distress in hospital physicians. *Scandinavian Journal of Public Health, 30,* 209–215.

Vahey, D. C., Aiken, L. H., Sloan, D. M., Clarke, S. P., & Vargas, D. (2004). Nurse burnout and patient satisfaction. *Medical Care, 42,* 57–66.

van Dierendonck, D., Schaefeli, W. B., & Buunk, B. P. (1998). The evaluation of an individual burnout intervention program: The role of inequity and social support. *Journal of Applied Psychology, 83,* 392–407.

Walster, E., Walster, G.W., & Bershcield, E. (1978). *Equity: Theory and research.* Boston: Allyn & Bacon.

CHAPTER 17

Toward an Integrative Theory of Care: Formal and Informal Intersections[1]

Virpi Timonen

Researchers have categorized the complex phenomenon of care into two distinct types: formal and informal. According to this accepted dichotomy, *informal* care is generally provided by untrained social network members (family or friends), usually in the absence of any monetary compensation (Walker, Pratt, & Eddy, 1995). Paid, professionally trained care workers, on the other hand, typically provide *formal* care. This two-dimensional classification of care does not adequately capture, however, the full spectrum of caregiving scenarios. Some formal caregivers work in institutions, others in home or community settings. Some receive their pay within the framework of taxes and social security, others as cash in hand. Most informal care takes place in the home of the care recipient or caregiver. However, informal caregivers can also play an important role in institutional long-term care settings where they offer companionship, emotional support, and assistance with daily activities (e.g., feeding). This chapter focuses on the care of older people because they are the fastest growing segment of the population and have a higher level of care needs than other age groups. I theorize primarily about home and community contexts because the number of older people receiving care is increasing more rapidly in this sector than in institutional settings. Formal and informal care occurs in tandem more prominently in the community context.

In this chapter, I initially review the caregiving literature to elucidate some of the persisting differences between formal and informal caregiving. Mapping out the *commonalities* and *intersections* between formal and informal care, however, is my primary aim. This is a daunting task since virtually all of the literature on caregiving discusses *either* informal *or* formal care, treating these realms as discrete entities. I base my rationale for teasing out the commonalities and intersections between formal and informal care on the fact that these categories increasingly co-exist and interact, especially in the home and community care contexts. This chapter also integrates the broader themes of this book through discussion of change, both at the individual caregiver level and the structural or policy level. I highlight the contexts that inform our understanding of these changes in the work and lives of both formal and informal caregivers, identifying antecedents and consequences of these changes. Lastly, the chapter presents the beginnings of an integrated theory of caregiving—one that straddles the formal and informal spheres.

The commonalities and intersections of formal and informal care are an almost entirely uncharted territory. In view of the relative novelty of formal and informal carers working in tandem, this is not surprising. The failure of scholars to address the overlapping aspects of these realms, however, has impeded the progress of both academic knowledge and long-term care policies. It is crucial that we begin to think of informal and formal caregiving within the same conceptual and theoretical framework. I theorize, therefore, within the context of the evolving and increasingly diverse profile of care in the home, where the interaction between formal and informal care is most visible. My aim is not to develop a grand theory of caregiving, but rather to reflect on how recent developments in formal and informal care should inform theory construction. Clearly, we can no longer think of caregiving as something confined to the informal, familial sphere. Similarly, we cannot theoretically conceptualize formal caregiving without consideration of the contributions made by informal caregivers. We need an integrated theory that recognizes the increasingly prevalent, complex, contexts of care: contexts in which informal and formal carers work alongside one another and interact in ways that reshape both realms of care.

THE CHANGING CONTEXTS OF CARE

Many researchers assume that caregiving today is essentially the same as in the past. However, fundamental changes have taken place in both the provision and contexts of care. In the informal realm, the extent to which different groups of kin provide care is changing. Several trends, including: (a) increasing life expectancies, (b) a narrowing in the gap between women's and men's life expectancies, (c) increased labor market participation among adult daughters, and (d) the preponderance of people entering old age with a partner, are diminishing the prominence of adult children as carers. Spousal caregivers constitute a growing proportion of informal caregivers, meaning care providers themselves increasingly face unique challenges stemming from their own age progression (McGee, Molloy, O'Hanlon, Layte, & Hickey, 2008). The growing care responsibilities of older adults have altered the caregiving landscape from the past, when adult children (daughters and daughters-in-law in particular) were the predominant providers of care.

In developed countries with institutional care provision, formal care has long occupied a very visible place in the public eye. Compared to informal venues of care, nursing homes and other residential settings absorb a disproportionate share of media and policy maker attention. A very diverse range of formal home and community care providers have proliferated in the care landscape, however, reshaping the sphere of care significantly (Doyle & Timonen, 2008). Because of these developments, some community-dwelling older persons are now receiving care exclusively from formal providers and an increasing number of older people are receiving care from both informal and formal sources. Although the majority of older adults are still reliant on informal care, informal care is converging with formal care in home and community settings. There is, however, very little literature that examines this intersection between formal and informal care. It is important that researchers begin to recognize this formal-informal nexus. Formal and informal care are not hermeneutically sealed off from one another. Rather, I hypothesize that the co-existence of informal and formal care of older people in the home is reshaping both types of care. It is therefore important to explore the evolving nature and mutual influence of these two types of care.

DIFFERENCES IN INFORMAL AND FORMAL CARE

Most of the caregiving literature argues or implicitly suggests that formal and informal caregiving are very different. Some of these differences pertain to the caregivers as individuals and others are structurally driven. Table 17.1 summarizes both types of differences.

Table 17.1. Differences in Formal and Informal Care

Formal Care	Informal Care
Caregiver Level	
Home usually separate from the workplace, except for live-in carers	Home and "workplace" usually coterminous
Typically, much younger than care recipient and generally of younger age than informal carers	Increasing prevalence of older, spousal carers and hence similarity in age between caregivers and care recipients
Clear majority female, often amounting to virtually 100 percent of workforce	Change in profile of informal caregivers from largely female adult children toward greater balance between male and female spousal carers
Increasing cultural, ethnic, linguistic, and other differences between care recipient and caregiver	Cultural, ethnic, linguistic similarities and familiarities between care recipient and caregiver
Degree of choice: in principle, considerable although powerful "pull and push" factors can be in operation	Degree of choice: often end up in caregiver role gradually, by default
Role adaptation: basic nature of caregiver-care recipient relationship does not usually change, although it often does evolve over time	Role adaptation: often required, sometimes very significant (e.g., from being the one who looks after others to becoming the one who is looked after)
Stress: can be high, but is usually interrupted by periods of rest, holiday, and so forth	Stress: varies from none to extreme (i.e., 24/7 care work)
Policy Level	
Paid, although level varies significantly between countries and systems	Usually unpaid, although increased availability of direct or indirect financial support and incentives in many countries
Increasingly regulated, concern with safety of both care recipient and caregiver	No or very light regulation in most countries

Informal carers usually reside with the care recipient, whereas formal caregivers typically return to their own home at the end of their working day or night. Live-in formal caregivers are an exception to this rule. These cohabitating formal care providers are increasingly prevalent in countries that have departed rapidly from an exclusive reliance on informal care provided by unpaid female family members but have not developed comprehensive long-term care policies. Spain, Italy, and Greece, for instance, have become highly reliant on migrant care workers from outside Europe who usually live with their clients (Socci, Melchiorre, Quattrini, & Lamura, 2003). This group of formal live-in care workers bears striking resemblance to informal caregivers.

The age, gender, and ethnic contexts of formal and informal caregiving are different. Concomitant with the shift from adult child to spousal caregivers, informal caregivers are increasingly similar in age to care recipients. Formal caregivers, in contrast, tend to be considerably younger than the people they look after. The overwhelming majority of formal caregivers are female. This is true even in countries, such as Sweden, that have demonstrated high levels of gender equality in other spheres of employment. The gender profile of informal caregivers was also highly feminized in the past, but this is changing (Finch & Groves, 1980). While female dominance has held steady in the formal care sector, male caregivers increasingly help shoulder the responsibility for informal care. This is due largely, again, to the growing prevalence of spousal caregiving (Calasanti & Slevin, 2006). While many formal caregivers are of a different ethnicity than their clients, informal caregivers and the relatives or friends they look after tend to be ethnically homogeneous, or at least have extensive familiarity with each other's ethnic and cultural backgrounds.

These differences between informal and formal caregivers help identify the antecedents of caregiving outcomes, and are primary to improved understanding of evolving care scenarios. Very little literature focuses on the pathways of formal caregivers into home care work. There has been some analysis of the "push" and "pull" factors affecting migrant care workers (Timonen & Doyle, 2008). This minimal attention to the dynamics of entry into formal care is dwarfed by the extensive literature that analyzes antecedents to engagement in an informal caregiver role (Pillemer & Suitor, 2006). Motivations to provide care and the duration of the caregiver role vary based on the relationship of the caregiver to the care recipient. Variables that influence which member of the family assumes the primary caregiver role (antecedents to informal caregiving) include gender, employment status, and material circumstances (Finch, 1989; Qureshi & Walker, 1989). Scholars have developed and tested several hypotheses pertaining to the differences between adult child and spousal carers. These hypotheses relate to, both the nature of caregiver obligations and responsibilities, and the impact of caregiving (i.e., the nature and causes of stress and the degree of stress experienced by different types of carers). For example, Lee, Colditz, Berkman, & Kawachi (2003) hypothesize that (female) spousal caregivers may be at a higher risk of developing coronary heart disease than those providing care to their parents.

Research on the socio-economic antecedents of caregiving demonstrates that individuals and families from lower socio-economic strata are more likely to end up in informal caregiving roles. Individuals from higher socio-economic classes have, and often take advantage of, greater financial flexibility to contract out all or some of their care work (Wall, Aboim, Cunha, & Vasconcelos, 2001). Research clearly shows that informal carers often have limited choice due to socio-economic limitations, the powerful norms that govern filial responsibility, and expectations attached to gender, marital, or family status (Finch & Mason, 1993). Entry into a formal caregiving role, in lieu of the obvious constraints faced by informal caregivers, may appear to result solely from personal choice. Formal caregiving, however, is often poorly paid and even exploitative work. Just as certain forces steer particular individuals into an informal care provider role, powerful factors are at work that make some individuals much more likely to enter the formal caregiver role than others. These areas, neglected in research, remain poorly understood.

The *consequences* of caregiving have received the most attention in the literature. Analysis of change as it pertains to caregivers has focused primarily on the physical and mental health impacts of caregiving, especially for informal caregivers. Many studies, in fact, address the impact of caregiving on informal carers. This body of research was founded almost entirely on the premise that caregiving is exhausting, demanding, and stressful, and therefore will have detrimental effects on physical and mental health. Scholars suggest that health impacts are particularly profound when caregiving is prolonged and support from other informal caregivers is absent. Numerous studies have produced evidence to support such hypotheses (e.g., Fast, Williamson, & Keating, 1999; Starrels, Ingersoll-Dayton, Dowler, & Neal, 1997). A growing body of research has also started to examine the possible positive impacts of informal caregiving (e.g., O'Reilly, Connolly, Rosato, & Patterson, 2008). Nonetheless, most studies have conceptualized change in the lives of informal caregivers as change toward negative outcomes. Scholars have additionally analyzed the economic, social, and emotional costs of caregiving, again largely in relation to informal caregivers (Andersson, Levin, & Emtinger, 2002; Opie, 1992; Ungerson, 1987). There is a dearth of literature dealing with the impact of caregiving on formal carers, especially those working in the home and community care sectors.

Some of the informal caregiving literature focuses on role adaptations that result from caregiving and receipt of care (Walker et al., 1995). Entry into the caregiver role can represent a major individual transformation. Some individuals who become care providers for older adults have prior caregiving experience. For instance, many older women have shouldered the bulk of care responsibilities for their children. They often have provided care for children well into early adulthood or beyond, especially in the case of children with disabilities. Although, care for a spouse or a parent is different from the care of a child, late life entry into the role of caregiver does not present these women with an entirely new prospect. For a man or woman who has no prior caregiving experience, however, the changes involved in becoming a carer are likely to be more momentous. For instance, a man with a long history of employment outside the home and very limited involvement in informal care of children or parents may find himself thrust into the role of a caregiver for his spouse. In this case, the carer takes on an entirely new role at an advanced stage in life: a stage where many researchers assume little change takes place.

While scholars recognize that radical role reversals can result from informal care demands, they tend to assume the roles and relationships between formal caregivers and care recipients are largely stable over time. Researchers, however, have not made a serious attempt to verify this stability through empirical research. For the increasing number of migrant care workers, for instance, assumption of a formal caregiving role necessitates dramatic life adjustments. A migrant's entry into this role can involve radical changes in living environment, proximity to family, daily schedules and routines (especially in home care settings), and dominant cultural and linguistic expectations. All of these changes demand considerable adaptation. The reasons for adaption may vary for informal and formal care providers. I hypothesize, though, that both types of caregivers frequently and continually must adapt to change within the contexts of their respective roles.

A growing body of literature examines the structures and policies that create differences between the formal and informal care realms (Ungerson & Yeandle, 2007). According to this policy research, the main, consistent difference between formal and informal care in most countries is monetary compensation; formal care workers receive pay (at varying rates), while informal care generally constitutes unpaid labor. However, many countries have recently developed new policies that offer incentives or actual compensation to those who provide informal care. Cash allowances, certain health benefits, and tax breaks have become available under various policies intended to improve support for informal care providers. Formal care, on the other hand, has been subject to increased regulation and monitoring. Intensified regulatory oversight aims to optimize the health, safety, and well being of both professional caregivers and care recipients in many countries. In contrast, only a handful of countries have implemented policies that safeguard informal caregivers in their workplaces. Germany, for example, offers professional training and home visit support to informal caregivers who receive long-term care insurance payments.

INFORMAL AND FORMAL CARE: COMMONALITIES AND INTERSECTIONS

Table 17.2 highlights some of the key contexts in which formal and informal caregivers interact and overlap with each other. Formal and informal carers often engage in similar care tasks and work in the same location—the care recipient's home. Currently there is very limited information regarding how the work profile of formal care providers differs from that of informal caregivers. There is some evidence that the *content* of informal care is changing, though, at least in countries where provision of formal care has become widespread in home and community settings. In these national contexts, such as Denmark, informal carers are shifting their focus *away* from tasks of physical care (i.e. help with activities of daily living), and *toward* lighter care tasks such as companionship and small-scale domestic repairs. The time devoted to informal care has held steady in these countries. In other words, it appears the content rather than the duration of informal care is altered when formal caregivers enter the home sphere (Attias-Donfut & Wolff, 2000; Motel-Klingebiel, Tesch-Roemer, & von Kondratowitz, 2005). Future research on both caregiver inputs and caregiving outcomes (e.g., stress, burden, institutionalization patterns) should therefore consider the coexistence of formal and informal carers in the home, and the division of labor between them.

Data on informal caregivers indicates that many work well in excess of "normal working hours" (over 40 hours per week). The growing number of live-in formal care workers, however, blur the distinctions between

Table 17.2. Commonalities and Intersections of Formal and Informal Care

Commonalities and Intersections	Explanation
Care tasks	In some contexts a "division of labor" between formal and informal carers may be emerging
Settings or contexts	Care recipient's home or the home of the informal caregiver
Long hours of work	Paid and unpaid
Inter-personal	Emotive nature of care work
Policy frameworks that encompass and influence both types of care	Payments that can be made for formal or informal caregivers
Communications and information	Focus on care recipient
Support	May be unidirectional or bidirectional
Negotiating role changes	When a formal caregiver starts participating in the care of a person who was previously exclusively looked after by an informal caregiver

very extensive (even 24/7) informal care work and the hours of formal care work, complicating researcher attempts to characterize working conditions. The overlapping work of both formal and informal caregivers often violates the norms established in employment regulations, but standard approaches to work hour calculations are inadequate for documenting these complex care contexts.

Both formal and informal caregiving can prove equally challenging, stressful, or even overwhelming. Despite these commonalities, research has usually sought only to measure the adverse health impacts of informal care. Moreover, researchers often measure the health consequences of informal work without consideration of potentially mitigating factors, such as the involvement of other (formal and informal) caregivers. We must improve the scope of health outcome measurement for informal caregivers, simultaneously extending such measurements to formal caregivers.

From accounts of both informal and formal care worker experiences, we know that both types of caregiving are inter-personal and often highly emotive in nature. However, while researchers have explored the inter-personal and emotive nature of informal care work at length, we have largely neglected these aspects of formal caregiving, especially in the home and community care contexts. There is an implicit assumption that formal caregiving is not as emotionally demanding, or rewarding, as informal caregiving. Yet, the limited qualitative data available on formal caregivers indicates that they experience intense emotions and significant impacts because of their care responsibilities. Formal care providers often describe their work as a labor of love. They also identify negative experiences and deteriorating relationships within and outside their caregiving domains. They describe, for example, how negative experiences with care recipients, in combination with other stressors, can erode the quality of relationships with family and friends. These consequences of the formal caregiver role remain largely unexplored.

In contexts where formal and informal caregivers are working together, or alternating care schedules, the need to communicate arises. Often this communication pertains to the needs of the care recipient (Geerlings, Pot, Twisk, & Deeg, 2005), but it can also involve the needs and experiences of the carers. Despite the obvious importance of such communication for both the well being of caregivers and the quality and consistency of care, these interactions remain very poorly understood. We know little about the ways in which formal and informal caregivers communicate with each other or how they negotiate the division of care tasks. Future research should explore the dynamics, changes, and outcomes that arise when an informal caregiver relinquishes a certain degree of care responsibility for a loved one over to a formal caregiver. The interactions between formal and informal caregivers, positive or negative, may be unidirectional or bidirectional: in the absence of research, we simply do not have enough data and insight to guide inductive theorizing.

Some of the literature has attempted to bridge the spheres of formal and informal care. Piercy (1998, p. 117) hypothesizes that:

> [o]lder persons with adult children as their primary caregivers are likely to exhibit different patterns of service utilization from older persons who have spouses as primary caregivers . . . adult children, in an effort to address the needs of their other family relationships, might seek services such as respite care, and home-delivered meals more readily and extensively than spouse caregivers.

Although this research alludes to why informal caregivers might seek assistance from formal sources, Piercy does not pursue investigation of the actual interactions that take place between the two realms of care once they are working in tandem.

Barer and Johnson (1990, p. 27) have argued that "the absence of attention to the total support network" has impeded progress in understanding care, and that future research should "focus on the total support process in later life . . . so that policy can best be designed to mesh the informal and formal support systems." In a similar vein, Cahill (1996, p. 41) has argued that "the distinctions between formal and informal, private and public, paid and unpaid work are false and misleading . . . all care entails both activity and feeling irrespective of the location in which it takes place." A comprehensive theory of caregiving will incorporate these important insights. Before presenting the key building blocks for an integrated theory of caregiving, however, I will outline the key reasons why theorizing about formal care has been inadequate and integrative theorizing has been virtually nonexistent.

LACK OF INTEGRATIVE THEORIZING ABOUT CARE

Scholars from a multitude of disciplinary perspectives have studied care of older adults, focusing primarily on informal caregiving. It is, of course, desirable that researchers approach a complex phenomenon such as caregiving from different angles and that many different disciplines mobilize their accumulated knowledge, methods, and tools to understand the dynamics of care. In practice, however, scholars from different disciplines rarely "talk" to each other. Because of this disconnect, a multi-disciplinary approach has arguably hampered the development of theory. In the area of caregiving research, scholars have paid extensive attention to the physical and mental impacts of caregiving on care provider health. While clearly an area that merits research, this dominant focus on the *physical* impacts of caring has diverted attention away from the radically changing context and nature of caregiving itself. As I have already discussed, caregivers are now increasingly older themselves (due to the growing prevalence of spousal caregivers), informal carers often work alongside formal caregivers, and many of these formal care workers are now "sourced" from countries outside the one where they provide services. The *face* of caregiving has therefore quite literally changed: it is older (in the case of informal caregivers) and more ethnically and culturally diverse (in the case of formal caregivers). It is imperative that we take into account these fundamental contextual changes when we formulate research questions and design studies of caregiving.

Formal caregiving in the home setting is a relatively novel phenomenon, one that has unfolded (and is unfolding) quickly in many parts of the world. The rapid increase in the *quantity* of formal caregiving (e.g., number of older people receiving some type of formal care in their home, the number and diversity of caregivers employed) has also led to major changes in how caregiving is experienced and approached. Despite these notable changes, very few studies of formal caregiving use a theoretical framework, let alone set out explicitly to test theories.

Most societies view all, or at least some aspects of care provision as problematic. The proposed solutions to these problems are always changing. Because of this solution-focused thinking, much of the research in the area of caregiving has a strong practice- and problem-orientation. This focus on practice is another central reason for the lack of theorizing in this field. The trend away from theory building stems from the widespread conceptualization of old age and care as problematic and costly. Concerns over the costs of care and the need to plan for the eventuality of increased costs have motivated researchers to explore only isolated aspects of care provision for older people such as the cost effectiveness of different care solutions. Often, researchers have not considered theory relevant to the very practical issues that they are seeking to disentangle and solve. It is too bad this artificial dichotomy between practice and theory characterizes the caregiving literature because much of the best policy- and practice-oriented research is driven and assisted by theory.

To summarize, I have highlighted several important features of formal care: (a) it is a relatively novel phenomenon in home and community settings, (b) this sphere has undergone qualitative change (increased diversity in care providers) and quantitative change (proliferation in home settings), and (c) it is commonly conceptualized as problematic and in need of "solutions" and interventions. Collectively, these facts have driven researchers to *describe* this new phenomenon or scrutinize isolated aspects of formal care. Indeed, this is the logical and correct first step in the process of seeking a theory of care: researchers cannot formulate explanations (and, to begin with, explanatory variables) if they do not have accurate characterization of what they are trying to explain (the dependent variables).

BUILDING BLOCKS OF AN INTEGRATIVE THEORY OF CARE

Despite the explanations and obstacles outlined above, scholars must begin to conceptualize informal and formal caregiving as overlapping entities. Adapting some of Settersten's (2006, p. 4) criteria for a good theory of aging to the field of caregiving research, I argue that an integrative theory of caregiving must take into account:

1. Caring along multiple dimensions (physical, psychological, social), by multiple providers (informal, formal), and in multiple spheres (home, community, institutions)
2. How experiences of caregiving are shaped by earlier life experiences (e.g., relationship quality before caregiving commenced, caregivers' background)
3. How caregiving involves distinct and important developmental experiences
4. How caregiving experiences are shaped by specific characteristics of and processes in a wide range of inter-connected social settings (both proximal settings of everyday life and distal settings such as the state and its policies)
5. Differentiation in care-related experiences across cohort, sex, race and social class groups

Most, if not all questions that can frame the exploration of informal care can also apply to formal care. However, scholars have rarely extended their inquiries to the field of formal care. Even in contexts where two types of carers are working alongside one another and interacting extensively, researchers have failed to apply questions across both sectors of care.

Caregiving, formal and informal, always takes place in an interpersonal context. Many caregiving studies have focused excessively on dyadic relationships (carer-care recipient), neglecting the broader context that may involve other informal and formal carers. Piercy (1998, p. 109) has highlighted "the importance of examining the role of multiple and extended family members to obtain a more complete picture of how families provide care to older members." Researchers must now extend this argument to *formal* carers who enter the care constellation because a growing number of countries are departing from exclusive reliance on informal care in home and community settings. Other areas of gerontology suffer from a similar, exclusive focus on individuals to the neglect of broader contexts and structures. For instance, Bass has argued that "[social gerontological theory] must integrate the experience of the individual with that of the larger environmental context . . . [i]t is this integration of individual and larger scale political economy which a unified theory should address" (Bass, 2006, p. 142).

Entry into the role of a formal or informal caregiver involves a major change and places the caregiver in a context that, by definition, entails (an)other person(s). The study of caregiving, therefore, forces researchers to think of the caregiver in relation to other individuals. Care providers are susceptible to the impacts of their surroundings. A caregiver is, by definition, embedded in social context. This context may begin with the care recipient, but it generally extends to encompass a much wider *constellation* of other caregivers. Caregiving therefore laces the individual in an inherently *social context* in relation to the person they are looking after, other carers, and social contacts (where these are present), and as such shifts the focus away from the individual providing care and toward the context in which they find themselves. Any attempt to understand caregiving, its antecedents, processes, and consequences, must take into account the broader context that involves at least three separate layers, namely:

1. *The care recipient*: his or her personality, life expectations, and reactions to the need for care
2. *The social and family network including formal carers where present*: their expectations, level of involvement, and recognition of the contributions made by the primary caregiver
3. *The social care system*: expectations, availability, and conditions attached to support; recognition and support of both informal and formal carers

The social care system is perhaps the most neglected external influence in care theory. With the exception of the *political economy of aging*, and *structured dependency theory* (which are largely overlapping), care-relevant theory in social gerontology has rarely taken the broader context of macro-level policies into account. Bengtson, Rice, and Johnson (1999, p. 17) call for:

> greater emphasis placed on macro-level phenomena and the structural contexts of aging . . . because there is increased awareness of structures as having effects on processes . . . independent of individual actions, and because of the recognition that structures and institutions are not socially constructed but have a certain facility . . . This shift in awareness may promote renewed interest in theory-building.

Care-related policies, expectations, and values vary greatly across countries. In some regions, a strong expectation prevails that close relatives will become caregivers when the need arises. In other countries, no such expectation exists (Timonen, 2005). In other words, caring is not a social or a policy issue in many national care systems. Rather, it has remained a private, family matter confined to the sphere of informal care. The state, in these cases, only intervenes when the family summarily fails to function as a care provider (e.g., in the case of people with no surviving close family members). What does the fact that family caregiving is expected in some cultural and policy contexts, but not others, tell researchers about the way in which family, social obligations, and old age are constructed in those different contexts? How do these contextual differences affect the experiences of caregivers who enter into the family caregiver role?

A theory of caregiving must account for both the micro and macro aspects of social context, hypothesizing at both individual and systemic levels. At the *micro* level, a theory must elucidate how and why potential informal and formal carers respond when called upon to enter into the caregiver role. How do formal care workers interact with informal caregivers, and to what extent does their presence mediate the caregiving experience? At the *macro* level, the theory must illuminate the impact that social and public policy structures and institutions have on the caregiver role(s), asking: Which caregiver roles does the policy encourage and reward, and which does it inhibit or discourage? Furthermore, an effective theory must link these two levels. Micro and macro levels of context are both so pivotal in determining experiences and outcomes of caregiving that any useful theory must extend itself to both. Bass (2006, p. 142) exhorts that "theory must be interactive in that social forces influence individuals, and, in exchange, individuals and groups influence these larger social forces." Focus on the micro and macro level social contexts also addresses the complexity and diversity of caregiving scenarios. "The development of theory will need to embrace complexity in terms of aging in a post-industrial context ... Anything but homogeneous, the aging society is one with enormous divergence ... [t]he theoretical framework must explicitly embrace this diversity and diffusion" (Bass, 2006, p. 142). Social and economic differences (class, ethnicity/race, gender, geographic location, religion, and age) shape experiences and provision of care, but so do "superstructures" such as social and public policies (e.g., income transfers to carers, subsidies and tax breaks for costs of care, direct provision of care).

In addition to the generic characteristics of theory, an integrative theory of caregiving should demonstrate the following properties:

1. It needs to be dynamic, helping scholars understand change and transformation in the kind and sources of care over time.
2. It needs to incorporate the care recipient, the carer(s), and their social context(s).
3. It must recognize both the micro and macro levels of social context (family, social network, society, social care, welfare state, political, and cultural levels).

Preliminary assumptions upon which I will construct an integrated theory include: (a) formal care as a large-scale, socially, politically, and economically significant phenomenon is very novel historically, (b) all societies and older individuals have adapted, and continue to adapt, to aging and care needs, and (c) in some societies adaptation is slow, while in others it is rapid. Societal responses to increasing care needs and national profiles of caregivers vary considerably. In some societies, there is a strong expectation that micro-level social units (individuals and families) absorb the bulk of economic and non-economic costs of care. As a result, care remains largely a private issue, with individuals and families almost entirely shouldering the costs of care (e.g., through informal caregiving, intra-familial transfers of income, or the use of private funds to pay formal caregivers). Other societies make macro-level adaptations to the changing care needs of an aging population. As a result, extensive policies that address the care needs of older adults have come into existence. In countries that make these macro-level changes, different age groups more evenly bear the costs of societal aging.

TOWARD AN INTEGRATIVE THEORY OF CARE

Theorizing on formal caregiving has been woefully underdeveloped for too long. Theoretical and conceptual frameworks that view formal and informal care through the same lens, and in interaction with each other, also are at an inchoate stage. In this chapter, I suggest the need for a new conceptual and theoretical framework that encompasses both informal and formal caregiving. I have argued that the informal and formal care realms have converged in home and community settings, that the two spheres of care increasingly overlap, and that they are reshaping each other. Ignoring these developments will result in the production of inadequate, possibly misleading information about caregiving. In order to be useful, the theoretical and methodological tools that scholars deploy to study caregiving have to account for the co-existence and co-evolution of formal and informal care.

The main argument of the chapter is that we can no longer conceptualize formal and informal care as fundamentally different. Though some differences do persist, these types of care do not exist in separate realms. The points of intersection between formal and informal care steer researchers toward an integrative theory of care. I have taken the first steps toward developing this integrative theory of care. A vast amount of work remains, however. To flesh-out this theoretical framework, we must continue to mine the resources of both existing literature and new exploratory studies.

Implications for Theory, Research, and Practice

The extensive body of theorizing on informal care contrasts starkly with the lack of theorizing on formal care. In view of the facts that (a) a growing number and share of the older population is receiving formal care and (b) the care industry now constitutes an important source of employment for a rapidly growing number of people, theorizing about formal care is imperative. Some may argue that theorizing about caregiving will distract researchers from practical considerations of care provision as a job, a sector of the economy, and a component of social policy. However, theory is not only scientifically necessary, but also highly practical and useful: "[it] informs the development of research questions, points to populations and samples, suggests variables and measures, and aids in interpreting study results" (Roberto, Bliezner, & Allen, 2006, p. 515). As Achenbaum and Bengtson (1994, p. 762) state, "there is nothing so practical as a good theory."

Scholars can no longer treat informal and formal care as separate spheres of research or view care policy and practice as fundamentally different from each other. Rather, formal and informal care often co-exist in complex ways, are arguably very similar in some respects, and are becoming more similar. Thus, both researchers and practitioners need an integrative theory of care. Such a theory would help researchers develop research designs that encompass both informal and formal care and caregiving and shed light on the interactions between the two. For example, studies that seek to gauge the impact of caregiving on informal caregivers should not assume that no formal caregivers are involved. The impact of formal supports in the home must be better understood. Researchers also need to develop instruments and measures that work for both formal and informal caregivers. Such instruments would enable us to collect data on the consequences of caregiving, formal or informal. Scholars could then test the hypothesis that these consequences can be similar (a possibility that the existing literature has largely discounted or ignored).

The implications for practice are equally extensive. If research can shed light on the ways in which formal and informal caregivers interact, and illuminate the differences and similarities between informal and formal caregiving, policy makers and practitioners will be in a better position to design policies and interventions that support both types of caregivers equally. For instance, if studies can demonstrate clear similarities in the impacts of extensive caregiving on formal and informal caregivers, both groups might gain access to interventions that mitigate such impacts. If a researcher identifies informal-formal caregiver conflict that has a detrimental impact on the quality of care, policy makers and practitioners can develop interventions that improve communication between the two types of caregivers. The possibilities for enhancing the work and the lives of all caregivers, and the quality of care provided to older adults who receive care from multiple sources, are endless.

NOTE

1. I would like to thank Dr. Suzanne Cahill and Ms. Martha Doyle, of Trinity College Dublin, and Amilcar Moreira, of Oslo University College, for reading early drafts of this chapter and giving me their (as always) constructive comments.

REFERENCES

Achenbaum, W. A., & Bengtson, V. L. (1994). Re-engaging the disengagement theory of aging: On the history and assessment of theory development in gerontology. *The Gerontologist, 34,* 756–763.

Andersson, A., Levin, L. A., & Emtinger, B.G. (2002). The economic burden of informal care. *International Journal of Technology Assessment in Health Care, 18*(1), 46–54.

Attias-Donfut, C., & Wolff, F. C. (2000). Complementarity between private and public transfers. In S. Arber & C. Attias-Donfut (Eds.), *The myth of generational conflict* (pp. 47–68). London: Routledge.

Barer, B. M., & Johnson, C. L. (1990). A critique of the caregiving literature. *The Gerontologist, 30*, 26–29.

Bass, S. A. (2006). Gerontological theory: The search for the Holy Grail. *The Gerontologist, 46*, 139–144.

Bengtson, V. L., Rice, C. J., & Johnson, M. L. (1999). Are theories of aging important? Models and explanations in gerontology at the turn of the century. In V. L. Bengtson & K. W. Schaie (Eds.), *Handbook of theories of aging* (pp. 3–20). New York: Springer.

Cahill, S. (1996). *"I wish I could have hung on longer": The choices and dilemmas of dementia care.* Unpublished doctoral dissertation, University of Queensland, Brisbane, Australia.

Calasanti, T., & Slevin, K. F. (Eds.) (2006). *Age matters: Re-aligning feminist thinking.* New York: Routledge.

Doyle, M., & Timonen, V. (2008). Breaking the mould: New trajectories in the domiciliary care of older people in Ireland. *International Journal of Social Welfare, 17*, 324–332.

Fast, J. E., Williamson, D. L., & Keating, N. C. (1999). The hidden costs of informal elder care. *Journal of Family and Economic Issues, 203*, 301–326.

Finch, J. (1989). *Family obligations and social change.* Cambridge: Polity.

Finch, J., & Groves, D. (1980). Community care and the family: A case for equal opportunities. *Journal of Social Policy, 9*, 487–511.

Finch, J., & Mason, J. (1993). *Negotiating family responsibilities.* New York: Tavistock and Routledge.

Geerlings, S. W., Pot, A. M., Twisk, J. W. R., & Deeg, D. J. H. (2005). Predicting transitions in the use of informal and professional care by older adults. *Ageing and Society, 25*, 111–130.

Lee, S., Colditz, G., Berkman, L., & Kawachi, I. (2003). Caregiving and risk of coronary heart disease in US women: A prospective study. *American Journal of Preventive Medicine, 24*, 113–119.

McGee, H., Molloy, G., O'Hanlon, A., Layte, R., & Hickey, A. (2008). Older people—recipients but also providers of informal care: An analysis among community samples in the Republic of Ireland and Northern Ireland. *Health and Social Care in the Community, 16*, 548–553.

Motel-Klingebiel, A., Tesch-Roemer, C., & von Kondratowitz, H. J. (2005). Welfare states do not crowd out the family: Evidence for mixed responsibility from comparative analyses. *Ageing and Society, 25*, 863–882.

Opie, A. (1992). *There's nobody there: Community care of the confused older person.* Auckland: Oxford University Press.

O'Reilly, D., Connolly, S., Rosato, M., & Patterson, C. (2008). Is caring associated with an increased risk of mortality? A longitudinal study. *Social Science and Medicine, 67*, 1282–1290.

Piercy, K. W. (1998). Theorizing about family caregiving: The role of responsibility. *Journal of Marriage and the Family, 60*, 109–118.

Pillemer, K., & Suitor, J. (2006). Making choices: A within-family study of caregiver selection. *The Gerontologist, 46*, 439–448.

Qureshi, H., & Walker, A. (1989). *The caring relationship: Elderly people and their families.* Philadelphia: Temple University Press.

Roberto, K. A., Bliezner, R., & Allen, K. R. (2006). Theorizing in family gerontology: New opportunities for research and practice. *Family Relations, 55*, 513–525.

Settersten, R. A. (2006). Aging and the life course. In R. H. Binstock & L. K. George (Eds.), *Handbook of aging and the social sciences* (6th ed.) (pp. 3–39). Burlington, MA: Elsevier.

Socci, M., Melchiorre, M. G., Quattrini, S., & Lamura, G. (2003). Elderly care provided by foreign immigrants: Lessons from the Italian case. *Generations Review, 13*(4), 9–13.

Starrels, M. E., Ingersoll-Dayton, B., Dowler, D. W., & Neal, M. B. (1997). The stress of caring for a parent: Effects of the elder's impairment on an employed adult child. *Journal of Marriage and the Family, 59*, 860–872.

Timonen. V. (2005). Policy paradigms and long-term care: Convergence or continuing differences? In P. Taylor-Gooby (Ed.), *Ideas and welfare state reform in Western Europe* (pp. 30–53). Basingstoke: Palgrave Macmillan.

Timonen. V., & Doyle, M. (2008). In search of security: Migrant care workers' understandings, experiences and expectations regarding social protection. *Journal of Social Policy, 38*, 157–175.

Ungerson, C. (1987). *Policy is personal: Sex, gender and informal care.* London: Tavistock.

Ungerson, C., & Yeandle, S. (Eds.) (2007). *Cash-for-care in developed welfare states.* Basingstoke: Palgrave.

Van Dyk, S. (2008, September). *Diversity and normalisation: The (self-)management of aging in times of individualized life courses.* Paper presented at the World Forum of the International Sociological Association, Barcelona, Spain.

Walker, A. J., Pratt, C. C., & Eddy, L. (1995). Informal caregiving to aging family members: A critical review. *Family Relations, 44*, 402–411.

Wall, K., Aboim, S., Cunha, V., & Vasconcelos, P. (2001). Families and informal support networks in Portugal: The reproduction of inequality. *Journal of European Social Policy, 11*, 213–233.

CHAPTER 18

From Welfare to Well-Being: Turning Things Around Among Homeless Veterans

Hugh Milroy

The process of change among homeless veterans in the United Kingdom (UK) comes under the care of Veterans Aid (VA). The seventy-seven year-old charity for homeless veterans is based in London and specializes in helping clients move away from *rough sleeping* to leading normal and stable lives in their own homes. Rough sleeping is defined as sleeping on the streets, although many homeless veterans exist in temporary accommodation. Success and failure regarding change with the client group is part of daily life within the charity. Traditionally, work with this client group has relied on welfare-based systems. In contrast, VA has developed a highly sophisticated well-being approach that has seen more than 200 successes in just over twenty months, sometimes from its drop-in center in Central London, but in the main from its hostel in East London. In some cases, this can be life changing. For example, four VA employees have a total nineteen years experience of rough sleeping between them but after graduating through VA's change process, they have totally reclaimed their lives.

This chapter illustrates VA's well-being approach and identifies stages of change progression and key pivotal points in this dynamic transformation process that leads to success or failure. I begin by highlighting key problems, either personal or contextual, which inhibit change and look at what creates sustained change for clients. In addition, I will demonstrate the necessity of interactivity between formal and informal types of support when dealing with change in the lives of those in crisis. Practitioners, as well as researchers, need to rethink the role and importance of each type of support in the change process, particularly where sustained change is the goal. I base my arguments entirely on a mix of my observations of successful and unsuccessful change interventions, through working experience within the Veterans Aid organization as well my own research on homeless veterans (Milroy, 2001). The foundation for the VA approach is imagination, teamwork, empathy, and a thorough knowledge of the pathways that lead into and out of homelessness for these veterans. For VA, and for me, this has been an evolutionary approach to the problem, based on years of experience of what works and what does not work in the circumstances for the total well-being of the client.

This well-being methodology is a distinctive, ground-breaking step away from traditional methods of intervention among homeless veterans and has the potential to reshape future intervention policy and practice for the socially excluded, be they veterans or otherwise. This is because the model is highly flexible, driven by the unique needs of the client, and is holistic; that is, problems are not seen in isolation in a client's life and the change process takes into account all aspects of somebody's physical, mental, and social conditions. In sum, a focused individual, well-being service is very useful for those in crisis whereas a large welfare type service cannot respond to complex and immediate need. The following case studies illustrate the complexity and fragility of change. I used pseudonyms to protect the identity of the clients throughout this chapter; however, all of the clients had similar backgrounds in terms of military service, socio-economic and familial contexts. Despite having access to the same support system designed to encourage a permanent move away from the street, there are different outcomes.

EVERYDAY VETERANS AID TALES

North Country Boy

This man came from the North of England and served two years with the British Army. He settled well in civilian life after his service in his home city which he loved, and had a good job in local government. After eight years, his partner died and in his grief, North Country Boy landed up on the streets in his home city. Despite having his mother and brothers in the same city, there had been a family background involving drug use, and he too sought respite in heroin and crack cocaine; this meant many terms in prison. Eventually, he drifted south to London and arrived at the VA office on a February morning, so cold that he could hardly speak. When recovered, he entered the VA hostel on the understanding that it was a drug-free facility. At forty-one, he wanted to recover so that he could return to live where he was raised and was willing to try to live in the hostel without drugs to do so. He built up trust with VA hostel staff; as long as he engaged with them while working toward a detoxification (detox) course, he could stay in the hostel. North Country Boy liked the hostel because of the military connections and progressed as far as contacting his mother telling her of his progress. Over a period of four months (the longest settled period in his life for some years), North Country Boy and the staff worked hard to break the grip that drugs had on his life; close personal support from staff was a vital element in this process. However, progress was not easy and despite the involvement of specialist drug workers he returned to the streets where he died from a drug overdose a week later. Later, the hostel staff received a letter from North Country Boy's mother thanking the staff for trying to help and saying how happy he was to have been back in an army environment. This case study illustrates the significance of trust building between the client and members of staff as they jointly try to expose and deal with deep-rooted personal problems. In addition, it demonstrates that the engagement and recovery process can be lengthy and that the military ethos of the hostel seems to be significant for clients. These themes constantly emerge as clients' progress though the VA system.

The Publican

This man was in his mid-fifties when he became involved with VA. He had served in the Royal Air Force for a few years. Without a trade, he drifted to London to set himself up in life and married in his thirties. The Publican became a bar-worker and eventually gained a bar of his own. However, his daily alcohol intake rose and he became a heavy drinker, drinking up to a liter and a half of spirits per day: this went on for twenty years. Inevitably, he lost his business and was left with debts. His family split up and he found himself rough sleeping. While with VA, he tried to stop drinking but frequently relapsed and each time, the staff provided support. As time went on the relapses were fewer and fewer. The persistent, openly caring, and non-judgmental approach by the staff eventually managed to persuade him to stop drinking. The change process was traumatic and life changing, not least because many of his friends were drinkers. In leaving alcohol behind, he had to change his life context to ensure that he was no longer dependent for support from others who were still drinking heavily. He was in the VA support system for a year and one of the key change factors was that this enabled him to make new friends. This informal support network (i.e., new friendships) continues to be critical to the maintenance of his new drink-free lifestyle. The Publican now works full-time, has a lovely house (facilitated by the formal support network), and is back in touch with his family. Although he has started drinking again, he has turned to the hostel for support. This case study demonstrates the importance of building a close network of supportive people, both formal (staff) and informal members (friends) that can intervene/support quickly and appropriately as problems emerge. While the staff can provide personal support if required (acting temporarily in an informal support capacity), the formal support system also facilitates and encourages conditions that promote new supportive friendships between clients. Experience shows that these friendships are vital to the recovery process. The case study also highlights the intrinsic weakness of a welfare system and the strength of a well-being approach to crisis intervention. In this scenario, because of the unique, personal, and immediate nature of the Publican's problems, he needs to talk to someone, at anytime day or night, as the urge to drink overwhelms him, in order to prevent the situation from deteriorating. Welfare systems cannot respond in such a situation.

Angry Man

An unhappy and lonely man, Angry Man is in prison for stabbing a police officer through the head. His childhood in Wales had been sad with both parents killed in a car accident, which resulted in relatives providing for his care. During this time, Angry Man did badly in school and was frequently in trouble with the law. As soon as he was able, he joined the army and served nine years. Although he enjoyed the lifestyle, his use of illegal drugs resulted in his eventual discharge (army policy). Without familial support, he started to drift, finding odd jobs to sustain his ever-increasing drug habit. Eventually, he ended up on the streets where his drug dependency became the driver for all his activity. By the age of twenty-nine, Angry Man was a hardened street-dweller. Despite spells in detox, his life became increasingly chaotic and very violent—anger management became a major issue for him and when he accessed hostels, he frequently took hostages and destroyed facilities. Eventually, banned from accessing most of the homeless hostels in London, Angry Man constantly lived rough. The only homeless project that would support him was VA, who provided humanitarian aid, but no money, because he would have used it to buy drugs. VA always gave help and treated Angry Man with respect, regardless of what he had done. While engaged with VA, he liked to discuss his army experiences. At one point, Angry Man was admitted to the VA hostel and stayed for a long period. Staff worked with him, despite his violent temper. He stopped using drugs and staff found him a suitable place to live but he relapsed and went back to the streets, ending up in a cycle of prison and rough sleeping. While in prison, he frequently wrote to the VA hostel manager apologizing for his behavior and pleading for readmission to the hostel. Because Angry Man's behavior was too chaotic for him to stay at the hostel, the VA directed him to more specialized help. Prior to his latest arrest, Angry Man was in turmoil as it was the twentieth anniversary of his parents' death. On the day of the incident, Angry Man came into the VA offices for some support. On leaving, he argued with a police support patrol and stabbed one of the officers. While in initial custody, he asked that VA staff be told of his predicament. He was sentenced to five years imprisonment. The fact that Angry Man kept returning to or connecting with VA staff in some way over the years indicates that he may regard VA as having a key support role in his life, almost like the family he had lost.

The case studies are examples of life-stories that VA staff deal with every day and serve to illustrate some of the key points of this chapter. This is particularly true about the validity of a well-being approach when assisting those in crisis. Traditional welfare systems cannot intervene effectively because they do not provide immediate intervention; something required frequently by most VA clients. In addition, a welfare system cannot generate a mutually supportive, safe, and empathetic network of friends; experience shows that this is a vital ingredient of the recovery process. Trust in staff and conformity to their interventions are key first steps in the progression and the three clients clearly recognized this as an important part of their transition even when they had failed.

A TYPICAL VETERANS AID CLIENT

Who are Veterans Aid Clients?

Although the terms rough-sleeper and homeless are frequently used to describe the same thing (i.e., street dwelling), in fact, they are not the same. Rough sleeping involves living and sleeping on the streets whereas homeless people may be sheltered, albeit in temporary accommodation such as hostels or bed and breakfasts. In London it is estimated that 1,000 veterans on any one day can be defined as homeless (Johnsen, Jones, & Rugg, 2008, p.viii); this is not to be confused with rough sleeping. Homeless veterans in the UK are thought by many casual commentators to make up 25 percent of the rough-sleeping population. Recent research by Johnson, Jones, and Rugg (2008) found that in London about 6 percent of rough-sleepers claim to have had a military background. The number of rough-sleepers, let alone the number of homeless veterans among that number, is subject to debate. There have been various attempts to understand homelessness among veterans focusing mainly on military-related factors. However, this provides only a partial understanding of the issues. Homeless veterans do not exist in isolation and all have a pre- and post-military existence that influences their lives. VA clients are usually in their mid-forties and have about two years of military service. Typically, they will have been out of the military for some years and be homeless for a variety of reasons. Military service is rarely a precursor to their homelessness. An understanding of family, childhood, adolescent, and community factors in addition to the military experience of the individual is vital to any comprehensive evaluation of the issues involved. To deal effectively with this combination of antecedents, and to move the clients away from the streets, VA has developed a unique well-being methodology to help clients. As part of this process, clients must normally overcome some serious personal issues.

Common Problems Facing Veterans Aid Clients

VA clients are homeless for a wide variety of reasons. Consequently, a multi-layered intervention is necessary for recovery. Successful change for a VA client is about returning to as normal a lifestyle as possible, abandoning harmful actions, and sustaining this new existence without close personal support from VA. However, there are many structural or contextual problems that are hurdles to, or inhibitors of, successful change including a lack of affordable and suitable housing, and poverty. Despite best intervention efforts, these problems often prevent or slow down the change process. Equally, inadequate mental health facilities or a lack of detox and rehabilitation places can also be major hurdles. Often researchers do not consider such variables when exploring issues surrounding homelessness among veterans (Green, O'Neill, & Walker, 2008; Lemos & Durkacz, 2005). Despite the profound influence of broader issues, the focus is frequently on seeking causal or linear links with military service. The change process is complex but the linkage between welfare, housing, and homelessness is clearly relevant (Stephens & Kirkpatrick, 2007). However, the cases of Angry Man, North Country Boy, and The Publican illustrate that housing alone was not the main problem; for these men, and many others, the inability to sustain housing was primarily due to mental health issues or alcohol and drugs misuse.

Alcohol misuse. Many VA clients suffer from alcohol misuse to varying degrees. In some cases, this can be a major hurdle to change even when the individual is not a full-blown alcoholic. Overcoming this is often the key to success or failure of the change process. The etiology of alcohol misuse among VA clients is always complex, but it is alcohol abuse, and not drug abuse, that is often connected with the clients. VA is not a specialist alcohol charity, but as this is a major problem among the client group, the organization made the decision to employ an alcohol specialist who, in a three-month period, placed nineteen clients in detox facilities. One seriously inhibiting factor when dealing with alcohol recovery is a paucity of detox and rehab facilities in general in the UK. Where such facilities exist, discharge from them is a particularly vulnerable time and a lack of support at this time can lead to relapse. The impact of alcohol on the clients can be life changing. For example, one recent VA client, who does not admit to having an addiction problem, spent his day sipping alcohol, vomiting after each mouthful, and never seemed to get drunk. Until he deals with his alcoholism, he cannot possibly move on with his life. Whatever the causal link, it is clear that for VA clients, dislocation from the primary personal support system is often associated with alcohol misuse. This was a recurring theme in my initial research, which explored the individual, family, and social issues that created homeless veterans (Milroy, 2001).

Mental health. Many VA clients have dual-diagnosis problems such as alcohol misuse combined with mental health issues. Accessing effective treatment for this combination is always problematic. While this drawn out process is underway, staff members try to provide close support to the client to look after their general well-being. An inability to sustain a home, be it financially, physically, or psychologically will almost certainly cause strain on any familial or community support network whether the client is a veteran or not. The cumulative effect of all of these issues may even exacerbate the mental health problems and create a vicious downward spiral. Treatment is often long and complex with uncertain outcomes. A lack of mental health support for the general community is a factor in the UK and non-acute VA clients often struggle to find adequate help.

FROM WELFARE TO WELL-BEING— A UNIQUE VETERANS AID APPROACH

Despite these serious hurdles, the charity continually manages to help clients rebuild their lives. VA has a unique understanding and empathy for its client group and has found that change, for these veterans, could best be effected by moving away from the provision of a general welfare service or programs, to provision of a well-being service that is needs driven, user-centered, and capable of dealing with clients holistically. Uniquely, VA overlays this approach with a military ethos to create a distinctive blend that is critical to successful transition among these veterans. As a veteran helping veteran organization, clients are reassured right from their first interaction that they are dealing with staff who understand them because of shared experience and this helps them settle into the hostel environment very quickly. This makes the VA model distinctive and provides the key to the *informal support* part of the process. However, there is still a place for a traditional welfare system support, particularly after the client leaves the VA. For example, financial support is often required in order for the clients to move into a self-sustaining position such as living in their own flat. This is the *formal* element of the intervention. The two approaches have different characteristics and as a corollary vary in effectiveness with clients in crisis. However, the roles within the VA model are clear. Interaction with the client during the change process is nearly always *informal* activity with *formal* intervention activity relegated to a support or facilitation function. Blending the two methodologies effectively is crucial, as they are quite different.

In terms of service delivery, this represents a significant step away from traditional approaches to support for veterans in crisis; this is a radical break with the past and is credible because it relates to successful outcomes. The implications of this within the veteran nonprofit world are wide-ranging for funding streams, structures and numbers of nonprofit organizations, the future policies on delivery of services, and ultimately, in the role of government welfare systems.

The Veterans Aid Philosophy of Intervention

Having demonstrated the effectiveness of blending informal and formal intervention process it is worth considering the philosophy behind it. The simplest way to understand the VA concept of operations is to view the process as a set of scales. On arrival, the client's scales are heavily weighted to one side with mostly personal problems. VA staff addresses the personal issues and take initiatives to begin to balance the load. Other homeless services also do this, but the VA intervention philosophy is built on the military welfare ethos: namely, that all military personnel know that someone in their management chain is specifically looking out for their welfare in a meaningful way, regardless of the crisis involved (just as a family would do). Within the VA environment, military service is openly acknowledged and understood; it operates in a similar way, but without the institutional aspects of military service. The message to all new arrivals is clear, "welcome back to a family who really cares and whom you can trust."

Practice of Intervention

Experience shows that the building of trust is the pivotal point in the whole intervention process. For example, hostel staff always note that a new client rarely looks them in the eye during initial engagement and that they do not like having conversations; staff persist in trying to engage regardless. However, after a week or so of this one-sided interface the client will start to look at the staff member and have a conversation. This low-key trust allows staff to treat the client holistically and to set the scene for next steps. The speed of this process allows staff and client to start with the process of intervention almost immediately.

There are four distinct phases involved in the intervention process: *Gateway Interventions, Unpacking, Getting Sorted Out, and Graduation.* This is a collaborative process between staff and client and repeated as often as necessary to enable progress. The four-phase process can take many months, even years; and, failure, leading back to the streets, is possible

336   HUGH MILROY

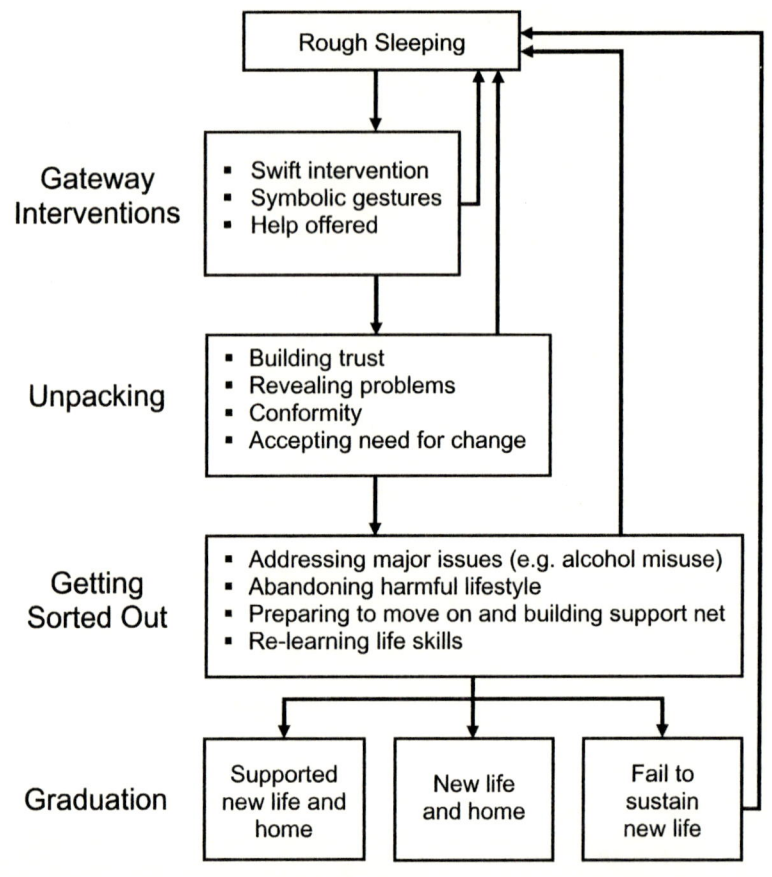

```
                    ┌─────────────────────┐
                    │   Rough Sleeping    │◄────────┐
                    └─────────┬───────────┘         │
                              │   ▲▲                │
                              ▼                     │
                    ┌─────────────────────┐         │
    Gateway         │ • Swift intervention│         │
   Interventions    │ • Symbolic gestures │         │
                    │ • Help offered      │         │
                    └─────────┬───────────┘         │
                              ▼                     │
                    ┌─────────────────────────┐     │
                    │ • Building trust        │     │
    Unpacking       │ • Revealing problems    │     │
                    │ • Conformity            │     │
                    │ • Accepting need for    │     │
                    │   change                │     │
                    └─────────┬───────────────┘     │
                              ▼                     │
                    ┌──────────────────────────────────────┐
                    │ • Addressing major issues (e.g.      │
    Getting         │   alcohol misuse)                    │
   Sorted Out       │ • Abandoning harmful lifestyle       │
                    │ • Preparing to move on and building  │
                    │   support net                        │
                    │ • Re-learning life skills            │
                    └──────┬────────┬────────┬─────────────┘
                           ▼        ▼        ▼
                    ┌──────────┐ ┌───────┐ ┌──────────┐
                    │Supported │ │New    │ │Fail to   │
   Graduation       │new life  │ │life   │ │sustain   │
                    │and home  │ │and home│ │new life │──┘
                    └──────────┘ └───────┘ └──────────┘
```

Figure 18.1. *Change Process—VA System*

even after *graduation*. However, the circular nature of the process is well suited to dealing with this (see figure 18.1).

Gateway Interventions. The first intervention is an immediate offer of accommodation at the charity hostel. In some cases, the time from first contact to having a room in the hostel can be less than an hour. Two very strong women run the hostel, which serves as a multi-purpose facility, providing such things as respite care or longer-term stays. On arrival, the client will immediately notice how clean, home-like, and open the entrance area is. Military symbols and pictures are on display to help new clients fit in quickly and to reassure them that they will be safe. Many of the long-term rough-sleepers will never have encountered such an open and friendly facility during their time as a homeless person. These gateway interventions and signs of their past are symbolic and vital to the process of change; for example, those with filthy clothes immediately receive new replacements. This is a unique part of VA's approach to help re-stock the client's dignity and self-respect as part of a stigma management strategy. The result is that, for at least a short period, when they put on these new clothes, the clients can feel the same as everyone else. All activity at this stage is a *swift intervention* that is designed to demonstrate that change is possible with VA and that they can trust the system. What does this look like in practice? During an interview on the day after his arrival, Rifleman (a serious crack addict), told a member of staff that he painted in oils and that he really wanted to get back to that to help him get over his time on the streets and to get his mind away from drugs. That same day, VA arranged for him to visit an art shop where he was given all the materials he needed to start painting again. From that moment, Rifleman seemed to understand that change was possible and he has been drug-free for several months.

Unpacking. After initial assessment, staff members, specialists, and clients work together to develop mutually agreed plans to address any personal issues that are causing problems (e.g., alcohol misuse). The ethos of the hostel is about directness and the building of trust and support. For example, if someone smells, they are told that they smell, then are offered new clothing, showers, and, if they want to keep their clothing, laundry facilities. Normally, staff members address clients' personal barriers in a very direct way. Overall, the service provided will be emblematic of change, entirely practical, robust, and as often as possible, immediate. The lengthy process of unpacking the underlying problems that may have initiated the decline into homelessness is often best dealt with in a low key manner and is always based on trust-building created during the arrival phase in the hostel when residents are allowed to rest. As the client feels more at home in the hostel and with the staff, a joint-plan between the individual and the staff key-worker is developed and main problems are addressed. Although every person has his own room, they are not allowed to hide in the shadows. A team of specialists including a psychiatrist, a psychotherapist, an alcohol specialist, a barrister (lawyer), a social worker, and specially trained hostel staff are available to address clients' personal problems.

Getting Sorted out. In this environment, change plays out in an unhindered way, which is when the client is getting sorted out. This is a process of dealing with the challenges preventing or hindering change and abandonment of the previous harmful lifestyle. Relapse is normal, but those who do may start over as long as they are willing to work toward change in their lives. The average length of stay is 9.6 months. Through experience, understanding, and simply knowing what will make an immediate change in peoples lives, VA staff are frequently successful in providing options that will help the resident to move away from homelessness. The aim is always to help clients lead as normal a life as possible—to be like everyone else. In the main, for clients, this involves, as a first step, moving on from the hostel and living successfully on their own. Life in the hostel is always dynamic with clients moving out and on regularly. New clients see others graduate and reclaim their lives. This success frequently spurs others on with the same process.

Graduation. When an individual is ready, the staff works with them to move-on from the hostel and to find new accommodation. Practical help at this point is critical so VA seeks money from the formal welfare system, such as the Royal British Legion, to ensure that new furniture, carpets, and curtains are included in the move-on package. Often, the hostel manager and other residents will help paint and prepare the new accommodation. When the move takes place, feelings of vulnerability and loneliness may overwhelm the client. VA then introduces a support worker whose role is to ensure tenancy sustainment during this period and clients are encouraged to keep close links with key staff members.

Fragility

Although the process from gateway interventions to graduation looks linear, it is in reality very complicated, with relapse and restart being key features. The hallmark of success is a self-sustained existence in a new home without a return to harmful habits (e.g., alcohol misuse). Typically, the transition process after graduation sees the client frequently returning to the hostel for reassurance; but as time goes on, and independence increases, this contact lessens. For the client, the pathway to recovery is very fragile and there can be triggers or circumstances that cause them suddenly to return to live on the streets or simply run away: but, in the main, the longer the client lasts in the new home the less the risk of walking away.

However, surprises still happen among those who seem settled. Recently, a graduate of the hostel was evicted from his new accommodation because he preferred to buy a new plasma television rather than pay his rent—he had been in the house for six months. Sometimes graduates who are failing return or make some sort of contact with the hostel manager to apologize for misdeeds or squandered opportunities, or to seek advice and guidance in dealing with a crisis. For example, when The Publican started to drink again he immediately came back for support and guidance. The hostel staff engaged with him immediately thus putting the well-being service in action. However, when problems happen and contact is made this often acts as a prelude to them seeking re-admittance in the same way as the "prodigal son" returned to find forgiveness, acceptance, and shelter from the parental figure. This is always based on promises of conformity and open acknowledgment that they cannot achieve change without staff (parental) guidance (e.g., Angry Man writing from prison). Sometimes some clients go through this whole process five or six times before they finally succeed. The following detailed accounts of Engineer and Marine Boy's time with VA illustrates the complexity of the change process, and in addition, clearly demonstrates the dynamic ebb and flow nature of the interaction between client and staff.

An ex-army sergeant, Engineer was so filthy after living on the streets for eleven years that it took the VA hostel team a day to get him clean. He was a chaotic street drinker with a history of depression. As is usual, the charity provided Engineer with new clothing. Once cleaned up, Engineer put his new clothes on and proudly showed them off to staff. The next morning he appeared in his old clothes, despite the fact the staff had thrown them in the garbage ... he had sold the new clothes for a drink. The staff started over again. Initially, Engineer could not sleep on the bed but slept on the floor. As a hardened street drinker, he found life in the VA hostel, which is a dry environment, doubly difficult. After many months of care and support, Engineer began to function much better than anyone thought possible and was able to cope with daily life in a "normal" situation. He went to alcohol counseling and remained closely supervised by staff. The key element in this process was that Engineer learned to trust the staff and to understand that they and others he met really cared about his welfare. For example, when he felt as if he was just about return to alcohol he would walk into the office and spend time with the staff until he got past the urge. All through this process, staff and friends disciplined him when his behavior was unacceptable.

Engineer went through this change process and after fourteen months of support and intervention, he graduated to a supported housing scheme. Staff members and his friends from the hostel painted his new flat. The charity bought the furniture and carpets, and the hostel manager made the curtains. During the first few days after graduation, Engineer frequently returned to the hostel seeking reassurance. Despite some relapses, he has never returned to the street but when he relapsed, Engineer immediately returned to the hostel for support because he trusted the staff to look after him regardless of his misdemeanor. While Engineer clearly responded well to VA interventions, Marine Boy did not.

Marine Boy lived under a bush in a London park for eleven years. Being an ex-commando, he was proud of this feat of endurance. His mental health began to deteriorate and he sought help from VA. On arrival at the hostel, staff discovered that he had lost all "normal" living skills. Marine Boy refused to listen to staff who told him that he had to learn to live normally if he was to change his situation and that some of his behavior was strange and unhealthy. For example, for four months, he defecated in the sink in his room thinking that this was "normal" behavior; he had lived in similar fashion under the bush. Staff encouraged him to change his habits by being very direct, but he regarded the interventions as an insult and interference with his freedom of choice. This prohibited the building of trust. He returned to the park, but came back three months later when VA arranged for him to move somewhere more appropriate. Gateway interventions were ineffective as he was almost feral due to the habits of his previous lifestyle. For Marine Boy, getting sorted out was never going to be an effective phase of intervention; however, the fact that he was not under the bush for some months was a form of success. The pathway to success is fragile and sometimes even the best well-being intervention can fail because there are key elements in the process that clients must address before progress can be made.

BLENDING CONTEXT AND PROCESS TO PROMOTE CHANGE

The military ethos of the charity and the hostel promotes an atmosphere of robust care, which is supported by a typical armed forces "can do" attitude from staff. Just as they did in their military service, clients soon learn that while the hostel will take care of their basic needs, they must take responsibility for their actions and do things for themselves. However, they do so secure in the knowledge that everyone in the organization is committed to their success and that the staff are there to catch them should they falter. The shared experience of military training helps clients accept intervention (e.g., very direct speaking and encouragement). Equally, the expectation is that they keep their rooms clean and tidy with staff inspections once per week (though not to the same military stringent standards). This helps remind them about responsibility and promotes relearning basic living skills. In nearly every case, clients immediately accept the rules and expectations as part of the regime. However, despite this context, there are certain key dynamics that, experience shows, tend to predict success or failure in the change process.

Trust and Conformity

Success in this change process, particularly in the *unpacking* and *getting sorted out* phases of the transformation process, is closely connected to trust building between the clients and staff member allocated to them, and conformity to staff interventions and direction. This is the single most pivotal point within the transition process. Clients who fail tend not to want to engage with the staff and are not able to admit that they have problems. However, if they engage, and trust emerges, the client is encouraged to admit that change is needed (conformity). Change cannot be imposed (unlike the military); the client must want to change. Many clients find this a difficult process mainly because they have not had someone else in their lives taking on a consultative or guidance role, similar to that of a parent, for many years.

As the trust develops, there must also be an acceptance that change must take place. Staff members tell clients in very clear terms that non-engagement or hiding from their problems is likely to lead to failure and possible eviction. For example, clients who are involved in substance misuse have three opportunities to engage. Failure to do so will result in a planned move-on to a more appropriate facility if they wish. This abandonment of aspects of the past way of life can be problematic (e.g., when the only friends the client had were other drinkers) and can lead sometimes to grieving at the loss of a previous way of life. In this phase, relapse is frequent. As long as the client still wants to change and is not violent, he can re-engage with the staff. Staff members are blunt at this point and tell clients where they went wrong. Acceptance back into the care system is conditional at this point. Failure to conform and start again will mean eviction: the choices are clear. Uniquely, this is where the military experience of discipline helps move clients forward. They know that a robust and up-front approach to wrongdoing from the authority figure is never personal and always geared to their well-being in the end. Equally, they know, just as they had experienced in the military, that the authority figure will, as long as they conform, work with them to overcome their problems. Owning up to their mistakes and taking responsibility is a critical part of this process and of conformity. Many clients respond well to this *unpacking* phase. When conformity takes place, the interaction between staff and client moves on to the *getting sorted out* phase. Here, the staff member works with the client to guide him through the rebuilding process. The relationship, while collaborative, is direct, much like a parent would teach new skills to a child.

Relationships

Within the change process, two types of relationships seem to be important: both are encouraged by the military context within the charity and by the shared military experience of the clients. Experience shows that much of the process depends on building relationships between staff members (authority figures) and clients. Initially, the dynamic of this interaction is similar to that acted out between a parent and a child, for example, the staff member acts as a competent, authoritative, and caring parent and the client as conforming child (Kuczynski & Hildebrand, 1997). As children, most of the clients would have had a significant person, like a mother, to turn to in times of stress and the shelter from this stress, in theory, would be a place of safety and survival—a home (something that for some VA clients never existed until their arrival in the hostel). The VA hostel aims to provide a similar environment. The atmosphere in the hostel is home-like and from the first moments, staff members make clients aware that someone is looking out for their welfare. Additionally, clients are told that engagement with staff is required. This is similar to the military welfare system but is different in that it is much less formal. There are clear rules of behavior and standards to which clients should aspire—just like living in a home or in military barracks.

The purpose of enforcing these rules is to help clients' re-learn living skills and to discard unacceptable behaviors that have been harmful to them and others. Being in a safe relationship with the staff member promotes a real sense of well-being just as in a healthy parent-child relationship. From this point of safety the clients can then start to reclaim their lives with confidence—if something goes wrong, they can rush back to the place of safety knowing that the parent figure will look after them and their interests. Like parental figures, staff members use the bond of trust to support, encourage, develop, guide, and where necessary chastise clients; this trust-based bond allows staff to tackle behaviors that may have been normal for the client, robustly and consistently just as a parent corrects a child. Most successful clients respond very well to this type of parent-child relationship but it is noticeable that informal support and understanding from peers is crucial to the transformation process.

New Friends

One of the most significant threads among those that achieve successful change is that clients are no longer alone. Loneliness will have been a key feature of the clients' homelessness or they had friends on the streets that may have had a negative impact on their lives. Successful transition seems to be related to the creation of close friends. Often other hostel residents become fictive kin who replace the family ties that had been lost with the previous lifestyle. These bonds can be enduring and are reciprocal in terms of care-giving and care-seeking. For some, the hostel manager remains a strong parental or friend figure whom they refer to in crisis. This bonding process is made easier because the clients are all in the same position, and as veterans, have an idea of the basic military care system of buddy-buddy; that is, you are expected to look after those around you. Staff members work in a variety of ways to foster this unique bond in order to help clients create new support/friendship networks. Those who fail to build friendships frequently struggle to graduate thus demonstrating the critical importance of a support network within the transformation process.

Not Playing

There are clients who do not want to change and want to continue with their behaviors regardless of the impact on them and on others. Experience shows those who are unsuccessful in transition are nearly always, for whatever reason, loners who do not make any friends within the hostel. Unlike the norm of a parent-child relationship, this adult relationship includes an option of choice. The care-seeker can ignore the advice, leave the hostel, or just not comply. The general weapon of non-compliance in this case is avoidance. In this scenario, the parent figure (caregiver) becomes much more of an authority figure. Within the hostel, this level of authority lies with the manager. The bidirectional interaction can be intense and frequently plays out as a mother correcting her children by telling them which behaviors will and will not be tolerated. Conflict often results where there is an unwillingness to adapt or live within the communal (family/hostel) way of life. These transactions are often not about conformity but about a client's unwillingness to abandon harmful behaviors.

TOWARD AN AGENDA FOR FUTURE PREVENTION AND INTERVENTION

Developing the Veterans Aid Model

The VA model of operations is adept at helping clients move forward and more importantly, at ensuring that those that go through the system do not end up back on the streets. This is a common problem in the world of homelessness, sometimes called the "revolving door." Other agencies are surprised at the lack of relapse among VA graduates. Despite this level of success, we need to understand what works and does not work for clients to enable the VA model to develop further. We know that a holistic and multi-agency approach works, but know little about what aspects of the military ethos are beneficial to the process. While it is also clear that the rebuilding process benefits greatly from informal relationships, it is clear that resilience seems to be a critical factor for the sustainment of new homes and lives. We know that this is important in the rebuilding process, but we need to know if this is something that is innate, develops because of the VA model, comes from the direct emotional and psychological support of close (new) friends or VA staff, or a combination of all three. More importantly, we need to know how best to encourage independence and to understand the cognitive aspects (e.g., what they think of the role of friends and staff) of the rebuilding process. This will highlight behaviors or emotional responses that may inhibit or damage the rebuilding process.

Finally, we continually strive to improve our service. More research is needed to identify how best to blend informal and formal support networks as independence grows; an aspect of the model that may have wider societal implications and use.

Implications for Veteran Welfare Organizations

Welfare or benevolent nonprofit organizations within the ex-service sector should recognize the worth and role of the VA well-being method of operation, in contrast to old welfare methodologies, as being an innovative and efficient way of effecting change for veterans in crisis. They should accept that in the future, despite their size, they might only ever have a support (funding) role in crisis intervention. Presently, in the UK, some larger ex-service charities are confused about their role and try to do both benevolence and welfare, neither of which, given the VA experience, are able to support veterans in times of crisis. To move forward, I believe that the larger benevolent charities have a duty to support smaller ex-service charities that provide effective well-being services that focus on prevention or early intervention of homelessness. The VA model highlights the unique benefits of a military ethos in promoting effective change for vulnerable veterans. Given these positive outcomes, large veteran organizations should, where possible, assist well-being focused veteran helping veteran organizations, rather than be influenced by trendy new initiatives from organizations that have little or no understanding of military life. From a national perspective, they also have a very important role in finding or creating prevention solutions for vulnerable veterans. This may involve developing veteran specific measures (e.g., supporting veteran poverty relief initiatives or lobbying for specific veteran housing policies). Equally, it just as vital to ensure that mainstream services, such as the UK National Health Service (NHS), play their part in supporting veterans in crisis (e.g., they should ensure that the NHS provides adequate mental health or detox facilities for veterans). In addition, it would be helpful if they encouraged the government to continue to promote a stronger veteran identity. Finally, the larger veteran organizations must strive to understand the impact of poverty on the veteran community and conduct research to discover if veterans are uniquely disadvantaged; if they are, then they must lobby government to tackle the issue.

Implications for Community Service Policy Makers

Practitioners from the social care sector may find this pioneering well-being model, with its immediacy and holistic approach, of interest. It provides an alternative methodology for social care support where change is required and is applicable well beyond the veteran community. As the 2009 recession takes hold, more people will find themselves in poverty, and for an increasing number, this will mean homelessness or social exclusion. As long as society believes that those in crisis should be cared for, it is the responsibility of those involved to create and provide effective, swift intervention services, similar to those run by VA. The current UK state welfare system fails many, which means that the nonprofit sector is coming under increasing pressure to pick up the pieces. The VA methodology is effective because the welfare (formal) model works in support of informal well-being interventions. In the future, due to financial constraints, a similar partnership model may need to develop between state and the nonprofit sector to ensure that society as a whole can effectively care for those who cannot fend for themselves. This will include, by definition, all veterans.

REFERENCES

Green, G., O'Neill D., & Walker, S. (2008). *Welfare and warfare . . . an uneasy mix*. Department of Health & Human Sciences: University of Essex.

Johnsen, S., Jones, A., & Rugg, J. (2008). *The experience of homeless ex-service personnel in London*. University of York, Centre for Housing Policy. York: University of York.

Kuczynski. L., & Hildebrandt, N. (1997). Models of conformity and resistance in socialization theory. In J. E. Grusec & L. Kuczynski (Eds.), *Parenting and children's internalization of values: A handbook of contemporary theory* (pp. 222–256). New York: Wiley.

Lemos, G., & Durkacz, S. (1995). *Military history: The experiences of people who become homeless after military service*. London: Lemos & Crane.

Milroy W. H. (2001). *Pathways to the streets for ex-service personnel*. Unpublished doctoral dissertation, University of East Anglia, Norwich, United Kingdom.

Stephens M., & Kirkpatrick S. (2007). Welfare regimes, housing systems and homelessness: How are they linked? *European Journal of Homelessness, 1*, 201–212.

Part V

THEORIZING HUMAN DEVELOPMENT AND CHANGE

CHAPTER 19

Theorizing about Human Development: Identifying Antecedents, Processes, and Consequences of Change

Karen A. Roberto and Jay A. Mancini

The intent of the 2008 summit sponsored by the Institute for Society, Culture and Environment (ISCE) at Virginia Polytechnic Institute and State University was to build cross-national capacity to investigate critical worldwide issues affecting human development. To that end, this volume represents the efforts of seventeen of the summit participants (and their colleagues) to explore the contexts in which individuals, families, and communities develop and change. The individual research agenda of each of the participants focuses, to some extent, on factors influencing risk and resilience among individuals situated at some stage of the lifespan. Their collective task was to step beyond their own empirical work and further inquire about human development using theory and their own theorizing about the antecedents, processes, and consequences of changes that take place throughout the lifespan and to identify potential strategies critical for enhancing developmental outcomes and thus, improving quality of individual, family, and community life.

In this chapter, we synthesize and reflect about the ideas and challenges put forth by the summit participants. As we listened and discussed the presentations at the summit as well as read and reread the resultant chapters, several themes emerged in the ways in which the contributors theorized about development, conceptualized change, and proposed future research and practices supporting individual, family, and community change.

THEORETICAL UNDERPINNINGS OF DEVELOPMENT

To advance understanding of human development required us to address issues related to definition of theory, stage of theory development, differences in theoretical assumptions, and application of theory within their research programs. Although there is differentiation among theories, perspectives, conceptual models, and frameworks, the authors frequently use the terms interchangeably. As we examined the multiple uses and integrations of theory to advance understanding of various aspects of human development, we acknowledged all types and levels of theorizing.

Foundational Theories

As shown in table 19.1, the contributors present a diverse array of intra- and interdisciplinary theories as they described, explored, and interpreted the complexities of human development. Their theorizing recognized that a single theory is rarely sufficient to understand all aspects of change. The interconnectedness among various dimensions and contexts of development necessitated the use of constructs from multiple extant theories to theorize about change.

As a foundation for their work, numerous contributors relied (explicitly or implicitly) upon constructs from Bronfenbrenner's ecological theory (1979), which encapsulates a multiplicity of systems, each pointing to interactions with others and the environment, as well as individual agency, as keys to development. For example, Lollis draws upon ecological theory as she considers different contexts (e.g., dyadic relationships, institutions, cultural ideology, laws) in which children experienced swift transformations in their personal relationships. She noted that regardless of the context, change occurs not only for individuals, but for their dyadic relationship as well. Few and Stephens' integration of ecological and womanist theory guided their theorizing about how Hip Hop culture influences the interaction of structures within and between ecological layers and shapes the sexual scripts enacted by African American female adolescents. They suggested that female adolescents make sense of the various meanings of and attitudes toward sexual behaviors embedded within the contexts in which they interact.

Other approaches that several authors incorporated into their theorizing included the life course perspective, models of stress and coping, personal relationship theories, and social capital frameworks. For example, Roberto assimilated elements from the life course perspective into her theoretical framework depicting how chronic health problems transform the everyday lives of older women. Specifically, she considered how personal

Table 19.1. Guiding Theories and Antecedents, Processes, and Consequences of Change

Chapter	Author(s)	Topic	Theories	Antecedents	Processes	Consequence
2	Gilligan	Positive Turning Points in Individual Development	Complexity Theory	Nature	Opportunity	Individual development
			Ecological Theory	Nurture	Readiness	
			Life Course Perspective	Random events	Agency	
			Resilience Theory		Sustaining Context	
3	Lollis	Children's Close Relationships	Interactional Model of Close Relationships	Interpersonal (relationship history)	Swift transformations	Relationship reformation
			Separation and Loss	Separation and Loss		
			Ecological Theory	Working models of relationships		
			Attachment Theory			
4	Holland	Changes and Continuities in Young Peoples Lives	Feminist Theory	Sociodemographic characteristics	Agency	Adult identity
			Life Course	Time (biological, social, historical)		
			Ecological Theory	Resources		
			Social Change (Giddens, Beck, Bauman, Bourdieu)	Environments		
				Critical moments		

(continued)

Table 19.1. (continued)

Chapter	Author(s)	Topic	Theories	Antecedents	Processes	Consequence
5	Roberto	Adaptation to Health-Related Trajectory Changes in Late Life	Life Course Model of Chronic Disease Management Selective Optimization with Compensation Model	Sociodemographic characteristics Intraindividual (biographies, values resources) Interpersonal (informal and formal relationships) Obstacles (intraindividual, interpersonal)	Adaption (selection, optimization, compensation)	Psychological well-being Quality of life
6	Ollendick	Social Anxiety Disorder in Youth	Development Theory Transactional Model	Intraindividual (genetics, temperament) Interpersonal (parental Influences, peer relations)	Interplay of person characteristics and informal relationships	Maladaptive social anxiety

7	Few & Stephens	African American Female Adolescent Sexuality	Ecological Theory	Sociodemographic characteristics	Sexual decision making (timing, practices, scripts)	Sexual health
			Womanist Theory	Culture		
			Sexual Health Model	Intraindividual (risk factors)		
				Interpersonal (protective factors-parental communication; peers)		
				Media		
8	Kim	Drug Use Among American Youth	Life-course-Persistent Trajectory	Intraindividual (parental involvement)	Transactional model	Antisocility
			Adolescent-limited Trajectory	Interpersonal (conduct problems, self-efficacy)		
			Social Causation	Environment		
			Social Selection			

(continued)

Table 19.1. *(continued)*

Chapter	Author(s)	Topic	Theories	Antecedents	Processes	Consequence
9	Kuczynski, Pitman, & Mitchell	Parent-Child Relationships	Social Relational Theory	Intraindividual (vulnerabilities)	Agency	Nature of parent/child relationships
			Dialectical Causality	Interpersonal (relationship history)	Bidirectional interactions	
			Transactional Model	Ambivalence		
			Stress and Coping Model	Ambiguity		
10	Dunsmore & Halberstadt	Parental Influences on Emotional Socialization of Children	Emotion Socialization	Culture	Socialization practices and choices	Emotional competence
			Model of Minority Children's Developmental Competencies	Situations/physical environments		
			Socialization of Emotion-Related Schemas	Intraindividual (parental beliefs; child's age and skills)		
			Cultural Socialization	Interpersonal (children's identities)		
11	Chuang	Parenthood-Immigration	Confucianism	Culture	Parental practices	Family functioning
			Family System	Economic environment		
				Political environment		

12	Dolbin-MacNab	Grandparents Raising Grandchildren	Ecological Theory	Sociodemographic characteristics	Risk accumulation	Adaptation
			Family Systems Theory	Intraindividual (cognitive appraisal & coping; ambivalence; role changes, vulnerabilities)	Adaptive resources and support	Stagnation
			Accumulation of Risk Model			Deterioration
			Double ABCX Model of Adjustment and Adaptation	Interpersonal (relationships; behaviors of others; social support)		
13	Huebner	Families Under Stress	Double ABCX Model of Adjustment and Adaptation	Stressors	Internal working models	Adaptation
				Resources		Adjustment
			Attachment Theory	Interpersonal (attachment security)		Child behavior
			Family Systems Theory			Attachment to child
14	Mancini & Bowen	Community Resilience	Social Organization	Risk exposure (internal, external, community conditions)	Community capacity	Improved lifestyles
					Social capital	Effective community responses
				Interpersonal (informal and formal networks)		Community resilience

(continued)

Table 19.1. (continued)

Chapter	Author(s)	Topic	Theories	Antecedents	Processes	Consequence
15	Edwards	Social Capital	Social Capital (Coleman, Putman, Bourdieu); Critical Theory	Sociodemographic characteristics	Social capital	Social change
16	Preyde	Psychosocial Impact of Illnesses	Stress and Coping; Cognitive-Behavioral; Social Support; Equity theory	Intraindividual (illness characteristics, beliefs, perceptions); Interpersonal (informal and formal relationships); Resources (treatment; intervention); Organizational culture	Coping	Well-being
17	Timonen	Integration of Formal and Informal Networks	Intersection of Informal–Formal Care	Sociodemographic characteristics; Interpersonal (communication); Environment	Role adaptation	Sustained or improved physical and mental health
18	Milroy	Homeless Veterans	Well-being	Intraindividual (personal problems); Interpersonal (relationship issues)	Gateway inventions; Unpacking (trust building, acceptance); Relationships (staff, new friends)	Independence

biographies and social systems shaped the women's beliefs about their health and their responses to illness-related challenges and constraints. Both Doblin-MacNab and Huebner incorporated assumptions from the Double ABCX Model of Adjustment and Adaptation (McCubbin & Patterson, 1983) in their discussions of families at-risk. Doblin-MacNab suggested that intrapersonal antecedents (i.e., cognitive and affective processes) are essential to explaining how an accumulation of risk factors influences adaptation of custodial grandparents. Similarly, Huebner contended that internal working models influence both the degree to which family members' perceived military deployment of a spouse or parent as stressful and beliefs about the availability of supportive resources. Social relational theory shaped Kuczynski, Pitman, and Mitchell's theorizing about change in parent-child relationships. They focused on the integration of assumptions about human agency and dialectics as they discussed interpretive processes related to parent-child perceptions of context and their evaluations of the significance of events that transform their relationship. Edwards noted that the socialization of children is a key, but underacknowledged issue in social capital theorizing. Her critical analysis of family and social change suggested that mainstream social capital theories reproduce and reify particular forms of family and community life and inherently marginalizes and obscures the main hierarchies and disparities of power and resources (e.g., age, gender, class, race, ethnicity).

The contributors also integrated constructs from a variety of other theories specific to topic area of interest to guide their individual research agendas. Although we would argue that the major tenets of most of these approaches fit loosely within the approaches just highlighted, they also contribute unique assumptions and propositions for the consideration of change. As an example, Dunsmore and Halberstadt integrated four heuristic models addressing culture and emotional socialization as they theorized about different pathways by which parental beliefs influence their socialization practices and choices and ultimately, their children's socioemotional development. Similarly, in her theorizing about parenting in Chinese societies, Chuang incorporates a discussion of the cultural history of Confucianism and its influence on parenting practices. Taking a somewhat different approach, Kim drew upon tenets of two trajectory taxonomies of antisocial behavior and substance abuse in putting forth a data-driven third trajectory of drug use among youth leading to antisocial behaviors as they move toward adulthood. These theoretical perspectives incorporate different characteristics, qualities, and contexts of human development, in effect, providing social and behavioral scientists various conceptual lenses and perspectives with which to consider individuals, families, and systems as they intersect with change.

Level of Theorizing

We placed the contributors theorizing about change on a commonly used continuum. At the extreme ends of the continuum are micro- and macro-theories, which differentiate change according to social structural and social psychological foci, respectively (Settersten, 1999). Here too, the authors combined different theoretical perspectives to develop their own theorizing about the antecedents, processes, and consequences of change.

Micro theoretical approaches incorporated particularly in the chapters presented in part II (*Individuals, Challenges, and Trajectories*) and part III (*Families, Relationships, and Transitions*) of this volume focus on subjective experiences and meanings created by individuals and families as they move through the life course. As expected from the disciplinary backgrounds of many of the contributors, their theorizing about change relied, at least in part, on micro-level analyses that seek to distinguish the characteristics of individuals who are most likely to respond to conditions that facilitate development. For example, Ollendick included theoretical constructs inherent to developmental psychology and psychopathology (e.g., heredity, temperament, parental influences, conditioning events, information processing styles) in his theorizing about the development of social anxiety disorders in youth, or "development gone awry." In contrast, Gilligan theorized about positive turning points, precipitated either by conscious intentions of the individual or by random events, in the pathways of development.

Conversely, macro-level theories are compelling in their breadth. They focus on the ways in which social systems, structures, and forces, including culture, institutions, and policy influence development throughout the life course. As suggested throughout the chapters in part IV of this volume (*Society, Systems, and Interventions*), macro-level theories provide a diverse set of constructs from which to examine change. For example, in their chapter on community resilience and change, Mancini and Bowen laid out a model of social organization that encompasses concepts that capture an array of community conditions and characteristics (antecedents), social actions (processes), and community results associated with resilience. Timonen put forward the beginnings of an integrative theory of caregiving that recognizes the commonalities and intersections of informal and formal care of older persons, which is inclusive of macro- as well as micro-contexts and processes.

Recognizing the intrinsic complexities in the study of human development, most contributors also included meso-level or middle-range theories, linking individual agency and social-structural influences, as vehicles for focusing on smaller parts of larger developmental phenomenon. Theorizing within this realm provides for contextualized frameworks that accommodate multiple perspectives and influences on development. For example, the work of Holland and her research group focused on core concepts of agency, values, and resources in conjunction with the social and material environment as they tracked trajectories of young people toward adulthood in different geographic and social contexts. Similarly, Milroy theorized about key personal and contextual problems, taking into consideration unique physical, mental, and social conditions that sustained or inhibited change in the lives of homeless veterans. Preyde's theorizing about psychosocial care recognized the need to incorporate hospital patients' experience of illness (e.g., cognitive appraisals and knowledge) as well as the influence of the stress inherent in the hospital environment (e.g., stressed medical personnel) in the development of interventions to promote positive individual and organizational change.

CONCEPTUALIZATIONS OF CHANGE

Also shown in table 19.1 are the ways in which the authors defined antecedents and contexts, processes (change mechanisms and pathways), and consequences (outcomes) of change. They operationalized these concepts based on their use of extant theories as well as their own theorizing. Thus, even when the authors identify the same or similar concepts of change, they did not always agree as to their significance within the change process. For example, Mancini and Bowen identified social capital constructs, including informal and formal networks, as processes of change. Although she also equates social capital constructs with processes of change, Edwards contends that social capital alone does not provide a sufficient explanation for understanding the influence of diversity on change.

Roberto described adaptation as a process that older women carry out when faced with deteriorating health and daily functioning whereas Huebner viewed adaptation as an outcome of successfully managing the stress associated with the military deployment of a family member. Regardless of the specific contexts and processes proposed, most authors framed the consequences of change as a positive development for which individuals, families, and communities strived.

Antecedents of Change

There is not one fundamental cause of change, but rather a multiplicity of variables working together to guide and facilitate the processes of change and contribute to either positive or negative outcomes of change. Although some variables may precede change, many are contextual and permeate throughout the change process. Understanding the interplay among multiple influences operating at the same or on different levels is a key challenge in formulating theory and executing empirical research. The authors frequently converged on the need to situate individual level constructs in larger social and historical contexts. Similarly, they often noted the interdependency among intraindividual, interpersonal, and environmental antecedents of change.

Intraindividual Antecedents. Intraindividual mechanisms include individual characteristics that shape development. For example, Dolbin-MacNab suggested that grandparents' cognitive appraisals are likely to be significant in determining how they respond to the changes and demands associated with caring for their grandchildren. Similarly, Preyde theorized that response to illness among hospital patients depends, at least in part, on individuals' interpretation of the stressors they face as well as their perceived resources, options, and constraints. As Ollendick pointed out in his chapter on the onset of social anxiety disorder in children, it is unlikely that one antecedent or mechanism is sufficient or necessary to influence change. Rather change is brought about by a complex array of interacting intraindividual factors that are dependent upon contextual factors and broader familial and community contexts in which the individual is embedded.

Almost all of the contributors viewed intraindividual antecedents as embedded within larger, and perhaps more powerful, social structures. Individuals have differential access to various opportunities and constraints based on various characteristics including gender, race, ethnicity, socioeconomic status, and so forth. These differentials translate into structural inequities beyond the individual person. Structural influences can have cumulative disadvantageous or advantageous effects over the life course; change cannot be achieved by the individuals themselves, but can occur only through larger structural societal changes. Inherent in most theorizing about structural influences as antecedents of change was the concept of intersectionality, which denotes the complexity and interconnectedness of myriad social structures.

Interpersonal Antecedents. Interpersonal antecedents encompass informal and formal relationships with others. According to Few and Stephens, inter- and cross-generational communications mediate Hip Hop consumption among African American female adolescents, which may counter high-risk Hip Hop sexual scripts and promote healthy sexual behaviors. The intersection of informal and formal care networks discussed by Timonen suggests the need to consider the influence of relationships within and among interpersonal relationships. Similarly, Mancini and Bowen viewed networks as "organic" and "malleable," which can be developed, aligned, and strengthened to support community change. In particular, they consider formal networks as primary vehicles for strengthening informal networks.

Environmental Antecedents. Environmental contexts also influence positive and negative change. For example, Milroy's analysis of intervention strategies implemented by Veterans Aid (VA) emphasized the importance of both the built environment (i.e., VA hostel) and social environment (e.g., relationships between the clients and staff) for reducing unhealthy behaviors among veterans. Similarly, Kim noted the role of neighborhood violence in the continued use of drugs among youth, whereas the presence of at least one prosocial adult (other than parent or sibling) deterred continual use. Chuang described how changes in the economic and political environments of China have instigated change in parents' socialization strategies and goals for their children and thus, transformed family dynamics and parenting processes.

Processes of Change

Articulating the mechanisms and pathways by which change occurs was not an easy task. There is not a simple means to address the complexity of the change process; any attempt to explain the processes of development must recognize the great variability in them. Several contributors alluded to the importance of understanding intraindividual variation in subjective experiences of development, emphasizing the role of individual interpretation and appraisal of the change process. For example, Gilligan proposed that random events might create positive turning points in individual paths of development, depending upon the manner in which the person responds. Similarly, Holland identified critical moments (e.g., family issues, illness and loss, educational issues) as young people transitioned to adulthood. The configuration and timing of such moments varied extremely and their significance depended upon the youths' social location and ability to respond (i.e., type of resources available).

The characteristics of members of dyadic relationships shape the growth and development of both individuals. Theoretical explanations purported by Dunsmore and Halberstadt acknowledged children's active role in evoking and shaping parent socialization patterns. They, like Kuczynski and his colleagues, emphasized the importance of interpretation in making meaning of the interaction and the bidirectionality of such interactions in the socialization process.

Typically, developmental changes result from a slow, gradual process. Contrary to this notion, Lollis noted that there are times of swift transformation wherein changes in relationships occur much more rapidly than normal, often associated with unexpected or unpredicted events. In these types of situations, expectations of the past are no longer useful for interpreting the present, and future outcomes appear uncertain.

Consequences of Change

The authors typically discussed outcomes, or the consequences of the contexts and processes of change, based on their particular unit of analyses. Some outcomes were very specific to the individual's personal development (e.g., emotional competence, independence, sexual health, relationship reformation, and adult identity), while others focused more exclusively on relational outcomes (e.g., parent-child attachment, parent-child socialization). The theorizing of several of the authors led them to outcomes related more generally to individual development, situational adaptation, and personal health and well-being whereas others focused on broader outcomes pertinent for communities and the larger society. Regardless of the point of emphasis, outcomes of change have direct and indirect consequences for the transformation of individuals, families, and communities.

INDIVIDUAL AND SOCIAL TRANSFORMATION: NEXT STEPS

Each of the contributors to the summit and this volume embraced the importance of studying change, and identifying the antecedents, contexts, and consequences of various experiences that shape development over the lifespan. Their own history of research and scholarship, and for several their own professional practice, informed their theorizing about change within individuals, families, and communities. The opportunity to engage in multiple discussions among newfound colleagues generated new ideas and helped crystallize others. Yet, much remains to be learned.

The contributors concluded their oral and written presentations by considering conceptual and methodological needs for advancing knowledge and informing professional practices. They provided specific suggestions for future research and implementation of the knowledge generated. We conclude this chapter by highlighting the overarching themes for research and intervention that emerged across the chapters.

Future Research

The recent advancement of methods and analytic strategies that are more sophisticated provide researchers and scholars the tools for examining and measuring antecedents, processes, and consequences of change that support theorizing on multiple levels. The effective use of theorizing in conjunction with these tools becomes increasingly important and complicated in the ever-changing world in which we live. There is a great need for well-crafted longitudinal investigations that allow for the study of the *dynamics* of change. Dynamics-centered research accounts for the motion, nuances, and forces associated with multiple elements located within and outside of individuals, their families, and their communities. Improved understanding of antecedents and change processes, and their specific linkages, will help clarify the variability in outcomes within and across individuals and systems.

There are also measurement challenges in the study of change. Several of the elements identified in the authors' theorizing are still at the conceptual stage; thus, requiring greater clarity of concepts and terms. They encouraged the use of qualitative data collection strategies as one means of informing the development of measures that are more precise, which researchers can then use in the implementation of larger, more encompassing quantatative investigations.

Opportunities and challenges experienced in individual lives and those with whom they interact merge to influence the dynamics of development. Thus, advancing the study of change requires shifts in the unit of analysis from a primary focus on individuals to the inclusion of influential others. Within this context, the authors reinforced the need for linking human agency with social structures that influence change throughout the life course. The inclusion of multi-layered and reciprocal influences on human development will further understanding of these interdependences on the mechanisms of change.

Intervention Strategies

In addition to the generation of new knowledge, another important contribution of theorized research in human development is its potential for improving the lives of individuals, families, and communities. Making meaningful connections among theory, research, and practice requires dynamic interchange among professionals working in a variety of venues. The authors commonly connected their theorizing and research with prevention and intervention efforts with regard to program development and evaluation, policy development and implementation, and capacity building. We end this volume with a summary of their specific suggestions for influencing and changing the pathways of human development.

1. *Creating and evaluating prevention and intervention (including crisis intervention) programs that promote positive change and reduce the influences of harmful or negative social structures.* Prevention and intervention efforts often lack the precision necessary to assess effectively whether change occurs, and more importantly, whether the change is attributable to a particular prevention or intervention practice. These social action efforts require intentional theoretical foundations because very often when programs do not result as intended, professionals are unable to differentiate theory failure (the

idea was deficient to begin with) from implementation failure (the idea was valid but how it was implemented was deficient).
2. *Developing tailored programs that acknowledge variability about constituents.* One size rarely fits all, at least not very well. Intentionality about exactly who is the target audience of, for example, individual interventions or family support programs, gives clarity and insight into how appropriate the program may be for others unlike the target audience. In the mix of these decisions is the importance of differentiating variability within a group and variability between groups; this includes recognizing that within-group variability is often greater than imagined.
3. *Using a variety of venues to inform and support positive change including the media, community groups, and public organizations.* In the twenty-first century we place a premium on information flow, making assumptions about how best to inform citizens without fully examining how people are informed, or what sorts of information attracts them and influences either positive or negative change. Professionals and communities must move beyond conventional or convenient approaches to practice and explore new avenues for promoting positive behavioral changes and supporting opportunities for healthy development.
4. *Building capacity within individuals, families, and communities.* Strategic approaches to improving the lives of individuals, families, and the neighborhoods in which they reside include several important elements: accurate assessments of current situations, including needs and assets people possess; clarity about what changes are desired in order to improves lives and situations; and exactly what should occur so that change is more attainable. The "what should occur" category is where capacity building resides, and pivots around potential, ability, power, mechanisms, and competence.
5. *Promoting and informing local, state, and national government policies that support change.* Most policies are better oriented toward maintenance of what is rather than toward what could be. Forward thinking policies can be substantially informed by the theories and theorizing found throughout this volume; although incomplete, they are forming a roadmap of how change occurs, and the leverage points that policies are best suited to address.

REFERENCES

Bronfenbrenner, U. (1979). *The ecology of human development: Experiments by nature and design.* Cambridge, MA: Harvard University Press.

McCubbin, H. I., & Patterson, J. M. (1983). The family stress process: The double ABCX model of adjustment and adaptation. *Marriage and Family Review, 6,* 7–37.

Settersten, R. A. (1999). *Lives in time and place: The problems and promises of developmental sciences.* Amityville, NY: Baywood.

Subject Index

Abbott, 17
ABCX model. *See* double ABCX model
able communities, 257, *258*
abuse, sexual, 26
accommodation, change and, 162, 163
acculturation, Chinese immigrant, 202–3
accumulation of risk model, 221, 222, *354*
Achenbaum, W. A., 323
Acquired Immune Deficiency Syndrome (AIDS), 75
adaptation: accumulation of risk model for, 221, 222, *354*; custodial grandparents', 209–10, 222–23; family adjustment model, *238*; formal/informal care and, 313; interacting components of, 133, 143; intervention programs for, 237–40; to military deployment/separation, 227–40, *230*, *236*; resilient, 32. *See also* double ABCX model
adaptation, to chronic illness, 128–46; case study, 139–43; future research/intervention for, 143–45; SOC model for, *135*, *136*, 139–43

Add Health Study. *See* National Longitudinal Study of Adolescent Health
adolescents: drug use among, 113–25, *119*, *353*; insecure attachments in, 232; parental involvement in lives of, drug use and, 119–20; parental military deployment and, 229; psychopathology/taxonomy theories of, 115–16; SAD symptoms in, 96; sexual abuse of female, 26; sexuality in, 78–80, 84–86, 91–92. *See also* drug use, in adolescents
adult(s): adult child caregivers, 311; marginalization of children/older, social capital, 274–75. *See also Inventing Adulthoods*
adversity, chronic/acute, 32
Afghanistan, 228
African Americans: grandparents, 207; Hip Hop sexual messaging on female, 75–92; hypersexualization of female, 81–84; sexual health intervention for male, 90
African-Caribbean youth: shifting identities among, 281; social capital/marginalization of, 275

367

age, 145; BI and, 103–4; caregiving and, 311, 319, 320, 321; emotion socialization linked to child's, 176; -graded trajectories, 114; -related health, 221; -related social evaluative anxiety, 95; SAD onset, 96
agency, 16, *351*; co-construction and, 163; late modern theorists on, 56–59; opportunities and, 17, 27, 29; transactional/dialectical theories view of, 154–56
AIDS (Acquired Immune Deficiency Syndrome), 75
Ainsworth, Mary, 39
alcohol misuse, VA clients, 333
Allatt, Pat, 272
ambiguity, in parent-child relationships, 159–62
ambivalence: attachment, 231–32; intergenerational, 212; in parent-child relationships, 157–59; psychological, 213–14
Americans. *See* adult(s); health, in older Americans; Native Americans; United States; women
amoral families, mainstream social capital theories', 278–79
Angry man (VA client), 330–31
antecedents, 4, 5, 7, *351–56*, 360–61; caregiving, 320–22; chronic illness in older women, 128; community, 249–51, *250*; drug use, 121–23; emotion socialization processes and, 176–81; environmental, 361; grandparent change, 211–21; illness as, 294–96; interpersonal, 215–18, 361; intraindividual, 360–61; intrapersonal, 212–15; networks as, 251–55; SAD, 100–106, *101–2*; social/personal overlapping, 140–41; sociodemographic, 212, 218–21; SOC model showing, *136*; swift transformations context, 38, 39; time-fixed, 121; time-varying, 122; veteran homelessness, 332
Anthias, F., 281
anxiety, age-related social evaluative, 95
approach-avoidance system, BI/SAD, 105–6
Arneil, Barbara, 279
artists, female Hip Hop, 77, 83
attachment theory, 38, *230*, 230–35, *238*, *355*; attachment security, *230*, 230–35, *236*; attachment styles in, 231–35; insecure attachment in adolescents, 232; mindfulness and, 238; working model from, 38
automatic processing, 162–63

Bailey, S. J., 214
Barer, B. M., 316–17
Baron, S., 285–86
Bass, S. A., 319
BD. *See* behavioral disinhibition
Beck, U., 56, 57
behavior: cognitive behavioral theory, 298–300, *356*; cognitive behavioral therapy, 238; integration of influences on, 78–79; life course trajectories of, 114, 129–31; SAD manifestations in, 96; sexual, 85–86, 89–90; trajectories of, 114–17
behavioral disinhibition (DB), 105, 107
behavioral inhibition (BI), 100, *101–2*, 103–6, 107; age and, 103–4; future research, 107–8;

genetic component in, 104; statistics on, 103
behavioral psychology, Skinner's mechanistic premise of, 97
beliefs, cultural, 181
Bengston, V. L., 320, 323
bereavement, 64
BI. *See* behavioral inhibition
bidirectionality, 37, 107, 151
biographical time, 54
biographies: choice, 56, 57–58; *Inventing Adulthoods* using model of, 60–61; normal, 56, 57–58, 61. *See also* personal biographies, women's
bonadaptation, 222, 223
bonding, social capital, 279–81, 282
Bourdieu, Pierre, 269, 272–73, 275, 277, *351*; on social capital bonding, 280; theoretical concepts treated by, 285, 286
Bowen, Gary L., 246, 250, 358–59
Bowlby, J., 233, 235
Brannen, J., 57–58
Breaking the Silence, 45
bridging: individual to community, 254; social capital, 280–81
Britain, 43; parenting focus of policy in, 270
British Army, veteran from, 328–29
British Columbia, 46
British North America Act, 43
Bronfenbrenner, Urie, 8, 39–47, 350; womanist theory integrated with ecological theory of, 78–80

Cahill, Suzanne, 317
Canada, 44, 158; Chinese immigrants in, 193; hospital environments in, 300, 301–2; internment camps in, 46; Vietnamese youth in, 165–66

cancer, swift transformations caused by sibling, 40–43
capacity, intervention for building, 365. *See also* community capacity
caregivers, attachment patterns among, 232
caregiving, formal/informal, 307–24, *310*, *315*; adult child v. spousal, 311; age and, 311, 319, 320, 321; antecedents of, 320–22; assumptions about demanding nature of, 315–16; building blocks of integrative theory of, 318–22; commonalities/intersections between, 307–8, 314–17, *315*, *356*; consequences of change, 312, 320–22; contexts of, 308–9, 320; cost-effectiveness focus on, 318; differences between, 309–14, *310*; ethnicity and, 311; as family matter, 321; future research on, 314, 316; gender/ethnicity and, 311; gender issues in, 311; home setting for, 310, *310*, 314–15, 317–18; implications for theory/research/practice, 323–24; important features of formal, 318; increase in quantity of, 318; informal "lighter" tasks in, 314; integrated theoretical approach to, 317–24; towards integrative theory of, 322–24; lack of integrated theorizing on, 317–18; live-in, 310; migrant, 310, 313; neglected external influence in, 320; policymaking and, *310*, 314, 321, 322; salary concerns in, 313–14; socioeconomics of, 312; total support process focus of, 316–17; trends in, 309; women, 313. *See also* Veterans Aid

Cartmel, F., 58
case studies: health adaptation in context, 139–43; veterans', 328–31, 339; youth transitions, 60, 64–65, 68–71
Center for Disease Control (CDC), 75
Center for Survey Research, 128
certainty, social capital and, 277–78. *See also* uncertainty
ceteris paribus, 8
chance, 17–18, 24–25
change: accommodation and, 162, 163; blending context/process to promote, 340–44; chronic illness and, 131; community capacity and, 260, 365; consequences of therapeutic, 303–4; continuity and, 53–72; in cultural context, 181–82; culturally relevant intervention model for, 90–91; custodial grandparent, 208–21; development and, 4; double ABCX Model processes of, 235–37; dynamics of, future research and, 363; elements influencing, 31–33; emotional return on investment, 29–31; emotion socialization and, 172, 176, 178–80; enduring, 27–31; events as sources of, 19–23; explaining, problem in, 18; five principles of, 36–37; four conditions for positive, 31; incremental, 165–66; novelty leading to, 162–67; pessimism towards, 15; qualitative, 156, 162, 163; quantitative, 165; refusal to, 343–44; second order, 162; social, 55, 56–61, 201, 284–87, 363–65; social organization and, 249–51, *250*; sustaining contexts for positive, 29–31; turning points in dynamics of, positive, 15–31. *See also* consequences of change; swift transformations, in close relationships
Chao, R. K., 197
Cheryl (case study/working class/ Protestant), 68–71
children: ambivalence in, 158–59; disabled, care of, 313; emotion socialization of, 171–89; grand-, 216; parents monitoring of, 124; readiness in, 181; reforming relationships, 49–50; relationship formation in, 37–38; SAD in, 95; socialization of minority, *173–75*, *176–77*, *354*; swift transformations experienced by, 39–40
China, 93; Sichaun earthquake, 35
Chinese National Bureau of Statistics, 198
Chinese societies: acculturation/ immigration process for, 202–3; Confucianism and, 195, 196, 198, 202; demographic trends in, 192–94; economic changes in, 200–201; parenting in, 192–204; social changes in, 201
choice biographies, 56, 57–58
chronic illness adaptation, 128–46, *135*, *136*; case study on, 139–43; life course model for, 129–31; in older women, 128–46; personal history context for, 128; research on, overview of, 127–28; trajectory model for, 131–32
Chuang, S. S., 199, *354*, 357
co-construction, 163
cognitive appraisal/coping, 294–96; custodial grandparent, 212–13; primary/secondary, 295

cognitive behavioral theories, 298–300, *356*; cognitive behavioral therapy, 238
cognitive reappraisal, 299
Coleman, James, 268, 271–72, 275, 277, 283–84
collective competence, 256–58, *258*
collectivist orientation. *See* individualist/collectivist cultures
communities: antecedents and, 249–51, *250*; bridging individual to, 254; collective competence, 256–58, *258*; consequences of change in, 249–51, *250*; as contexts, 246–48; at risk, 245–46; typology of, 257–58, *258*
community capacity, 260, 365; shared responsibility/collective competence as, 256–58, *258*
community resilience, 245–63, *250*, *258*; definition of, 248–49; determination of, 249; leverage points for, 258–60; networks in, 251–55; results definition for, 262; silo approaches to, 253; social capital and, 254–55; social organization elements of, 249–58, *258*
compensation: adaptation component, 134, 138; SOC process, 138
competence, collective, 256–58, *258*
complexity theory, 16, 32, *351*
compliance, 163
condoms, 87
conformity, VA trust and, 341–42
Confucianism, 195, 196, 198, 202
consequences of change, 4–5, 6–7, 132, *351–56*, 362–63; caregiving, 312, 320–22; community, 249–51, *250*; custodial grandparents, 208–11, 221–23; Rhonda's/case study,

142–43; sexual health intervention beyond, 76; SOC model showing, *136*; theorizing process in, 168; therapeutic, 303–4
consequences of change, custodial grandparents, 208–11, 221–23; accumulation of risk model, 221, 222, *354*; physical/mental health, 208–9
construction of object, 284–87
constructivism, 140, 154–55
consumption: Hip Hop, 78, 88; *Inventing Adulthoods* study and, 67
contexts: antecedent/swift transformation, 38, 39; caregiving, 308–9, 320; change from blending process with, 340–44; chronosystem, 40; communities as, 246–48; constructivist view of, 154–55; developmental contextualism and, 98; distinguishing qualities of, 9; ecological, 47–48, 247; emotion socialization, 172–76, *173–75*, 178–79; exosystem, 84–86; hospital, 291, 292–93, 301–3; human development and, 8–9; mesosystem, 86–87; microsystem, 87–89; parent-child relationship, 155; past/future, 37–38; resilience development, 47–48; SAD, 96; social, 71–72, 140–41; SOC model with, 134–38, *135*, *136*; stress coping, 295; sustaining, 29–31; theorizing, 153–54; time in cultural, 182–83; transactional, 154–58; womanist theory and, 90; words expressive of, 8. *See also* dynamic cultural context; ecology theory

continuity: attachment styles, 234–35; change and, 53–72; women's life course value as, *136*, 136–37; in youth's lives, 71–72
contradiction, dialectics addressing, 157–59
contributors: contexts discussion by, 8–9; six questions asked by, 6; theoretical perspectives of, 350–51, *351–56*
coping. *See* stress, coping with
couples. *See* dyadic relationships
critical moments, 59, 61; employment factor in, 67, 69; *Inventing Adulthoods* study, 59, 62–64; marijuana bust, 64–65; material conditions and, 64; relationships as source of, 62–64. *See also* turning points
cross-cultural research, 183–84
cultural capital, parents as, 65
cultural socialization, *173–75*, 178–79, 181–82, *354*
culture(s): definitions of, 172, 178, 191–92; of distress, 301; dynamic context of, 171–89; emotion socialization and, 172–76, *173–75*, 178–79, 181–82; individualist/collectivist, 185–86, 187, 194–95; parenting and, 194–99, 203–4; sexual health intervention through understanding, 76, 80, 89–91; strip club, 81–82; synthesis of Vietnamese/Canadian, 165–66; time in context of, 182–83; transforming views/assumptions about, 203–4; within/across, 188
custodial grandparents, 207–25; accumulation of risk for, 221; adaptation of, 209–10, 222–23; ambivalence in, 213–14; antecedents to, 211–21; change for, 208–21; consequences of change for, 208–11, 221–23; deterioration of, 209–10; double ABCX model, 222–23; grandparent-to-parent transition, 215–18; health issues for, 208–9, 220, 221, 222; policy and, 224–25; professional practice implications for, 223–25; stagnation of, 209–10; statistics on, 207; trajectories for, 209–11
cyclone, Nargis, 35

Dahlen, P., 214
daily functioning, SOC process, 138
daily transitions, 182
data, iterative process of theory and, 59–61
death(s): baby's, young mother's, 63; grandparents', 62–63; GWOT service members, 228
defensive exclusion, 235
delinquents, early-onset, 115, 117–21, *119*, 124
demographic trends, Chinese society, 192–94
Denmark, 314
Densho Project, 46
Department of Defense, 228
desistor trajectory, drug use, 117–21, *119*
deterioration, custodial grandparents', 209–10
development, human: age-related anxiety in normal, 95; change and, 4; contexts of, 8–9; cultural beliefs about, 181; dialectics perspective on, 153–54; ecological approach, 6; hurricane analogy for, 16–17; mechanistic model of, 97; minority children emotion socialization and,

176–77; organismic model of, 97, 98; pathological, 99–100; plasticity in, 133; six questions approach to, 6; social relational theory of, 152, 153; SOC on individual, 132–34, *135*; theoretical underpinnings of, 349–59; theorizing, 349–65; transactional model of, 98–99, 154; understanding, 3–10. *See also* ecological development; intervention; theory(ies)
developmental contextualism, 98
developmentalists, challenge for, 7
developmental psychopathology, 99–100; implications for theory/research/practice, 106–8; as macroparadigm, 100
developmental theory, *352*; *ceteris paribus* principle of, 8; criteria for, 4; ecology approach to, 6, 8, 39–40, 47–48, 204, 350, *352*, *354*; heterogenous trajectories for drug use, 114–17; premises of, 97–99; special considerations in, 4; theorizing and, 9–10
deviant peers, drug use antecedent, 122
dialectics, *353*; agency and, 154–56; assumptions of, 153–54; dialectical causality, 152; novelty causing change perspective of, 162–67
Dirty South rap, 81
disaster preparedness, community resilience and, 259
disease. *See* chronic illness adaptation; illness
disengaged communities, 257, *258*
distress: culture of, 301; detection of patient, 302; illness, 292, 293; patient psychosocial, 292, 301–2
divorce rates, Chinese, 201

Dolbin-MacNab, Megan L., *354*, 357, 360
domestic arena, *Inventing Adulthoods* study and, 67–68
double ABCX model, 222–23, 229–31, *230*, *355*; application of expanded, 237–40; internal working model with, 234; intervention utilization explained by, lack of, 239–40; military deployment adjustment in, 229–31, *230*; processes of change in, 235–37
downward phase, trajectory, 131–32
drug use, in adolescents, 113–25, *119*, *353*; antecedents for, 121–23; early onset, 115, 117–21, *119*, 124; late onset adolescent, 115; odds ratios for, *119*; prevention/intervention implications for, 123–24; risk/protective factors for American youth, 113–25, *119*; statistics on, 113; trajectories of, 114–21, 124, *353*; transactional model for, 114, *122*, 122–23
Du Bois-Reymond, M., 57
Dunsmore, Julie C., *354*, *354*, 357, 362
dyadic relationships, 35–40, 48, 87–89, 144, 155, 165–66, 245, 319, 362; late modern theorists and, 57
dynamic cultural context, emotion socialization, 171–89
dynamic cultural context, measuring, 183–87; change and, 187; dialogue with cultural informants, 183–84; multiple indices for, 184–85; race/ethnicity in, 185–86; social class in, 186–87
dynamics of change, 363

early-onset delinquents, 115, 124; desistance pattern in, 117–21, *119*
earthquake, Sichaun, 35
ecological development, SAD in youth from perspective of, 95–109
ecological-womanist analysis: deconstructing symbolism in, 89–90; intersectional, 80–89
ecology theory, 6, 8, 39–40, 47–48, 247, 350, *352*, *354*; fathers/parenting, 204
economics: Chinese societies' changes in, 200–201; economic independence in youth transitions, 60; misattribution of rationality in, 277–78
education policy, 43–45
Edwards, Rosalinde, 127, 255, *355*
effortful processing, 162–63
Elder, G., 140
electrical workshop example, 22
emotion: caregiving and, 315–16; coping, 213, 296
emotional distress: culture of distress, 301; illness causing, 292, 293; medical personnel, 292; patient, 292; perception of patient's, lack of, 302
emotional return on investment, 29–31
emotion socialization, 171–89, *173–75*, *354*; antecedents/processes, 176–81; change and, 172, 176, 178–80; change conceptualized in, 181–83; change in cultural context for, 181–82; conceptual model comparison, culture in, 172–76, *173–75*; content v. sequence in, 179; cultural, *173–75*, 178–79, 181–82, *354*; dialogue with cultural informants, 183–84; integration of conceptual models for, 179–81; measuring dynamic cultural context of, 183–87; multiple indices for research on, 184–85; social class and, 186–87; socioecological approach, 180–81; structural approach, 179–80; time concept and, 182–83
employment: *Inventing Adulthoods* study and, 67, 69; mothers', 280
engagement, women's life course value, 136
Engineer (VA client), 339–40
enjoyment, women's life course value as, *136*, 137
environment: antecedents of, 361; transactions between individuals and, 154–56; VA hostel, 342–43
epistemological fallacy, 58
equifinality principle, 99
equity theory, 301–3, *356*
ethnicity: caregiving and, 311; cultural context measurement and, 185–86. *See also* race/ethnicity
ethnocentrism, 183–84
events: levels of, 19–20; as sources of change, 19–23
exclusion, social, 268–69
exosystem: adolescent sexuality analyzed at level of, 84–86; mass media as, 84–86; swift transformations at level of, 43–45
expectations, transformative power of, 22–23, 32, 42–43
extended family, 188, 216–17, 319

family(ies), 88; adaptation to military deployment/separation, 227–40; amoral, 278–79; caregiving as private matter for, 321; care provided by, 319; Chinese, 197, 200–202; deficiencies, 276;

extended, 188, 216–17, 319; internment camps for Japanese, 45–47; life course perspective for, 130–31; military deployment theoretical framework for, 229–31, *230*; models of socialization, 151–52; nuclear/traditional concept of, 270, 271–74, 283–84; reconnections, 49–50; social capital and, 271–74, 287n1; socialization, 151–52, 177; transnational, 281; welfare, 284; as zombie category, 58–59. *See also* custodial grandparents; fathers/fathering; mothers
family adjustment model, *238*
family system theory, 217–18, *236*, 236–37, *354*
fateful moments, 59
fathers/fathering: accessibility of, 198; authoritarian/authoritative, 202; Chinese immigrant, 202–3; Confucianism on role of, 195, 196, 198, 202; contemporary views on, 197–99; ecology approach to research on, 204; household chores done by, 198, 199; interviews of, 199; research on, 191, 204
females, Hip Hop artists, 77, 83
feminists, 53, 279, *351*
Few, April L., 350, *352*
filial piety, 195
financial resources, custodial grandparents', 219–20
Finland, military in, 23
First Nations Health Commission, 44, 49
First Nations people, 43–45, 49–50
Folkman, S., 212–13, 294, 299
formal caregiving. *See* caregiving, formal/informal

formal networks, 252–54, 255, 261
foster care, 23, 207, 210, 224; transition to, 164–65
fragility, VA client process, 338–40
Fujii, Frank, 46–47
Furlong, A., 58
future research: adaptation to chronic illness in older women, 143–45; BI, 107–8; caregiving, 314, 316; emotion socialization, 187–88; immigrant families, 203–4; *Inventing Adulthoods* and, 71–72; measurement tools in conjunction with theorizing, 363–64; parent-child relationships, 152, 161, 162; policy and, 365

gangsta rap, 81
Garcia Coll, C., 176–77
gateway interventions, VA intervention phase, 335, *336*, 336–37
gender, 53, 57; grandparenting antecedent, 220–21; Hip Hop and, 77; social capital and, 279–80; SOC model and, 144–45; -specific filter, 79; youth transitions and, 70
gender relations: mesosystemic analysis of, 86–87; social capital and, 273–74
gender socialization, microsystem level, 87–89
gender specific normal biography, 57
generations, bonding social capital within/across, 279–80
genetic factors: BI, 104; SAD, *101*
Germany, caregiving support in, 314
getting sorted out, VA intervention phase, 335, *336*, 337–38, 341
Giddens, A., 56, 57, 59
Gilligan, Robbie, *351*, 358, 362

Gillum, T. L., 86
Global War on Terrorism (GWOT), 228–29, 233
goodness of fit, 28, 179
government. *See* policy
graduation, VA intervention phase, 335, *336*, 338
grandparents: African American, 207; death of both, 62–63. *See also* custodial grandparents
grandparent-to-parent transition, 215–18
grants, TANF, 224–25
GWOT. *See* Global War on Terrorism

Halberstadt, Amy G., *171*, *173*, *354*, 357
Hamstead Nurseries, 38–39
healing model, family reconnections with, 49–50
health, caregiver, 317
health, in older Americans: adaptation case study, 139–43; age-related, 221; custodial grandparents, 208–9, 220, 221, 222; research on illness and, 127–28, 143–45; SOC model for, 129, 132–34, *135*, *136*; statistics on, 127; theoretical framework for research on, 129–38. *See also* adult(s); chronic illness adaptation; women, chronic illness in older
heart disease, spousal caregivers risk of, 311
heterogeneity: chronic illness in older women and, 128; drug use trajectory, 114–17, 124; social capital homogeneity and, 281; within-group, 185
heteronormativity, 82
Hinde, Robert, 36–37

Hip Hop culture: African American female sexuality in context of, 75–92; consumption of, 78, 88; female artists, 77, 83; transformational force of, 77–78
Hirshfeld-Becker, D. R., 105
historical time, 54
Hofstede, G., 172
Holland, Janet, 55, *351*, 359
homeless: antecedents to veteran, 332; revolving door of, 344; rough sleeper v., 331–32. *See also* Veterans Aid
home setting, caregiving in, 310, *310*, 314–15, 317–18
horizontal networks, 279
hospital-based psychosocial intervention, 291, 293, 297–300; theoretical foundations for, 297–98
hospitals, 39; contexts of, 291, 292–93, 301–3; environments of, 300, 301–2; organizational culture in context of, 301–3; research in setting of, 291; transformation within, 292–93
hostel, VA. *See* Veterans Aid (VA)
household chores, fathers doing, 198, 199
Huebner, Angela J., 229, *355*, 357
human development. *See* development, human; theory(ies); *specific theories*; *specific topics*
hurricane analogy, 16–17
Hutchinson, J. F., 87
hypersexualization, African American female, 81–84

identity: African-Caribbean youth, 281; bad boy, 65
illness: consequences of therapeutic change for, 303–4; organizational

culture in hospital context and, 301–3; psychosocial impact of, 291–304; transformative power of, 294–96; uncertainty and, 291, 292, 298–300, 303–4. *See also* chronic illness adaptation
immigration: Chinese, 193–94, 202–4; future research on family, 203–4
Immigration Act of 1952, 193
incarceration, African American male, 90
independence, women's life course value, 136, *136*
Indian Act, 43
indices, multiple, 184–85
individual(s): trajectories of, social contexts for, 71–72; transactions between environment and, 154–56; transformation, social and, 363–65
individualist/collectivist cultures, 185–86, 187, 194–95
individualization, 56, 58–59
inequalities: resource, 283; social capital theories reinforcing, 268, 273, 280–81, 282, 284
infant(s): with ambivalent attachments, 231–32; death of young mom's, 63
informal networks, 252, 253, 255, 261, 280
informational interventions, 297
Institute for Society, Culture and Environment (ISCE), 349
integrated theoretical approach: adolescent sexuality studied through, 78–80; building blocks of, 318–22; caregiving, 317–24; emotion socialization, 179–81
intentionality, intervention programs, 239–40

interactional model: adaptation and, 133, 143; of close relationships, 36–38, 45, *351*; slow transformations in, 37, 40–41; themes of interaction, 38
interdependence, 196
intergenerational ambivalence, 212
intergenerational closure, Coleman's, 272
intergenerational socialization, 271–73
intergenerational transmission, 151–52, 163
internalization, sexual messages, 76
internal working models, 42; military deployment separation and, 230–31, 233–34; as relationship-specific, 234
internment camps, 45–47
interpersonal antecedents, 361; grandparent, 215–18
interpretation, 362. *See also* meaning(s)
intersections, 3; care, formal/informal, 307–8, 314–17; contextual, 9; ecological-womanist, 80–89; between formal/informal care, 307–8; grandparents as surrogate parents and, 211–12; network, 254
intervention, 83, 364–65; context-process blend in, 340–44; culturally relevant sexual health, 76, 80, 89–91; double ABCX Model application for, 237–40; evidence base for psychosocial, 294, 299; formal/informal, 334; future programs for, 364–65; hospital-based psychosocial, 291, 293, 297–300; implications for drug use, 123–24; informational, 297; intentionality and, 239–40; military deployment separation

adaptation, 227–40, *230*, *236*; one-stop shopping approach to, 224; Sexual Health Model for, 90–91; stress coping capacities for effective, 296–97; swift transformation implications for, 47–50; tailored programs for, 365; utilization, 239–40; VA model for future, 344–46; VA philosophy of, 335, *336*; VA well being approach to, 327, 328, 331, 332, 334–44, *336*. *See also* policy
interviews: adaptation to chronic illness project, 128–29; emotion socialization, 184; of fathers, 199; internment camp individuals, 46–47; *Inventing Adulthoods*, 60–61; military deployment spouse, 237
intraindividual antecedents, 360–61
intrapersonal antecedents, 212–15; cognitive appraisal/coping in, 212–13; role timing/conflict, 214–15
Inventing Adulthoods (UK study), 53–71, 72n1; adulthood models and, 65–68; biographical model in, 60–61; case studies in, 60, 64–65, 68–71; critical moments in, 59, 62–64; design/method/interpretation for, 54–56; domestic arena in, 67–68; employment and, 67, 69; fateful v. critical moments and, 59; findings from, 60, 62–71; future spaces and, 71–72; interview overview for, 60–61; leisure/consumption and, 67
Iraq, 228
Ireland, Northern, 275
Irish saying, 25

ISCE. *See* Institute for Society, Culture and Environment

Japanese families, placed in internment camps, 45–47
Johnson, C. L., 316–17
Johnson, M. L., 320

Kagiti çibasi, C., 196
Kim, Kee Jeong, 123, *353*
Kuczynski, Leon, 37, 157, 164, *353*, 357

late modernity: risk society and, 56–59; theories in, 53–54, 56–59
Lazarus, R. S., 212–13, 299
leadership, community, 261
leisure, *Inventing Adulthoods* study and, 67
Letiecq, B. L., 214
life course perspective, 114, 115–17, 129–43, *135*, *136*, *351*; case study on health adaptation using, 139–43; families, 130–31; for health issues in older women, 129–31, *136*, 136–37; life-course-persistent antisocial syndrome, 115; life-course-persistent trajectory, drug use, 115–17, *353*; SOC from, 129–34, *135*, *136*, 137, 140
linearity, avoiding excessive, 31
linked lives, life course model principle, 130
live-in caregivers, 310
local events, 20
logic of research, social capital, 285
Lollis, Susan, 350, *351*, 362
London, Tavistock Child Development Research Unit in, 39
Lumbee Native Americans, 187

macro external population level, events, 19–20; swift transformations from, 45–47
macrosystem: caregiving at level of, 320, 321; qualitative change on level of, 164–65; swift transformations level of, 45–47; theories on level of, 358
maladaptation, 222–23
males, African American, 90
Mancini, Jay A., 5, *355*, 358–59
marginalization, social capital and, 274–76; of children/older adults, 274–75
marijuana, 64–65, 113
Marine Boy (VA client), 339, 340
marriage enrichment programs, 239
mass media, as exosystem, 84–86
material conditions, critical moments and, 64
maturity gap, 115
meaning(s), 4, 362; construction of, parent-child relationship, 154–56; emotion socialization and, 180–81; Hip Hop culture and, 89–91
meaningful activities/relationships, SOC process, 138
measurement, 144; caregiving, 324; dynamic cultural context, 183–87; social capital, 285–87; theorizing with new tools for, 363–64
mechanistic model, 97
media: caregiving in, 309; exosystem as mass, 84–86
medical personnel, emotional distress in, 292, 293, 301–3
mental health, VA clients', 333–34
mesosystemic analysis, 359; gender relations, 86–87

microsystem level: caregiving on, 321; changes on, 53; gender/racial socialization at, 87–89; swift transformations at, 41–43; theories on, 358; transactions as meaning making on, 155
middle class, 58, 282
migrant caregivers, 310
military, 254–55, 328–30; in Finland, 23; United States, community resilience research in, 246; veterans homelessness and, 332
military deployment separation: adaptation to, 227–40, *230*, *236*; attachment security and, *230*, 230–35; definition of, 228; double ABCX model for, 229–31, *230*; internal working models and, 230–31, 233–34; intervention programs for adaptation to, 237–40; previous research on, 227–28; statistics on, 228–29
Milroy, W. Hugh, 333, *356*, 359, 361
mindfulness, 238
minorities, 192; emotion socialization of children, *173–75*, 176–77; minority children developmental competency model, *173–75*, 176–77, *354*
Mitchell, Monique B., 156, 159–61, 164–65, *353*, 357
models. *See* theory(ies)
modernity. *See* late modernity
Moffitt, T. E., 114
moral generalized trust, 278
mothers, 63; informal networks between, 280
multifinality principle, 99–100
Myanmar, 35

Narayan, D., 255
Nargis cyclone, 35
National Comorbidity Survey, 96
National Guard, 254–55
National Health Service (NHS), 345
National Indian Brotherhood of Canada, 44
National Longitudinal Study of Adolescent Health (Add Health Study), 117–21, *119*, 125n1
Native Americans: Lumbee, 187; time concept for traditional, 183
networks: for community resilience, 251–55; intersections of, 254; social capital and, 279–80
NHS. *See* National Health Service
Nilsen, A., 57–58
non-gender specific choice biography, 57
nonlinear time, 183
normal biographies, 56, 57–58; UK's youth, 61
normative events, 20
North Country boy (VA client), 328–29
Northern Ireland, 275
novelty, change resulting from, 162–67

obstacles, life course element, SOC and, 134, *135*, *136*, 137, 140
odds ratios, drug use, *119*
Ollendick, Thomas H., *352*, 358
one-child policy, 201
one-stop shopping approach, 224
Operation Desert Storm, 233
opportunities: grasping of, 25–27; recurrence of, 32; turning points, 17, *27*, 27–29; unpredictability of, 24–25

opportunity, good fit between readiness and, 26
optimization: adaptation component, 133–34, 138, 143; SOC process, 138
organismic model, 97, 98
organizational culture: definition of, 301; in hospital context, 301–3
outcomes. *See* consequences of change

parent-child relationships, 151–68; ambiguity in, 159–62; ambivalence in, 157–59; attachment security in, *230*, 230–35, *236*; changes/micro transactions, 166–67; contexts in, 155; dialectics of change from novelty in, 162–67; drug-use trajectories and, 114–15, 119–20; emotion socialization in, 176; family systems theory for, *236*, 236–37; intervention through, 83; parents as cultural capital, 65; past/future in, 37–38; research on, contemporary, 151–52; social relational theory and, 152, 154–55; theorizing, 151–52; transactional model of, 152, 154–56. *See also* custodial grandparents; emotion socialization
parents/parenting: adolescents of deployed, 229; attachment patterns in, 232; children monitored by, 124; in Chinese societies, 192–204; culture and, 194–99, 203–4; ecology approach to, 204; involvement in adolescents, drug use tied to, 119–20; socialization by, 87–89. *See also* custodial grandparents; grandparents
Parkin, C. M., 157

partners, socialization by, 87–89. *See also* dyadic relationships
paternal engagement, 198
patients, psychosocial distress in, 292, 301–2
pediatric cancer, 40–43
peers: deviant, 122; socialization by, 87–89
People's Republic of China, 193
performers, Hip Hop women artists limited to role of, 83
peripheral variable, culture as more than, 203
personal biographies, women's: as context, 128, 134; SOC model and, 128, 134–37, *135*, *136*, 140
personological factors, SOC model, 129–30
pessimism, 15
phases, trajectory, 131–32. *See also* Veterans Aid
Phillips, L., 79, 82
Piercy, K. W., 316, 319
Pitman, Robyn, *353*
place approach, to communities, 247
policy: Britain's focus on parenting and, 270; care-related, *310*, 314, 321, 322; community service, 346; education, 43–45; future research and, 365; government shifting responsibility to individual, 58; grandparenting and, 224–25; immigration, 193; informal care and, 314; one-child, 201; social capital and, 268–69, 283; third-way paradigm for, 270. *See also* intervention; prevention
political economy of aging, care theory and, 320
politics, Chinese societies' changes in, 201

Polytechnic Institute, Virginia, 349
Ponthieux, S., 285
population: Chinese immigrant, 193–94; Chinese percentage in world, 193; displacement, 20
pornography, 86
post-modern theories. *See* late modernity
praxis, theorizing and, 9
pre-conditions, sequence of turning point, *27*
predictions, hurricane analogy and, 16–17
prevention: chronic illness in older women and, 145; communities and, 247–48; implications for drug use, 123–24; pathway-specific, 113; science, 261; VA model for future, 344–46
Preyde, Michèle, *356*, 360
primary cognitive appraisal, 295
problem-focused coping, 296
processes, 316–17, 334, *351–56*, 361–62; acculturation, 202–3; automatic/effortful, 162–63; care, 320–22; change from blending context with, 340–44; double ABCX model for change, 235–37; emotion socialization antecedents and, 176–81; fragility in VA client, 338–40; iterative data, 59–61; SOC, 138; social action, 249–51, *250*; social capital, 284–87; structures v., 5; theorizing outcome, 168; understanding development with, 4, 5–6, 7
psychological ambivalence, grandparent, 213–14
psychopathology: adolescent, 115–16. *See also* developmental psychopathology

psychosocial impact, illness, 291–304
psychosocial intervention: active ingredients of, 299–300; referral patients to, lack of, 302; services included in, 297
publican (veteran case study), 329–30, 339
Putnam, Robert D., 254, 268, 271, 275, 279, 284; bonding/bridging viewed by, 281

Qin, D., 202

race/ethnicity, 185–86; AIDS disparities and, 75; dynamic cultural context measurement and, 185–86; emotion socialization theories accounting for, 177–78; grandparenting antecedent, 219; social capital and, 275–76
random developmental noise, 16
rap, 81
rape, Hip Hop culture and, 86
rationality, misattribution of economic, 277–78
readiness: children's emotion socialization, 181; community capacity and, 256–58; good fit between opportunity and, 26; for turning points, 26, 28–29
Reay, Diane, 269
reflexive project of self, 55, 56
reflexivity, social capital and, 286
relapse, VA client, 338–39
relational communities, 257, *258*
relationships: change events supported by, 21; children's formation of, 37–38; couple, late modern theorists and, 57; as critical moments source, 62–64; dyadic, 35–40, 48, 57, 144, 155, 165–66, 245, 319, 362; family adjustment model for attachment, *238*; interactional model of close, 36–38, 45, *351*; linked lives principle of, 130; peer, 88–89; power of positive, 21–22; reforming, 49–50; SOC and, 138; socialization of partner, 87–89; swift transformations in close, 35–50; VA approach and, 342–43; working model in formation of, 38, 42. *See also* family(ies); networks; parent-child relationships; partners
research: on adolescence, 91–92; care/caregiver, 312–13; caregiving implications for theory/practice and, 323–24; cross-cultural, 183–84; developmental psychopathology implications for, 106–8; emotion socialization, 176–81; ethnocentrism in, 183–84; family stress from military deployment, 227–28, 229; on fathering, 191, 204; on health/illness in older Americans, 127–28, 143–45; in hospital settings, 291; logic of, social capital, 285; multiple indices in, 184–85; parent-child relationships, contemporary, 151–52; SOC guided, 134, *135*; social capital implications for, 284–87; U.S. military used for, 246. *See also* case studies; future research; measurement; studies; theory(ies)
researcher-ese, 184
resilience, *351*; adaptation, 32; community, 245–63, *250*, *258*; contexts for development of, 47–48; drug use and, 114

resources: community capacity and, 256; custodial grandparents' financial, 219–20; gendered, 276; inequality of, 283; life course element, 134, *135*, *136*, 137, 139–40; perception of, 237–38
return on investment, emotional, 29–31
revolving door, homelessness, 344
Rhonda (health adaptation case study), 139–43
Rice, C. J., 320
risk(s): accumulation of risk model, 221, *354*; caregiver, 311; community, 245–46; drug use among American youth, 113–25, *119*; SAD, *101–2*; society, 56–59, 269, 277–78
risk-taking, sexual, 85–86
rituals, transition, 182
Roberto, Karen A., 350, *352*, 359–60
Robertson, James, 39
Robin (case study/busted for marijuana), 64–65
role timing/conflict, interpersonal antecedents, 214–15
rough sleeping, 327, 329, *336*; homelessness v., 331–32
Royal Air Force (veteran from), 329–30
Rutter, M., 99

SAD. *See* social anxiety disorder, in youth
salary, caregiving, formal/informal, 313–14
Sameroff, A., 162
SAS TRAJ statistical programs, 116, 118
school transitions, 43–45
Schoon, I., 16

Schuller, T., 269
secondary cognitive appraisal, 295
second order change, 162
security, attachment, *230*, 230–35
selection, adaptation component, 133, 140–42, 143
selective optimization with compensation (SOC), 129–45, *135*, *136*; case study on health adaptation using, 139–43; contextualized, 134–38, *135*, *136*; gender issues for use of, 144–45; life course model, 129–34, *135*, *136*, 137, 140; processes, 138; sociological/personological factors informing, 129–31
self-esteem: attachment security and, 232; drug use and, 120
semi-parametric mixture model, drug use and, 118
separation/loss, 35, 38–39, *351*; cancer in sibling causing, 40–43; internment camps and, 45–47; military deployment, 227–40, *230*, *236*
serendipity, 24–25
Settersten, R., 319
sexual abuse, 26, 85
sexual behavior: risk-taking, 85–86; sexual practices shift from, 89–90
sexuality: adolescent, 78–80, 84–86, 91–92; Hip Hop context for African American females, 75–92; sexual health model, 76, 80, 89–91, *352*
sexually-transmitted diseases (STDs), 75
siblings, cancer in, 40–43
silo approaches, to community support, 253
Skinner, B. F., 97

slow transformations, interactional model applying to, 37, 40–41
SOC. *See* selective optimization with compensation
social action processes, community resilience and, 249–51, *250*
social anxiety disorder (SAD), in youth, 95–109, *101–2*; in adolescents, 96; antecedents to, 100–106, *101–2*; approach-avoidance system for BI and, 105–6; BI and, 103, 104–5; context for, most significant, 96; definition of, 95–97; future studies on, 107–8; prevalence rates for, 96; risk factors for, *101–2*
social breakdown, families, 45
social capital, 21, 72n3, 267–87, *355*; bridging/bonding, 279–81, 282; communities and, 254–55; as declining, 271, 273, 275–76; definition of, 255, 268–69; economic rationality and, 277–78; families and, 271–74, 287n1; gender/generation and, 279–80; gender relations and, 273–74; implications for object construction of, 284–87; information aspect of, 259; interest in, 269–70; mainstream theories of, 267–68, 274–76, 284–85; marginalization and, 274–76; networks and, 279–80; politico-psycho-anthropological view of, 269; problematic mainstream conception of, 267–68; as public good, 268; public/private spheres of, 277–80; race/ethnicity and, 275–76; reflexivity and, 286; social mobility and, 282–84

social capital lost, theory of, 271, 273, 275–76, 279
social causation theory, 122, *353*
social change, 363–65; Chinese societies, 201; next steps in individual and, 363–65; social capital implications/object construction and, 284–87; theory, 55, 56–61
social class, 58, 68–71; care/caregivers and, 312; emotion socialization and, 186–87; late modern theories and, 57, 58–59; social capital and, 275–76, 282; youth transitions and, 57, 58, 66, 70
social cognitive theory, 98
social contexts, 140–41; individual trajectories and, 71–72
social evaluative anxiety, age-related, 95
social exclusion, 268–69
socialization: Chinese parents' strategies for, 200–201; cultural, *173–74*, 178–79, 181–82, *354*; emotion, 171–89, *173–75*, *354*; of emotion-related schemas, 177–78, *354*; family, 151–52, 177; intergenerational, 271–73; parent-child relationships and, 151–68; by parent/partners/peers, 87–89; sexual, 80–81
social mobility, social capital and, 282–84
social organization theory, 245–63, *250*, *258*, *355*; change and, 249–51, *250*; community resilience elements of, 249–58, *258*; theorizing implications of, 260–63
social relational theory: assumptions of, 153; parent-child relationships in, 152, 154–55, *353*

social selection theory, 122, *122*, *353*
social support theory, 297–98, *356*;
   grandparents and, 218
social time, 54
social transformation, next steps in
   individual and, 363–65. *See also*
   change; social change
society, risk, 56–59, 269, 277–78. *See
   also* Chinese societies
sociodemographic antecedents, 212,
   218–21; age-related health issues
   as, 221; financial resources, 219–
   20; gender-based, 220–21; race/
   ethnicity in, 219
socioecological approach, emotion
   socialization, 180–81
socioeconomics, caregiving, formal/
   informal, 312
sociological factors, SOC model,
   129–30
soft individualism, 186
special considerations, 4
spousal caregivers, adult child v., 311.
   See also wives
stable phase, trajectory, 131
statistics: BI, 103; custodial
   grandparents, 207; drug use, 113;
   military deployment, 228–29;
   older Americans, 127; SAS TRAJ
   programs, 116, 118
STDs. *See* sexually-transmitted
   diseases
Stephens, Diane P., 350, *352*
Stevenson-Hinde, Joan, 36–37
stress: family, military deployment
   separation causing, 227–40;
   grandparents as surrogate parents,
   216, 223; illness as cause of,
   291–304; psychosocial, 292,
   301–2; uncertainty, 291, 292,
   298–300, 303–4

stress, coping with, 212–13, 303–4,
   356; eight ways of, 295–96;
   functions of, 294–96; intervention
   effectiveness, 296–97; problem-
   focused/emotion-focused, 296
strip club culture, 81–82
Stroufe, L. A., 99
structure: culture in emotion
   socialization theoretical, 179–80;
   invisible forces of, 58; process v., 5
structured dependency theory, care
   and, 320
studies: BI/SAD future, 107–8;
   Inventing Adulthoods, 53, 54–61,
   72n1; wives of deployed military
   service members pilot, 237. *See
   also* case studies; future research;
   research
Su, Y., 199
swift intervention, VA, 337
swift transformations, in close
   relationships, 35–50; in children,
   39–40; exosystem level of, 43–45;
   intervention implications in, 47–50;
   micro-system level, 41–43; school
   transitions causing, 43–45; slow
   transformation model and, 40–41;
   translocation/macrosystem level,
   45–47. *See also* change
synergetic communities, 257, *258*
synthesis, cultural, 165–66

tabula rasa recipients, children as,
   274–75
TANF grants, 224–25
targets, communities as prevention,
   247
Tavistock Child Development
   Research Unit, 39
taxonomy theories, drug use,
   115–17

theoretical perspectives, contributors', 350–51, *351–56*
theorizing, 9–10; development/change, 349–65; foundations for hospital-based psychosocial intervention, 297–98; integrated caregiving, 317–24; outcomes in process, 168; social organizational theory implications for, 260–63; theoretical context of, 153–54
theory(ies): of acceptance, 292, 298–300, 303–4; accumulation of risk model, 221, 222, *354*; adolescent-limited trajectory, 113–25, *119*, *353*; attachment, 38, *230*, 230–35, 238, *351*, *355*; chronic illness management, 128–46; cognitive behavioral, 298–300, *356*; complexity, 16, 32, *351*; Confucianism, 195, 196, 198, 202; cultural socialization, 172–76, *173–75*, 178–79, *354*; desistor trajectory, 117–21; developmental psychopathology implications for, 106–8; development underpinnings in, 349–59; dialectical causality, 154–56, *353*; ecology, 6, 8, 39–40, 47–48, 204, 247, 350, *352*, *354*; emotion socialization, 171–89, *173–75*, *354*; equity, 301–3, 301–3. *356*; families experiencing military deployment, 229–31; family system, 217–18, *236*, 236–37, *354*; feminist, 53, 279, *351*; health issues in later life, 129–38; integrated, 78–80, 179–81, 317–24; interactional model of close relationships, 36–38, 45, *351*; iterative process of data and, 59–61; late modern, 53–54; macro level, 358; microsystem, 358; minority children developmental competency, *173–75*, 176–77, *354*; practicalities of, 9; resilience, 32, 47–48, 114, 245–63, *250*, *258*, *351*; separation/loss, 35, 38–39, 40–43, 45–47, 227–40, *230*, *351*; sexual health model, 76, 80, 89–91, *352*; social capital lost, 271, 273, 275–76, 279; social causation, 122, *353*; social change, 55, 56–61; socialization of emotion-related schemas, 177–78, *354*; social organization, 245–63, *250*, *258*, *355*; social relational, *353*; social selection, 122, *122*, *353*; social support, 218, 297–98, *356*; stress/coping, 212–13, 227–40, 294–97, 303–4, *356*; structured dependency, 320; taxonomy, drug use, 115–17; theory-practice gap, 151; time, 54, *351*; transactional model, 98–99, 114, *122*, 122–23, 152, 154, 155–58, *352*, *353*; Victorian era and, 292; well being approach, 327, 328, 331, 332, 334–44, *336*, *356*; womanist, 78–80, 86, 90, *352*. *See also* caregiving, formal/informal; developmental theory; double ABCX model; life course perspective; selective optimization with compensation; social capital; trajectories
Theory of Stress and Coping (Lazarus/Folkman), 294
time: chronosystem context of, 40; cultural context for concepts of, 182–83; levels of, 54
time-fixed antecedents, 121
time-varying antecedents, 122
Timonen, Virpi, *356*, 359

trajectories: age-graded, 114; chronic illness management, 131–32; drug use, 114–21, 124, *353*; grandparents' change, 209–11; health, 130, 131; life course, 114, 129–31. *See also* life course perspective

transactional model, *352, 353*; agency in, 154–56; contexts in, 155–58; development, 98–99, 154; for drug use risk/resilience factors, 114, *122*, 122–23; parent-child relationships in, 152

transactions: micro-macro, 164–65; transitions from micro, 167–68

transformations: expectations and, 22–23, 32, 42–43; Hip Hop culture as force of, 77–78; illness having power of, 294–96; individual/social, next steps in, 363–65; slow, 37, 40–41. *See also* change; swift transformations, in close relationships

transitions: daily, 182; foster care, 164–65; grandparent-to-parent, 215–18; Inventing Adulthoods study and, 59–61; life course model on sequence of, 130; micro-macro transactions leading to, 164–65; rituals for, 182; time concepts for, 182–83; youth, 61–72, *66*

transnational families, 281

Triandis, H. C., 194–95

trust: moral generalized, 278; VA conformity and, 341–42

turning points: bereavement as, 64; in dynamics of change, 15–31; electrical workshop example of, 22; new models of, 27–31; opportunities as, *27*, 27–29; personal story of, 23–27; power of relationships in, 21–22; promise of positive, 31–33; readiness for, 26, 28–29; sequence of pre-conditions for enduring, *27*; use of term, 17. *See also* critical moments

A Two-year old Goes to the Hospital, 39

UK. *See* United Kingdom

uncertainty: dialectics and, 156, 162; illness causing, 291, 292, 298–300, 303–4; theory of acceptance approach to, 292, 298–300, 303–4. *See also* ambiguity; ambivalence; certainty, social capital and

United Kingdom (UK): NHS in, 345; VA in, 327–28; youth transitions in, 61–62, *66*. *See also Inventing Adulthoods*

United States (U.S.): drug use epidemic in, 123; internment camps in, 45–47; research using military of, 246; risk factors for drug use among youth in, 113–25, *119*; SAD in adolescents, prevalence rate of, 96. *See also* military

universality, assumption of, 191, 197

unpacking, VA intervention phase, 335, *336*, 337, 341

unpredictability: change, 18; opportunity, 24–25

unstable phase, trajectory, 131

VA. *See* Veterans Aid

values: intergenerational transmission of, 151–52; life course/SOC element, 134, *135, 136*, 136–37; in Rhonda's case, 139; working models of, 163 veterans, 255; alcohol misuse by, 333; fragility in healing process for, 338–40; homeless, 327–46; mental health problems among VA client, 333–34

Veterans Aid (VA), 327–46; case studies, 328–31, 339–40; change from context-process blend, 340–44; community service policy and, 346; formal/informal support processes of, 334; hostel environment of, 342–43; as model for future prevention/intervention, 344–46; new friends and, 343; organization, 327–28; philosophy of intervention, 335, *336*; practice of intervention by, 335–38; refusal to change, 343–44; relapse and, 338–39; trust/conformity and, 341–42; typical clients of, 331–34; welfare organizations based on, 345; well being approach of, 327, 328, 331, 332, 334–44, *336*, *356*

Victorian era, 292
Vietnamese youth, 165–66
violence, sexual, 26, 85
Virginia Polytechnic Institute, 128, 349
Virginia State University, 349
Vormbrock, J., 233

Wacquant, L., 285
Weigert, A. J., 161
Weiss, C. H., 9, 261
welfare: family, 284; VA organizations, 345
well being approach, VA's, 327, 328, 331, 332, 334–40, *336*, *356*; context-process blend in, 340–44; fragility in, 338–40; relationships in, 342–43

Western families, Chinese v., 197
wives, deployed military service members, 236–37
womanhood, African American, eight scripts portraying, 83
womanist theory, 86, *352*; characteristics of womanism, 79; context and, 90; core characteristics of, 79; ecological theory integrated with, 78–80
women, 236–37, 280; caregivers as older, 313; as custodial grandparents, 220; Hip Hop artists, 77, 83; sacred/disposable view of, 86; SOC processes used by, 138
women, chronic illness in older, 128–46; adaptation project, 128–29; case study on adaptation to, 139–43; future directions for studying, 143–45; life course perspective on, 129–31, *136*, 136–37; personal biography context for, 128, 134–37, *135*, *136*, 140; prevention strategies and, 145; research on, overview of, 127–28
Woolcock, M., 255
working models: attachment theory, 38; internal, 42, 230–31, 233–34; long relationships use of, 41; of values, 163
World War II, 45

Yamagishi, M., 186
Yamagishi, T., 186
youth: African-Caribbean, 275, 281; change in lives of, 53–54; risks for drug use among U.S., 113–25, *119*; SAD in, 95–109, *101–2*; studies, 57, 58, 66; Vietnamese, 165–66

youth transitions, 61–72, *66*; case studies of, 60, 64–65, 68–71; continuity found in, 71–72; dimensions/fields of, *66*; economic independence and, 60; social class and, 57, 58, 66, 70; in UK, 61–62, 66. *See also Inventing Adulthoods*

Zetterberg, H., 7
zombie category, family as, 58–59

About the Contributors

Gary L. Bowen, PhD, ACSW is Kenan Distinguished Professor in the School of Social Work at the University of North Carolina at Chapel Hill, NC 27597. Working in the context of the public schools and the United States military, his research addresses ways in which elements of the social structure frame and influence individual and collective orientations and behavioral choices. Recent publications have appeared in *Family Relations* and the *Journal of Early Adolescence*. E-mail address: glbowen@email.unc.edu. Website address: www.schoolsuccessprofile.org.

Susan S. Chuang, PhD is associate professor in the Department of Family Relations and Applied Nutrition at the University of Guelph, Guelph, ON, Canada, N1G 2W1. Her research focuses on cross-cultural and immigrant families and children, with particular focuses on fathering and parent-child relationships. She recently co-edited a book (with R. Moreno), *On New Shores: Understanding Immigrant Fathers in North America* (2008), and co-edited a special issue of *Sex Roles* (with C. Tamis-LeMonda). E-mail address: schuang@uoguelph.ca. Website address: www.familyuoguelph.ca/page.cfm?id=693.

Megan L. Dolbin-MacNab, PhD, LMFT is assistant professor in the Department of Human Development at Virginia Polytechnic Institute and State University, Blacksburg, VA 24061. Her research interests include grandparent-headed families and systemic approaches to intervention and prevention. Recent publications have appeared in *Family Relations* and *Parenting the Custodial Grandchild: Implications for Clinical Practice*. Email address: mdolbinm@vt.edu. Website address: www.humandevelopment.vt.edu/dolbin-macnab.html.

Julie C. Dunsmore, PhD is assistant professor of psychology at Virginia Polytechnic Institute and State University, Blacksburg, VA 24061. Her research focuses on parents' role in children's social and emotional development. Recent publications have appeared in *Early Education & Development*, the *International Journal of Behavioral Development*, and *Social Development*. E-mail address: jdunsmor@vt.edu. Website address: www.psyc.vt.edu/labs/socdev.

Rosalind Edwards, PhD is professor in social policy and director of the Families & Social Capital Research Group at London South Bank University, London SE1 0AA. Her research focuses on family lives, from the perspectives of both adults and children. Recent publications include *Key Concepts in Family Studies* (with J. McCarthy, 2009) and *Researching Families and Communities: Social and Generational Change* (2008). She is founding and co-editor of the *International Journal of Social Research Methodology*. E-mail address: edwardra@lsbu.ac.uk. Website address: myprofile.cos.com/edwardra.

April L. Few, PhD is associate professor in the Department of Human Development at Virginia Polytechnic Institute and State University, Blacksburg, VA 24061. Her research interests include minority adolescent sexuality, intimate violence, racial-ethnic identity development as contextualized through lifespan and black feminist theoretical contexts. Recent publications have appeared in *Sexuality and Culture* and *Sex Roles*. She is co-editor of the *Handbook of Feminist Family Studies* (with S. A. Lloyd & K. R. Allen, 2009). E-mail address: alfew@vt.edu. Website address: www.humandevelopment.vt.edu/few.html.

Robbie Gilligan, MA is professor of social work and social policy and head of the School of Social Work and Social Policy at Trinity College, Dublin, Ireland. His research focuses on support for vulnerable children and young people, especially those in public care. Recent publications include *Promoting Resilience* (2nd Ed., 2009), and articles in *Journal of Social Work Practice* and *Children and Society*. E-mail address: Robbie.gilligan@tcd.ie/. Website address: http://tcdlocalportal.tcd.ie/pls/public/staff.detail?p_unit=swsp&p_name=rgillign.

Amy G. Halberstadt, PhD is professor of psychology at North Carolina State University, Raleigh, NC, 27695. Her research focuses on socialization of emotion in and across families and cultures. Recent publications have appeared in the *Journal of Family Psychology*, *Child Development*, and *Social Development*. E-mail address: Amy_Halberstadt@ncsu.edu. Website address: www4.ncsu.edu/~halbers/index.html.

Janet Holland, PhD is professor of social research at London South Bank University, London, SE1 0AA and co-director of *Timescapes* (www.timescapes.leeds.ac.uk). Research interests include youth, education, gender, intimacy, sexuality, families, and methodology. Recent publications have appeared in *Young* and *International Journal of Social Research Methodology*. Her latest book (with S. Henderson, S. McGrellis, S. Sharpe, and R. Thomson) is *Inventing Adulthoods: A Biographical Approach to Youth Transitions* (2007). E-mail address: hollanj@lsbu.ac.uk. Web address: www.lsbu.ac.uk/inventingadulthoods.

Angela Huebner, PhD is associate professor in the Department of Human Development at Virginia Polytechnic Institute and State University, Northern Virginia Center in Falls Church, VA, 22043. Her recent qualitative work has focused on stressors facing spouses and adolescents in military families. Research publications have appeared in *Family Relations, Journal of Adolescent Health*, and *Youth & Society*. E-mail address: ahuebner@vt.edu. Website address: www.nvc.vt.edu/mft/huebner.html.

Kee Jeong Kim, PhD is assistant professor in the Department of Human Development at Virginia Polytechnic Institute and State University, Blacksburg, VA 24061. Her major research interests are in examining developmental trajectories of adolescent externalizing and internalizing problems and applying advanced statistical methods to the analysis of longitudinal data. Her recent research has been published in *Child Development* and the *Annals of the New York Academy of Sciences*. E-mail address: keekim@vt.edu. Web address: www.humandevelopment.vt.edu/kim.html.

Leon Kuczynski, PhD is professor at the Department of Family Relations and Applied Nutrition at the University of Guelph, Guelph, Ontario, Canada. His research concerns dynamic processes in parent-child interactions and relationships and topics such as socialization, child agency and resistance, and relationship formation. He has edited two books:

Handbook of Dynamics in Parent-Child Relations (2003) and *Parenting and the Internalization of Values: A Handbook of Contemporary Theory* (with J. E. Grusec, 1997) E-mail address: lkuczyns@uoguelph.ca. Website address: stage.web.uoguelph.ca/fran/page.cfm?id=698.

Susan Lollis, PhD, C. Psych. is professor in the Department of Family Relations and Applied Nutrition, University of Guelph, Guelph, Ontario, Canada. Her research focuses on the close relationships that children and adolescents develop with peers, siblings, and parents. She is particularly interested in the dynamic tensions between attachment/affiliation and separation/individuation in children's close relationships. Recent publications have appeared in *Family Process, Journal of Marital and Family Therapy*, and *Journal of Social and Personal Relationships*. E-mail address: slollis@uoguelph.ca. Website address: www.family.uoguelph.ca/page.cfm?id=700.

Jay A. Mancini, PhD is the senior research fellow with the Institute for Society, Culture and Environment, and professor in the Department of Human Development at Virginia Polytechnic Institute and State University, Blacksburg, VA 24061. His research focuses on vulnerable families and the relationships between families and their communities. Recent publications have appeared in *Family Relations* and the *Journal of Community Practice*. Email address: mancini@vt.edu. Website address: www.humandevelopment.vt.edu/mancini.html.

Hugh Milroy, PhD is chief executive of Veterans Aid, a charity for homeless veterans based in London, England. He served in the Royal Air Force for seventeen years where his final position was as head of community support. A veteran of the Gulf War 1991, his research and practice has focused on military community well-being and homelessness/social exclusion among veterans. He is also the national chair of the Ex-Service Action Group on Homelessness in the United Kingdom. E-mail address: ceo@veterans-aid.net. Website address: www.veterans-aid.net.

Monique B. Mitchell, PhD is an instructor in the Department of Family Relations and Applied Nutrition at the University of Guelph-Humber Toronto, Ontario, Canada. Her research interests include children's experience of foster care and institutionalized care, life transitions, transactions, cognitive appraisals, ambiguity, stress and coping, and social support. E-mail address: mitchelm@unoguelph.ca.

Thomas H. Ollendick, PhD is University Distinguished Professor of Psychology and director of the Child Study Center at Virginia Polytechnic Institute and State University, Blacksburg, VA 24061. A social learning theorist, his research focuses on the developmental psychopathology and treatment of various childhood and adolescent behavioral disorders. Recent publications have appeared in *Behavior Therapy* and the *Journal of Consulting and Clinical Psychology*. E-mail address: tho@vt.edu. Website address: www.psych.vt.edu/centers/csc/.

Robyn Pitman, MA is a doctoral student in the Department of Family Relations and Applied Nutrition at the University of Guelph, Guelph, Ontario, Canada. Her research interests include the relationship between social networks and well-being during adolescence and young adulthood and the dynamics of relational maintenance during middle childhood in parent-child relationships. E-mail address: rpitman@uoguelph.ca.

Michèle Preyde, PhD is associate professor in the Department of Family Relations and Applied Nutrition at the University of Guelph, Guelph Ontario, Canada. Her research focuses on the psychosocial impact of illness and children's mental health. Recent publications have appeared in *Journal of Evidence-based Social Work*, *Residential Treatment for Children & Youth*, and *Social Work in Health Care*. E-mail address: mpreyde@uoguelph.ca. Website address: http://www.family.uoguelphca/page.cfm?id=703.

Karen A. Roberto, PhD is professor and director of the Institute for Society, Culture and Environment and the Center for Gerontology at Virginia Polytechnic Institute and State University, Blacksburg, VA 24061. Her research focuses on older women's management of chronic health conditions, family caregiving, and elder mistreatment. Recent publications have appeared in *Family Relations*, *Journal of Women & Aging,* and *The Gerontologist*. E-mail address: kroberto@vt.edu. Website address: www.isce.vt.edu.

Dionne P. Stephens, PhD is assistant professor in the Department of Psychology at Florida International University. Her research examines socio-historical factors shaping minority populations sexual health processes, with emphasis on gender and racial-ethnic identity development and sexual scripting. Recent publications have appeared in the *Handbook of Feminist Family Studies*, *Sexuality and Culture*, and *Sex Roles*. E-mail address: stephens@fiu.edu. Website address: www.fiu.edu/~stephens/.

Virpi Timonen, DPhil is director of the Social Policy and Ageing Research Centre in Trinity College Dublin, Dublin 2, Ireland. Her research focuses on long-term care for older people, the political and societal drivers of welfare state reforms, and the social policy ramifications of (im)migration. Recent articles have appeared in the *Journal of Aging Studies* and *Ageing & Society*. E-mail address: timonenv@tcd.ie. Website address: www.sparc.tcd.ie.